I0835869

Metcalfe & Son, *Lithe* Cambridge.

COMMODUS AND MARCIA.

(Frontispiece.)

HANDBOOK

OF

ENGRAVED GEMS.

BY

C. W. KING, M.A.

"In tenui labor, at tenuis non gloria si quem
Numina læva sinunt, auditque vocatus Apollo."

Fredonia Books
Amsterdam, The Netherlands

Handbook of Engraved Gems

by
C. W. King

ISBN: 1-4101-0348-X

Reprinted from the 1885 edition

Fredonia Books
Amsterdam, The Netherlands
http://www.fredoniabooks.com

In order to make original editions of historical works available to scholars at an economical price, this facsimile of the original edition of 1885 is reproduced from the best available copy and has been digitally enhanced to improve legibility, but the text remains unaltered to retain historical authenticity.

CONTENTS.

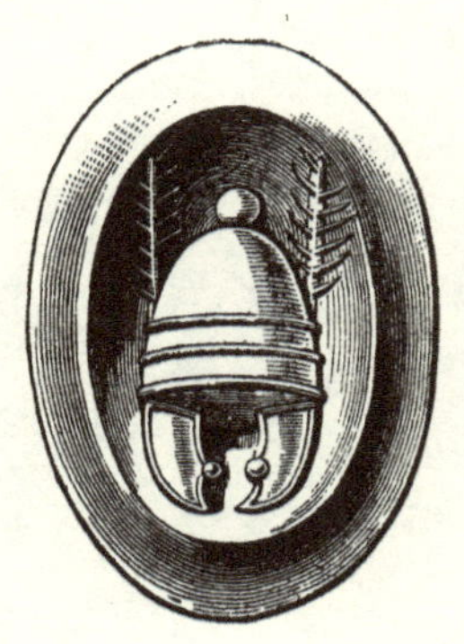

PREFACE.

My 'Antique Gems and Rings' is now out of print; and will not be republished. During the interval since its appearance, so much additional information has flowed in upon me, more particularly from the Oriental quarter, that I should not be satisfied with another edition of that work, unless the great stock of fresh materials which I have collected should be incorporated; and also large additions made—a long and laborious undertaking for which present circumstances have rendered me totally unfit. But as the Publishers are contemplating a fresh edition of my smaller Treatise upon the same subject, a way seems opened out to me of carrying knowledge forward (at least in some degree) towards the point at which I have myself arrived. The chief utility of a Treatise of this nature lies in its bringing under the eye of the student the largest possible number of examples that shall illustrate the rules laid down in the text, and for this purpose I have selected the most important gems from amongst those figured in the previous edition of the two books. Interspersed with these will be found newly executed engravings of curious and unpublished types, which recent discoveries have brought within my reach. These additions have afforded me an opportunity of leading the reader, with little trouble, into "fresh fields and pastures new." This plan, besides the being more simple and expeditious than that of blending the new matter with the original text, has the advantage of bringing it more prominently under the student's notice, because the "Description of the Plates" usually finds more readers than any other part of the volume. Of these new lights, the most novel, and to my mind the most interesting, are the series of ***Roman-British Signets***, for what curious thoughts do they not stir up through their connexion with the earliest history of our country? and of such memorials the kindness of friends has enabled me to exhibit a much larger array than I had hoped, on first attempting their collection for the present purpose.

Phœnician Art had previously been left almost entirely without representatives, from the want of specimens within my reach, but the recent discoveries made by General Cesnola in Cyprus have amply filled up that deficiency, and now give me many remarkable types that serve admirably to illustrate the remarks made in the text upon the rise and diffusion of the Glyptic Art upon the shores of the Mediterranean. The selected examples are full of instruction; their types clearly demonstrate the mingled influences of Assyria and Egypt upon the *thought* of those who wore these gems; of whom the *practical* genius is put in the strongest light by the immense improvement so conspicuous in the technical part of these embodiments of borrowed ideas. To the *Christian* and *Gnostic* classes Fortune has supplied me with many valuable additions which, as regards the first, have considerably increased the list of these monuments of the early ages of the Church—monuments full of interest, but yet so strangely overlooked by all previous writers upon gems, until five and twenty years ago when I first called attention to them by publishing the very few specimens that were at the time accessible to me. Although more than ever convinced by lengthened experience that the specious fabric of "Artists' Signatures" had its foundation laid in error and was built up to its present towering height by Fraud and Credulity going hand in hand, yet I have retained my translation of Dr. Brunn's 'Catalogue of Artists,' for the benefit of the multitude naturally unwilling to part with so pleasing a delusion; as well as of the knowing few who have the best of all reasons to shout with Demetrius the silversmith, "Great is Diana of the Ephesians!" . . . . . .

"For sure the pleasure is as great
In *being* cheated as to *cheat*."

C. W. KING.

TRINITY COLLEGE.
August 5, 1885.

DESCRIPTION OF WOODCUTS IN THE TEXT.

Frontispiece.—The Marlborough Cameo, long known as "Didius Julian and Manlia Scantilla," but now to be restored to the true originals, Commodus and Marcia, for reasons set forth at length in my 'Early Christian Numismatics,' p. 363. A recent explanation of the subject, as representing Julian the philosopher and Isis, evinces such complete ignorance of the necessary conditions of history, and of the Glyptic Art, that it may be passed by with a smile. (This drawing is made to the exact size of the cameo.)

Titlepage.—*Victory*, advancing, holding out the laurel crown, and in her left the palm-branch. Sard, set in a solid gold ring of truly republican simplicity. Few relics of the kind possess deeper historic interest than this, for it was found in the coffin of a Scipio, and given by Pope Clement XIII. to M. Dutens, tutor to Lord Beverley, on their visit to Rome, shortly after the discovery of the burialplace of the Cornelia family. (Alnwick Castle.)

Page iii.—Gladiator's Helmet, with palm-branch on each side instead of plume. It has a *vizor* of novel construction, being in two pieces, the *button* on each showing that they were intended to be slid laterally together so as to cover the whole face, leaving only a horizontal aperture for the sight. Carbuncle. (S. S. Lewis.)

Page vi.—Horse feeding, with the name of his owner, "Heraclides." Small sard, set in a silver ring, found at Dover.

Page ix.—Clepsydra: the Dolphin serves for index to a revolving dial.

Page 3.—A very remarkable type, being the Grecian Hermes in Asiatic costume. He wears the Persian gown (*candys*), and on his head the leathern helmet (*cidaris*); were it not for the caduceus and the lotus in his hands, and the little wings attached to his ankles, the figure might well pass for an Achæmenian Satrap. Before him stands an eagle instead of Hermes' regular attribute, the cock. Engraved with great minuteness on the base of an octangular cone of sappharine calcedony. (New York.)

Page 8.—The Drunken Hercules steadying himself with one hand placed upon his club. Greco-Bactrian work, a most instructive specimen of the transition of the bold Hellenic style into Puranic softness. The legend in Bactrian Pali (not yet read) doubtless gives the owner's name. Intaglio in a very fine sard, the history of which illustrates a curious phase in the progress of forgery. A cast from the intaglio came into the hands of the clever (no longer "mild") Hindoo now so busily at work in supplying the demands of Indian archæologists. He has used it for the type of a solid gold ring; but unaware that the irregularity at the foot was due to the fracture of the sard, he has represented the swelling in the wax by a corresponding indentation of the gold beasil. I have already seen two such rings, exact counterparts of each other, and which have imposed upon collectors of much experience. Let the rest take warning. (General Pearse.)

Page 11.—The most ancient example of a *genuine* Hebrew inscription to be found on a gem; being probably as old as the 5th century of our era. The type is the *Lulab*, the bunch of palm, olive, and willow, and the Esthropp, citron, which are carried by the Jews at the Feast of Tabernacles, and therefore are assumed as the national emblem. Of the various readings proposed for the rudely cut legend, I prefer that of the celebrated Hebrewist, Dr. Ginsberg, who makes it to be "Hillel Rabbi, bar Mosheh," *i. e.*, the Rabbi Hillel, son of Moses. Brown garnet. (Hertz, now British Museum.)

Page 19.—The Five Heroes in council. *See* pp. 17, 29.

Page 30.—Frog: the seal-device of Mecænas. If Isaac Taylor be right in interpreting his *Etruscan* name, MAIKNE, as Frog-man (analogous to the Italian "Ranuccio"), the great statesman had put in his seal a rebus on his name, after the so common fashion of his contemporaries. Calcedony scarabæus. (Praun.)

Page 33.—Lion, pulling down a Bull. The national Phœnician device typifying the power of the sun upon the earth. Sard scarabæus. (Praun.)

Page 37.—Head of Hercules encircled with a wreath of his own tree, the poplar. A work in the bold, heavy manner of the Greco-Egyptian school. Sard, from the collection of Giovanni di Dimitrio. (New York.)

Page 70.—A Christian intaglio, of very early date, apparently representing the Call of an Apostle. Christ, whose character is distinctly made known by the letters placed in the field above him, is seen, by his gesture, summoning a man, who seemingly holds back, whilst another, on the other side, appears to be hastening away to do his Master's bidding.

The mystic meaning of the legend IXΘYC will be found explained at p. 74; but it may be added here, that according to the great authority of Rashi (dec. 1105) the "Fish" does not stand for the Messiah himself, but for Leviathan, whose flesh is to be served up at the grand feast to be held at his coming. Red jasper. (S. S. Lewis.)

Page 122.—Head of the Chimæra: being that of a lion armed with the horns of a goat: a condensed expression of the composite figure in that monster. The two letters in the field are the beginning of the owner's name, cut short as was the early rule for Grecian signatures. A beautiful example of the Asiatic-Greek style. Yellow sard, from the Beckford Cabinet.

Page 133.—Psyche, stealthily opening the Box of Beauty, intrusted to her by Proserpine to carry to Venus. On her so doing, a poisonous vapour issues from it which throws her into a death-like swoon. There is extreme diversity in the merit of the Poniatowsky Gems; many being weak in design, and vile in execution: others, again, perfect in both respects, as this specimen shows, but in conception and treatment totally differing from the antique. Amethyst. (New York.)

Page 156.—Elephant, emerging from a snail-shell: one of the cleverest of these fanciful unions of the most inconsistent elements: the object of which was to *surprise.* The letters in the field are no more than the owner's initials. Sard. (New York.)

Page 100.—Antique intaglio of a lion, set in a private seal of the 13th century, as may be deduced from the Lombardic lettering of the legend. The words "Ira Regia, &c." refer to a verse of Solomon's: "The wrath of a king is as the roaring of a lion;" hence we may suppose the jewel to have served for talisman to a courtier. Drawn to the actual size.

Page 179.—Girl, with dishevelled hair, advancing on tip-toe, amidst a profusion of floating drapery. This figure has hitherto passed for a Mænad in Bacchic frenzy—but as she carries none of the indispensable symbols of Dionysiac worship, neither the thyrsus nor the ivy-wreath, she can be no other than a dancing-girl, Juvenal's "choro Gaditana canoro:" clothed, or rather, unclothed, in the transparent loose gauze, which this representation shows to have really merited its name of "Ventus textilis." Plasma of the finest quality, and uncommon size. (Praun.)

Page 200.—Bust of Vahrahran Kermanshah: upon his tiara is emblazoned the symbol known as the Standard of the Empire. Drawn to double the size from the masterpiece of Sassanian art, the Devonshire Amethyst.

Page 282.—The Philoctetes of Böethus. (Beverley.)

Page 287.—Head of the Etruscan Jupiter. (Blacas.)

TRIUMPH OF LICINIUS.

(*Vide* p. 50.)

(From Duruy's '*Histoire Romaine*,' vii. p. 27.)

To face p. 1

A HANDBOOK OF ENGRAVED GEMS.

HISTORY OF THE GLYPTIC ART.

I.

THE prophet Enoch has recorded (viii. 1) that it was Azazyel, the chief of the angels who took unto themselves wives from among the daughters of men, who first taught "the use of stones of every valuable and select kind;" and although the "seventh from Adam" is no longer regarded as a canonical authority, yet history and archæology combine to point out the first cradle of the human race as the region where originated the notion of applying stones, recommended by their beauty of appearance, to the purposes of personal decoration, and of serving for signets. It is a remarkable fact that, whilst the old Greek mythologists have ascribed to some particular divinity, or hero of their race, the authorship of almost every other useful or ornamental art, and of the instruments employed therein (as of ship-building and of the loom to Pallas, of the saw and the auger to Dædalus, of the working in metal with the hammer and anvil to Cinyras the Cyprian, of the lathe to Theodorus of Samos, &c.), they should have left unnoticed the inventor of the several processes employed by the glyptic art. And this neglect is the more surprising, from the art being, according to their habits of thought, of such extreme importance, and this infinitely more on account of its subservience, during the greater part of its flourishing existence, to the uses of public and private life, than to the mere gratification of taste and the love of the Beautiful. This silence on the part of the Greek mythographers, ever ready as they were to claim for their own countrymen the credit of every discovery in science or invention in manufacture (even when manifestly due to foreigners, and merely naturalised and perfected upon Hellenic soil), sufficiently declares both the undeniably exotic origin of the art of engraving upon gems, and also its comparatively recent introduction into Greece and Italy. The negative testimony, too, of Homer upon this point is justly adduced by Pliny (xxxiii. 4) in proof of the same thing. He observes that no mention whatever of signet rings is to be discovered amongst that poet's minute descriptions of ornamental jewels, although he particularly specifies ear-rings, necklaces, and hair-cauls, the work of the Olympic court-jeweller, Vulcan. In fact, it is apparent that gems, even in their native state, were totally unknown to Homer; *amber* (and possibly *pearls*, in the solitary instance of Juno's τρίγλῃνα, "triple-eyed" ear-rings) are the sole materials, besides gold, that enter into the composition of his jewelry; and yet he describes it with great exactness, and with an evident appreciation of the artistic skill displayed in its workmanship; for example, when he vividly pictures to us the brooch of Ulysses chased with the group of a hound pulling down a "sorely-panting fawn," "which all gazed at with wonder to see how the two, though formed in gold, seemed, the one barking as he throttled the deer, the other, struggling to get loose, kept beating with her fore-feet" (Od. xix. 227). But it is a truth that the real precious stones were till long after but little known to the Greeks, before, first, Asia was opened up to them by their intercourse, both hostile and amicable, with the Persians, and subsequently by the conquests of Alexander.

Again, a still more convincing proof that signets were not in use with the Greeks in the Homeric age, is that whenever the poet has occasion to speak of the securing of treasures, that end is always effected by the means of an artfully-tied knot, the unfastening of which is only understood by its maker; not by the imposition of a seal, in after times the regular substitute for a lock amongst both Greeks and Romans. Furthermore, the treacherous letter carried by Bellerophon to Iobates has no seal upon it that is mentioned, it is simply called "a folded tablet;" and, again, when the heroes cast lots, before the duel with Hector, it is done with marked sticks, and not with the signet-ring of each, which became the established method after the latter ornament had come into general use.

Later poets, indeed, transfer to the Heroic ages the customs of their own times; the dread of an anachronism being a feeling of purely modern growth. Sophocles, for example, makes Electra recognise her brother Orestes upon his producing the signet of his father Agamemnon:

"Art thou then he?" "Cast but thine eye on this,
My father's seat, and learn if I speak truth."

And similarly the Theseus of Euripides exclaims, on beholding Phædra's accusing letter, discovered by him upon her corpse,—

> "And lo! the impress of the gold-wrought signet
> Of her that is no more salutes mine eye."

But the Athenian poets, as just remarked, never troubled themselves about archæological accuracy. In fact, Lessing, in his dissertation upon the famous "Ring of Polycrates," boldly maintains that the Greeks did not begin to wear signet-rings at all before the date of the Peloponnesian War (B.C. 431). In this he is probably correct, if his dictum be restricted, in our sense of the word, to the *actual ring*, containing the engraved gem, the true signet, *σφραγίς*. For had it been a regular fashion with his countrymen, at the time when Herodotus flourished, to wear the engraved stone set in a ring upon the *finger*, that observant traveller would have noticed as a striking peculiarity in the Babylonian customs (fond as he was of putting down such like contraventions of Grecian manners) their mode of wearing the signet, "which every man there possessed," by means of a string suspended from the *wrist* or *neck*. His silence on this point proves that he passed the fashion over unnoticed, as a matter of course, and familiar to him at home.

II.

But if from Greece we turn to Asia, signets appear as far back as historic records extend, holding a highly-important place in the usages of the most antique amongst civilized nations, the Assyrians and the Egyptians. We find the signet of Judah the Syrian pledged as a security for a promised payment; that of King Pharaoh given to Joseph as a badge of his investiture with vicarious authority; the treasure-chamber of Rhampsinitus secured by the impression of his seal (Herod. ii. 121); the temple of Belus sealed up with the signet of Darius; the stone closing in the den of lions and their fellow-prisoner Daniel sealed "with the signet of the same king, and with the signet of his nobles," &c. All these circumstances declare that this contrivance for securing property had been known in the East from time immemorial; in fact, was almost coeval with the very institution of the right of property. For it must be remembered that in both these centres of primæval civilization, the plastic clay of the two parent rivers, the Tigris and the Nile, supplied the inhabitants with the material for almost all their requirements—their houses, store-vessels, memorandum-books, historical monuments, and, lastly, their coffins. The idea, therefore, must naturally have suggested itself to the first individual who deposited his property in a closed vessel, that it might be protected against pilferers by a plaster of clay laid round the junction of the lid, and rolled flat with the joint of a reed. Hence the first origin of the perforated *cylinder*, of which the bit of reed was the true prototype, both as to its form and its mode of application, and way of carriage.

Something analogous to this is to be met with even in Grecian usage, and as late as the times of Aristophanes, who makes Euripides recommend to suspicious husbands similar nature-signets ("worm-eaten bits of wood") as seals proof against all forgery, to which the more elaborate productions of the gem-engraver were then so much exposed. From the natural markings upon the reed-joint, or the fantastically perforated wood, employed to impress the clay, the transition was easy to some definite device scratched around the circumference of the former by the owner, and appropriated to himself as his own peculiar mark. This instinct of possession extending itself to the assumption of exclusive ownership in certain configurations of lines, or rude delineations of natural objects, is a universal impulse of man's nature, and one found existing amongst all savage nations when first discovered, wheresoever the faintest traces of social life and polity have begun to develop themselves. Thus the Red Indian has, besides the mark of his tribe, that of the individual (his *totem*) wherewith to identify his own property or the game he may kill. The South Sea Islander carries the tattooed pattern (*amoco*) that distinguishes his particular family imprinted in his skin, and also draws the same upon his credentials, like a regular coat of arms.

These simple signets, with their artless carvings, preceded by a long space the invention of hieroglyphics, or any other arbitrary mode of denoting ideas; for the earlier Assyrian cylinders present nothing but rude human and animal figures, or else religious symbols engraved upon them, and never exhibit the cuneiform legends that so commonly illustrate the design upon those belonging to a more advanced stage of civilization. And yet even this later date is anterior by several generations to the first appearance of anything like an engraved gem amongst the nations of Europe. Again, if we look towards Egypt, the incredible abundance of *scarabæi*, formed of terra-cotta glazed, or of a soft stone, of the same period with the primitive cylinders, still remaining above ground (and how small a tithe these of the millions still buried!), strikingly demonstrates the long-established use, and the great importance of the purposes for which they were there employed. And this was amongst the inhabitants of the land that ever boasted itself the true fountain-head of all ancient civilization. In fact, the vast quantities in which scarabæi must have been manufactured during the entire continuance of Egyptian independence, has been sagaciously accounted for by a theory founded upon an expression of Plato's, in his 'Eryxias,' "in Ethiopia they use *engraved stones* instead of money," that they passed amongst the natives as representatives of trifling values, in lieu of small change (larger sums being paid in rings of gold and silver), like the earthen and leather tokens of early Rome recorded by Suidas, or the cowries of our own times amongst the natives of Hindostan. And speaking of the latter, by a singular coincidence, these cowries are actually manufactured in *china* at our potteries for exportation thither, it having been discovered that the artificial shell can be supplied in sufficient quantities more cheaply than the natural one; another point of analogy to the use above suggested as the real object of the terra-cotta scarabæi.

III.

Thus far, however, we have come upon no traces, in these earliest of signets, of the ***true process*** of gem-engraving, for all the designs they bear have been incised by means of some cutting-instrument, whether flint or bronze, capable of operating upon a comparatively soft material. Herodotus (vii. 69) describes the Ethiopian contingent, in the host of Xerxes, as equipped with reed-arrows tipped with the stone, sharpened to a point, "by means of which they engrave their seals." Arrows, flint-headed, found in the mummy-pits certify us of what kind this stone was. The first Assyrian cylinders were made of ***serpentine***, green or red; a material recommended by its pleasing colour, susceptibility of fine polish, and facility of carving; the first Egyptian scarabæi are in ***steaschist***, a cognate material, and prized for the same qualities, or else in glazed terra-cotta. The actual invention of the true art of gem-engraving (the incising a gem by means of a drill charged with the powder of a harder mineral) is undoubtedly due to the seal-cutters of Nineveh, and that at a date shortly preceding the times of Urukh; that is as early as the year B.C. 2000. This is the era at which cylinders begin to make their appearance in the so-called "Hard Stones" (better termed by the French *Pierres Fines*)—onyx, agate, calcedony, crystal—covered with engravings executed in precisely the same style with the Archaic Greek intagli, and marked by the same minuteness of detail and elaborateness of finish.

The delicate execution of the best engravings referable to this period manifests that their authors had already invented the use of the *diamond-point* applied in the manner described by Pliny: "These minute splinters [of the crushed diamond] gem-engravers greatly value, and mount them in an iron tool; there being nothing so hard that they will not hollow out with facility." And the same instrument is distinctly referred to in the most venerable of all historical records: "The sin of Israel is written with a pen of iron, *and* with the point of a diamond; it is graven on the table of their hearts" (Jer. xvii. 1). The passage (evidently allusive to the stones of the High Priest's breastplate) is more correctly rendered by Jerome: "Stylo ferreo in *ungue* adamantino:" the *adamas* of those primitive times being beyond all question the *corundum*, the great agent of the Hindoo lapidary to the present day. Amongst their works, the signet of Sennacherib (now preserved in the British Museum) may be quoted as an example fully justifying this assertion, for it is made out of one of the finest substances known to the lapidary, the Oriental Amazon-stone; and nevertheless presents an intaglio that, by the extreme precision and complicated detail of its drawing, strikingly declares the perfection to which the art had thus early attained: a perfection, too, indicative of the long practice of the school capable of such a performance. Cylinders of a merit nearly commensurate with this, besides a large number of others inferior but still praiseworthy for execution, done in the same style and by the same perfected process, continued to be produced during the whole succeeding period down to the close of the first Persian Empire. The collection just cited also possesses the very royal signet of some Darius (it may be the identical one that secured the prophet's dungeon), engraved in a greenish calcedony, and having for its type the king in his car, with the legend, "I Darius the king," thrice repeated in the principal dialects current in his dominions.

IV.

As regards the *materials* appropriated to itself by the Glyptic Art amongst the Assyrians, it is apparent, from the numerous specimens of their jewelry still preserved, that neither this nation nor the Egyptians were as yet acquainted with the true "precious stones," the exclusive productions of India. The first rank with them for rarity as well as for beauty was assigned to the lapis-lazuli and the common amethyst; gems supplied to them by the veins of their own mountains, or by the beds of the torrents issuing therefrom. But of the Tyrian merchant the jewel-casket was far more richly furnished, and that, too, at a period anterior to Nebuchadnezzar's invasion of his country. The prophet Ezekiel calls up before our minds how the merchants of Saba (South Arabia) and of Raema brought to the marts of "the renowned city that was strong in the sea" all manner of spices, of *precious stones*, and of gold." These caravans from South Arabia had doubtless brought with them the choicest exports of their Indian neighbours; and that these included every species of the true precious stones we are assured on the testimony of the evidently well-informed Dionysius Periegetes, writing some eight centuries after the times of the prophet. All of them, even including the diamond, are named by him as gleaned by the Ariani of Paropamisus from the beds of their mountain streams. The Hebrew poet, in his gorgeous picture of the Prince of Tyrus: "The anointed cherub that covereth—thou that sealest up the sum, full of wisdom, perfect in beauty," set him before us as blazing in jewels; "Thou hast been in Eden, the garden of God, every precious stone was thy covering," proceeding to enumerate the sard, topaz, and jasper; the chrysolite, onyx, and beryl; the sapphire, carbuncle, and emerald. Or as Jerome more truly renders the passage, the Prince is termed "signaculum similitudinis," "the impression (or seal) of the Divine image;" he also gives "chrysolithus" (*Oriental topaz*) where our version has "diamond;" and his authority as to the Latin equivalents to the Hebrew terms of the sort is deserving, from the circumstances of his period and opportunities, of the very greatest respect.

Before quitting the subject of material it may be appropriately added here, that in the age of Alexander, the Greeks already possessed (as the descriptive list compiled by Theophrastus puts beyond question) all the true precious stones (except the diamond), including the real Indian ruby. Even without his authority the inspection of the Etruscan and Greek jewelry, brought to light of late years, would tell us as much, for these relics exhibit unmistakable, though minute, specimens of the native ruby, sapphire, and emerald.

V.

The affinity between the Assyrian style of *Design* and that of Archaic Greek Art, as exhibited in all its remains, cannot but strike every one who examines each with intelligence. The subjects, for example, that decorate the earliest Greek vases, the sole existing specimens of the painting of their times, are purely Assyrian both in nature and in treatment. They consist entirely of sphinxes, gryphons, harpies, and similar composite monsters such as were being contemporaneously depicted upon the walls, "portrayed in vermilion," of Susa and Persepolis.

In this branch, therefore, of art, the parentage of the Grecian is sufficiently obvious: that of the special subject of this inquiry shall be indicated in its proper place. Neither must it be overlooked that Pliny, going upon ancient tradition, asserts that Grecian *sculptura* in marble (in contradistinction to the more ancient *statuaria* in bronze) was invented by Scyllis and Dercyllides, in Crete, whilst that island still belonged to the Persian dominions. There is therefore nothing to surprise us in the Persepolitan air of the Metopes of Selinus, or even in much of the Eginetan marbles.

It only remains to be noticed here that the Greek art of vase-painting became known to the Etruscans at an early period of their establishment in Italy as a distinct nationality, a fact shadowed forth in the legend concerning the two companions of Demaratus upon his emigration from Corinth to Tarquinii; they were the *painter* Eugrammos, and the *potter* Eucheir. Nevertheless the Etruscans found it more convenient in general to make use of the Grecian manufacture, which may either have been imported as an article of commerce through Tarquinii, Ardea, and other maritime towns; or else (a theory serving better to explain certain existing facts) the ware was made in the country by a colony of Greek potters there domiciled, particularly in the district about Vulci. Proportionally few vases, and those in *artistic* value far below the rest, are inscribed with legends in the *Etruscan* language. Such examples, when they *do* occur, supply a trustworthy criterion for distinguishing between the Greek and the Etruscan fabrique. Out of the innumerable vases found at Vulci, not more than three (according to K. O. Müller) present indubitably Etruscan inscriptions; and the total number of such known to exist, says Millingen, amounts only to seven. A singular contrast this to the lesson taught us by the bronze *mirrors*, that specially national manufacture, where a true Greek inscription amongst the hundreds of Etruscan now collected, would form, if ever discovered, a most interesting exception. The Etruscans were the great metal-workers of the ancient world, favoured as they were with the possession of the inexhaustible copper-mines of Monte Catino. Even in the age of Socrates they maintained their pre-eminence for the making of gold plate and "of all bronze vessels required either for domestic use or ornament," as his disciple Critias informs us in a fragment of a poem preserved by Athenæus. In the latter manufacture they continued to compete with Greece long after art had been fully perfected there, for Horace alludes to the "Tyrrhena sigilla," or *bronze statuettes*, as being held in as high estimation by the dilettanti of the Augustan age as now by those of our own. These, too, were the "Signa Tuscanica" of Pliny, mentioned by him as then diffused all over the civilized world. Besides, the Etruscan statuaries were capable of the boldest flights; the same author cites their colossus of Apollo, fifty feet high, standing then in the Palatine Library; and is at a loss which most to admire, the excellence of the workmanship or the beauty of the metal.

VI.

But to return to gem-engraving. The Egyptians did not generally adopt the improved but more laborious process by that time established in the ateliers of Nineveh or Babylon, but continued the practice of carving or chiselling out their rude hieroglyphics upon the softer materials until the times of the Ptolemies. The signets of their kings and great men were engraved in gold, those of the commonalty upon the easily-worked substances, a fine limestone and steaschists of various colours, and in the manner already described. The circumstance that even in the age of Theophrastus the best material (ἀκόναι) used in engraving gems was still brought all the way from *Armenia*, points of itself to that quarter as the locality where the use of that agent was first discovered and generally adopted by the practitioners of the art.

This new method of rendering available for signets even the "hard stones," although neglected by the Egyptians, was speedily taken up by the ingenious *Phœnicians*, the allies or tributaries of the Assyrian and the Persian kings. In attestation of this, many seals are found, Egyptian indeed, in form, being regular scarabæi, but purely Phœnician in style and subjects, though of a very early date, and bearing also inscriptions in the Semitic character, of which that people were the first inventors. There are even some cylinders known that, from similar reasons, must be assigned to the Phœnician school. Their traders may have diffused the knowledge of this as well as of other decorative arts amongst the European and insular Greeks. Homer alludes to the Tyrian merchant-ships voyaging about amongst the islands of the Ægean sea, and trafficking in ornaments and jewelry with their inhabitants. His Tyrian captain offers for sale to the Queen of Syra a necklace of gold with pendants in amber; the latter probably carved into scarabæi, or such like symbolical figures, as they so frequently occur in similar ornaments of the Etruscan ladies (Od. xv. 460).

The Asiatic Greeks, however, who seem to have flourished as independent communities previous to the reign of Crœsus (noted by Herodotus as the first subjugator of the Ionians) learnt this art, simultaneously with the Phœnicians, from their Assyrian neighbours, to whom they were indebted as pointed out above, for all the other arts of design. Like the vase-paintings, the first intagli produced amongst the inhabitants of the sea-board of Asia Minor, bear the unmistakable impress of a Ninevitish or Babylonian origin in their stiffly-drawn, carefully-executed figures of animals; lions or bulls, for the most part, supplying the device for the signet of the newly-planted Æolian or Ionian colonist. And such a restriction was to be looked for in this class, for it will be observed that the designs upon the scarabæi of the Phœnicians also deviate but little from the strict rules of the Assyrian code of art; a point which of late years has been remarkably illustrated by the numerous engraved gems brought to light in the cemeteries of their most ancient European colony, Tharros in Sardinia. But the Phœnicians were an imitative, not an inventive race: thus they fabricated jewelry and porcelain ornaments in the Egyptian style for the Etruscan trade, copying the hieroglyphics of their patterns with precisely the same degree of intelligence as a Birmingham manufacturer evinces in his now so fashionable *caricatures* of antique medals.

VII.

From Asia Minor to Greece Proper the transition of fashion was expeditious, and the signet, now for the first time worn mounted as a *finger-ring*, came into universal favour amongst all the Hellenic population. This was a new method for securing the engraved stone; for the original inventors of seal-engraving had worn and continued to wear, down to the very close of their history (even to the date of the Arabian conquest), the cylinder or the conical seal as the ornament of the bracelet or the necklace. In fact, the curious necklace regularly borne by gods and royal personages in Assyrian sculptures appears to be entirely made up of cylinders separated by round beads. This explanation is supported by the practice, doubtless traditionary, of the Arab women of thus utilising, as an adjunct to other beads, all the antique cylinders picked up by them in the ruins of Hilleh, Khorsabad, &c.; a fashion which, until lately, was the only source supplying archæologists with these interesting relics. This primitive mode of carrying about one's signet seems, as the negative testimony of Herodotus above quoted shows, to have been in the first instance the usual one with the Asiatic Greeks; they had, however, modified the shape of the gem into the *scarabæid*, an elliptical disc convex at the back and perforated through its axis; a convenient pattern, the mean between the Persian cone and the Egyptian scarabæus. This fashion appears to have been first devised and made popular by that practical people the Phœnicians, to judge from its general use for signets, whose devices are in their national style. Its general adoption by the Ionians is established by one conclusive example upon a painted vase (figured by Visconti). Jupiter himself appears with his imperial signet thus shaped and tied round his wrist with a fine string.

Mythologists told an ingenious fable to account for the origin of the finger-ring. Jove, upon loosing the Titan Prometheus from the bonds to which he had been condemned to eternity, obliged him as a perpetual penance, as an equivalent to his original sentence, to wear for ever upon his finger a link of the chain enchased with a fragment of the Caucasian rock of torture. Thus ornamented, Catullus introduces him at the Wedding of Peleus (l. 295).

> "Came wise Prometheus; on his hand he wore
> The slender symbol of his doom of yore,
> When fettered fast with adamantine chain
> Hung from the craggy steep, he groaned in endless pain."

That this invention should be ascribed to Prometheus, a Grecian hero, and its designation δακτύλιος, a word of native origin (unlike those of many other personal ornaments evidently of a foreign root, μανιάκης ψέλλιον, for example), are considerations going far to prove that this latest and most permanent fashion was purely an innovation of the Greeks. Besides this, we have the express statement of Pliny (xxxiii. 4), that the use of the finger-ring was introduced amongst the Romans from Greece. "E Grecia fuit origo unde hic annulorum usus venit." The comparative lateness of the fashion is also indicated by the fact that all Greek intagli in the Archaic manner are found upon gems shaped as scarabæids. Even actual scarabæi have been discovered in the Greek islands; and although many of these may have been imported by Phœnician or Etruscan traders and colonists, yet a few are known of indisputably Hellenic origin. The strange corruption of the commonest Greek names to be seen on the most finished works of the *Etruscan* engraver betrays the efforts of an Oriental tongue to express sounds entirely new to it in a novel alphabet, whereas the very rare scarabæi in question exhibit the names of their proprietors, written according to the correct though antiquated spelling, intended to read from right to left on the *impression*—a convincing proof of their very early date. Of these, the finest examples are the one with the type of a beetle with expanded wings, reading in boldly-cut characters ΑΔΙΤΝΟƎꟼꓘ, discovered by Finlay the historian in a tomb in Egina; and another from the plain of Troy, finely engraved with a girl kneeling at a fountain, with the name ƩΟΝΟΜΕƩ.

But whatever their nature, signets of some sort or other must have been in general use amongst the Greeks 600 years before our era; for, shortly after that date, we find Solon enacting, amongst his other laws, that the *gem-engravers* (already, therefore, constituting a distinct profession) should not keep by them the copy of any signet once sold. The object of this regulation was to prevent the fradulent use of another person's seal through the obtaining a counterpart of the same from its engraver. About this date also Herodotus mentions the famous emerald signet of Polycrates, and the celebrity of the man who engraved it, Theodorus the Samian, as a jeweller and a worker in metal. It may be remarked here that this island, Samos, was the focus of the glyptic art, as far as Greece was concerned. According to the records, now lost, to which Apuleius had access (Florid. ii. 15), Mnesarchus, the father of Pythagoras (B.C. 570), "amongst the sedentary artists working there, sought rather for fame than for riches by engraving gems in the most skilful manner."

VIII.

The Etruscans, or, as they called themselves, the *Rasenæ*, were of a race very distinct from the Hellenic, as their language proves, which has more analogy to the Armenian than to any other, although there is no doubt that Lydia was their latest seat, and their ruling family of Assyrian stock, for the kings styled themselves *Sandonidæ* as the descendants of *Sandon*, the Hercules of the Babylonians. Nevertheless, they speedily adopted Hellenic culture and art, and that to an extent infinitely greater than any other foreign race in those remote times. The cause was due apparently to the colony of Pelasgic Tyrrhenes, driven out of Southern Lydia (Torrhebis), and which settled in Italy around the cities of Cære and Tarquinii. The latter place long maintained its rank as the metropolis of the Etruscan confederation, and ever remained the principal channel through which Greek civilization flowed into the rest of the country, chiefly from Corinth, the city of potters and metal-chasers. Besides, the Etruscans acquired much that was Hellenic through their intercourse with the Dorian colonies in Lower Italy, especially after they had themselves gotten a settlement at Vulturnum and Nola; as well as, still later, by their direct trade with Corinth and Phocæa.

This wealthy and luxurious nation (infamous on both accounts amongst the poor and ever-envious Greeks, as the stories Timæus retails about their licentious manners sufficiently indicate) were eager to decorate their persons by every means imaginable, and consequently were passionate lovers of jewelry. From the earliest period of their national existence they gave employment to a multitude of engravers in "fine stones." The majority of the subjects upon their gems, and particularly those the most archaic in style, are proved by the localities where they are discovered so plentifully now, and still more by the strangely-distorted spelling of the Greek names in the legends occurring upon some of their number, to be beyond all question Etruscan works, and not old Greek imported from abroad, as some archæologists have endeavoured to establish.

These intagli display the steps by which the art advanced, from the production of figures composed entirely by the juxtaposition of drill-holes up to those executed in the most elaborate and highly finished manner, and which exhibit marked vestiges of the extensive employment of the diamond-point. In the highest style attained to by the Etruscans, their gem-work combines a wonderful delicacy of execution with a love for violent action and an exaggerated drawing of the muscular parts of the figures introduced—considerations that often seem to have dictated the choice of the subjects.

The distinctive character of art amongst the early Greeks and the Etruscans cannot be better described than by quoting the masterly definition of Winckelmann's when treating of the famous Tydeus of Stosch's cabinet (*Pierres Gravées*, p. 348):—"Carnelian. Tydeus, one of the seven heroes of the Argive League against Thebes, who, having received a wound, is plucking the dart out of his right leg; with his name in Etruscan characters ƎTVT. If the intaglio of the Five Heroes be, as I have stated, the most ancient monument of the art in general, this gem is assuredly one displaying the highest perfection of the same art amongst the Etruscans. It is executed with a precision and delicacy which yield in no point to the finest Greek engravings. Here we are enabled to do more than merely form conjectures as to the state in which the art was at that period; nay, can decide upon it, as it were, without risk of error, and by combining the lights furnished to us by the other Etruscan monuments, we can determine by the means of this figure of Tydeus the character and the peculiarities of design among the Etruscans.

"The proportions of the *figure* in general are here already established upon the rules of harmony deduced by them from the study of Nature in her finest forms; and the figure is finished and easy to quite the same degree as the most beautiful Grecian statues. The engraver's profound knowledge of anatomy is everywhere conspicuous, each part is in its own place and is marked out with sureness; and in truth the subject chosen by the artist was of a character to display the entire extent of the study he had pursued of Nature. The acute pain felt by Tydeus and the efforts that he makes to pull the dart out of his leg demanded an attitude full of violence, with all the muscles in motion and under irritation. And this was precisely the limit of the skill of the master, who had not advanced as yet as far as the notion of Ideal Beauty. In fact, the head of Tydeus presents neither nobleness nor elevation of feeling, the idea of it is borrowed from ordinary nature. Another defect is that by the effort of the artist to show off so ostentatiously the whole of his anatomical knowledge, he has become exaggerated and stiff; all the parts are too strongly marked; and though the pain by which Tydeus was agitated demanded that the muscles should be swollen, yet the bones are too distinctly shown and the joints too loose and strained. To give an idea of all this to such as may not have the opportunity of seeing the gem or even the impression, I venture to compare this figure with the drawing of M. Angelo: there is the same relation between the manner of our figure with the Greek as between the drawing of M. Angelo and Raffaele's. The drawing, however, in this work must not be regarded as a personal peculiarity of the artist individually; the stiffness of the outline and the exaggerated rendering of the parts was the character of Etruscan art in general.

"The arts make their way towards perfection by means of exactitude and precision; but these two qualities are liable to go astray wherever they are coupled with the defects I have just particularised, and the eagerness of the artist to display his knowledge does not always confine itself within the bounds of simplicity. The exaggerated style of M. Angelo depends upon these causes; and (not to refer it to the national genius) it was these very causes that formed the characteristics of the Etruscan artists. Although it be true that amongst the Greeks design only attained to its sublime elevation by passing through the same gradations, it must be remarked that the circumstances were very different; by the time that the arts were in their fullest perfection in Greece, the Etruscans were worn out by continual wars, and at last remained subjugated by the Romans. It is therefore probable that even had the manners and form of government among the Etruscans been as well adapted to favour the progress of the arts as they were among the Greeks, yet the complete perfection of art amongst the former people was rendered impracticable, inasmuch as its accomplishment was cut short by the fall of their commonwealth. Such is the judgment which the examination of this intaglio induces us to pass."

A summary of the remarks of the same great critic upon the more complicated design of 'The Five Heroes before Thebes,' will render this portion of our subject complete:—"The reader must be apprized at starting that this stone is not only the most ancient monument of the art of the Etruscans, but also of art in general. For the shapes of the characters and the spelling of the words differ much from the ordinary Etruscan usage, and approximate more to the Pelasgic language, which is regarded by the learned as the mother as well of the Etruscan as of the Greek.

"In the next place, the engraving is executed with extraordinary carefulness, and exhibits a degree of finish far beyond one's preconceived idea of the productions of so remote a period. It is in this respect that it authorises us to judge, on sure grounds, of the 'First Manner' of the art of design. In fact, this gem, with the Tydeus, comprehends, so to speak, the complete system of Etruscan art; and the knowledge to be derived from them is much more to be relied upon than that furnished by the urns and painted vases which are only the productions of artists of an inferior rank.

"We discover in the Five Heroes the drawing of a master who belonged to a period when the Beautiful was not the primary object of art, as neither was it with the Greeks at the date of the earliest medals of Syracuse, Messina, Crotona, Athens, and other states, which subsequently all distinguished themselves by their inimitable coinage. The expression in the heads, which is very commonplace and without any individuality, justifies us in forming this judgment.

"Similarly the due proportions of the bodies were not as yet established: we perceive that the heads of our heroes are certainly larger than the seventh part of the entire figure. Consequently this period was the same one wherein architecture had not attained to those elegant proportions in columns that constitute all the beauty of them: witness the temples of Pesto, or Girgenti, and one of the temples in Attica. Lastly, there did not at that time exist any idea of beautiful variety in the grouping: Tydeus and Polynices are placed the one next to the other in the same attitude; and the latter, being opposite to Amphiaraus, is seated exactly like him without the least variation in the pose. The folds in the draperies of Parthenopæus and Polynices are parallel to one another, and of the same thickness—an indubitable characteristic of the most ancient style.

"Nevertheless the artists belonging to that primitive age of art very well understood the *material* of the human figure; and at least they knew how to draw those portions thereof in which nothing is left to the imagination. The feet here are drawn with elegance, and the ankle, notwithstanding the minuteness of the figures, is indicated upon them without harshness, nay, with grace; we even can discern the veins in the arm of Polynices. Amphiaraus has his breast protuberant exactly as we see him represented in statues in the finest style.

"The extreme finish of the engraving is likewise a proof that skill in the mechanical part of the art reached its perfection long before artists had attained to beauty in the drawing—an observation applicable to the works of the painters preceding Raffaele, for their pictures are very highly finished. This gem, therefore, holds the same place amongst other engraved gems that Homer does amongst the poets; no collection can boast of possessing another monument, in the way of engraving, equally valuable.

"This gem would supply many illustrations of the science

of archæology, but which would overpass the limits which our plan obliges us to observe. For instance, the shield of Amphiaraus has two grooves in the sides, after the pattern of the shields seen upon the medals of Argos, and of the one carved in relief upon the ruins of the Temple of Apollo at Amyclæ."

IX.

Rings formed entirely of gold have also been brought to light in considerable numbers by recent excavations, having their faces engraved or punched out in arabesque figures (*graffiti*) of an unmistakably Oriental character. In all such there manifests itself an aiming at monstrous combinations which clearly points to the true source whence the artist drew his inspiration—the Babylonian or Phœnician works of the same description. Compare the Etruscan arabesques, the border-patterns (for example, the so-called honeysuckle), the winged deities, and the symbolical animals, the harpies, sphinxes, gryphons,—in short, every design of the incised ornamentation decorating the Assyrian bronze *pateræ* lately discovered,—compare all these with the *graffiti* on either the rings or the mirrors of the Etruscans, and the immediate derivation of the latter style from Assyria becomes incontrovertibly obvious. Through the study of these relics, joined to the recognition of Oriental workmanship in all Etruscan jewelry, the crowns, bracelets (chiefly discovered about Vulci), &c., has the traditional Asiatic origin of the nation, as well as their love for personal decoration, so often noticed by ancient writers, received in our times the most conspicuous verification.

Again: if we proceed to consider their *scarabæi*, more especially those whose style betokens an earlier date, these, equally in material, form, and taste, point to Asia as the genuine land of their nativity. Their favourite stone, the Oriental sard, bears testimony, by its very name (from the Persian *sered*,) equally as decisive as to the country that supplied it. Together with the gem, came into Italy the art of engraving upon it; nay, more, the engravers themselves by a continuous immigration. There is a striking analogy in the mode of producing the designs upon the scarabæi in question by means of unassisted drill-holes, and the technique characterising the agate and calcedony cylinders belonging to the Second Period of Assyrian Art.

X.

These signets, like the Phœnician, retain the form of the *Beetle.* Why both nations should have conceived so persistent a partiality for that Egyptian fashion can only be a matter for conjecture. But it may be that, as the received symbol of the sun, this insect-form had recommended itself to the Phœnicians—those exclusive worshippers of that luminary, under the name of Baal: the beetle having acquired this honourable distinction amongst the Egyptians from its habit of forming globes, types of the world, as receptacles for its eggs, thus symbolising the creation and its Author (Plin. xxx. 30). Ælian, moreover, states that the warrior-caste amongst the Egyptians wore *beetles* in their rings as a badge of their profession, because the insect typified *manliness*, being, according to the popular belief, exclusively of the male sex. From this notice of Ælian's, Köhler ingeniously conjectures that amongst the Etruscans also this was at first the distinction of the military class (as the gold ring was of the Roman *knights*); and upon this hypothesis he proceeds to account for the exclusively martial character of the devices—heroes and combats—to be found upon the scarabæi that he refers to the most ancient of his three classes. If this explanation be the correct one, the shape, in the sense of a talisman, survived the fall of Etruria, and even of Rome herself; for one, engraved with Hercules at the fountain, had been deposited along with his other jewels in the sepulchre of the Frankish king Childeric at Tournay, evidently from a lingering belief in its prophylactic virtue (Chiflet's 'Anastasis').

XI.

As for the *subjects* constituting the signet itself, the majority of the scarabæi that come to light (more particularly those whose elaborate gold mountings indicate a period of extreme opulence in the first owners) bear only the delineations of animals domestic or wild, or else the single figures of deities and men. It would seem that it was not until after their intercourse with the Greeks had been long established, that they began to attempt embodying upon the field of the signet the personages and the scenes derived immediately from the mythology and poetry of that people. This circumstance was the necessary consequence of their national origin (which has been already established from other considerations) concerning which the *ancients* were unanimously agreed; that the *Rasenæ* or ruling caste amongst the Etrurians were a civilizing colony from Lydia, who planted amongst the rude aborigines of Central Italy arts of luxury already flourishing in their former home. Their predecessors, the *Pelasgi*, of the same stock, had already founded cities, like Cære, there, and speedily became amalgamated with the new comers.

The colonists of Doric race in the southern parts of the peninsula, the flourishing states of Magna Grecia, seem to have adopted from the Etruscans the peculiar form of the scarabæus-signet, and in all likelihood actually to have first learnt from them the art of engraving gems. For Castellani informed me that in the innumerable tombs of the earliest Greek colonists (notably at Cumae founded a thousand years before our era) opened by him in the search for painted vases, he had never been able to discover a single *engraved gem;* nothing else but rings, cut as signets, rudely formed in *silver.* These Dorians, in their turn, communicated a tincture of their own mythological and poetical learning, together with, it is natural to suppose, the improvement in design that now becomes conspicuous in Etruscan works, the result of their own greater advancement in modelling, vase-painting, and sculpture.

This secondary process of education may possibly explain the circumstance, at first sight so puzzling, the apparent contemporaneous production of two classes of scarabæi; the one extremely barbarous, the other most exquisitely finished as regards the *intagli* upon them. This latter restriction is necessary; for it is indeed a remarkable fact that we often meet with large scarabæi of the finest sard, in which the beetle itself is modelled with perfect skill, and mounted in elaborate and costly settings, whilst their devices in *intaglio* appear to betoken the very infancy of the art.

The first gem-engraver on record, *Mnesarchus*, the father of Pythagoras, we have already found practising his art at Samos, close to the Lydian coast, before the year B.C. 570; and he is said by Aristotle (as quoted by Diogenes Laertius) to have been by birth a *Tyrrhene* belonging to one of the islands seized upon by the Athenians. This event may be connected with the expulsion of the Pelasgi from Lemnos (detailed by Herodotus), which took place about this period. Mnesarchus, thus driven from home, takes refuge in Samos, probably still in the possession of a kindred race. In this brief notice of Aristotle's, two important facts for our purpose are involved: it records a *Tyrrhene* exercising the profession of a gem-engraver, and likewise the causes that dispersed such artists, with the rest of their brethren, far and wide over the coasts of the Mediterranean; for his illustrious son, doubtless, according to ancient rule, trained up in the paternal trade, subsequently establishes himself and philosophy at Metapontum.

XII.

The point next to be considered, namely, the motive dictating the choice of the signet-types, may possibly derive some elucidation from certain historical conditions already alluded to. The royal line of the Asiatic Tyrrhenes called themselves *Sandonidæ*, which patronymic the Greeks rendered by the equivalent *Heraclidæ*, substituting, with close accuracy, the Hellenic *Heracles* for the Assyrian *Sandon*. This tradition is alone enough to account for the continual appearance in Etruscan art of that demigod, in a semi-Grecised shape, it is true, but retaining his national Assyrian weapons, the metal mace (not the more picturesque club assigned him by later art) and the bow; for so he figures more especially upon the gems of the earlier times. The Florentines, the

> . . . . "popolo maligno
> Che discese da Fiesole *ab antiquo*,"

preserving the ancestral tradition, still retain Hercules for one of the supporters of the City Arms, the other being his lion under his strange-sounding, perhaps original, name of *Marzocco;* figures certainly continually repeated, and in much the same relation to each other, upon the cylinders of their Assyrian progenitors.

The origin of the royal line solves the mystery, wherefore the lion should have been as great an Etruscan as he is now a British *institution*, from the time when Meles, their ancient king, carried him—the monster-birth of his concubine—round the walls of his new-built capital, Sardis, at the bidding of the oracle, so to render it impregnable; why his figure should have crowned the tumulus of every *Lucumo:* should have been the favourite impress for his signet—the finest Etruscan ring known, the Canino (British Museum), is modelled into the forms of two lions supporting a frame containing a scarabæus engraved in its turn with a lion regardant—and finally why "Evviva Marzocco!" was the Florentine war-cry down to the very extinction of the Republic.

One peculiarity difficult to account for, although hitherto unnoticed by any who have treated of Etruscan art, has arrested my attention whilst examining the numerous casts from scarabæi which I have had occasion to study whilst investigating this very interesting division of my subject. This peculiarity is, the narrow limits within which the gem-artists of Etruria have confined their choice of things and personages to be engraved upon the scarabæus, and which they never seemed to have overstepped so long as this form of the signet continued in fashion. The principal divisions under which their subjects fall have therefore been briefly marked out in the following attempt at their classification in the order of antiquity. The question seems one of a certain ulterior importance; for it is not improbable that, by directing the attention of archæologists to this point, some valuable results may accrue, bearing upon the first colonisation of Italy and the introduction of the arts of design into that country.

The first and by far the largest class of scarabæi with the rude designs in drill-work already noticed (and which may safely be assumed as the productions of the first ages of the Etruscan commonwealth), present the collector with subjects rarely having any mythological import, nor attempting representation of an event in fable or action requiring the introduction of two figures. Fantastic animals, like those on the *graffiti*, the gryphons, winged lions, &c., clearly indicate the Eastern origin of the notions embodied on the gems: Fauns busied about some Bacchic ceremony (Fauns and Nymphs are spoken of by Evander as the aboriginal population of Latium); or else Hercules, who figures in works of this style, to the almost entire exclusion of other deities and heroes—sometimes in the posture of defence, resting on one knee and brandishing his club, or letting fly an arrow; sometimes rushing forward to the attack, or engaged in the chase, and holding aloft some huge beast, the trophy of his success; or lastly (what his worshipper must have thought a favourite amusement of the demigod's, to judge from its frequent repetition), floating along upon a raft borne up by *Amphoræ*, now steering it with his club and holding up an empty wine-skin or bowl to serve for a sail, now extended hopelessly drunk upon his back. This last notion is a curious one, for it seems to have been imported from the Nile (along with the little idols found about Vulci), on whose flood rafts thus buoyed up are even now commonly to be seen. Juvenal also notices the Tentyrites as accustomed

> "On boats of potteryware to spread the sail
> And push with oars their varnished vessels frail."

Dionysius, "the Brazen," seems to have had in view these bacchanalian voyages of Hercules, in the lines quoted by Athenæus (x. 61):—

> "Some carrying wine, the Bacchic crew increased,
> *Rowers* of cups, and *sailors* of the feast."

And the famous voyage of the same hero in the borrowed Cup of the Sun, the mystery involved in which tradition was the fertile source of discussion with the later mythologists, may perhaps have had its origin in the commonplace expedient depicted by the archaic engraver. Other scarabæi bear the emblems of his different labours, the Nemean lion, and the tripleheaded giant Geryon; and again allusions to his imitator Theseus in the figure of the Minotaur, a man with the head only of a bull.

The rings with hollow faces made out of thin gold-plate, and evidently intended as mere ornaments for the finger, not for signets (for which their slightness renders them unsuitable), exhibit devices of a yet more marked Asiatic character, in their fantastic monsters and sacred trees, so strongly suggestive of Assyria. As none of the *graffiti* manifest in their designs any influence of Greek ideas, they may justly be put down to the account of the original Lydian colonists, or their fellow-settlers, the Asiatic Pelasgi.

But in that other class of scarabæi characterised by the extreme finish and minuteness of detail already pointed out as its distinctive marks, we meet with pictures of events taken from mythic history and represented in a style that forcibly recalls Pausanias's description of the same scenes in the ivory bas-reliefs panelling the Coffer of Cypselus (Eliac. i. 7). Now if Cypselus did actually dedicate this Coffer (his hiding-place in infancy), and there is little reason to doubt the truth of the old tradition, these carvings must have been done sometime before B.C. 660, the date of his usurping the supreme power at Corinth. He belonged to the indigenous Æolic stock ("being a Lapith and descendant of Cæneus," says Herodotus), and the Bacchiadæ whose rule he overthrew were the Doric conquerors who had changed the original name of the city, *Ephyre* into *Corinthus.*

Amongst the personages upon these gems we remark three as principally figuring: *Minerva,* usually represented with wings and occasionally with four (an attribute speaking plainly of an Asiatic origin, and always drawn in the stiff manner of the archaic bronzes); Hermes with his wand, and usually in his character of conductor of souls to Hades; and Hercules, who again supplies nearly as many illustrations to the graver as in the foregoing category. But in all Etruscan art the demigod does not combat clad in the lion's hide, and having for weapon the knotted wild-olive trunk assigned him by the Greeks; he is either nude or wears the customary heroic panoply, whilst his arms are purely Asiatic, being the strangely-shaped angular bow, and the slender-handled metal mace ending in a knob, such as his prototype Sandon wields in his encounters with the lion or Minotaur in the Babylonian sculptures. But *now* Hercules figures as the actor in some mythical scene; in combat with Cycnus, or with the Scythian gryphons, or carrying in triumph the vulture of Prometheus transfixed by his arrows.

There seems reason to conjecture that he is so great a favourite at this particular period of *Etruscan* art in consequence of his connection with Thebes, a city whose primeval history was the inexhaustible source whence the Pelasgian artists drew their ideas. A singular confirmation of this is supplied by Virgil (Æn. viii.), where he depicts Hercules as the patron god of the first occupants of the site of Rome, Evander and his Arcadians: a race who to the latest times of Greece boasted of their pure Pelasgic blood. And farther, Bœotia is named as the first seat of the Pelasgi, who were afterwards driven out from thence into the islands of the northern Ægean. Besides this, Thebes—surnamed *Ogygiæ,* to mark its antiquity—was the earliest centre of civilization in prehistoric Greece; and its legends, therefore, had become interwoven with the creed of all the colonists issuing therefrom. Thus upon our gems we find Cadmus, her traditional founder, approaching the dragon-guarded fount, or sowing in the earth the serpent's teeth fated to bring forth his new citizens replacing his devoured Phœnicians. Then succeed in regular series all the events of the memorable siege: the chiefs in council; the brothers in deadly conflict; Tydeus waylaid, wounded; severing the head of Melanippus; Capaneus struck by lightning; and so forth.

To the list of the long-celebrated Etruscan masterpieces described by Winckelmann (which were the Five Heroes in Council, Theseus in the shades, Tydeus purifying himself, Peleus returning from the Nereid's cave, and wringing out the brine from his flowing locks) may now be added others recently discovered and of fully equal excellence, namely:—the Hercules striking down Cycnus; the seated and pensive Hercules; the same hero opening the amphora of Pholus; the Capaneus, and some others found in the environs of Vulci and Chiusi. A very complete collection of these later discoveries, both in the perfected and in the more primitive styles, and also of the *graffiti*, will be found in the 'Impronte Gemmarie,' Cent. I., Nos. 1 to 50, and Cent. III., Nos. 1 to 65.

The classical reader will remark that the above-named subjects constitute likewise the main repertory of the early tragedians, "Thebes or Pelops' line" supplying them with infinitely a larger number of themes than does "the tale of Troy divine." For Argos, another centre of civilization which disputed with Thebes the priority of date, claiming an Egyptian as the other did a Phœnician planter, furnishes, in the story of Bellerophon and the Chimera, matter for many of these admirable engravings. Frequently, too, do we meet with Philoctetes, the companion, and, though more rarely, Theseus, the successor of Hercules in the task of clearing the earth of monsters and tyrants. Although other gods than the three above-mentioned are seldom brought upon the scene, yet one of the most perfect compositions in this style, commemorating another legend of Thebes, displays Jupiter, an aged venerable figure, long robed and with mighty wings, descending amidst a shower of lightnings upon the dying Semele; whilst a second exhibits Neptune, here a youthful beardless divinity (but recognised by his name annexed), tearing asunder the rocks which barred the course of the Peneus; for which service the Thessalians worshipped him under the epithet of *Petræos*.

All these scenes come out of legends belonging to Greece Proper, and of which the date is laid long before the Dorian invasion, when these rude restless hordes expelled or enslaved the peaceful industrious Pelasgi,—traditions of whose superiority in the arts of peace, particularly in architecture, were long prevalent amongst the successors to their territories. And the exiled artisan-people (like the *Dwarfs* amongst the Teutons) equally preserved the memory of their birthplace, notices of which perpetually turn up in the early historians. Thus Herodotus (vii. 95) describes the *Æolians* of Asia Minor as armed after the Grecian fashion, and named in ancient times Pelasgi, according to the tradition of the Greeks. Furthermore, he records that the Asiatic Ionians had been formerly called "the Pelasgi of the Coast," when they occupied the part of the Peloponnesus afterwards named Achaia.

Again, these stories are all of them pre-Homeric: the poems of Homer (an Asiatic Greek) were unknown to the primitive inhabitants of the mainland—perhaps, indeed, not composed when these intagli were executed, certainly not before the expulsion of their engravers. Moreover, the language of his verse was to them a foreign idiom in the times when they wandered forth to occupy the coasts of the Mediterranean.

Traditions of descent from the heroes of the Theban War were long kept up in the more ancient Latin towns. The natives of Tibur, even in Pliny's age, boasted of their founder Tiburtus as being the son of Amphiaraus, the wisest of the Seven Chiefs at the memorable Siege (xvi. 87). And Virgil (viii. 600) describes a grove near Cære dedicated to Sylvanus by the Pelasgi, "the ancient occupants of the Latin soil."

The frequent repetition of the same incidents, coupled with their limited number, affords some grounds for the supposition that such were purposely selected as conveying some moral lesson or warning to the wearer of the gem embodying them. According to this view he would have set before him in the Hercules an example of patient endurance; a moral, indeed, expressly pointed out upon a work of later date, "The Repose of Hercules," by the inscription ΠΟΝΟΣ ΤΟΥ ΚΑΛΩΣ ΗΣΥΧΑΖΕΙΝ ΑΙΤΙΟΣ, "Labour is the foundation of glorious repose;" or, again, in his helpless drunkenness a hint against the resistless power of wine that could thus overthrow the conqueror of every other force,—an idea elegantly turned in the lines inscribed under the statue of the 'Drunken Hercules:'—

> "The all-subduing hero, theme of song
> For Labours Twelve, for might of body strong,
> Burthened with wine as from the feast he reels,
> Soft Bacchus, victor in each member feels!"

The Philoctetes, serpent-stung in the act of betraying the deposit of Hercules, gave a warning how divine vengeance ever follows upon the violation of a promise; the Tydeus, wounded but unconquered, a pattern of invincible courage disdaining to yield to any odds; the Capaneus, struck by Jove's bolt, and tumbling headlong from the towers he had sworn to scale even in despite of heaven, taught a striking lesson against presumption and impiety, which again is repeated by the figure of the despairing Theseus, fixed eternally upon his iron chair at the gates of Hell, thus to atone for his audacious attempt upon the consort of Aidoneus.

Thus far the scarabæi. On the ring-stones, however, the abundance and extreme refinement of which convincingly proclaim, beyond all their other remains, the opulence and the taste of the *Greek* colonisers of Italy, we find, in addition to these earliest portions of the Epic Cycle, scenes unmistakably drawn from Homer, and where the meaning is placed beyond all doubt by the insertion of the names of the actors. Such intagli give us Achilles and Ulysses in conference; the parting of the former from Peleus; the episode of Dolon; and Hector dragged behind the victor's chariot. The Odyssey, however, is the repertory for incidents far more largely drawn upon by this class than the Iliad; the nature of its story necessarily rendering it the more popular of the two with an adventurous and maritime people, upon whose coast also the scene of many of its incidents is laid. On such intagli, therefore, Ulysses perpetually comes in as busied in building his ship on Calypso's island and cutting out with his adze the *aplustre*—the ornament for the stern-post—or carrying the bag of Æolus swollen with the imprisoned winds, or presenting the bowl of wine to Polyphemus; the Syrens also frequently adorn the works of this same period with their graceful figures.

Now, too, the Argonautic expedition begins to make its events visible in the labours of the gem-engraver, few subjects being so popular with the Greco-Italians of the time as Argus shaping the timbers of the Heroes' bark, or Jason consulting the Pythian Oracle, typified by a serpent-encircled column, concerning the success of his projected expedition. The legend of Perseus still continues to inspire many admirable works; and the Gorgon appears in all her traditional horrors, as upon the coinage of the same date, always in full face with protruded tongue; the beautiful *profile* of the same monster being the later birth of the more refined taste of Greece, that excluded from the domains of art everything grotesque or hideous.

The inscriptions supply strong grounds for the belief that the primitive language of the Pelasgi was the earliest form of the Æolic, which, mixed with the aboriginal Oscan, became the base of the Latin. In the age of Herodotus it had become a tongue whose affinity to his own no Greek could recognise: Herodotus expressly describing it as "barbarian," meaning thereby quite foreign. In the times of Alexander, the Macedonian language (probably the old unchanged Pelasgic) could only be understood by the Greeks through the medium of an interpreter: a very remarkable but hitherto unnoticed fact. This appears from what occurred on the trial of Philotas, Parmenio's son (Quint. Curt. vi. 9), where Alexander asks him whether he prefers making his defence in his *native* tongue or in Greek; and his reply, that, since the king had made the accusation in the latter for all the army to hear it, so would he defend himself in the same against his charges. And this decision the king spitefully construes into a contempt for the national language, akin to that he had previously displayed for the national simplicity of manners.

The alphabet used upon these gems is very limited, although the letters are universally formed with the utmost neatness, and microscopic delicacy, often not discernible to the ordinary sight without the aid of a magnifying lens. To specify the most obvious peculiarities of this alphabet: it possesses but three vowels, A, E, V, the last standing for O, Ω, and Υ; H is merely the sign of aspiration. D is written for P, and P for Π; Λ is always inverted, but somewhat obliquely, thus V; the vertical stroke of the K is dropped, and the angular part becomes the parent of the hard Roman C; Σ is written 8 reversed. For T, Θ is frequently substituted, always so for Δ, which last character is also replaced by T; for X a form like Ψ is invariably used. Here we see at once the source of the Latin alphabet, and of its variations from the Ionic Greek which became afterwards the universal character, as belonging to the language of literature, "adopted by the universal consent of mankind," to use Pliny's words. He remarks (VII. 58) the almost exact identity of the *ancient* Greek alphabet with the modern Latin, and quotes in illustration a bronze tablet then in the Imperial Palace, in the Library of Minerva, dedicated by "Nausicrates, an Athenian," and consequently of Pelasgic race. The scantiness of this alphabet is explained by the tradition that only sixteen letters were brought by Cadmus into Greece (VII. 57)—a tradition that, whether true or false, points to Thebes as the place where written characters first came into general use. Another proof of the claim of the Ogygian city to her old renown for primeval wealth and power is to be found in the fact, that of Thebes alone, in Europe, are gold coins of the true archaic character known to exist.

The legends themselves for the most part read from right to left upon the *impression*, and in this peculiarity corroborate the universal tradition as to their Phœnician origin. Occasionally, and upon the same stone as in the famous "Five Heroes," some read in the other direction; and Pausanias remarked upon the Coffer of Cypselus (made early in the 7th century B.C.), that the descriptive distichs were written *βουστροφηδὸν*, *i.e.* each line running in an opposite direction. Thus, upon the above-named celebrated intaglio (the base of a scarab found at Perugia), "holding the same place amongst engraved gems that Homer does amongst the poets," these peculiarities strike us in the spelling of the Heroes' names, and exemplify the foregoing remarks upon their alphabet. Amphiaraus is written ƎᗡAITΦMA; Adrastus, ATDESΘE; Parthenopæus, PADΘA-NAPES; Tydeus, ƎTVT; Polynices, ƎƆIN⅃VΦ. As a general rule, the final Σ is omitted, and E is used for the O of the last syllable; whilst the limited employment of the vowels, of which the short ones are usually dropped, bears another testimony to the Semitic origin of this method of writing. Such a distortion of names so famous, and so closely interwoven with all the historical associations of the people who have thus immortalised their ancient bearers by choosing them for the devices of their signets, goes far to support the assertion of Herodotus, that the few Pelasgians yet existing in his day spoke a barbarian tongue, *i.e.* one not a current dialect of the Greek then in use. But again he proves undesignedly that their tongue was not the Etruscan, by taking one of his examples from a community dwelling among the Tyrrheni; otherwise, what distinction could he have observed between the two races of Tyrrhene and Pelasgian settlers? It is no wonder that this ancient speech sounded so foreign to the ears of Herodotus, that he could not detect in it the parent of his own expanded and flowing Ionic: the distortion of classic names, the abbreviations, and the substitution of harsh aspirates like the Θ for T would seem to betoken a strong affinity between this primeval tongue and the Celtic.

Another circumstance has struck me connected with these inscriptions, that they solely occur upon scarabæi of the very finest work, and belonging to the perfected style of Etruscan art: hence their rarity, and the vast increase of value added by them to the gems so inscribed. They are never found upon that infinitely more numerous class where the rude designs, entirely drill-wrought, bespeak the workmanship of a far less civilized race, apparently as yet unacquainted with the use of letters, the introduction of which into Italy had by constant tradition been ascribed to the Pelasgi (Plin. VII. 57). These *legended* gems, therefore (to be distinguished as the Archaic Italiote), present us with both Greek art and Greek letters in their primitive form, thus illustrating a period in the history of both, preceding by some ages the appearance of any coins bearing inscriptions; though, in truth, the meagreness of the legends upon the Greek mintage, even in its full glory, must often have provoked every numismatist. As monuments, therefore, of palæography, they are perhaps of yet more importance than as illustrations of the state of art in the age that produced them.

These considerations will elucidate another anomaly, so unaccountable at first sight, and which must have puzzled many a classical student, and that is, the strange alteration the names of the Greek gods and heroes exhibit in their Latin form—Diana for Artemis, Hercules for Heracles, Ulysses for Odysseus, Pollux for Polydeuces, but the mode of spelling them (Hercle, Thana, *Tanait*, Ulxe, Polluce)—on these gems, the very ornaments of the Tuscan teachers to whom the Roman youths were, in the early times of the Republic, sent for their education, as in after ages to Greece, will explain in a most satisfactory manner the cause of this singular transformation.*

* The analogy between this language and Latin finds, to me, a convincing testimony in the title VƎV LEO, placed over a lion attacked by a hound, an excellent work of this kind (Impronte, iii. 58). I have never seen upon these gems the purely Etruscan names of the deities, so Celtic in sound, which are affixed to their representations on the metal mirrors. This is a natural consequence of the fact that the Etruscans had gained distinction as workers in metals long before the Greeks, and therefore these mirrors were produced by native artists, and adorned with the same designs in outline that had been used for their original and Asiatic gold tablets, though Greek fable now supplied the subjects. The Etruscan Vulcan was Sethlans; Venus, Turan; Juno, Thalna: Bacchus, Pupluns; Jupiter, Tinia, the fire-god (from Tan, *fire*, Celtic). Hermes is written Mercurius; Athena, Minerva; Selene, Losna; and Artemis, Thana. In Losna we see the early form of Luna, the medial S being a characteristic of ancient Latin forms; and in the times of Nigidius (Sat. i. 9), the rustic still called the moon Iana, to which the D was prefixed for the sake of euphony.

XIII.

Gem-engraving, like the cognate art of die-sinking, attained to its highest perfection first in Sicily and Magna Græcia. Greece itself was ever a poor country and distracted by perpetual wars and revolutions, whereas the colonies she had sent forth were on all sides advancing through commerce or agriculture to a degree of opulence now hardly credible. What city of Greece Proper, Athens excepted, could vie in wealth and population with Syracuse, Velia, Sybaris, or Tarentum? And what bears directly upon our subject, in one Dorian colony and that the most remote of all, Cyrene, Ælian particularly notices the wonderful multitude and skill of the gem-engravers, and to express the ostentation of the inhabitants in this article of luxury, adds that the very poorest of them possessed rings worth ten minæ (30*l.*). Cyprus again is named by Pliny as the locality from whence the fame of an engraved *emerald* had reached the ears of the conceited, purse-proud musician Ismenias at Athens.

Many of the finest gems that grace our cabinets manifest, by the identity of their style, that they proceed from the same hands that cut the dies for the beautiful coinages of the cities just mentioned. The graceful "Etruscan border" incloses the type upon several mintages of Magna Græcia, as it does the designs upon the contemporaneous signets of the coinless Tyrrhenes of Upper Italy. After this period the establishment of Greek kingdoms in Asia, and the enjoyment of boundless wealth in the long accumulated hoards of the Persian kings, conduced greatly to the encouragement of this art, pre-eminently the handmaid of tasteful opulence. In the generation following Alexander, the advance of luxury displaying itself amongst the rest in the decoration of the fingers with rings, brought the glyptic everywhere to the highest perfection attainable by it in its relation to the other branches of creative art. History, however, has preserved no name of the celebrities of this period besides that of Pyrgoteles, engraver of the Macedonian conqueror's signet.

It is the opinion of K. O. Müller, that although we may occasionally trace in gem-works a treatment of form and a composition of groups corresponding to those of the sculptures of Phidias, yet vastly more numerous are the works of the class in which the spirit of the school of Praxiteles manifests itself in both these particulars. The observation of Nature, coupled with the study of the early masters, which Lysippus intimately combined in his practice, led the artists who followed after him to many refinements in details (*argutiæ operum*). Thus it is noticed that Lysippus arranged the hair more naturally, meaning, it would seem, with greater regard to artistic effect. In addition to this, the succeeding school of Polycletus devoted their most earnest study to the proportions of the human body, in pursuing which they were seduced, by their endeavours to exalt Nature (especially in the case of portrait statues) beyond human measurement, into an exaggerated slenderness of forms, and this was carried to a new, totally artificial, system of more attenuated proportions in the figure. This system, inaugurated by Euphranor in sculpture, by Zeuxis in painting, was first carried out in its full harmony by Lysippus, and thenceforward became the dominant one in Greek Art.

Lysippus is said "to have greatly advanced the art of statuary by making the heads of his figures smaller than had been the rule with the artists preceding him." "Euphranor," observes Pliny, "though the first to pay any attention to symmetry, was too attenuated in his bodies, too big in his heads and joints." Lysippus, on the contrary, made the limbs more slender and somewhat less fleshy, in order to exaggerate the apparent height of the whole figure (Plin. xxxiv. 19, 6). It must, however, be observed that this system originated less in a vivid and intimate comprehension of Nature (which, in Greece especially, displays itself with more of beauty in such forms as are of a slender make) than out of the ambition to elevate the production of Art above the beauty of Nature herself. Moreover, in the works of this Alexandrian school there already betrays itself that prevailing inclination towards the colossal which in the next period of the history of Grecian sculpture shows itself as the predominant feeling.

Pliny's acute criticism upon the style of these statuaries affords us the soundest data for determining the periods which produced the Greek gem-works that may come under our examination. In how many of them belonging to the Archaic period, corresponding to the flourishing times of Etruria, are we struck by the exaggeration in the size of the heads and the undue prominence given to the joints, and the skeleton-like attenuation of the bodies, that betray the epoch of Euphranor; whilst in the grander and freer works of the mature art, with their general slenderness of proportions, and aiming at loftiness in the figure, the innovations of Lysippus are equally conspicuous.

The Glyptic art indeed was, by its very nature, ancillary to Sculpture, and its productions, in order to be effective, are strictly tied down by the same rules as a bas-relief in stone or metal. To go beyond these limits, and ambitiously to invade the proper province of Painting, always results in egregious failure, as the over-refined works of the Cinque Cento school painfully attest, despite the immense practical skill and ingenuity they brought to the impossible undertaking. Yet, if we bear in mind that the painting of the Greeks was as simple in the rules for composition as was Sculpture itself, many gems may be supposed, with the best reasons, to preserve to us copies of celebrated pictures, and in the same proportion as they confessedly do of world-famous pieces of sculpture. In the fine intaglio by Nisus (Orleans) we have transmitted to us a faithful reduction in miniature of that masterpiece of Apelles for which he received the fabulous remuneration of twenty talents (nearly one *ton* weight) of gold pieces. We recognise in the gem all the particulars given by Pliny of his picture in the temple at Ephesus, "Alexander holding the thunder-bolt of Jove," where his fingers seemed to project and the thunder-bolt to stand out of the painting. And to return to Sculpture—that greatly admired work of the very early statuary Canachus, an Apollo holding up a stag by the forefeet, which stood when Pliny described it in the Didymæum at Miletus, has left behind it no other vestige of its existence save the tiny sard formerly discovered by me amongst the Praun gems. Another intaglio of the same cabinet enables us to appreciate the justice of the same critic's encomium upon that piece by Leochares, "the eagle sensible of *what* he is carrying off in Ganymede, and to *whom* he is carrying it, and using his talons gently not to hurt the boy through his garments." And in reading the poetical Catalogue composed by the ingenious Byzantine Christodorus of the sixty-eight masterpieces of Greek statuary in bronze, then standing in the Gymnasium of Zeuxippus (shortly afterwards destroyed by fire), how many, both groups and single figures, upon gems are we enabled to identify from his accurate delineation of their prototypes!

XIV.

"Painting amongst the Greeks was at first divided into two schools—the Asiatic and the Helladic." This is an important record for the history of our special subject. The existence of the former school sufficiently explains the appearance upon vases, chasings, and gems, of the strange monsters and fanciful arabesques already adverted to as full of the taste of Babylon and Persepolis. The Helladic, on the other hand, has left us the stiff drawings—eternised in the contemporary gems—of gods and heroes, and scenes drawn from mythology and the Epic Cycle, all framed within the elaborately *engrailed* borders popularly known as Etruscan.

Subsequently the high reputation of Eupompus of Sicyon occasioned the subdivision of the Helladic school into three—the Ionic, Sicyonic, and Attic. The most distinguished pupil of Eupompus, Pamphilus, a Macedonian by birth, was also a proficient in every branch of learning, especially in arithmetic and geometry, without which two sciences he declared that excellence in painting was not to be attained. By his influence he brought it about, at Sicyon first, and afterwards all over Greece, that the children at the public schools should be taught before anything else the art of drawing (*graphice, i. e.* sketching in outline) upon a boxwood panel, and that this art should be reckoned the first step amongst those termed the "liberal arts." Indeed such respect had always been paid in Greece to painting, that it was exclusively practised by persons of free, and afterwards even of noble birth—there being a standing prohibition against teaching it to slaves; and this is the reason, says Pliny (xxxv. 36, 9), why no works of note exist, either in painting or sculpture, executed by one of servile condition.

Even the severe Romans of the Primitive Republic held this art in the highest reverence. The head of the patrician clan, the Fabii, gloried in the surname of *Pictor*, conferred upon him for having decorated with his own hands the Temple of Concord. And later Augustus recommended that a deaf and dumb boy, a relative of his, Q. Pedius, should be brought up to this profession; in which the youth made great progress, but was cut off at an early age. M. Aurelius studied painting under Diognetus; Alexander Severus, that model of a perfect prince, "pinxit mire," to use the expression of his biographer Lampridius. Even Valentinian, distinguished as he was for his military abilities, added to his other merits in the estimation of the honest old soldier Ammian that "of writing a beautiful hand, and modelling in wax and painting with much elegance." No wonder that, with such a training, the Romans so well appreciated the artistic value of engraved gems.

But to return to Greece in its best times. Hippias, the sophist, the contemporary of Socrates, is described by Apuleius (Flor. p. 112, ed. Bipont.) as coming to the Olympic games and boasting that everything he wore was manufactured by himself, and at the same time perfect in its kind, including his gold ring, which he had wrought with his own hands, and the gem in it, which he had engraved most artistically and set: "Et annulum in læva aureum faberrimo signaculo quem ostendebat ipse, ejus annuli et orbiculam circulaverat, et palam clauserat, et gemmam insculpserat."

XV.

Proceeding now to the epoch of the full development of the Glyptic Art, under Alexander and his immediate successors: this period presents us for the first time with contemporary portraits of princes, whose heads begin to replace the national deities upon the stone of the signet, as they were doing at the same date upon the obverse of the coin.

From several allusions of classic writers (to be quoted under "Signets") it appears that the official seal of every person of importance was, as a rule, the likeness of himself. This fact, to give an example, seems implied in Cicero's warning to his brother Quintus, concerning the cautious use of his official seal during his government of the province assigned him. "Look upon your signet, not as a mere instrument, but as your *own self;* not as the agent of another person's will, but as the attestation of your own." The example of this substitution was probably set by Alexander; and the exchange of the god for the king was connected with his own assumption of divinity: certain it is, that the first authentic portraits of him are those partially deified by the assumption of the horn of Ammon. This consideration likewise serves to explain the motive for restricting the privilege of engraving the sacred features to Pyrgoteles, the first master in the art. This indeed is the reason actually assigned by Apuleius (*l. c.*, p. 118), who subjoins, after mentioning the restriction,—"Threatening that if any other artist should be discovered to have put his hand to the *most sacred* image of the Sovereign, the same punishment should be inflicted upon him as was appointed for sacrilege." In fact, it is obvious, from their style, that the numerous gem-portraits of the hero now to be seen are mostly long posterior to his times, and belong to the school of the Roman Empire when such heads were in high repute as amulets. And this virtue extended to his likeness impressed upon his medals; as Trebellius, writing in Constantine's days, incidentally informs us.

With this period, also, a new branch of the art—*cameo-engraving*—is first inaugurated. The term signifies work in relief upon stones of two or more differently-coloured layers, affording a background and a contrast. The word, which first appears in the thirteenth century as *camahutum*, is usually derived from the Syriac *chemeia*, "a charm," from the light in which such relics were universally considered in those ages by both Orientals and Europeans. There may, however, be some truth in Von Hammer's conjecture, who makes it the same with *camaut*, "the camel's hump," applied metaphorically to anything prominent, and therefore to gems in relief, as distinguished from signet-stones.

The Etruscans had, indeed, made some small attempts in that style by carving the backs of scarabæi into figures in relief, but these instances are of such extreme rarity, that they may be put out of the question. The earliest indubitable example of a true cameo possessing the necessary quality of a distinction of colours, the date of which can be certainly fixed, is that presenting the heads conjoined of Demetrius Soter and his wife Laodice (B.C. 162–150). This precious monument of the first days of the invention, though inconsiderable in point of magnitude, if compared with similar works of Roman date, being only 1¼ × 1 inch in measurement, is executed with admirable skill, and the sardonyx of three layers is of surpassing beauty. It originally decorated a cabinet made for Cardinal Grimani in the sixteenth century, which long stood in the *sala* of the Ducal Palace, Venice. The gem was extracted in 1797, and presented by the municipality to M. Lallemand, the French Commissary, who, later, ceded it to the gem-loving Empress Josephine.

Previously to the establishment of Macedonian kingdoms in Persia and Bactria, we may infer, from the confused expressions of Theophrastus, in speaking of the use of fire in making the artificial stones "which are brought out of Asia," that the special material for the cameo, the sardonyx, was but little known to the Greeks, and was mistaken by them for an artificial composition of the Indian jeweller.

Thus the art advanced with rapid strides towards its culminating point, its practitioners ranking high amongst the artists of their times, and their performances deemed not unworthy of being sung by the court poets, nay, by kings themselves. Tryphon's *Galene* is immortalised by Addæus, Satyreius's *Arsinoe* by Diodorus, whilst king Polemo bestows an ingenious conceit upon a group of *seven cows* which seem alive and browsing, on a green jasper. They enjoyed the patronage of the most powerful monarchs. Antiochus Epiphanes delighted to spend his leisure hours in the *ateliers* of his artist-goldsmiths and jewellers, greatly to the scandal of that stiff pedant, Polybius. Mithridates is recorded as the founder of the first royal cabinet of gems; and a treatise upon stones (unfortunately no longer extant) was dedicated to him by Zachalias of Babylon. The very nature of the destination of their works, to serve the important office of public signets, has, unhappily for us, precluded the engravers from marking them with their *own* names, the rule then prevailing in all the other departments of creative art. Hence it is that, before the age of Augustus, the sole masters belonging to this era of perfection, of whom any historical notice is preserved, are, in addition to Pyrgoteles, Cronius, and Apollonides, the two already mentioned as enshrined in the Anthology, and the most ancient in the list (after Theodorus), Nausias the Athenian, incidentally vilified by the orator Lysias.

XVI.

It is but natural to suppose that the *Romans*, in the beginning, took the Etruscans for their masters in the Glyptic as they are known to have done in all the other arts of peace, such as their coinage (the *æs grave* cast, not struck as was the invariable plan with the Greeks), their bronze statuary fictile works, and architecture. "Before the building of this temple (of Ceres, embellished with paintings and terra-cottas by two renowned Greek masters, Demophilus and Gorgasus) both the temples and all their ornaments were of *Etruscan* work, as Varro states" (Plin. xxxv. 45).

The primitive senator or knight must consequently have adopted the *scarabæus* for his signet whenever he aspired to the luxury of an engraved gem. For the old tradition quoted by Maccrobius from the eminent antiquary Ateius Capito, related that, consistently with pristine simplicity, their signet-devices were merely cut in the metal of their *iron* rings. In fact, scarabæi often occur in which the more recent treatment of the subjects would lead one to believe that they date from the later times of the Republic. Signet-rings, however, seem from the beginning to have occupied the place of this primitive form of the seal with the Romans as with the first Greek colonists of Southern Italy. Pliny notices, that amongst the statues of the kings of Rome, two only—Numa and Servius Tullius—were represented as wearing rings. Now these statues must have been the work of Etruscan artists and contemporary with their originals, it being contrary to all probability that the succeeding Republic should thus have commemorated a detested order. And further, the authorship of these regal statues is placed beyond all doubt by the portraits (which could only have been derived from them) placed long after upon the mintage of the families claiming descent from the most venerated of the ancient line. Thus the gens Pomponia assumes the head of Numa, the Marcia of Ancus Martius, the Tituria of Tatius; and these heads are in the exact style of the most archaic Etruscan statuettes.

These rings, however, were not set with engraved gems, but had the devices cut in the solid metal, whether that were iron or gold. But after the use of gold rings as common ornaments had been introduced amongst them by the *Greeks*, to follow Pliny's authority (those of Sicily, other circumstances would lead us to infer), engraved gems immediately began to be admired and sought after for their own sake. This change of taste, which came in towards the later ages of the Commonwealth, produced that class of intagli so abundantly turned up in the vicinity of Rome, which distinguish themselves equally from the Greek as from the Imperial Roman by their deeply-cut figures retaining much of the old Etruscan manner, and in other points exhibiting their relationship to their predecessors, the scarabæi of that nation. The most valuable relic in this style known to me—for it commemorates an important event which, in its turn, furnishes us with the exact date of the work—is the signet of Q. Cornelius Lupus (Waterton) referring to the victory of his kinsman Cornelius Cethegus over the confederate Insubres and Cænomani upon the Mincio (B.C. 197).

Of such intagli many bear traces of having originally been set in rings of iron, and thus, as well as by their style, indicate the period when engraved gems began to grow popular amongst the Romans.

The taste for these objects of luxury was hardly introduced into the Republic, than—like that for other works of art a little later—it grew into an ungovernable passion, and was pushed by its noble votaries to the last degree of extravagance. Pliny seriously attributes to nothing else the ultimate downfall of the Republic; for it was in a quarrel about a ring at a certain auction that the feud originated between the famous demagogue Drusus and the chief-senator Cæpio, which led to the breaking out of the Social War, and to all its fatal consequences. A jewel this, if I may be allowed an expression quite in Pliny's style, that ought to have been dedicated thereafter in some conspicuous place in the temple of Nemesis. Julius Cæsar, again, was an enthusiastic collector of works of art, and of this sort more particularly, for Suetonius (47) in describing his tastes, heads the list with them: "Gems, chasings, statues, paintings by the old masters, he always collected with the utmost avidity." Seneca relates a singular anecdote of this mania of the Dictator. When he gave Pompeius Pennus his life—"if not taking away may be called giving"—he held out his foot for him to kiss in returning thanks, an action that scandalised all the beholders, but for which his friends made the excuse that it was not done out of arrogance, but merely to show off the fine gems with which his boots were studded. He further testified his judgment of their importance by dedicating six cabinets of gems (dactyliothecæ) in the temple of his patron-goddess Venus Victrix (Plin. xxxvii. 6) as his great rival had, some years before, done with that of Mithridates to the Capitoline Jupiter.

XVII.

These favourites of the First Cæsar were, it may be inferred from the qualification, "antiqui operis," works due to the eminent masters of bygone times who had flourished in Greece and Asia; they were in great measure the spoils of Mithridates and the Ptolemies. But under Augustus the art was more zealously cultivated than ever, and for the first time found a domicile in Rome. It again reached a very high degree of excellence, more particularly in the department of portraits, in which indeed lies the great strength of the imperial school. Under the enlightened patronage of Mæcenas, a man as passionately fond of gems as any of his Etruscan ancestry, flourished Dioscorides and a host of others, his scholars or his rivals; all the best hands of Greece in this line were now drawn together in the metropolis of the world; either attracted thither as the place offering the most promising field for the exercise of their talents, or else conveyed there in the first instance as the slaves of those nobles whose family names they assumed, according to the Roman custom, upon their manumission. Augustus himself had inherited the taste of his adoptive father in this particular, for an inscription yet extant commemorates one Julius Philargyrus by the title of "Keeper of his Cabinet of Gems" (libertus a dactyliotheca Cæsaris). Now for the first time (according to the received opinion of archæologists) was the gem-artist permitted to place his name upon his best works, a convincing proof of the estimation in which his genius was held, his thus being allowed to commemorate himself upon the ornaments of the highest personages! The Greek engravers of the best times had contented themselves with the easily-worked though beautiful gems of the quartz species—the sard, banded agate, and amethyst—as the materials for their art. The Roman, from a false ambition, chose to heighten art by the value of the medium displaying it, "ut alibi ars, alibi materia esset in pretio," as Pliny hath it, and therefore attacked the most precious stones, in spite of their hardness,—the ruby, the sapphire, and the emerald. The Marlborough Cabinet boasts of a head of Caracalla in a large and fine sapphire; but nothing in this class approximates in splendour to the signet of Constantius (to be particularly described hereafter), also in a sapphire, but of the extraordinary weight of fifty-three carats. And that masterpiece of Roman portraiture, the *Julia* of Evodus, is engraved in an immense aquamarine, long regarded from its fine quality as a priceless emerald.

"Valuable data for the history of Roman art, and of equal importance with those derived from the portrait-statues, are supplied," observes Müller, "by these gems. Though Dioscorides was the most distinguished engraver in intaglio of that period, still more important than the gems now extant under his name is the series of *camei* that represent the Julian and Claudian families at different epochs, and which besides the beauty of the material and its skilful employment, deserve admiration upon many other grounds. In all the principal works of this kind the same system prevails: the representation of these princes as lords of the universe and dispensers of its blessings, as present impersonations of the higher gods. The drawing is expressive and accurate, although the same spirit in the treatment of the forms as in the Ptolemaic camei is no longer to be found. On the contrary, in these works as in the bas-reliefs upon the triumphal arches, and in many statues of the Cæsars, the eye is struck by a peculiar *Roman build* in the bodies that is markedly distinguished from the Greek manner by a peculiar hardness of the forms. For example, the body is too long in proportion to the extremities, a natural peculiarity still observable in the modern Romans." Now, indeed, commences the golden age of camei, whether heads, single figures, or groups, for works in this style that can be attributed with certainty to the pure Greek period are of the utmost possible rarity. The regular commercial intercourse by this time established with the interior of Asia, and with the emporia on the coast of India, Baroche, Barcellore, and Pultaneh, supplied the special material of the art, the *sardonyx*, in masses of dimensions and of a perfection totally unattainable in modern times. Down to Severus inclusive, the most meritorious productions of the Roman school consist in the cameo-portraits of the emperors and their immediate relations. By Pliny's strange and exaggerated parlance, "the Emperor Claudius used to *clothe* himself (induebat) with emeralds and sardonyx-stones," the use of such gems as decorations for the dress, and not as mere small ring-stones, is plainly intimated. This predilection of the pedantic Cæsar is a sufficient reason for the existence of so large a number of cameo-portraits of himself and his connections.

Roman art reached its culminating point in this as in all its other branches under the zealous and judicious patronage of Hadrian, himself an accomplished sculptor, as his contemporary Florus records, a proficient too in painting, adds the later Spartianus. His taste as regards engraved gems is immortalised by the numerous portraits of Antinous which have come down to us (amongst which the Marlborough sard takes the lead), works that, like the busts in marble of the same deified beauty, are the very first of their kind. It needed not the express testimony of Capitolinus to tell us of his private gem-cabinet, the contents whereof ("gemmas e repositorio sanctiore Hadriani") were sold by auction, together with all the other valuables of the palace by the philosopher M. Aurelius, in order to raise funds for carrying on the Marcomannic war.

Even after the Glyptic art, as far as regards the production of fine or even of mediocre *intaglio*-work, was utterly extinct, the branch of cameo-engraving still lingered, and actually revived, together with the reviving prosperity of the empire, under Constantine's encouragement, so as to give birth to certain very important monuments. They are somewhat spiritless, it is true, but display unabated mechanical skill in their execution, and amongst them the *aliter* Triumph of Constantius in the Biehler Cabinet may be quoted as the finest example.

XVIII.

Some notion of the magnificence of the gem-works in relief executed under the first Cæsars, and the immense amount of talent and of labour expended upon them, may be derived from a fuller account of the two chief camei now extant: the "Agathe de la Sainte Chapelle," Paris, and the "Gemma Augustea" of the Imperial Museum, Vienna.

The former was included amongst those treasures of real or imaginary value—the Crown of Thorns, the swaddling clothes of the infant Saviour, &c.—pawned by Baldwin, the last Frankish emperor of Constantinople, to St. Louis, for various large sums, vainly expended in the defence of his tottering throne.

Its exact valuation *then* has not been stated; but it is believed to have been included in the list of the *reliquaries* of the imperial chapel of Byzantium, for which, as security, Baldwin obtained an advance of 10,000 marks of silver (6666⅔ pounds troy), or 20,000*l.*, a sum equivalent to twenty times that amount in the currency of our times. But the pious monarch paid thus high for the sanctity of the relics, not for the intrinsic value of their casings: he had previously acquired the Crown of Thorns from the royal supplicant, singly, for a similar consideration. The cameo was regarded as a loan, not as a gift from Louis, to the treasury of the Sainte Chapelle, as the term "bailla," used in the inscription, shows.

For the comparison of prices, it may here be noted that four centuries later, Rudolf II., that truly imperial virtuoso, is reported to have acquired the Vienna Cameo at the almost incredible price of 12,000 gold ducats (6,000*l.*) at a time when the artistic and mineralogical value of the monument was alone taken into the account.

In the year 1343, Philippe VI. sent to Rome to gratify the curiosity of the reigning Pope, all the other relics, and "spécialement un joel appellé 'Le Camahieu,'" in the charge of the treasurer of the Chapelle.

A replica of this cameo (omitting the lowermost group) exists on a fine sardonyx, 3½ by 2½ inches in dimension. It is judged by J. C. Robinson to be a contemporary work, and in the same style: a most interesting coincidence, if his judgment be correct, for it is much more probable that such a piece is a copy executed for François I. by some of the skilful Italians in his employ. So famous a monument would be amongst the first to excite their wonted emulation of the antique. (Now in the possession of Heywood Hawkins, of Bignor.)

The original is described in the ancient inventories as "Le grand Camahieu;" later as "Le grand Camée de la Ste. Chapelle;" or "Agathe de Tibère." During the whole course of the Middle Ages it was understood as representing "the Triumph of Joseph in Egypt," and was therefore venerated as a most holy relic. It was not until 1619 that the learned Peiresc presumed to restore to its subject its proper designation, "the Apotheosis of Augustus."

In dimensions it far exceeds all other works of the kind (the Carpegna excepted), being 30 c. high by 26 c. wide (about 13 × 11 inches); whereas the Gemma Augustea, its superior in point of art, is but 21 c. by 18 c. (9 × 8 inches). The former, too, is a sardonyx of five layers, the latter of only two, a pure white on a transparent ground.

It is evident, from the arrangement of the design, that the artist allowed the stone to retain its native outline, that its extraordinary volume might not in the least degree be diminished by its reduction to a regular shape. On its deposition in the Ste. Chapelle, it served, set in a silver frame, for a cover to a copy of the Gospels: the date of which has not been noticed.

The design is highly allegorical, and therefore susceptible of diverse explanation, in what follows, therefore Millin's interpretation of the groups has been condensed and adopted; with occasional modifications, however, in some points where he has obviously mistaken the intention of the designer.

Germanicus, the principal erect figure, upon his return from his glorious German campaign, is received and adopted by Tiberius and Livia, both seated upon the same throne. The emperor holds in one hand the sceptre, in the other the lituus, badges of the supreme ruler and Pontifex Maximus; the ægis spread upon his lap betokens a time of peace, being no longer required as armour for the breast; and he wears a laurel wreath in honour of the recent victories. A similar wreath encircles the head of his mother Livia, who, depicted in her favourite character of Ceres, holds forth a bunch of wheat-ears and poppy-heads, symbol of fecundity. Before them stands Germanicus fully armed, as about to start upon his second expedition into Asia: he therefore sets firmly upon his head the helmet which his mother Antonia appears attempting to remove. Behind him stands his wife, Agrippina, holding a scroll and leaning upon his shield; his son Caligula, also in full armour, is shown hastening eagerly away to the scene of new triumphs. At the back of the throne of Tiberius is seen an armed warrior engaged in erecting a trophy, supposed by Millin to be Drusus, the emperor's only son. The seated lady on a throne, supported by sphinxes, is his wife Livilla, sister to Germanicus. A seated and mourning figure, in Asiatic attire, typifies Armenia soliciting the Roman aid against her Parthian invaders.

The entire space, or exergue, below the central group is filled up with barbarian captives seated in attitudes of grief amidst their scattered armour and weapons.

Now we come to the third group filling the upper portion of the tableau, the actual Apotheosis of Augustus, that gives its name to the whole work. Here, the principal figure, his head veiled and radiated, the established symbols of deification, and holding a sceptre, floats in the air upborne by another in Persian costume bearing a globe in his hand. Millin takes the pair for Romulus and Æneas, but, as it seems to me, erroneously. From the analogy of the bas-relief figured by him (Gal. Myth. clxxx.), representing the Apotheosis of Antoninus Pius and Faustina, where they appear carried heavenwards upon the back of a gigantic genius in the same action as this Oriental personage, and like him bearing the orb, and whom Millin there understands as the genius of the world, Αἴων; or else, as Eternity personified, it seems more natural to infer that this Persian-clad deity is meant for the Solar genius, Mithras; whilst the person enthroned upon him is Augustus himself. *Romulus* he certainly is not, for the founder of Rome is always sculptured with a beard after the fashion of his own primitive times. This central group is flanked by two supporters; one a warrior holding up a shield, like a mirror, perhaps Mars or Julius hastening to greet his adopted son; the other coming from the opposite direction, mounted upon Pegasus, whom Cupid leads by the bridle, may represent Drusus the Elder, father of Germanicus, and deceased several years before the death of Augustus. According to Millin, however, this last is the figure that actually expresses the idea of the ascending up to heaven of the deified emperor. But such an arrangement would be at variance with all the rules of these compositions; for he is evidently introduced here as a character subordinate to the principal personage who is deified (as Augustus is supposed to be by the express design of the complete tableau), and whose figure is, for that reason, made the principal one in the foreground.

Equal to this in archæological importance, but far above it in the gracefulness of design and in its character of a perfect work of art, as a composition displaying every excellence required in a bas-relief, is the Cameo of Vienna, the "Coronation of Augustus." This prize, wrested by Philippe le Bel from the Knights of Jerusalem, and presented by him to the Abbaye de Poissy, was stolen thence in the civil wars of the sixteenth century, and ultimately found its way into the collection of that Coryphæus of royal amateurs, the Emperor Rudolf II., himself a zealous student of mineralogy as well as of the occult sciences, and who paid the enormous sum already specified, probably more for the rarity of the material than for the merit or historical interest of the relief upon it. The form of this sardonyx is nearly elliptical (9 × 8 inches), and the principal group occupies about two-thirds of the height, arranged on a line parallel with the longest axis. Augustus, in the character of Jupiter, is seated on a throne, holding the lituus, and leaning on a long sceptre; a shield serves for his footstool, emblem of profound peace; the eagle stands beneath. Above his head is Capricorn, his horoscope, surrounded with rays like a sun. Behind the throne stands Neptune, easily recognisable by his dripping locks, thick beard and stern aspect; and Cybele, veiled and crowned with towers. She is placing a civic crown upon the head of Augustus, in allusion to the peace he had restored to the commonwealth, thus indicating him as the saviour of the state. The two deities are introduced to proclaim his sovereignty over land and sea. By the side of the emperor, and upon his throne, is seated Livia, as the goddess Roma; she wears a triple-crested helmet, her right hand supports her lance, her left is laid on the hilt of the sword hanging from the belt, a shield rests against her knee, and a pile of armour serves for a footstool. The next figure is Drusus (her son) in full armour, but bareheaded, with his hand also upon his sword-hilt; behind him Tiberius in a toga with his head laureated, a sceptre in one hand, a scroll in the other, is descending from a triumphal car guided by a Victory—an allusion to his Pannonian triumph. On the left of Augustus is seated Antonia, wife of Drusus, in the character of Abundantia, crowned with ivy, and bearing a cornucopia; at her knees stand her two infant sons, Germanicus and Claudius, one of whom holds out a bunch of wheat-ears, a symbol again relating to the character sustained by his mother. Millin indeed sees, in this family, Germanicus, Agrippina and their children, which could not have been intended by the artist, as his design was evidently to commemorate the victories of Tiberius and his brother Drusus over the Rhæti and Vindelici, B.C. 17, when Germanicus was but three years old.

In the exergue, on one side Roman soldiers are erecting a trophy, under which, seated on the earth, are a barbarian man with hands tied behind him, and a woman weeping. On the other, two warriors in Greek costume, one equipped as a *peltastes* with two javelins, the other, wearing the Macedonian *causia*, are dragging along an aged barbarian, who kneels in supplication, and a female in thickly-folded drapery.

In the first-mentioned group, attached to the trophy, will be observed an *Amazonian* shield, device a scorpion (Scorpio being the horoscopical sign of Tiberius, whose birthday fell in November). The classical scholar will recollect that Horace, in his magnificent ode upon this very victory of Drusus, expresses his wonder how the "Rhæti should carry for arms the Amazonian battle-axe," with the use of which such a shape of buckler was always united. The second group refers to the contemporaneous successes of Tiberius over the Pannonians; one division of whom had invaded Macedonia, whilst the other moved upon Italy. For these the Senate had decreed him the honour of a triumph, as we have seen denoted by his appearance in the car above.

Nothing can be conceived more satisfactory, in every point of view, as a work of art, than the whole of this composition; the grouping of the main design displays the most consummate skill, and is, in that respect, the finest ancient picture preserved to us; the accessory figures tell their own story, without any far-fetched allegory, and by certifying the design of the whole, add infinitely to the historical value of the monument. In the grace and easy movement of the figures it shows more of the Greek taste than does the Apotheosis; the latter already manifesting, in the attitudes of the terrestrial actors, some of the stiffness that marks the Roman hand. The events recorded on the two camei, themselves indicate a lapse of thirty-four years (if my explanation be correct) between the execution of each; that is, the space between the Pannonian triumph of Tiberius and the German of *his nephew Germanicus.*

Yet a third cameo is illustrated by Millin (Pl. ccxxvii.) possessing (in addition to its great elegance in drawing) a higher interest to the English archæologist, as commemorating the Conquest of Britain by the Emperor Claudius. The idea of the piece is borrowed from that favourite subject of antiquity, the triumphal march of Bacchus and Ariadne after his Indian victory; doubtless a covert compliment of the designer comparing the equal remoteness of the two scenes of glory, of the god and of the imperial hero. This idea is made more obvious by the vast goblet thrown beneath the wheels of the Cæsar's car, which, drawn by centaurs, the usual equipage of Bacchus, points again to his resemblance to the first-recorded conqueror of distant and barbaric regions. On the car reclines, in the post of honour, Messalina, with the attributes of Ceres; her uxorious lord is seated next, with his arm thrown round her neck, and grasping a thunderbolt as the terrestrial Jupiter. In front stands the little Britannicus in complete armour, his name being derived from this victory; and behind, his elder sister Octavia, all with their heads laureated. One of the Centaurs bears on his shoulder a trophy, a coat of scale armour (the usual defence of the barbarian cavalry, the Sarmatians for example), and the pointed oval shield with which the Briton appears equipped on certain Consular denarii. They trample upon two prostrate enemies, one holding a quiver, the other a buckler, and dressed in tunics of many folds. Over all soars a Victory, about to place a laurel wreath upon the brows of the triumphant *Imperator.*

This most important monument (even as regards size, being 10 inches square) was, when Millin described it (1811), in the possession of a Dutch family.*

The "Apotheosis of Germanicus" is a piece that, for the excellence of its work as well as for the beauty of the stone—a sardonyx, 4 inches (10 c.) in diameter—has always held the next place in the French Cabinet to "Le Grand Camée." Upon this gem the ill-fated hero appears armed in the ægis, the lituus and cornucopia in his hands, and soaring heavenwards upon the wings of a mighty eagle, which bears in its talons a crown of laurel and a palm-branch.

* According to Müller, it has since passed into the Cabinet of the Hague.

Victory, hovering above, places upon his brow the triumphal garland.

For six centuries this cameo passed for the authentic likeness of St. John the Evangelist, on the strength of the eagle, which forms so prominent a feature in the composition, and was therefore treasured up with the utmost veneration by the monks of St. Evre de Toul, to which cathedral Bishop Humbert had presented it upon his return from Constantinople, whither he had been sent as his envoy by Pope Leo IX., in 1049. Louis XIV., upon founding the *Cabinet d'antiquités* at Versailles, begged this invaluable work from the fraternity of St. Evre, and compensated their house for the sacrifice by the princely donation of 7000 crowns.

The idea of that magnificent piece of adulation, " The Triumph of Claudius," above described, seems to have been taken from the vast cameo of the Vatican, formerly belonging to Cardinal Carpegna. It is well described by Buonarotti, who gives a fine plate of it, the actual size, in his 'Medaglioni,' published in 1698. This is by far the largest cameo remaining, being sixteen inches long by twelve deep, thus greatly surpassing in extent the "Great Cameo of France" usually quoted as the first in this respect. The stone is a sardonyx of five strata, in which the figures are worked in very flat relief, so as to preserve for each a distinct colour, and every detail made out with the most scrupulous fidelity. A certain grand simplicity in the design, joined to the beauty of the composition, places it (besides its extraordinary magnitude) at the head of all such works. The subject is the "Pompa di Bacco," or Bacchus and Ceres, Virgil's "duo clarissima mundi lumina" as symbolising the sun and moon, standing up in a magnificent car; the god holding a vase and a thyrsus, the goddess her bunch of wheat-ears. On his right stands a youthful winged figure, Comus. The car is drawn by four centaurs, two male, two female; the first bears a rhyton and a thyrsus, the second a torch, whilst he snaps the fingers of his right hand; one centauress plays the double flute, the other a tambourine. On the ground lie the mystic basket and two huge vases. The whole composition is given in a front view, and this difficult arrangement is carried out with admirable art, so that nothing can surpass the gracefulness of the effect. The purity and force of the outlines seem to indicate a Grecian rather than an imperial epoch; it may well be ascribed to some of the munificent patrons of art amongst the Syrian princes. The top and sides are framed in a simple bead-cornice worked out of the stone, an elegant border of the acanthus-leaf finishes the bottom, a novel feature, forming an appropriate exergue to the picture.

The better-known "Odescalchi Cameo" first appeared to the world in the Gonzaga Cabinet, Mantua. After the dispersion of the collection at the sacking of that city, in 1629, we next find it in the possession of Queen Christina, then of Prince Odescalchi, and lastly (at the date of Visconti's 'Icon Græca') of the Empress Josephine. What was its fate on the breaking up of her collection is unknown to me. The male head has a nascent beard and moustache, and wears a Roman helmet adorned with a winged serpent and a star upon the side; the lady's hair is bound by an olive-wreath, in the character of Peace, as her consort figures in that of Mars. His breast is covered with the ægis adorned with the Gorgon's head, and a large mask, full-faced, of Jupiter. The faces are in white, on a black ground, the helmet and ægis in light brown, the work in high relief. The stone is a perfect oval of 6 by 5 inches.

Nothing except the inveterate prejudice of his day that every fine work must belong to purely Grecian times, could have induced Visconti to discover in these heads portraits of Ptolemies, to whose strongly-marked type of face the profile bears not the slightest resemblance. Besides, the regal portraits of that date are always beardless, leaving out of the question the established fact that all important camei commence with the Augustan age. The costume of the male is the regular Imperial Roman, there being a close resemblance between the ornamentation of the ægis and that worn by the Strozzi Augustus. The winged serpent on the helm may allude to the tale concerning Nero's guardian genius, preserved by Suetonius. The lady is unmistakably Agrippina; and Nero's beard shows that the cameo was done before her murder, and his twentieth year, after which he, as the other Cæsars, appears close shaven. To judge from Visconti's beautiful engraving, there may even be grounds for supposing this grand work to be no more than the production of some great Renaissance artist; there is a freedom and lightness in its treatment superior to the style of Nero's period.

Although almost unknown to the world, in consequence of its seclusion in the all but inaccessible Cabinet at Blenheim, the Marlborough "Didius Julian," in point of mineralogical interest, surpasses, and in dimensions (8 inches wide by 6 deep) falls little short of, the world-famed examples already passed in review. It presents the confronted busts of a Roman emperor and empress; the former invested with the horn of Ammon and the oak-wreath of Dodonæan Jove; the latter crowned with a similar wreath, but in which are interwoven the wheat-ears and poppies of Ceres. The faces are certainly not those of the sexagenarian usurper * and his wife, Manlia Scantilla, to whom they are given by the inscription upon the setting, being of much too youthful a cast. In fact, the male portrait very much resembles that of Commodus upon his earlier medals; whilst the lady, though not his wife Crispina (unless her hard features have been largely flattered by the engraver) may very likely be his more beloved concubine Marcia.

The sardonyx exhibits four distinct strata, one being a rich purple, altogether unique in this stone; of which contrasted colours an intelligent use has been made by the artist in rendering the different tints of the flesh, drapery, and decorations. The slab, an irregular ellipse in shape, has been broken across, but skilfully reunited and mounted in a chased frame of silver gilt, with a backing. On the latter is the inscription: "Ingens anaglyphicum opus, olim Sannesiorum ducum, nunc vero pretio acquisitum in Fontesiano cimelio asservatum." As to the former of these, its owners, I have been able to discover nothing; but it is more than conjectural that the latter name refers to the Marquis de *Fuentes*, Portuguese Ambassador at the Papal Court in the year 1720, mentioned by Mariette as a well-known amateur in this branch of art, and the first patron of Dom Landi.

Amongst the relics of the expiring taste and opulence of the Lower Empire, few are so valuable historically as the piece acquired by the Bibliothèque Impériale in 1851, and explained, on good grounds, by Chabouillet as commemorating the triumph of Licinius, Constantine's early colleague in the empire. In form it is an oval, of 4 by 2¼ inches, and exhibits, in flat relief, the emperor erect upon his triumphal quadriga, seen in front face. Over his head on either side float Sol and Luna, each bearing a long flambeau to indicate their character, and each presenting to him a globe, to typify the East and the West obedient to his power. Two Victories lead the off-horses; one bears a trophy, the other the *labarum*, emblazoned with the portraits of *two* emperors; an important circumstance, upon which the attribution of the subject to Licinius is principally founded. On the foreground are strewn the corpses of the vanquished foe, artistically grouped in various attitudes of prostration. The design has considerable merit in point of composition, although the figures themselves betray the stiffness marking the period, and

* The shortness of whose reign—only sixty-five days—quite suffices to overthrow the usual attribution of the portraits. A work of this magnitude requires several months of unremitting labour to complete. Guay expended two years of continuous toil upon his bust of Louis XV., a piece of considerably smaller dimensions.

bear much analogy in execution to the earliest productions of the regular Byzantine school.

Last in order of time comes the magnificent cameo (once belonging to Charles I.) of Her Majesty's collection. The form is a perfect oval, 7½ by 5½ inches in measurement, and the relief is enclosed within an elegant "egg-and-tongue" moulding, instead of the customary simple reserved rim. It presents the profile bust of Constantius II.* in mezzo-relievo, represented according to traditional usage (notwithstanding his Christian profession) as a Jupiter, the ægis on his breast, the sceptre resting on his shoulder, and the laurel-wreath encircling his brows. Upon the ægis the Gorgon in white, the eagle's plumes in brown, are worked out with marvellous skill. The portrait, however, as was to be expected in so late a monument, is tame and destitute of individuality, and, indeed, would serve equally well for that of any of the three imperial brothers. The sardonyx has four well-defined layers, employed by the artist with much effect to render the laurel-wreath in brown, the flesh in pearly white, and the ægis in a darker brown, which heightens the effect of the Gorgoneion set upon it. The stone has unfortunately been much fractured, a piece of mischief attributed by Vanderdort (keeper of Charles's antiquities) to the notorious Countess of Somerset.

Beger ('Thes. Palat.' p. 92) figures a bust of *Constans* with laureated head, a well-executed cameo, 2 by 1½ inches in size. On the reverse is cut the head of a negress in three-quarters face, which Beger understands as symbolising the province of Africa, which fell to the share of Constans upon the partition of the empire. The grotesque treatment, however, of the subject manifests it to be the work of some Cinque-cento hand availing himself of the black base of the sardonyx for producing in its natural colour a figure wonderfully popular with the amateurs of that period.

From the small number of such works preserved, it is worth while noticing here another cameo of the same epoch of the Decline, which I discovered amongst the Royal Gems. It is a remarkably beautiful sardonyx, in shape a long oval, and bears, in very low relief, the heads of two boys facing each other, each wearing the close helmet of the Lower Empire. This adjunct, together with the peculiar cutting of the relief, renders it certain that we have here portraits of the two elder sons of Constantine. Both quality of gem and manner of execution of the heads exactly correspond with those distinguishing a magnificent cameo of that

* It is really Claudius, and the likeness cannot be disputed. It was mended anew, and framed by Spilling, and deposited in the British Museum (1874).

emperor in the Marlborough Cabinet. This cameo is curious on another account; upon the reverse is rudely engraved the Abraxas god, surrounded by an illegible inscription, the addition of a later age, with the view of augmenting the value of this fine gem by endowing it with talismanic virtues.

But of all these monuments of the last days of Roman Art, there is none so interesting historically, or more precious artistically (if Gori's attribution of it be correct) than the immense cameo of the same family, representing the Emperor Julian and his wife Helena; the one as Mars, wearing a dragon-crested helmet, the other as Isis, bearing a star-tipped sceptre, standing at each side of a low altar, upon which a Cupid is throwing incense. The execution, indeed, seems far above the epoch of this prince; but the examples already quoted point to a revival of taste, about this time, that renders such a mode of judgment fallacious, whilst the profile of the chief personage certainly bears a stronger resemblance to the last imperial philosopher than to any other prince in the later series (Florence).

Millin cites as a Byzantine work the cameo (then Lord Carlisle's) figured by Gori as the frontispiece to his 'Thesaurus Diptychorum.' It is a sardonyx of large dimensions, being an oval of 3 by 2½ inches; the subject, Noah and his Family about to enter into the Ark, the foreground filled with the various animals that accompanied them. Noah in full robes, an angel hovering above his head, holds open one of the folding-doors of the ark, which is represented on a diminutive scale, and its model evidently taken from the Ark of the Covenant, as conventionally depicted on Jewish monuments. Noah's sons and the four wives are artistically grouped upon the other side. It is, however, quite impossible to consider this fine work as a production of the Byzantine school, even in its best days, for many reasons. The first is the classical treatment of the figures of the sons, and the studied display of the nude in their attitudes,—a thing utterly repugnant to Byzantine taste, but quite in accordance with that of the latter part of the Quattro-cento period; and, indeed, this group might very well have come from Pollaiulo of his scholars. Again, the doors of the Ark terminate in double ogee-curves, savouring mightily of the lingering reminiscences or the Flamboyant Gothic, but the very last pattern to be found in a Greek design. Upon these doors is engraved LAV MED, not as in the case of Lorenzo's undoubted
R
antique camei, in large lettering upon the field merely to mark ownership, but here, from the peculiar position, seeming to me

to indicate a piece of work actually executed to his order. The subject is one quite in accordance with the taste of his times, so is the attempt to treat it classically; and certainly both the attempt and the success with which it has been carried out involve conditions of thought that never existed amongst the Greek cameo-cutters of Constantinople.

XIX.

With the empire opens the grand era of *portraits* upon gems, the countless offspring of adulation, love, affection, and friendship. The purely Greek period had produced nothing but *ideal* heads, with the exception of those rare cases where his own image was required for the personal seal of the sovereign or his representative. But with the Romans the love for perpetuating the memory of their ancestors, by means of collections of family portraits, had from the earliest times shown itself a ruling passion: their *atria* were lined with heads of their predecessors, modelled in wax after the life, for many generations back, ensconced each one in its own little shrine (*armarium*)—monuments, in virtue of their composition, that set decay at defiance. In the later Republican times, after gem-engraving had come into fashion, these wax-casts furnished authentic originals for the family-portraits embellishing signets of the kind to be more particularly described in their due place. But as soon as the despotic power of the Cæsars was established, it became a mark of loyalty to adorn either one's house or one's hand with the visible presence of the sovereign. Capitolinus notices that the individual was looked upon as an impious wretch who, having the means, did not set up at home a statue of M. Aurelius; and, a century later, the Senate obliged by an edict every householder to keep a picture of the restorer of the empire, Aurelian. That officials wore such portraits in their rings as an indispensable mark of distinction may be deduced from the regulation of Claudius (preserved by Pliny), confining the *entrée* at court to such as had received from him a gold ring having the imperial bust carved upon it. There was, however, another and a deeper motive for the wide prevalence of the fashion. Certain passages from writers of the time* (first pointed out by

* Firmicus the astrologer (ii. 33), and Ammian the historian. The latter's words are (xvii. 12) "Opinantur quidam Fatum vinci principum fortuna, vel fieri."

Buonarotti, *l.c.*, p. 413) give evidence of the general existence of a belief that the *Genius* of the Emperor (accounted of higher power than Fortune herself) was propitiated to extend his patronage over the individual who, by assuming this badge of subservience, put himself under his protection.

Numerous gem-portraits of Augustus, including the very finest specimens of the Roman school, are to be admired in every large cabinet; and he, we know, was even in life regarded as a "præsens deus." The *Augustus*, it must be borne in mind, united in one person the most sacred offices of religion as well as of the state; he was *Pontifex Maximus* and *Tribunus Plebis* at once; his person was therefore *sacrosancta*, and all offences committed against it became of the nature of sacrilege. Still more abundant (and where now they would be least expected) are they of the last of his line, the present synonym for all that is detestable—Nero. But the anomaly is explained by the youthful age of all his portraits; the nascent beard to be remarked upon all of them proves them to date from the first four years of his reign; for it was in his twentieth year that he first shaved, instituting—to commemorate that important epoch in his life—the festival *Juvenalia*. These same four years were a season of the brightest promise to the Roman world, that had for nearly half a century lain groaning under the tyranny of the malignant Tiberius, the maniac Caligula, and the dotard Claudius. The same cause explains the almost equal frequency of the youthful Caracalla, depicted usually as Mercury, the "Very-bountiful," to use the Homeric epithet best descriptive of his godship, or else of the equally auspicious Bonus Eventus. This prince also had in his youth been as conspicuous for the clemency and amiability of his temper as he afterwards became infamous, during his short tenure of empire, for cruelty and moroseness.

The educated classes, who so greatly affected the study of philosophy, esteemed their claims to the honourable title established in Juvenal's days—

> "Si quis Aristotelem similem vel Pittacon emit
> Et jubet architypos pluteum servare Cleanthis."

Cicero also laughs at the fondness of his friends belonging to the Epicurean sect for carrying about their master's likeness in their rings. And the innumerable heads of Socrates, all of Roman workmanship, speak to the wide spread of the theosophy (the sole vital religion of the times) elaborated by his successor Plato.

Living men of letters, the popular authors of the day, received from all admirers a similar homage. To this practice Ovid, writing from his far-distant place of banishment, pathetically alludes :—

> "Hoc tibi dissimulas sentis tamen, optime, dici
> In digito qui me fersque refersque tuo ;
> Effigiemque meam fulvo complexus in auro
> Cara relegati qua potes ora vides."

One of the most tantalising things in this study is, in fact, the continually meeting with faces upon our gems full of genius and of energy, unmistakably belonging to the bright spirits of the first two centuries, but which rest to us voiceless and lifeless from the loss of all means of identifying them with their originals, still eternised by history. The matter-of-fact Etruscans, when they drew a god or hero, were careful to add his name "for the benefit of country gentlemen:" it is infinitely to be regretted their successors thought scorn of the good old rule of their ancient preceptors in the arts—even a few initials would in many cases have imparted a transcendent interest to these, now silent, monuments.

Names, indeed, are often to be discovered accompanying portraits upon gems; but it so happens that they are invariably the names of *nobodies*, for they are only found annexed to the heads of the bride and bridegroom engraved upon the stone that decorated the wedding-ring (under the Later Empire), and replaced the more ancient *clasped-hands* or *Fides*, which likewise, as a rule, commemorated the names of the pair.

After these mementos of the nuptial ceremony succeed others, still placing before our indifferent eyes its natural consequences—chubby *baby-faces*, whose sight, some eighteen centuries ago, called up many a smile upon those just alluded to—little bubbles rising up and breaking unnoticed upon the ocean of eternity, of whom nought is left save these tiny but imperishable records. These full-faced, laughter-stirring visages had also a further object: like the other masks thus represented, they had virtue as amulets. Cut in relief, and perhaps then allusive to *Horus* (the vernal Sun-god), they, with the Gorgon's, embellished the phaleræ of the knight, becoming thus—

> "Decus et tutamen in armis."

Lastly, as large a class as any of the foregoing owes its birth to the "love free as air," who—

> ". . . . . at sight of human ties,
> Shakes his light wings, and in a moment flies."

These fair faces once gave a soul to rings intended either for mutual exchange or to be worn for the sake of the constant enjoyment, in some sort, of the company of the beloved original. The preacher of the new and rigid code of morals, Clemens Alexandrinus, fails not to inveigh against the fashion "of the licentious world of keeping in their rings the likenesses of their naked mistresses or other favourites, so that they are never left for a moment free from the torments of desire."

XX.

During the first two centuries of the empire, the art of making *Pastes* was cultivated to an incredible extent, in order to meet the requirements of the poorer classes (Pliny terming them "Gemmæ vitreæ ex vulgi annulis"), persons who were unable either to dispense with the use of so necessary an appendage as a signet, or to afford the cost of an engraved gem of sufficient merit to satisfy their innate love of perfection in form. Through these ingenious multiplications which afforded them almost the full enjoyment of all the *artistic* merit of the originals, the poorest were enabled to gratify both taste and vanity at a very trifling outlay. Under so powerful an impulse this branch of the glass-maker's art throve prodigiously, and has bequeathed to us many extraordinary specimens of skill in the chemical composition of the material, and of ingenuity and dexterity in its manipulation. These reproductions of glyptic works appear to have come to an end in the third century, simultaneously with the extinction (as far as high art is concerned) of the production of their prototypes in real stones. Nevertheless the making of imitative precious stones and also of ornamental glass for the table, continued a flourishing manufacture at Constantinople until late in the Middle Ages, when Venice succeeded to the inheritance of its secrets and of its prosecution.

In the better days of the Roman practice, camei of large size were counterfeited with wonderful fidelity in pastes of many strata, and in a close imitation (sometimes even surpassing Nature) of the colours of the original; to be distinguished with difficulty from the true, in those examples where the cast has been gone over and polished by the same *technique* as was employed for the actual gem. Equally successful were the old *vitriarii* in reproducing the then very rare and highly-esteemed lapis-lazuli (*sapphirus*) the "royal stone," as the Greeks designated it. The Bonus Eventus, or

Caracalla, thus deified (Townley) in half-relief upon a plaque eight inches square, is a superb monument of the proficiency of his age in this curious manufacture.

XXI.

When the times of the Decline had lost all power of producing anything of merit in this branch of art, it is evident, from various allusions in the later historians, that fine works were (perhaps the more so on that very account) still held in the highest estimation. Though the power of imitation was lost, the faculty of admiration of the Beautiful long survived. Lampridius (Hel. 23) expresses this sentiment by the way in which he puts down amongst the most wanton extravagances of Heliogabalus, "his wearing upon his shoes gems, and those, too, engraved; a caprice that set everybody laughing, as if the engravings of *celebrated artists* could be seen in gems that were fastened upon the foot." Again, the detailed and elegant description of the signet of King Hydaspes—an amethyst with a shepherd-boy piping to his flock—upon which the tasteful Bishop of Tricca, Heliodorus, has lavished all his eloquence, abundantly manifests his admiration for excellence in this line. So does the spirited epigram of the still later Marcus Argentarius, upon the gem presenting Cupid mounted on the lion.

It now remains for us to trace the sad and precipitous course of the decadence of this Art; pointing out the causes that occasioned it, and briefly describing the very remarkable monuments that the same causes generated with fantastic prodigality. It must be premised that the most important amongst the camei preserved to us may, from the circumstances of their history (related in the preceding description), be supposed to have ever been the foremost in their class, for, as far back as they can be traced, they have without interruption figured as the choicest ornaments of regal or sacerdotal treasuries. Although the grandest examples, as my foregoing list of them has shown, all belong to the early part of the first century, yet camei in sardonyx and lapis-lazuli, important both for workmanship and material, continued to be executed in profusion throughout the whole of the succeeding century. This latter period indeed, was that when the sister-art of die-sinking was in its most flourishing condition in the Roman mint; the age of magnificent and numerous medallions may be said to commence with Trajan and to end with Commodus. Several camei bear the artist's signature in *relief*, and such signatures are almost the only memorials of the great masters in this line that are placed beyond the suspicion of modern forgery, or of misapplication.

Although, as already observed, the best period of Roman art terminates with the luxurious reign of the tasteful tyrant Commodus; nevertheless, very creditable performances in this particular department are due to the patronage of the learned African Severus and perpetuate the faces of all the members of his family. Of his successor Caracalla, who, ferocious soldier as he is represented by history, nevertheless fostered the art of gem-engraving with much liberality, the cameo-portraits are far from uncommon and are done with singular (and unflattering) fidelity of expression, and neatness of *technique*.

After his times, however, gem-engraving, already on the decline as far as the *intaglio*-branch thereof was concerned, degenerated, and became, so to speak, extinct, with a rapidity at first sight incomprehensible. But sundry powerful causes worked simultaneously together for its overthrow. The ruling spirit of the empire was the military, and that now more than half barbarian; the greatest of the later emperors being by birth Illyrians, their highest officers, their own countrymen, then Franks, and last of all Goths. In personal decorations, therefore, intrinsic value came to be the only thing regarded by the possessor; precious stones, as a natural consequence, in their native state, speedily drove engraved gems out of fashion. Vast gold medallions for the wealthy, the current *aurei* for the commonalty, now superseded the cameo-head of the reigning prince in the pendant (*stellatura*), and in the ring. Add to this that the spread of Christianity precluded a large class from patronising the representation of the forms emanating from the elegant mythology of the preceding times, whilst with those who still adhered to Paganism the only subjects in favour were those suggested by the revolution, which had imperceptibly, though completely, metamorphosed their own religious ideas. Oriental mysticism had by this time respectfully dethroned the proper gods of Greece and Italy. Its votaries demanded nothing more from the engraver than the barbarous symbolical monsters engendered by the prevailing syncretism of old Egytian, Zoroastrian, and newly imported Buddhistic ideas.

In fact, even under the Middle Empire, and before the Glyptic Art had begun to betray any marked symptoms of decay, its finest productions are connected with the worship of Serapis and of

Mithras, and thus are tinged with the spirit of Egypt and of Persia; or else they are *Grylli*, those fantastic combinations, talismanic and astrological in their hidden import, which, nevertheless, exhibit much ingenuity and taste in their invention, and equal skill in their execution. Such designs, all impregnated with a profound, practical feeling of mystic superstition, already oust from the gem the graceful forms of the deities created by the ancient Hellenic and Hesperian nature-worship.

XXII.

By the name *Grylli* are understood those grotesque figures of which the Romans were so fond, to judge from the immense number of them in existence. They are formed out of portions of various animals, of the most diverse species, combined into the outline of a single monster, that generally takes the form of a bird, a horse, an eagle's head, or a helmet. They have been called *Chimæræ*, because that fabulous monster was similarly multiform, being a goat, a lion, and a dragon united into one; *Symplegmata*, in the sense of the *embracing* or *copulation* of the discordant components; *Grylli*, from the Italian *grillo*, signifying a cricket and a caprice or fancy. For the last designation a classical origin has been sought in the "Gryllus" of Pliny, who states (xxv. 37) "Antiphilus jocosis (tabulis) nomine *Gryllum* deridiculi habitus pinxit, unde id genus picturae *grylli* vocantur." But it is evident that Pliny here employs the word in the exact sense of our "caricature," implying a style that got its name from one Gryllus, a person of grotesque appearance, who had been taken off by Antiphilus (the inventor of caricature and *genre*-painting), who first degraded thus the dignity of the art, which before had been sacred and heroic in its essential nature.

These caprices are often wrongly called *Basilidan Figures*, and classed amongst Gnostic remains, to which category, however, they are very far from belonging: for besides never exhibiting the symbols, or the siglæ, or the legends that characterise the entire Gnostic family—all more or less betraying an Egyptian origin—the style of work exhibited upon them sufficiently proclaims to the least experienced eye that the Grylli belong to a much earlier date, the flourishing period of Roman Art.

Nevertheless, in one point are they cognate to the Basilidan stones. Like them, they were designed for talismans and amulets,* but the notions they embody are purely *astrological* or else springing out of the ancient religion of Greece and Rome, and are never tinctured with the exotic doctrines of the Alexandrine Kabala. Although the period which produced them in the greatest abundance was the first two centuries of the Empire, after which they entirely vanish, driven from the field by the countless barbaric swarms of the offspring of the Alexandrine Gnosis, yet some of these composite heads, human and bestial in one, are to be found on much more ancient relics: for example, upon the Phœnician scarabæi of Tharros. One of these (Brett Collection) would seem to refer to the Orphic cosmogony (as preserved by Athenagoras), "*Water* and *mud* † were the first principles of creation; from their union proceeded a being having the body of a serpent, with the heads of a bull and a lion, and a man's in the middle. This being was named Hercules, or Chronos, and laid an egg, out of which came forth the god *Phanes*: of the two halves of the shell were formed heaven and earth."

Of all such compositions that in which a mystic meaning is the most immediately obvious to the sense is the symplegma, combining the fore-quarters of two beasts, as the lion and the bull, the bull and the goat, which are clearly *Zodiacal* in their origin. Frequently we have three in one—the bull, sheep, swine; the combination borne up upon wings, like the bust of a Magian divinity. The explanation of the latter configuration as referring to the sacrifice *Suovetaurilia* is by no means satisfactory; for what had such an idea to do with the choice of the signet-device,—a thing ever regarded as in some sort a talisman and securing to the bearer the protection of the deity thereby indicated either expressly or by a symbol? Such pairs of combined heads are seen on the primitive coins of Samos; Müller thinks they were

* "But especially in all combinations of various animal forms which had indeed been partly originated by an Oriental influence, but were perfected in a pure Hellenic feeling, does a spirit manifest itself which grasps the life of Nature in her creative omnipotence with equal truth and boldness. Hence such figures meet us as real and actually existing objects. A far different spirit from this simple feeling for Nature speaks to us out of the grylli of a later period, on gems; humour displayed in the putting together of the most incongruous ideas: where also often an allegorically expressed meaning lies at the bottom of the whole."

In this opinion of the great archæologist I cannot acquiesce. The very introduction of the symbols of various deities, so frequent in them, is in itself a proof that they were designed for talismans.

† Eva and Adam. *Eva* is water in the ancient Celtic (still preserved in the Piedmontese dialect), whence comes the French *eau*.

suggested by Asiatic forms derived from Persepolis, and originally Assyrian. The grave, severe character of this early religion necessitates our believing that some deep mystery was couched in this union of different beasts; perhaps pairs or triplets of divinities expressed by the animal attributes of each. The beings (Izeds) seen by Ezekiel on the Chebar had conjoined heads of a man, lion, ox, and eagle.

And descending to later times, the symbolism of our *symplegmata* becomes an admitted fact, if we accept Quatremère de Quincy's explanation of the passage in Pliny, describing how Parrhasius embodied in painting his conception of the Athenian Democracy, "wishing to represent it as feeble, passionate, unjust, inconsistent, yet at the same time placable, merciful, tender-hearted, haughty, vain-glorious, abject, bold, and timorous, all at one and the same time." De Quincy supposes that all these conflicting qualities thus united in one were typified by the figure of an owl (the national emblem), furnished with the *heads* of the various animals the recognised emblems for these different qualities. More probably they were all combined into the general *outline* of the Athenian fowl, else there would have been but little cleverness in the invention lauded by Pliny as "ingenioso argumento." The prosaic Müller rejects as fanciful the hypothesis of the ingenious Frenchman, but it appears to me as correct as it is acute. When Horace styles the Roman Public "a beast with many heads," some such picture as this Parrhasian *Demos* must have floated before his mind's eye, and not the Hydra, as the passage is commonly understood. The poet is alluding to the *diversity* of tastes amongst his readers, not to their *cruelty*, the sole quality for which the many-headed Lernæan foe of Hercules was notorious.

That the intention of an amulet lay at the bottom of such fantastic compositions in general is nowhere so clearly perceptible as in the class now to be considered.

"The objects that are fastened up as means to keep off witchcraft," says Plutarch, in a remarkable passage ('Sympos.,' v. 7), where he is attempting to explain everything by natural causes, "derive their efficacy from the fact that they act through the strangeness and ridiculousness of their forms, which fix the mischief-working evil eye upon themselves." Exactly such is the case with the grotesque distorted *masks*, which seem to have derived their name of *Oscilla* from the grimace of the wide-open mouth. People thought, by the suspension of such caricature masks, which threatened to swallow up everything in their gaping jaws, to counteract the pernicious influence of envy and of witchcraft. Thus superstition knew how to derive comfort out of the most hideous shapes. The workers in metal, clay, and wax were ready to make their profit out of the demand for such protective bugbears; but with the progress of art they softened down that ugliness so repugnant to their feeling, for the Beautiful, and left but so much of their original form as was absolutely necessary for the expression of the primitive idea. Thus the Gorgon's head, with flaring snaky hair, protuded tongue, and hideous death contortions (Hecate's "facies Erebi"), a mere amulet at first on the warrior's breast and shield, grew by gradual refinement into the ideal of female beauty, the Strozzi Medusa.

"This leads us to the true derivation of the word *Mask*, which is not, as Orientalists will have it, the Arabic, *Maskara*, 'a juggler,' nor *Makelung*, 'to besmut the face,' as in the primitive theatre, but the corruption of a Greek term, preserved by Hesychius, *βασκὰ* = *δείκελα*, *masks*; *βασκανία*, fascina, *amulets*. Hence by the common commutation of the initials we get *Maska*. This derivation is due to Salmasius. In Low Latin (Ducange) *Masca* and *Talamasca* signified a goblin, witch, or monster—whence also the French *grimace*. From this custom of regarding hideous masks as amulets can be explained a circumstance otherwise a problem to every archæologist—the vast number of such subjects we meet with in antique gems. More than two thousand of them have been already published. As they evidently came from the best artists of the time, there must have been some more potent reason for the demand than the mere love of the ancients for dramatic matters or their connection with the Bacchic mysteries." (Böttiger, 'Ueber das Wort "Maske."')

The importance attached by the Romans to this class of subjects is manifested not only by the vast numbers in which they have come down to us, but by the circumstance that the highest skill of the artist under the Cæsars and the "Five good Emperors" was lavished upon the engraving of Masks, whether single or combined.

In the latter the designer ever sought to produce the strongest possible contrasts by putting together visages the most incongruous in expression, as a satyr's and a beautiful nymph's side by side, or back to back Janus-like, a stern tragic with a laughing wide-mouthed comic; and an infinity of similar ill-paired couples, for the most part brought together with singular skill. The special stone for all such subjects is the red jasper: its colour caused it to be almost exclusively dedicated to the purpose, being that sacred to Bacchus, the "rosy god," * whose statues were regularly painted with vermilion, as Pausanias inform us.

One of the most ingenious of these combinations, and, as its outline bespeaks, especially devised in his honour, represents a noble bunch of grapes, with stalk and tendril, the separate berries being five masks, the two upper satyric, the three lower comic, the outline filled up with a few more: an idea perhaps unique, and carried out in this instance with the utmost skill.

The conjunction of the three masks expressing the ancient division of the Drama into tragic, comic, satyric, has given birth to the finest examples we have of Roman gem-engraving: witness the beautiful sard in the Marlborough Cabinet, and another, equally admirable, lately in the Fould. Another and a very favourite arrangement was to make a charming youthful profile covered with a congeries of several grotesque visages, all amalgamated into the form of a helmet. Again, we are presented with a tragic mask in full face, every feature distorted and horrific, coupled with a comic profile full of a mild and cheerful serenity.† In fact, every collection will supply new proofs of the old engravers' skill in producing an endless variety of such fantastic unions.

Similar antique combinations of grotesque masks may have suggested to Dante his description of Lucifer, according to the usual transmutation of the antique comic into the mediæval horrible :—

"Oh ! quanto parve a me gran maraviglia
Quando vidi *Tre facce* alla sua testa :
L' una dinanzi, e quella era vermiglia ;
Le altre eran due che si aggiungén a questa,
Sovresso il mezzo di ciascuna spalla,
E si giungóno al loco della cresta :
E la destra parea tra bianca e gialla,
La sinistra a vedere era tal quale
Vengon di là ove il Nilo s' avvalla."

---

* Before masks came into use, the Greek actors stained their faces with wine-lees.

"Dicitur, et plaustris vexisse poëmata Thespis,
Quæ canerent agerentque peruncti fæcibus ora.

The engravers evidently aimed at selecting gems analogous to the subjects they were to present ; thus Venus will generally be found on the *sea-green* plasma, Jupiter on the *cerulean* jasper, Serapes the "blood-drinker" on the sanguine kind.

† A religious notion may possibly be hidden here: the secret teaching of the Phrygian mysteries represented the Supreme One Deity as at once male and female.

In the next phase, the human wizard was coupled with the head of some beast, which latter, if viewed in one direction, forms a head-covering for it: an idea evidently borrowed from the ancient Heroic heads enveloped in the hide of the fore-part of a lion, a bull, or a goat. In this way an old man's (Socrates) face, backed by the head of a boar, a ram, or an elephant, are amongst the most common in the series.

By adding to this compound the head and neck of a horse or of a bird, and then mounting it upon the legs of the latter, a complete animal *sui generis* was the result, often serving for a steed to a little Genius,—a parody upon that favourite type the God of Love bestriding the lion. Another "strange fowl" was created by giving a peacock's head and neck to a body built up out of satyric masks, or rather the repeated head of Silenus (itself a potent amulet), a ram's and a cornucopia, with wheat-ears doing duty for the tail. This creature usually stands upon a dolphin or a lizard, and the first idea of it seems suggested by the Ibis destroying reptiles,—a frequent picture on the Roman walls when the Egyptian was the fashionable superstition of the day.

There seems good reason to suspect that India—the true source of the various new Theosophies, however externally differing, that in the same ages were overflooding the Roman Empire—was likewise the original parent of these fantastic multiform creations. *Chrishna*, the chief avatar of Vishnu, seems to have been in many points the prototype of Apollo. He appears as *Pythius* slaying the serpent Kalya, and as *Nomios* piping to the flocks of the shepherd his foster-father, and accompanied by the *Nine* "Gupta" or milkmaids, who dance to his music. These maidens interweave themselves into the forms of different animals (precisely as the Indian jugglers perform the same feat in our day), an *elephant*, a *horse*, a *peacock*, or a *palky*, and carry about their beloved playmate mounted upon this extemporised vehicle. Such composite creatures are in their nature identical with the grylli, built up out of numerous heads and serving for a steed to Cupid. The astrological character of these devices affords another argument in support of their Oriental origin. Chares, an eye-witness, mentions *Indian* jugglers as exhibiting at the festivities of Alexander's wedding at Ecbatana. Such is the unchangeableness of everything Hindoo that we may be sure this very combination of themselves into the form of a single animal was one of the tricks that astonished the Macedonian and Persian feasters upon that occasion. And that these living patterns were actually introduced in the shows of the Romans we have the express testimony of Martial. In an elegant epigram (Spect. 26) he describes a chorus of Nereids disporting upon the lake brought in to fill the arena, and forming themselves into a trident, an anchor, an oar, a ship, the twin stars of the Dioscuri, and a sail swollen by the wind. Fantastic alliances like these must have been in Horace's view when he laughs at the painter who should "fasten a horse's neck to a human head, and clothe with motley feathers the miscellaneous members of the whole, got together from all parts of creation."

It will be found on examination that these monsters, however diverse in outline—whether that be a cock, a horse, or a headpiece—admit of very little variety in their component parts; the Silenus mask, ram's head, dolphin, mouse, and cornucopia evidently having been deemed essential elements in their creation. It may hence safely be concluded that these objects—emblems of the sun, earth, air, and ocean—were employed in a definite relation to each other, and the resulting figures conveyed a deep and mystic virtue, like the famed Ephesian spell, which was no other than the names of the sun and the elements in some forgotten primæval tongue. That all were in their nature astrological appears from the solar and lunar symbols with the caduceus and the thunderbolt so frequently introduced. In some, indeed, the astrological character is unmistakable, as in one of my own, which gives a Janus-head of Neptune and Bacchus (here the solar god), with the trident and thyrsus in the field, crowned by the eagle of Jove, that most propitious horoscope, and accompanied by Cancer and the letters AIH, antique name for the earth.

There is another consideration that comes in support of this view; it is hardly probable that devices of this nature should have risen into such general favour for signets, and all at a time when good taste still reigned in Italy, if they had been mere caprices of the artist. In the latter case, moreover, we should now perceive an endless variety in the component elements selected, instead of that marked restriction to the narrow limits above enumerated.

This hypothesis—which I originally deduced for myself from the careful study of this interesting class—I subsequently was gratified to discover had long ago received the sanction of that very acute and experienced archæologist Böttiger, who says ('Kleine Schriften,' iii. 9):—"The *bird-chimæra* is, through its constituent parts, the cock, the ram, and the mask, an unmistakable amulet. The cock was in all antiquity, on account of his fiery nature, the symbol of the sun,* as the principle of light and of all good. For this reason we find upon Egyptian amulets a peculiar genius

* Which makes him the favourite decoration of the *Rhodian* pottery.

having the head of a cock (Abraxas). The ram is the emblem of fecundity,* and therefore the cornucopia is placed upon his head. The Silenus-mark set upon the cock's breast in front is the so-called *oscillum*, or amulet-mask, which used to be hung up on trees, house-doors, and fixed on shields, for the purpose of scaring away evil spirits and for the promotion of fruitfulness. The ram holds the hare (rabbit) by the tail, and the cock bestrides the dolphin. The hare stands here as the representative of the beasts of the land, as the dolphin for those of the sea. The meaning of the whole allegory may therefore be read:—'Sunshine, abundance, and protection against all evil both by sea and land be unto thee that wearest this ring!'"

That Böttiger is right in assigning a protective virtue to these talismans in their securing for the wearer the patronage of the four elements, is, in my opinion, clearly established by another shape into which the same components are frequently worked up. This is the type where the owner's head is portrayed covered with the chimera-helmet, or where, as frequently, the latter is represented alone. Of this the finest example known to me is most ingeniously put together.† A boar's head forms the frontlet, a ram's the neckpiece, a wolf couchant the crown, whose bushy tail hanging down finishes the crest; the chinstrap is a lizard. Here are united the attributes of Hercules, of Mercury, and of Mars; whilst the lizard, Egyptian emblem of the Logos, is a frequent attribute of Minerva. Its aspect also was considered beneficial to the sight, probably on account of its agreeable emerald hue. On another gem, the wolf's head becomes the neckpiece of a casque in which the body is completed by two doves (bringing in the influence of Venus), pecking together at a fig which stands for the ear of the helmeted personage.

There is yet another and a frequent type of the head of an *elephant* made up out of several masks, in which the Silenus is ever the main feature, and holding in its trunk a caduceus. This is usually explained as an amulet against the disease called elephantiasis, but this is mere conjecture. Orpheus, indeed (though in his extant verses he does not keep his promise) declares that—

"The wretch dashed to the ground in that dread hour
When reels his brain beneath fell Luna's power,
I'll teach his cure; and how the pest to tame
That from the *elephant* derives its name."

* Besides being the special attribute of Mercury, the patron of shepherds.

† I cannot help thinking the first idea of these figures was suggested by the helmets of the Gauls, which, according to Diodorus Siculus, were carried up into

But the whole tenor of his work manifests that these remedies were to be sought for in the specific virtues of certain stones, and not in the sigils or formulæ to be inscribed upon them.*

Another most convincing proof of the importance attached to these symbolical figures is that they were admitted amongst the types of the national coinage. Thus we have that very ancient gryllus on the silver of Halicarnassus, known as "the Winged Sow," apparently compounded of that beast and the cock; and the yet more singular composite put upon their denarii by the family Valeria, a long-legged crane furnished with a helmeted female head, a serpent encircling the neck, a bearded mask on the breast, armed with a buckler and two javelins and trampling upon a lizard. Müller can discern in this nothing more than all Minerva's attributes combined into the outline of her own bird: but this interpretation will not stand the test of examination, for the bird's figure is manifestly not an *owl's;* neither does Pallas carry a pair of javelins, but the long Homeric spear. More probably it represents one of the "Birds of Mars," inhabiting the isle Aretias in the Euxine, which shot forth their feathers like arrows in their flight upon the approach of the Argo, and wounded Oïleus in the shoulder (Ap. Rhod. ii. 1060). The device was evidently chosen as a rebus on the name *Valeria*, being to the eye the personification of *strength* and *valour*, and is one amongst many of what heralds call the "canting arms" in which the consular Romans so much delighted; examples whereof are the *burning* sun of Aburius, the *elephant* of Cæsar (so-called in Punic), the butting *bull* of Thorius, &c. Havercamp, indeed, thinks it may be one of the Stymphalian Birds, which, as the story goes, were invulnerable themselves, but could pierce through the strongest armour with their beaks—a power typified by the darts. They consequently set Hercules and his arrows at defiance, until Pallas coming to his aid gave him a bronze rattle wherewith to scare them away to the shores of the Red Sea. There their progeny still flourish, for the officers employed in the late nautical survey of that coast discovered upon the sandhills the deserted nests of a gigantic crane infinitely exceeding in measurement anything before known to belong to that species. Interwoven into the structure of one of them were discovered the bones and tattered clothing of some poor shipwrecked mariner, still

---

the shape of the heads of beasts or birds, all forged out of the same metal. They must have resembled the towering tilting-helmets thus adorned, that came into fashion in 1450.

* In fact, this specific virtue is assigned by Psellus, drawing from the same sources, to the emerald.

retaining his silver watch, a convincing testimony of the recent building of the pile.

Legends, when they occur on such *intagli* (for strangely enough a *cameo* in this style is not known), are always as enigmatical as the device itself, and, when they can be read at all, must be read from the middle towards each end; but for the most part give no intelligible sense to the uninitiated. More frequently only detached letters or mysterious-looking characters are found inscribed; the latter may be supposed either astrological cyphers, or the *siglæ* of the Roman shorthand, and containing, could they be interpreted, the key to the enigma.

On this interesting subject—the stenography of the ancients—a few words will not be out of place here, where the compression of numerous ideas into one figure is the topic under consideration. The use of shorthand, or the expressing entire words by a single arbitrary cypher, "*fictis* notare verba *signis*," as Prudentius calls it (P., S. Cassiani), was first brought to a regular system by the famous Tiro, who invented or adapted 1500 of them. Seneca in the following century augmented them to the number of 5000. A few of those most commonly required are preserved in the MSS. of Cicero.* The principle of their formation was to take the initial of the particular word, and then to add a stroke, which, by varying its inflections, denotes the remainder of the several words beginning with the same letter. A contrivance happily and tersely described by Manilius in the line—

"Hic et scriptor erit velox cui litera verbum est,"

"The *native* shall be a rapid scribe to whom one letter stands for the whole word."

By constant practice these *Notarii* attained to extraordinary facility in the use of the cyphers, so that Martial says of one—

"Currant verba licet manus est velocior illis;
Nondum lingua suum, dextra peregit opus."

"Though swift your words, his fingers swifter run;
Before your tongue, his pen its task hath done."

These *Notæ* had all to be learnt by heart,† and the tax upon the memory must have been most distressing; hence the notarii were trained from childhood in schools kept expressly for that purpose, and a truly distasteful discipline was the study to

* Kopp, in his 'Tachygraphia Veterum,' gives a large quarto full of them. A very copious list is also appended to Gruter's 'Inscriptions.'

† As in Chinese at present.

the youthful mind, as Prudentius remarks in the poem above quoted; for—

> "Verba notis brevibus comprendere cuncta peritus
> Raptimque punctis dicta præpetibus sequi."
>
> "Skilled in brief marks all words soe'er to bind,
> And follow speech in cyphers swift as wind."——

Cassianus, the unlucky preceptor, an obstinate Christian, was given up by order of the Pagan judge, naked, to his infuriated pupils, who pricked him to death with their styli.

In other *capricci*, however, it is apparent that nothing recondite lies hid under the design, and that the ludicrous alone is the thing aimed at. But even here an important object was kept in view for the grotesque, or the unexpected put prominently forward was deemed the surest means of baffling the stroke of the universally dreaded Evil Eye or Βασκανία. In this belief we have the motive for those combinations of the mightiest with the most fragile of things created: such as a lion or an elephant emerging from a snailshell in the place of its proper molluscous inhabitant; or that where a Pygmy fisherman, similarly housed, is diverting himself by angling with a rod and line. From the same motive springs also the predilection for the combat between a Pygmy and a crane as a device for the signet; not to add that the warrior ever exhibits in a most exaggerated form that object (fascinum), the figure of which was the most ancient and most efficient of all amulets.

It is often impossible to avoid being astonished with what ingenuity the designer of these trifles has contrived to work elements so incongruous into one complete and graceful whole; and this, coupled with their usually finished execution, convincingly demonstrates that the best engravers of the age did not look upon such embodied *jeux d'esprit* as beneath their attention.

The same observation applies to yet another class where insects, usually the *grillo** or mole-cricket, figure engaged in all the occupations of the human race. Thus on one gem the cricket acts as a porter with a long pole slung over his shoulders, and packages on each end; on another he marches along with a vast cornucopia upon his arm, whence issue Capricorn and a bee; in a third a couple appear equipped as gladiators, one with the trident

* This insect swarms in the Italian copses during the summer months, and is still (as by the ancients) kept in paper cages by children for the sake of its low monotonous note. It seems to have been the ἄκρις to which Meleager addresses a pretty epigram.

and net of the *retiarius*, the other with the shield and falchion of the *secutor*, as if matched together in the arena. The cricket figured so largely in these half-comic, half-serious representations for a very singular reason; there was current a strange notion suggested by its withered skeleton form and subterranean habitat, that it was the express image of a ghost, and on that account it is actually styled "larvalis imago." Hence the humour of making it thus occupied in the daily avocations of this life; it was the graceful embodiment of the same moral that the gloomy imagination of the mediæval artist, "fed full upon horrors," delighted to image forth in his ghastly Dance of Death.

To close the list, a pretty and frequent composition may be quoted—the lyre of Apollo made out of a mask for sounding-board, with the arms formed by two dolphins, creatures supposed to be passionately fond of music. It is supported by ravens or hoopooes, birds sacred to Apollo, or by the owl of Pallas; the meaning couched in the whole presenting an enigma by no means difficult to be solved. But to pursue this subject further would be an endless task, inasmuch as every gem-cabinet presents new examples of these whimsical yet elegant fancies, born of the same taste that adorned the walls of every Roman saloon, with the graceful and ever-varying arabesques which we cannot help admiring although so strongly condemned by Vitruvius as derogatory to the dignity of art.

XXIII.

Gnosticism was the pretension to the true knowledge of divine things, as enveloped in the outward forms of Paganism as well as of Christianity. The Ophites, or serpent-worshippers, the most ancient of the school, and who exclusively arrogated to themselves the title of *Gnostics*, were accustomed, says Hippolytus, assiduously to attend the celebration of all the heathen Mysteries, and to pretend that in their transcendental *knowledge* they possessed the key to all the deep truths symbolically expressed in the rites. For the same reason they boldly maintained that they were the only real Christians. To express in a visible form their own doctrines, they availed themselves of the emblems and iconology of two religions principally. The first of these was the Egyptian, then (the second century) very fashionable at Rome; besides which Alexandria was the fountain-head of Gnosticism, and its greatest lights, Basilides and Valentinus, were inhabitants of that city. The second source whence they drew their materials was the Mithraic creed, a modification of the Zoroastrian, introduced into Rome after the conquest of Pontus, and flourishing there so amazingly as, with the first-named, to have nearly superseded every other form of religious belief. This Mithraic religion was, from its nature, essentially astrological; the sun-god being its special object of adoration, and the planetary genii playing important parts in the scheme as his subordinate ministers. The Jewish Kabala was likewise the offspring of the union of Zoroastrism with the "traditions of the Elders." The Magi on one side, the Jewish astrologers on the other, were the missionaries of the new religion, and diffused its notions—

> "All that on Folly Frenzy could beget,"

through the length and breadth of the empire—Mithraicism, accepted as cognate to the national Druidical system, being universal in Gaul, Germany, and Britain.

From the Egyptian worship the Gnostics borrowed many types to engrave upon the gems, which were to serve them both for talismans for the good of their souls and bodies and for means of mutual recognition between the *illuminati*. In special veneration with them were the figure of the jackal-headed Anubis, the guide of souls to the other world; the solar serpent with a lion's head radiated, originally an amulet for the protection of the chest, but now interpreted in a more spiritual sense; the infant Horus (another personification of the sun) seated upon the lotus, the emblem of fecundity: the *cynocephalus* baboon, the peculiar attribute of the moon, and therefore generally represented as adoring the triangle, the received symbol of that luminary; and, above all, that peculiar creation of the Basilidan sect, the *Abraxas*-god Iao, a *pantheus* made up out of the symbols of the four elements—the serpent, eagle, the human trunk, and the scourge; or perhaps combining in himself so many attributes of the solar divinity alone. His title *Abraxas*, "The Blessed Name," had the grand virtue of containing in the sum of its letters, taken according to Greek numeration, the solar period of 365. All these types the Gnostics interpreted as shadowing forth the Christ, "the Sun of Righteousness." From Mithraicism they obtained and used with equal profusion the Belus mounted on his lion, and the mystic many-winged and armed figures of the planetary genii. And lastly the Kabala (whose grand school was previously established at Alexandria) furnished them with interminable inscriptions in corrupt Hebrew or Syriac, and with series of mystic numerals, which cover the reverses, and often the fields, of their talismanic stones. Of such inscriptions the most frequent are ΙΑΩ, "Jehovah," always given to Abraxas himself; ΑΔΟΝΑΙ "The Lord;" ϹЄΜЄϹ ΕΙΛΑΜ, "The Eternal Sun;" ΑΒΛΑΝΑ-ΘΑΝΑΛΒΑ, "Thou art our Father;" and last, but not least, the seven Greek vowels, symbolising the seven heavens, whose mystic harmony kept the whole universe together, and which, if rightly uttered with their forty-nine Powers, were of force (teaches *Pistis-Sophia*) to make the great First-Father himself tremble, and to deliver souls out of the deepest dungeons of the Dragon of Outer Darkness. The other inscriptions, often occupying entire gems, whenever they can be made out contain the names of the Jewish angels regarded as rulers of their respective planets, or else of equivalent divinities holding corresponding places in the theology of the Magians.

With very few exceptions, all the engravings belonging to this numerous and far-extending family are executed in a barbarous and careless style: it was the sigil and the spell of their own essence, no matter whether well or ill represented, that gave its power to the talisman. Occasionally the Gnostics, practically carrying out in this particular the grand principle of their theosophy—the discovery of the same one and grand truth in all religious systems, however diverse in outward appearance—converted to their own ends the monuments of a better period that presented figures susceptible of the desired interpretation, such as Phœbus, Pallas, and their attributes. This adaptation was effected by adding in the field, or reverse of the gem, the formulæ of their own system, of which examples are given above.* Astrological intagli again, whence originated the name of talisman (ἀποτέλεσμα, a planetary influence), are as numerous and in point of art belong to the same category as the Gnostic works.

XXIV.

Primitive Christianity has been as remarkably unproductive in glyptic monuments, as its grand rival, the Gnosis, has been fruitful. The latter, well described as "the *spirit* of the ancient religions warring against the Church," had availed itself of all their machinery, and notably of the powerful media talismans and amulets, to establish its empire over the soul; whereas the former, long tinctured by the Judaical habits of thought of its first preachers, regarded with horror every representation of the human form, much more any attempt to image forth divine personages.

The feeling of the Primitive Church upon this point is clearly expressed in the directions Clemens Alexandrinus, writing in the middle of the second century, gives to his flock concerning what signets they ought to use. He restricts the choice of the devices to a few simple emblems—the Anchor, the Lyre, the Ship under sail, the Dove, and the Fisherman. It will be observed that he does not include in the list the figure of the Good Shepherd, which in somewhat later times became the established emblem of the Faith, and in that acceptation appears upon the signets, tombs, churches, and as Tertullian notices, even upon the drinking-glasses of the Christians, long before the reign of Constantine. Doubtless the Alexandrine teacher and his disciples would, at their early date, have regarded such a direct personification of the Saviour as verging too closely upon the audacious and idolatrous. The types Clemens actually recommends have so much that is curious in their origin, and go so far back in the history of symbolism, as well to merit a few words of explanation. The *anchor* had been the family badge of the Seleucidæ (the offspring as they boasted of Apollo), and every legitimate scion of the family was believed to bear it naturally impressed upon his thigh. From them, their

* Gnosticism, and the various sources whence it was derived, more especially with reference to the memorials it has left behind, have been fully treated of by me in a separate volume, illustrated with the largest collection of such remains that has ever yet been brought together.

former slaves the Asmonæan kings of Judea adopted it as the type upon their coinage, and thence it descended to the Christians, being furthermore recommended by the similarity of its outline to the Cross. The *lyre* had been the engraving upon the most celebrated signet of all antiquity, the emerald of Polycrates; and also by a very intelligible symbolism taught the lesson of mutual harmony and concord. The *ship* flying before the wind pointed out that life is but a voyage across a stormy ocean to a better land. But in the *dove* a deeper abundance of mysteries were involved. The bird had ever been, both to Assyrians and Syrians, the special emblem of the Godhead, from the time when the Ninevite sculptor typified the Supreme Being by an orb, with the tail and wings of a dove (the *Mir*), hovering above the head of his sovereign, and fabled that the most illustrious of the line, Semiramis, had assumed its shape upon quitting earth, down to the commencement of our era when Propertius alludes to

"Alba Palæstino sancta columba Syro."

Again, in sacred history, the Dove is associated with the Second Founder of the human race, and with the immediate manifestation of the Divinity at the Saviour's baptism. But what completed the mystic importance of the emblem was the discovery made by some Christianised adept in the Kabala, that the sum of the numeral letters in its Greek name, *περιστερά*, amounted to 801, and therefore the value of the word was identical with that of A and Ω, which the Lord had assumed for His own proper title upon His last manifestation in His glory. The *fisherman* was instructive, as Clemens explains, by his occupation reminding the beholder of "little children drawn up out of the waters," that is, of the story of Moses, whose name is so interpreted, and who thus in the outset of his career foreshadowed the doctrine of baptismal regeneration. The grand type of all, though not mentioned by Clemens, was the *fish* itself, a figure equally replete with mystic significance as that of the dove. The fish consecrated to Atergatis, or Venus, had ever been held sacred by the Syrians, to whom the eating thereof had consequently been interdicted from the earliest times. The Dagon of Philistia and the corresponding deity of the Phœnicians were imaged under this form. It was probably owing to the influence of the superstition of their neighbours that the Kabalists, although assigning a much more occult reason, gave the name of *Dag* (the Fish) to their expected Messiah, and taught that the "sign of His coming" would be the conjunction of Jupiter and

Saturn in the *sign* Pisces. And, to crown all, the type of the fish had become to Christians a hieroglyphical confession of faith on account of the certainly singular coincidence that the elements of the Greek word form the initials in the sentence Ἰησοῦς Χριστὸς Θεοῦ Υἱὸς Σωτήρ, "Jesus Christ, the Son of God, the Saviour." Early Christian remains of all classes often exhibit a simple but expressive mark of religious profession in the *Chrisma*, where the letters X P, ingeniously united in a monogram, contain all the elements of the name XPICTOC, and are so disposed as to present the image of the instrument of salvation. The yet lingering gleams of antique taste often introduce this simple monogram with much elegance upon the signet, sometimes elevated upon the head of a Cupid, christened for the nonce into an angel, sometimes forming the shank to the Anchor of Hope, from the arms whereof is suspended the sacred fish in pairs, and sometimes grasped in the crossed hands, the long-established symbol of good faith.

From the foregoing particulars, and from the very nature of the case, one would be led to infer that no attempts at the direct portraiture of the Redeemer would be met with before both religion and art had entered upon their purely Byzantine phase. And such is actually the case; the earliest heads of Christ that are met with upon gems being in cameo upon plasma or jasper, in a style whose exact agreement with that of the same representations upon the reverse of the bezants immediately indicates the date of their execution. How impossible their existence at an earlier period of Christianity is sufficiently exemplified by a single fact, Epiphanius' winding up his long list of the heresies of the Carpocratians (Gnostics admitting more of the Pagan element into their theosophy than any of their brethren) with the charge that they had and adored images of Christ which they pretended had been made by order of Pilate when He was amongst men. There can, therefore, be little hazard of mistake in pronouncing the first direct representations of Divine personages upon gems to be those works of the Sassanian engravers of which some, though rare, examples are known to exist; such as the Head of Christ, beardless (Paris), the Annunciation, the Greeting of Mary and Elizabeth, &c. The cursive form of the Pehlevi lettering in the legends apprises the Orientalist that these intagli are due to the Nestorians who found an asylum in the Persian empire during the century or two before its fall.

But to conclude this Section, the notoriety given by its recent publication to the pretended "Emerald of the Vatican" necessitates a brief notice here of that audacious imposture. According to the legend that goes with it this gem had been engraved with an intaglio portrait of Christ by Pilate's order, and by him presented to Tiberius. Thenceforward it had been treasured up by the Roman and Byzantine Cæsars and their Ottoman successors until paid by the Sultan to Innocent VIII. as a more than equivalent ransom for his brother, who had fallen into the Pope's hands. It would be mere waste of time to point out all the historical absurdities involved in this fable: to view it on the side of art is quite sufficient to decide the question. This *contemporary* portrait is treated in neither the antique nor even the Byzantine manner, but most unmistakably in that of the Italian Revival; in fact, is merely a copy of a medal belonging to the times of the Pontif, whose name is commemorated in its legend.

XXV.

Thus, in the fifth century, the Glyptic Art amongst the Romans entirely disappears, its last traces fading away in the swarms of ill-cut, worse-drawn, *abraxas* and Manichean talismans that have for their material stones of *virtue*, not of beauty; the coarse jaspers and loadstones of the fountain-heads of the doctrines, Egypt and Assyria. The Byzantines, indeed, kept up, though very languidly, the art of engraving camei, but entirely dropped that of working in intaglio upon hard stones. An imperial *atelier* for the former art seems to have been long supported as a necessary appendage to the pomp of the Byzantine Cæsars: the "artifices Palatini," in the sense of gem-engravers, are mentioned in a law of the Emperor Leo's (886–911). Their works in cameo were exclusively designed for enriching the vessels intended for the service of the altar; their subjects are therefore scriptural only—such as the Annunciation or the Salutation; or else they are the single figures or busts of the Saviour, the Virgin, or the Saints. They are cut in bloodstone, plasma, sardonyx, and lapis-lazuli. The Emperor Heraclius presented to King Dagobert a magnificent oval plaque of the last, which bore on one side the bust of the Saviour, on the other that of His Mother. It was dedicated by the king, and remained for a thousand years in the Treasury of St. Denys.

At this time the official signets of the great were made of metal entirely, charged with the letters of the cognomen quaintly arranged in the form of a cross—as that of Clementinus, consul A. D. 513, appears figured upon his diptych. The few men of taste yet surviving treasured up the gems, the legacy of better times, exactly as we do now, as precious articles of *virtù*, not to be profaned by modern use. That they viewed them in this light is apparent from their poems upon certain *chefs-d'œuvre* of the class, preserved in the Anthology, to which allusion has been made on a former occasion.

This state of things gave birth to a new class of gems that may properly be designated "complimentary," or "motto-camei." They present short sentences enclosed within a myrtle wreath, or a plain circle, of an import showing that they were designed for ornamenting rings and other small jewels intended for new-year's gifts (strenæ) or birthday presents. The lettering of these inscriptions is the peculiar, neat character which came into use under Diocletian, and is seen on the gold coinage of his successors down to the fall of the Western Empire. The spelling renders the fact indubitable, that the so-called modern-Greek pronunciation was already established as the fashionable one at Rome. The mottoes are for the most part appropriate to the occasion for which I have supposed them engraved: for example ΖΗϹΕϹ ΑΚΑΚΙ—"Long life to thee, Acacius;" ΜΑΚΡΙΝΕ ΖΗϹΑΙϹ ΠΟΛΛΟΙϹ ЄΤЄϹΙΝ—"Mayest thou live many years, Macrinus;" ЄΥΤΥΧΙ ЄΥϹЄΒΙ—Prosper, Eusebius;" ΠΑΛΛΑΔΙ ЄΥΤΥΧΙ ΜΕΤΑ ЄΙЄΡΟΚΛΙΗϹ—"Prosper, Palladius, together with Hieroclea." A longer formula, ЄΥΦΗΜΗΤΩ ΑΙΘΗΡ ΚΑΙ ΓΑ ϹΤΑΤΩ Δ' ΑΗΡ ϹΤΑΤΩ ΠΟΝΤΟϹ, is, in substance, the same good wish that Propertius sends his beloved Cynthia for her natal day—

"Transeat hic sine nube dies, stent æthere venti,
Ponat et in sicco molliter unda minas."

A frequent one indicates a keepsake on departure—ΜΝΗΜΟΝЄΥЄ ΜΟΥ ΤΗϹ ΚΑΛΗϹ ΨΥΧΗϹ—"Remember me, thy pretty sweetheart;" accompanying the device of a hand pinching an ear, the seat of the memory according to the then popular notion—

"Cynthius aurem—vellit et admonuit."

Lastly, some preach a moral to the recipient: take this very common one for a specimen, and which, Caylus says, should be the motto of every philosopher— ΛΕΓΟΥϹΙΝ Α ΘΕΛΟΥϹΙΝ ΛΕΓΕΤΩϹΑΝ ΟΥ ΜΕΛΕΙ ΜΟΙ, aptly rendered in the motto inscribed by the old Scots baron over the door of his mansion—

"Men saye: what saye they?
Wha cares: let them saye."

XXVI.

The simple cruciform arrangement of the letters of the name, of which the signet of Clementinus has been quoted as an example, and which also was adopted on much of the Byzantine coinage, was, somewhat later, superseded by the more complicated form of the *monogram.* The use of the latter, so general throughout *Romanesque* Europe (following servilely the example of the focus of Christian art) was, strange to say, only the resuscitation, doubtless undesigned, of a very ancient fashion. *Monograms*—or the compression of an entire word into the outline of a single letter written with one stroke of the pen, as the compound term expresses, that letter being the initial—had been in great favour with the Greeks at a very early period. Under such a form do the names of the mint-masters appear upon the coinage of the best times of art; and yet it was very long before this convenient form of the signature came to be generally adopted upon the seal. Although it had been from the first customary with the Romans to have the person's name added to the family device upon his signet, yet it was either written in full, or else expressed by the separated initials of the *prænomen*, *nomen*, and *cognomen.* The earliest example of a true monogram known to me is the name *Antoninus*, so disposed on a red jasper of Lower-Empire work (Bosanquet Collection). But after the sixth century the fashion became universal. Avitus, Bishop of Vienne, orders such to be cut for the device of his episcopal signet (an *iron* ring having two dolphins for the shank): " Si quæras quid insculpendum sigillo, signum *monogrammatis* mei per gyrum scripti nominis legatur indicio " (Ep. VII. Mabillon, De Re Diplom. p. 132). Symmachus, writing early in the fifth century, alludes to a seal of his own, " which rather *hinted* at his name than expressed it openly." Kirchmann, in his learned treatise ' De Annulis,' supposes this seal was some figure that embodied the idea conveyed in the Greek word, which signifies a *helper ;* but the age was too low down in the Decline to admit of similar ingenuity, Symmachus evidently meaning nothing more by this circuitous expression than his own monogram.

The names of the *cities*, as well as those of the magistrates, often occur upon the Greek coinage in very complicated monograms. This makes it still more surprising that no one should have adopted the same conceit for his seal before the ages of barbarism. But no sooner had Byzantium set the fashion than it became universal throughout Europe, to which that capital long continued the fountain-head of Art. The obverse of the *deniers* of the Carlovingian kings is for the most part occupied by the monogram of the name—in the case of Charlemagne's, very ingeniously constructed; and the contemporary Anglo-Saxon pennies clumsily attempt to copy the same novelty.

XXVII.

In the mean time the Glyptic Art, thus rapidly dying out in Europe, the scene of its greatest triumphs, had sought a refuge, and again grown strong, in the very cradle of its infancy. The young and vigorous Sassanian monarchy of Persia had resuscitated, together with the ancient royal line, the religion also of the Achæmenidæ. Gem-engraving, ever the favourite vehicle for the ideas of the Assyrian creeds, for the second time found its productions in as great request as in the ages preceding the Macedonian conquest, that have bequeathed to us such stores of Ninevitish and Babylonian cylinders and seals. During the four centuries of the domination of the Parthians (a truly Turkish race) these very regions had been singularly non-productive in engraved stones—nay, it may be said, entirely barren, so dubious are any intagli that may be referred to the *Arsacidæ*. Of their long series not a single portrait is now known to exist upon a gem, although Pliny the Younger, in a letter to Trajan, mentions one engraved with the figure of Pacorus in his royal robes, brought from his court by an escaped Roman slave. This peculiarity had, indeed, attracted the notice of his learned uncle, who remarks: "Even in the present day the East and Egypt do not use seals, but are satisfied with the mere writing (of the name)." Pliny's "East," was the vast Parthian Empire—that "second world," as Manilius phrases it—

"Parthique vel alter . . . . orbis."

But the truth is that many of its subject-races, instead of having never *learnt* the use of signets, as the great naturalist supposes, had on the contrary, from some unknown cause, discontinued the very practice of which they themselves had been the first inventors.

But now a complete revolution in taste sets in: the succeeding four centuries of the revived native Persian rule (by a strange coincidence commensurate in extent with the previous blank) have handed down to us innumerable memorials of the sovereigns, and of their religion, in works somewhat rude, it must be confessed, yet of transcendent merit, if compared with the contemporary productions of the effete civilization of Byzantium. Extremely valuable, too, is this series in the historical point of view, on account of the Pehlevi legends which usually surround the monarch's portrait, setting forth his name and high-sounding titles. Barbarous as the style of many of these intagli is, and coarsely sunk as are the lines into the stone, there is yet a force and an individuality of expression about the drawing that declare the engraver's knowledge of the true principles of his art. The masterpiece of this school, and one without a rival, is the Devonshire amethyst, displaying the bust, not of Sapor I., as it long was named, but of the illustrious descendant of that conqueror, *Vahrahran Kermanshah*. His features are full of a stern majesty; his hair falls in long curled tresses from beneath his pearl-bordered tiara: his name and numerous titles surround the field in two lines of elegantly-cut Pehlevi characters.

These Sassanian works have another interest, and that is their mineralogical; no other series being so rich in point of *material*, presenting us largely with splendid spinels, jacinths, and almandines, tributes from their far-extended Indian dominions. The supply is continued without abatement in quantity, though with a sad falling off in workmanship, down to the very epoch of the Mohammedan conquest, in the year 632, when it comes to a sudden close, together with the dynasty whose features this last survivor of the *ancient* schools of gem-engraving had so long and sedulously perpetuated.

Their place is taken by the only forms permitted by the religion of the victors, inscriptions in the *Cufic* or modified Sassanian letter. This character took its name from the town of Cufa, where it was adopted by the first Arabian transcribers of the Koran. Ouseley gives a specimen of a MS. held by the Persians in the highest veneration, as being in the handwriting of Ali himself; the characters vary but little from those seen on the later Sassanian gems.

These Cufic seal-inscriptions are wrought tastefully, and with perfect technical mastery, in the choicest Oriental gems, and even in the hardest precious stones, the sapphire and the ruby. The demand throughout the whole Mohammedan world for such signets, and the skill required for the effective combination of the flowing curves that constitute the chief elements of Arabic calligraphy, often into the outline of various objects, a horse, a bird, a balance, &c., kept alive all the technical processes of the art down to the period when favouring circumstances brought about its revival in Italy.

XXVIII.

The Byzantine school during the same interval merely deserves a passing notice, the sole evidence of its existence remaining to us being a few camei of religious subjects, in which the unskilful execution aptly harmonises with the tastelessness of the drawing. And both these are kept in countenance by the strange corruption of orthography in the legends, exactly corresponding to that of the modern Romaic, of which a single example will suffice: "ΧΕΡΕ ΚΑΙ ΧΑΡΙΤΟΜΕΝΕ," accompanying the group of the Annunciation upon a splendid sardonyx (Brit. Mus.), would puzzle an etymological Œdipus did he not, by pronouncing the formula aloud, recognise therein the precisely equivalent sounds of the angelic salutation, "χαῖρε κεχαριτομένη."

But all over the West, during these same ten centuries—that millennium of darkness—gem-engraving may be regarded as virtually extinct, for the few barbarous and perhaps disputable evidences of its latent vitality can hardly be said to affect the question. These instances, curious both from their rarity and on several other accounts, will be fully considered in the next chapter to which the remainder of *this* will serve for introduction. *Signets* indeed, were in as much demand and for the same important uses throughout mediæval Europe as they had been in the ancient world; but they were for the most part cut in metal. For *personal* seals all who could procure them employed antique intagli (recommended to them by their firmly-believed-in mystic virtues), their subjects being generally interpreted of the personages of Scripture, whence their popular name "pierres d'Israel." The *official* seals, however, were large and elaborate designs cut in matrices of metal, brass (*latten*) or pewter, silver being reserved for royalty; and usually, according to the taste of the times, completely architectural in character. The king and the noble placed their own figures on their great seals portrayed in their appropriate characters—the former seated on his throne administering justice, the latter in full armour upon his war-horse, discharging his duty as a knight. These designs, though accurate as to costume, make no pretensions to be considered portraits. But it is a curious fact that *ecclesiastics* occasionally attempt to give actual likenesses, from the life, of their own faces in profile, upon their small personal seals, engraved in the metal. And some such portraits have lately been brought under my notice (all of them, to judge from the lettering, of the Edwardian era), which are executed with a spirit and an evident fidelity to nature that could not have been expected at so early a date. One such tonsured head—a first-class specimen of mediæval portraiture—bears a motto seemingly the most inappropriate of all to the celibate vow of its proprietor, CRESCITE ET MVLTIPLICAMINI. But the increase wished for was doubtless meant of his coin, not of his olive-branches.

This resumption of the ancient practice of sealing with one's own likeness appears to have been made long before the date above given, and indeed may be said never to have been totally dropped; for St. Bernard, writing to Eugenius III. (1145–53), complains that many forged epistles were circulating under his name, and that therefore in future none were to be accounted genuine unless they bore his seal engraved with his own likeness and superscription. Both were probably rude enough, if we may form an opinion from the very remarkable seal, attempting the same thing, ascribed by tradition to St. Servatius (d. 389), and preserved in Mæstricht Cathedral, attached to a porphyry slab, known from the same tradition as the Saints' portable altar. This seal, a circular jasper, three inches in diameter, bears on one side the Gorgon's head, with a legend seemingly in corrupt phonetic Greek, and intended for Μοῖρα μελαινομένη ὓς ὄφις, a spell to be found on certain Byzantine bronze amulets. The other side has a bust in front-face, with an attempt at O A (γιος) in the field, and a legend, baffling all interpretation, but possibly a continuation of the formula on the other side, running around. The style of the intaglio is certainly not that of the saint's own times, but of some six or seven centuries later. But with laymen the demand for antique intagli to mount in their *secreta* or personal seals was evidently enormous; the desire for their possession, however, was not inspired by their beauty as artistic objects, but by the nature of the figures cut upon them in accordance with the universal belief in the virtues of *sigils*, as such figures were properly termed. These virtues were exactly described and the sigils possessing them minutely specified in the various *Lapidaria* in which those times were so rife—examples of which I purpose adducing for the edification or amusement of my reader when I come to treat of the employment of antique gems in the Middle Ages.

XXIX.

All who have written upon our subject assume that gem-engraving was utterly extinct in Europe during the whole extent of the Middle Ages—that is, from the coronation of Charlemagne as Emperor of the West in the year 800 down to the middle of the fifteenth century (1453), when Greek fugitives from Constantinople re-established its practice in Italy. The continuance of the art within the Greek empire during that period does not enter into the question, for this, together with all the other arts of antiquity, maintained a feeble existence there down to the very last, as numerous camei, some in fine sardonyx but the greater part in bloodstone, remain to testify. The agreement of these in style with the bezants of John Zimisses and the Comneni shows that the manufacture of such ecclesiastical decorations (their subjects are always Scriptural) was prosecuted with considerable briskness between the tenth century and the thirteenth. No Byzantine *intagli* (except a few amulets) were, however, produced during the same period, for if such had existed, they would be easily recognisable by the same unmistakable stamp of the epoch impressed upon them, both as to subjects and their treatment, that marks the Byzantine camei and ivory carvings. The reason for this extinction of intaglio-engraving is obvious enough; signets cut in hard stones were no longer in request, the official seals for stamping the leaden bullæ authenticating public documents were, like coin-dies, sunk in iron; whilst those for personal use were engraved in the precious metals.

Camei were the ornaments above all others deemed appropriate for reliquaries and similar furniture of the altar; a tradition dating from imperial times. In the estimate of art then current, the value of the material and the time expended in elaborating it counted for much. Another consideration also influenced this preference, the greater facility of executing a tolerable work in relief than in intaglio; a fact declared from the first by the nascent art producing the perfectly modelled Etruscan scarabæi that serve as vehicles for such barbarous intagli upon their bases as we have above noticed, and confirmed by this second childhood of the Byzantine school.

It is at first sight apparent, from many considerations, that the genuine Gothic artists never attempted engraving upon hard stones. The first, and this is an argument of the greatest weight, is that no gems are to be met with exhibiting purely Gothic designs. We know from the innumerable seals preserved, both official and personal, many of them most elaborately drawn and artistically executed, what would be the designs that gems engraved by a worker contemporary with these seals must necessarily have exhibited; for, as the analogy of the two arts requires, the same hand would have cut the intagli in stone and the seals in metal. Thus at a later time we find that the famous gem-engravers of the Revival, such as Il Greco, Matteo del Nazzaro, and Valerio Belli, were also die-sinkers. Any gems, therefore, engraved either in Italy, France, or Germany between the years 800 and 1453 would necessarily present such subjects as Saints in ecclesiastical or monastic costume, Knights arrayed in the armour of their times, and, above all, architectural accessories, canopies, niches, and diapering, the customary decorations of the mediæval seals in metal.

Besides this restriction as to subjects, the drawing of those ages has, even in its highest correctness, a peculiar character never to be mistaken, and which even pervades the paintings of the Italian school down to late in the fifteenth century, and those of the German for a century longer. Lastly, a class of subjects distinct from any known to antique glyptic art, *armorial bearings* arranged according to the rules of heraldry, would have constituted a large portion of anything executed in those times for seals, and yet such are wholly deficient. Again, in the choice of the antique intagli set in mediæval seals, there is often evident a desire to pick out some figure agreeing with the owner's cognisance. On the other hand some of the metal seals exhibit in their heraldic animals an attempt to copy representations of the like objects upon gems. Antiques of the class being so highly esteemed on the score of the supposed mystic virtues of both substance and sigil, doubtless, had it been within the mediæval engraver's power, a "stone of virtue" would have been preferred by him for the purpose when about to execute the signet of a wealthy patron.

On this consideration our second argument is founded. The great number of antique gems set in mediæval privy seals sufficiently proves how much such works were in request. The legends added upon the metal settings enchasing them show how the subjects were interpreted to suit the spirit of the times, often in a sense so forced as must have tried the faith of even their simple-minded owners. Certainly, had it been possible to execute in such valued materials designs better assimilated to the notions they desired to embody, such would have been attempted in a manner more or less successful, but still bearing unmistakably the stamp of Gothic Art. This remark applies exactly to the latest intagli of antiquity, or rather to the earliest of mediæval times, the date of which can be accurately ascertained, the signets of the Emperor Lotharius. One is set in the cross which he presented to the Cathedral of Aix-la-Chapelle, an oval crystal, $1\frac{3}{4} \times 1\frac{1}{2}$ inch in dimensions, engraved with his head in profile covered with the closely fitting Roman helmet seen upon the contemporary coinage. Around runs this legend cut in the stone, in imitation of a favourite Byzantine invocation which is found upon the *aurei* of the same epoch—

+ XPE ADIVVA HLOTHARIVM REG.

—"Christe adjuva Hlotharium Regem."—Both the style of the portrait and the lettering agree with those seen on the Carlovingian *sous d'or.*

Still more curious, because betraying more of a national character, is the other seal of Lotharius,* of which an impression only exists attached to a document, dated 877, preserved in the archives of the department of the Haute-Marne. It shows the Emperor's bust in full face, the hair long and parted, with seemingly a nimbus over the head, having the hand upon his breast, and in the field something like an arrow, perhaps intended for a palm-branch. The entire design is replete with the taste of the age, retaining no reminiscence of the antique even in its lowest decline.† The bevelled edge indicates that the stone was a nicolo about $1\frac{1}{4} \times 1$ inch in size. On the metal setting is the legend, cut in large letters—

LOTHARIUS DEI GRACIA REX.

The Byzantine camei themselves supply a further illustration; they exactly agree in character with other bas-reliefs of the same origin in whatever materials they may be executed, ivory, boxwood, marble, or bronze.

The British Museum has lately acquired two most interesting memorials of this monarch's patronage of the fast dying art. The first is the *morse* which from time immemorial served to fasten the robes of the Abbot of Vézor on the Meuse, when in full pontificals. It is a circular plaque of crystal 6 inches in diameter, with the story of Susanna and the Elders (conveying an apt and humorous moral to the wearer) engraved or rather faintly etched in separate

* Figured in the 'Revue Archéologique' for 1858.

† See the 'Trésor de Conques,' quoted further on, for the strange intaglio of the Saviour in amethyst, of this period.

scenes depicted in the true Anglo-Saxon taste, each with an explanatory inscription below. But what gives the piece the greatest value is the circular legend in the centre, LOTHARIUS REX ME FIERI FECIT. The reversing of the letters proves that the engraving was intended to be seen *through* the crystal, being laid upon a coloured backing as was the rule in that age. The setting of silver gilt, though ascribed as a matter of course to St. Eloi, is in reality of late Gothic workmanship. The second piece, the Crucifixion, cut upon the plane face of an enormous crystal *cabochon*, 8 inches long, is manifestly from its peculiar technique due to the same school, probably to the same hand as the first.

In the treasury of Noyon Cathedral there was preserved down to the time of the Revolution "the small seal (secretum) on crystal, mounted in gilt bronze, that had belonged to St. Eloi, dec. 659." La Croix, however, says nothing about the engraving upon it; a most provoking piece of negligence, inasmuch as the material of the signet, crystal, seldom used by the ancients for that purpose, makes it more than probable that the intaglio was of the times, perhaps actually from the hand of the goldsmith-saint. We are certified of his skill in the cognate art of die-sinking, the elegant (for the age) solidi of his sovereign Dagobert remaining to attest the same.

Amongst the Transalpine nations, at least during the last two centuries of the period above indicated, heraldic devices would have been beyond all others the subjects to employ the seal-engraver in preference to those of a religious character. In fact, the learned Dutchman Agricola writing soon after 1450 mentions the engraving of coats of arms upon the German onyx as then in common use, without the slightest allusion to that art as having been but recently introduced into Holland. And such was the material of the signet of Charles the Bold (slain 1477) which Comines describes as "Un anneau et y avoit un fusil (*spindle* heraldic) entaillé en un *camayieu* où estoient ses armes;" *camayieu* at the time signifying only the *stone* onyx or agate, not the *work* upon it. However, as Bruges was then famed for its jewellers (L. de Berquem flourished there at that time), no doubt every new invention in the lapidary's art speedily found its way thither, and was cultivated to the utmost. It is on record how munificently similar discoveries were remunerated by the wealthy of those ages, as the same Duke's liberality to the inventor of diamond-cutting conspicuously testifies.

Briefly to sum up the substance of the preceding arguments. For the space of five centuries the Gothic seal-engravers were employed in executing an infinite number of signets in metal, to which business all their skill was devoted, as the elaborateness and occasional merit of the work manifestly proved. The designs on these seals are invariably in the taste of their age, being either religious or heraldic, and generally accompanied by architectural decorations. The style of all these ages has an unmistakable character of its own, from which the simplicity of the artists could never deviate by an attempt to revert to antique models; indeed, whatsoever Gothic art has bequeathed to us shows the exact date, almost the very year of its production. Yet nothing, to speak generally, displaying the Gothic style has ever come to light amongst the profusion of engraved stones then used, not even amongst those set in church plate, which would have admitted as more appropriate in its own destination any contemporary work, had such been attainable. As a proof of this, immediately upon the Revival we find the most eminent gem-engravers employed almost exclusively in executing crystal plaques with intagli of Scriptural subjects for the furniture of the altar, by the order of Popes and Cardinals.

Nor did such an exclusion of contemporary works (had any existed) arise from a disregard of the productions of the glyptic art. The rudest works of antiquity are to be seen enchased in Gothic goldsmiths' work, and honoured there with the same precious mountings as the finest and most costly stones. It was enough that the subject suited the taste of the goldsmith, the art exhibited therein was altogether disregarded. It is very plain besides, that, in consequence of the prevalent belief in the virtue of sigils, all engraved stones were esteemed as more valuable than those not engraved, even though the latter were of a more precious species. Again, we must remember it was not its mere antiquity that gave the sigil its virtue: *that* was derived entirely from the planetary influence under which it had been made, and therefore the same and invariable whatever was the date of its execution. For example, we have abundant proof that, as soon as the art was revived, the manufacture of astrological talismans flourished quite as vigorously as of old under the Later Empire. The case therefore stands thus. We find signets as important as ever, and their execution employing the best skill of the age, but taking for their material only metal; whilst, nevertheless, antique intagli in gems were more prized than before, and were adapted to the prevailing notions by the most forced interpretations. We find the supply, too, falling so short of the demand that the very rudest were accepted and highly estimated by persons not destitute of an appreciation of the Beautiful, or at least of the highly finished and, nevertheless, in spite of all this love of engraved stones, scarcely one production existing of the sort that can be assigned to a truly Gothic artist. From these considerations we are forced to agree that the general conclusion of archæologists is well founded, and that the art during all the period above specified was totally extinct in Europe except within the precincts of Constantinople.

It is true that a passage or two in the works of mediæval writers seem to contravene this conclusion,—for example, where Marbodus, writing at the close of the eleventh century, directs how to engrave particular sigils on the proper gems: such as a vine entwined with ivy on the sard; a lobster with a raven on the beryl; Mars and Virgo holding a branch on the calcedony, &c.; directions which at first sight would appear to indicate the existence of workers capable of executing his directions. But in reality the passage proves nothing, being no doubt merely transcribed from the same more ancient sources whence he drew the materials for his Lapidarium.

We come now to consider a most interesting class of monuments, and which may be pronounced exceptions establishing the rule; few indeed in number, and their origin forming the most difficult problem to be encountered in the history of this art. These exceptional pieces are what Vasari alludes to (Vita di Valerio Belli), where, treating of the engravers of his own age, the Cinque-Cento, he has these remarkable words:—"The art of engraving on hard stones and precious stones (*gioie*) was lost together with the other arts of design after the fall of Greece and Rome. For many and many a year it continued lost so that nobody was found to attend to it, and although something was still done, yet it was not of the kind that one should take account thereof. And, so far as there is any record, there is no one to be found who began to work well and to get into the good way (dar nel buono), except in the times of Martin V. and of Paul II. (1417 and 1464). Thenceforward it went on improving until Lorenzo the Magnificent," &c. Vasari's "*buono*" always means the classic style; the expression "although something was still done," cannot be understood as having reference to nothing more than the Byzantine camei that occasionally found their way into Italy, or to works done in that country by the Greek artists, so much employed before the springing up of a native school, as painters and architects, like Buschetus, the builder of the Duomo at Pisa, and those who raised S. Marco at Venice in its purely Byzantine style. The mention of the two Popes indicates the place of the practice and the improvement of the art as Rome itself; in fact, we know that Paul II. was a passionate lover of gems, and left to his heirs a magnificent collection. A cameo portrait of the pontiff amongst them is said by Giulianelli to be a fine performance, and to show the hand of an accomplished artist, affording the best confirmation of Vasari's statement.

But to go back to the very earliest times in which any traces of the art appear, Scipio Ammirato (Hist. Flor. p. 741) mentions a certain Peruzzi, "il quale era singolare intagliatore di pietre," as forging the seal of Carlo di Durazzo. This was in the year 1379. Here then is an instance, not to be looked for at so early a period, of a prince having for his seal an engraved gem, and that apparently not an antique, else the Florentine artist had not been competent to imitate it so exactly. Again, Giulianelli (p. 76) quotes Gori's Adversaria to the effect that before the year 1300 the Florentine Republic used two seals—both engraved stones. The first, large, for sealing public documents, was a plasma engraved with a Hercules (one of the supporters of the city arms), with the legend running round it—SIGILLVM FLORENTINORVM. The other, small, for letters, bore the Florentine lily; legend—SIGILLVM PRIORVM. The mention of the *large size* of the former seal, as well as the subject in such a stone, suffice to show that this plasma was not an antique intaglio fitted into the seal with the legend added upon the metal; whilst the engraving upon the second must necessarily have been done expressly, as no such device could have been supplied by the relics of antiquity. Giulianelli also remarks, with some plausibility, that, in the same way as the art of mosaic-working was kept up at Rome during the ages following the fall of the Western Empire, there is reason to believe that the art of gem-engraving may in like manner have been maintained there.*

The signet of Jean sans Peur, Duke of Burgundy (d. 1417), is preserved. His arms are engraved upon a pale sapphire, which is coloured underneath with the proper heraldic tinctures. In the Waterton Collection I observed a shield of arms very skilfully cut in a fine jacinth, and set in a ring evidently by its fashion belonging to the first half of the fifteenth century. 'Le Trésor Sacré de Sainct Denys' (1646), describes,—"L'anneau du mesme glorieux Roy Sainct Louis qui est precieux: Il est d'or semé de fleurs de lys, garny d'un grand saphyr quarré sur lequel est gravée l'image du mesme sainct avec les lettres S. L., qui veulent dire *Sigillum Lodovici.* Sur le rond de l'anneau par le dedans sont gravez ces mots, *C'est le Signet du Roy S. Louis,* qui y ont esté

* The inventory of the Duc d'Anjou contains a sapphire ring engraved with a *Dux,* given him by Phil. de Valois. Bar. Pichon has lately bought a sapphire ($\frac{1}{2} \times \frac{3}{8}$ inch); type, a prince on throne, rude mediæval, which may be the same.

adjoustez après sa mort" (p. 107). The wedding-ring of the same prince is said to have been set with a sapphire engraved with the Crucifixion; the shank covered with lilies and *marguerites*, allusive to his own name and his wife's. This attribution of the first is a mere *custode's* story. Mr. Waterton lately examined the gem, and puts it down at a much later age: the king, a full length, has the *nimbus*, proof positive that the figure is posterior to his beatification. It probably belongs to Louis XII.'s reign. That the Italian lapidaries could at all times shape, facet, and polish the softer stones, such as amethysts, garnets, emeralds, is apparent from the number of antique gems of those species extant, but recut into the then fashionable octagonal form for the purpose of setting in mediæval rings.

Vasari's second date indeed, 1464, might be supposed to have some connection with the influx of Greek fugitives after the fall of Constantinople eleven years before. But Vasari would certainly not have discerned any "improvement" in what *they* were capable of producing, for Italian plastic art was by that time fully developed, as we see by Luca della Robbia's terra-cottas, not to mention the bas-reliefs of Ghiberti and Donatello. And again, in all probability very few of the artist class fled from Constantinople, the Greeks naturally enough preferring the tolerant Mohammedans to their persecuting, more detested rivals of the Latin Church. The emigrants were the nobles, special objects of jealousy to the conquerors, and the grammarians, whose teaching was greatly sought after in Italy and most liberally remunerated. Besides this, Byzantium, when the empire was once more re-established after the expulsion of the Franks, who had held the city during the first half of the thirteenth century, did nothing more for art, her vitality having been utterly exhausted by the grinding tyranny of those barbarians. When Vasari specifies two particular periods after 1400, and quotes the pontificates of two Popes as manifest epochs of improvement in gem-works, he must be referring to pieces done in Italy and by Italians. It is very provoking that Vasari, usually so loquacious, should have passed over this most interesting dawn of the art with such contemptuous brevity. He mentions no engraver by name antecedent to Gio. delle Corniuole, who worked for Lorenzo dei Medici, and had learnt the art from "masters of different countries" brought to Florence by Lorenzo and Piero his son, to repair (*rassettare*) the antiques they had collected. These expressions prove that gem-engraving was flourishing already in other places before it was domiciled in Florence; and this very probably is the reason why the patriotic Messer Giorgio passes so slightingly over these earlier celebrities—"vixere fortes ante Agamenona." Milan was long before noted for its jewellers; Antellotto Bracciaforte was celebrated in the fourteenth century. These lapidaries cut into tables and pyramids the harder precious stones, such as spinels and balais rubies, and even *polished* the diamond before L. de Berquem's discovery in 1475 of the mode of *cutting* that stone; and therefore, as far as the mechanical process was concerned, they were fully competent to engrave intagli. The engravers named by Camillo (*Spec. tap.*), as flourishing in 1502, may have been Vasari's "foreign masters;" they will be considered when we come to treat of the Revival.

It was in the year 1488 that Lorenzo founded the Accademia di S. Marco, appointing as president the aged Bertaldo, the favourite pupil of Donatello, for the cultivation of all the fine arts, including the glyptic. But it was long before this, and in his father's lifetime, that he had summoned the foreign engravers above alluded to. Inasmuch as Gio. delle Corniuole learned the art from them it must have before been extinct at Florence. Vasari's expression, "diversi paesi," would, in the language of his times, apply to the states of northern Italy almost as strongly as to Flanders, or to Alexandria, for to the Tuscan even those of the next city (like Pistoia) were foreigners and "natural enemies."

The die-sinkers of Vasari's age being, as a matter of course, the most eminent gem-engravers, such was probably the case in the century before; and Pollaiuolo, whose dies for the Papal coinage he so highly extols, may be supposed likewise to have tried his skill upon gems, and to have inaugurated the improvement that dawned in his times at Rome, where he and his brother worked till their death in 1498. And since the earliest works quoted by Vasari are both portraits in intaglio—that of Savonarola (put to death in 1498), by Gio. delle Corniuole, and the head of Ludovico Sforza (Duke of Milan from 1494 to 1500), executed in ruby by Domenico dei Camei *—we may conclude that the pieces done in 1417 and 1464, which began to show signs of improvement, were similarly portraits, and in intaglio. Such was naturally the first method in which the die-sinker would essay his skill upon the new and refractory material, and the one in which the result would be most serviceable to his patron. No camei of that age are to be found that can be imagined to exhibit the improvement

* Who doubtless executed in the same precious material the portrait *in relief* of his conqueror, Louis XII. (now in her Majesty's Collection).

mentioned by Vasari, and the supposed cameo portrait of Paul II., above quoted, I very much suspect belongs to a later pontificate.*

Vasari's hints, coupled with these facts, throw some light upon the origin of that rare class of intagli mounted in massy gold rings made after the mediæval fashion, which, both by the intrinsic value of the stone and of the setting, evince they were designed for personages of the highest rank. On this very account such are the precise objects likely to exhibit the most novel and most admired improvements in the art. First amongst these ranks the Marlborough spinel engraved with a youthful head in front-face, wearing a crown of three fleur-de-lys. The intaglio, in a small square stone, is deep-cut and neatly done, but the face is quite the conventional Gothic head seen on coins, and exhibits no individuality whatever to guide us in attributing it to any particular personage. It is set in a massy gold ring ribbed longitudinally, and chased with flowers in the style prevailing about the middle of the fifteenth century, a date further indicated by the lettering of the motto engraved around it on the beasil—tel il nest—" There is no one like him." It is evident that both intaglio and ring are of the same date, for, besides the Gothic fashion of the crown, the work of the intaglio has nothing of the antique character, and, though highly polished internally, does not appear to have been sunk by the ancient process; this last remark, indeed, applies to the entire class now under consideration. The portrait may be intended for some Italian prince of the age. The only circumstance against this explanation is that the motto is in black letter, a Tedescan barbarism unknown in Italy, where the round Lombardic continued in use until superseded by the revived Roman about the date of 1450. The species of the gem at first suggests to us the famous portrait of Ludovico Sforza already noticed; but, that being on a ruby the size of a *giulio* (*i. e.*, an inch in diameter), it follows necessarily almost that, like the heads on the improved coinage of the times (imitated by Henry VII., and by James IV. of Scotland in his bonnet-pieces), the latter would have been in profile in somewhat slight intaglio, stiffly drawn, yet full of character, like the contemporary relief in ruby of Louis XII.

The Marlborough gem is (it ought to be mentioned) described in the old catalogue as the "Head of a Lombard king;" but not only does the form of the crown contravene this explanation, for these barbarians, as the coins and the contemporary Frankish *sous d'or*

* No cameo portrait of certain attribution is known to me of an earlier date than that of Louis XII. in agate-onyx (Orleans).

attest, aped the diadem of the Byzantine Cæsars; whilst for their signets they had their own image and superscription cut on gold rings, of which Childeric's is a specimen, or on large gems of the softer kinds, as in the two seals of Lotharius above described.

Mr. Albert Way discovers in this little portrait a resemblance to that of our Henry VI. upon his great seal. Of this similarity there can be no doubt; yet, unfortunately, such a coincidence is far from deciding the question, such portraits being entirely conventional, and suiting equally well any number of contemporary princes. He conjectures that the ring, a lady's from its small dimensions, may have belonged to Margaret of Anjou, which is, indeed, supported by the loving motto, "There is no one like him." This pleasing and romantic theory has, doubtless, several circumstances in its favour. This princess coming from the south of France, if we allow that the art in Italy was sufficiently advanced to produce such a work, her position would have enabled her to procure its best and earliest performances. Her marriage with Henry VI. took place in 1445, a sufficient space of time after the first epoch (1415), named as that of an improvement in the art in Italy. Her father, the "good king René," had been dispossessed of Naples in 1442, only three years before; he was himself a painter as well as a poet, and introduced many useful arts into Provence, glass-making amongst the rest. The last being then chiefly cultivated with a reference to art in the production of elegant vessels or of painted windows, there is a probability that gem-engraving likewise may have shared his patronage. Such an attribution of the ring would also explain the appearance of the black letter, used till late in the following century by the French, for *posies;* and the general style of the jewel itself, which certainly is not of Italian workmanship. But enough of attributions founded upon mere probabilities. In the Uzielli Collection there was a somewhat similar work (procured in France by Bőőcke), a female head in front-face very deeply cut in an octagonal amethyst, but quite in the stiff Gothic manner of a metal seal, and certainly not antique, nor even to be referred to the Lower Empire. It was set in a very heavy gold ring made like a many-stranded cable, a fashion much used throughout the fifteenth century, and, indeed, extremely tasteful. Here, also, both gem and ring are apparently of the same date, but there is no inscription of any kind to assist conjecture. Of such heads given in full face more shall be said when we come to another and a particularly interesting specimen of the kind.

A greater affinity to the "Henry VI.," both in material, execution, and lettering, is the jacinth intaglio now in the Braybrooke Collection, set in a weighty though plain ring, which is said to have been found in Warwickshire. The device is a triple face combined in one head, seen in front, but differing altogether in treatment from the three masks thus united so common in Roman work. Here, indeed, a certain Gothic grimness pervades the design, and the hair is done in a manner totally different from the ancient, being represented by thick straight strokes, each terminating in a drill-hole. The intaglio, highly polished, is deeply sunk in the stone, and executed with the very greatest precision. On the beasil is the motto noel twice repeated. This triune face is the cognisance of the noble Milanese family, Trivulzi, being the rebus on the name, "quasi tres vultus." The style of this intaglio, so bold and forcible, yet full of a Gothic quaintness, has no similarity whatever to the Roman antique. There can be little doubt that we have here an actual gem cut at Milan about the year 1450. A conjecture that would account for the use of the black letter in the motto, will plausibly indicate at the same time the former owner of this valuable signet. Gian Giacomo Trivulzio, surnamed "the Great," born in 1441, having been slighted by Ludovico Sforza, became the most active partisan of his mortal enemy, Charles VIII., and afterwards of Louis XII. and François I. What, then, more natural than that he, a general in the French service, should inscribe upon his family signet the well-known Gallic war-cry, "Noel," *i. e.* Emanuel, "God be with us," and written in the character still prevailing in his adopted country?

Our third example is analogous to the last in many respects. It also is cut in a precious material, a large and good sapphire, and is a female face in profile, the head covered with a cloth after the fashion of a Roman *contadina.* It is worked out in a manner resembling the preceding, allowance being made for the difference necessitated by the superior hardness of the stone, the most difficult (after the diamond) that ever taxes the engraver's skill. The intaglio has an extraordinary polish, but in technique equally as in design it differs totally from the rare antiques extant in this stone, and yet more from the numerous examples in it executed after the Renaissance. Round the beasil, in neat Lombard letters, runs the warning, TECTA LEGE LECTA TEGE, a favourite motto for mediæval seals. On the sole ground of this motto the signet has been attributed to Matthew Paris, and the head-cloth fancied to be a Benedictine hood; apart from all other considerations, so valuable a ring was beyond the station of a monk like that chronicler. The Lombard character may appear on works made in the same year as others inscribed in the black letter, supposing the former executed in Italy, the latter by a French or German jeweller. The subject is undoubtedly the very one that we should expect a mediæval engraver to select for so valuable a stone—the Head of the Madonna. There is an attempt to represent curls where the hair is disclosed beneath the head-cloth, the conventional drapery for such a type; blue is, moreover, the colour appropriated to the Virgin Mary. This ring, also massy and intrinsically valuable, was found in cleaning out an old well at Hereford. Thus we have, within the limited circle of my own experience, three intagli on precious stones, and bearing a certain family resemblance to each other.

Last to be described, but not the least important, is an intaglio on an occidental cornelian, not a *sard*. It is a female bust in front face; upon the head is a sort of diadem, placed horizontally; round the neck is a chain, supporting a small undefined ornament. At first sight this bust strongly reminds one of the type upon the coins of Licinia Eudoxia in the fifth century; but there can be no doubt, after examination, that it is designed for a Madonna. The work indeed is very tolerable, but the face has the usual impudent and smirking expression that marks the female heads of the later ages of Gothic taste; certainly such a manner was foreign to the Roman hand, even in the lowest stages of the Decline. Imperial portraits, even after the execution had become quite barbarous, are still successful in preserving a certain rude expression of dignity and repose. This stone is not set as a ring, but in an octagonal silver seal, in shape far from inelegant. The legend on the setting —PRIVE SVI E POY CONV—" Privé suis et peu connu," is well cut in bold Lombardic letters, like that on the ring last mentioned. This seal, found at Childerley, Suffolk, in 1861, was ceded by the late Mr. Litchfield of Cambridge to the Prince of Wales.

All the above described engravings distinguish themselves at the very first glance from the innumerable examples of really antique intagli adapted to mediæval usages. The latter, whether the finest Greek or the rudest colonial Roman, have an air of antiquity about them which cannot be mistaken, in addition to the characteristic shaping of the stone itself. For all antique gems (excepting the sard, the red jasper, and the sardonyx, when cut transversely by the older Greeks) have always a surface more or less convex, and more especially so in the case of the three precious kinds we have been considering—this in all the instances cited is perfectly plane. The work also betrays in every line the heavy touch of the engraver accustomed to cut seals in metal.

It is only a matter of wonder why the Italians (at least in the great trading cities, Pisa, Venice, Genoa) did not sooner turn their attention to gem-engraving; in constant intercourse as they were with the natives of Alexandria and of the Syrian ports, to say nothing of their artistic relations with the Byzantine Greeks. In all these regions the art was at the time extensively practised, the more especially amongst the Mohammedans, in the cutting of Cufic, and later of Persian calligraphy with the accompanying arabesques and floral decorations. This is the more singular as the Italians are known to have learnt many arts from the Arabians, chiefly those established in Spain, such as the manufacture of ornamental glass, enamelled wares or Majolica, and damascening metal. Many Italian words relating to the arts betray the source whence the latter were derived, being pure Arabic, such as *zecca*, *tazza*, *gala*, perhaps also *cameo*, &c. It is not, however, unlikely that some amongst the ruder talismans, on which Hebrew letters appear, were made in the interval preceding the date of 1417, hinted at by Vasari as the space when something continued to be done, although it was of no account. Yet, had the Italians, before the year 1400, practised gem-engraving even to this limited extent, we should expect to find a class of intagli existing, of which no examples have yet presented themselves; namely, the patron saints of the respective cities, just as the contemporary Byzantines were doing with their St. George, Demetrius, and Nicolas on plasma and bloodstone, and their own mintmasters in the types of their national coinages. We should expect often to find on gems the well-known figure of St John of Florence and *her* old lion "Marzocco;" the "Tota Pulchra" of Pisa; the Santo Volto of Lucca, and her St. Martin; and above all the Winged Lion of Venice. The last was the device beyond all others the one for a merchant's signet, and therefore does it figure on so many counters or Nuremburg Rechenpfennings.

Sometimes indeed a calcedony or cornelian is found bearing a regular "merchant's mark," but all known to me seem posterior to the year 1500, and may have been engraved as late as Elizabeth's reign, which has left abundance of signets of this sort in metal.

To return to the triple face on the jacinth above described: its most weird magical-looking aspect irresistibly suggests an equally strange hypothesis to account for it. It strongly resembles the heads of certain mysterious statuettes bearing Arabic legends of darkly obscene purport, published by Von Hammer (Mines de l'Orient, vol. vi.) as the very images of *Baphomet* which the Templars were accused of worshipping. It certainly would well represent the "capita quorum aliqua habebant *tres* facies" specified in the articles of accusation. Hence sprung the but too seductive idea that some dignitary of the Order, stationed in the East, had possibly employed a native engraver to execute after his instructions this image on a precious stone, whilst the same theory would account for the other female heads similarly on precious stones, whose style is evidently contemporary with this triplet's. In that case all such female heads would typify the Female Principle, that important element in the Gnostic scheme, their Achamoth, or Wisdom. As on the Roman talismans of the sect, a Venus appears in her place to the eyes of the uninitiated, so a bust that would do duty for a Madonna might have served to baffle the curiosity of the profane, when adopted by these latest cultivators of the Gnosis, to typify their mystic *Metis.*

In such a sense the enigmatical motto "I am secret, and little known," and the injunctions to silence would be highly appropriate, the true meaning of the devices being only understood by the "free, equal, and admitted brother;" but such an explanation, tempting as it is, will not stand a closer investigation, for it is based upon a mere chimera. The figures so laboriously collected, so ingeniously interpreted by Von Hammer, manifest in everything the spirit of the Cinque-Cento and a certain inspiration of Roman art, for in some the idea has evidently been borrowed from the Hercules wrapped in his lion's skin, whilst the armour in others is much too classical in its details to have been of the work of the Templar times. The astrological symbols, too, so profusely interspersed, are not even as ancient in form as those employed by the Gothic architects in their sculptured decorations, but exactly correspond with those found in printed books of the sixteenth century. The Arabic inscriptions also are in the modern Neskhi, which had not superseded the Cufic in the ages in question; and this circumstance alone suffices to demolish the whole fabric he has so ingeniously reared. All these considerations united show that these *Teraphim*, if not altogether modern forgeries, were made to serve some purpose in the proceedings of the alchemists or astrologers in the train of the emperor Rudolf II., or perhaps, as certain Masonic emblems denote, they had reference to the arcana of the Rosicrucians. The latter flourished amazingly in Germany about the opening of the seventeenth century, and before they were merged into the Freemasons sometime in the succeeding; and, seeing that the *motives* of these statuettes are palpably borrowed from Florentine bronzes, the latter explanation is, perhaps, the nearest to the truth. At the assigned date the notions of the Kabala and mysticism of every kind flourished most vigorously;

indeed the astrology and alchemy of the preceding ages were simple science conducting its investigations according to the rules of common sense, when compared to the extravagant theosophy established by Paracelsus and his disciples.

From all this we are driven back to the conclusion before attained from other data, that these mysterious intagli, instead of being purely mediæval works, are specimens of the dawning Revival, and belong to the school of the Quattrocentisti. By the very beginning of that age the Italians already sought after engraved gems as works of art, as appears from Cyriac of Ancona's letter respecting the coins and gems collected by the Venetian admiral, Giovanni Delfin, the first possessor of that famous amethyst, the Pallas of Eutyches. His words describing the latter prove that the merit of a fine intaglio was perfectly appreciated in the year 1445.

Mr. Albert Way has favoured me with an impression of a seal containing an intaglio, perhaps the most indubitable example of a mediæval engraving of all yet mentioned. It is a female bust, with a band around the head, and another under the chin: the hair is tied in a large bunch at the back of the head, a fashion peculiar to the early part of the fourteenth century. In front is a spray with flowers: a Gothic lily in its conventional form. The execution of the intaglio, highly polished inside, though far from rude, differs entirely from the antique. The subject, I have no hesitation in pronouncing "Santa Maria del fiore," and engraved by an early Florentine; perhaps an actual specimen of the skill of Peruzzi, that "singolare intagliatore di pietre." An artist capable of such a performance in that age would well merit such a reputation.

The engraved stones set in mediæval metal works, even in the most important pieces remaining, such as the Shrine at Cologne, and that of St. Elizabeth at Marburg, to be described hereafter, are all of Roman date and of trifling artistic value—probably because they were extracted out of Roman jewelry then in existence belonging to the latest times of the Empire. The finer works of Greek art, *ancient* even to the Romans themselves, in the age of Julius Cæsar, as we have already seen, had, one may well suppose, disappeared in the ages following the fall of the Empire, and those we now enjoy are the fruit of modern research amongst the remains of long-buried Italian and Grecian opulence. Of this fact, the scarabæi are a proof, now so abundant, yet unknown to the mediæval jeweller, or to the earlier collectors after the Revival, almost in the same degree. In fact, the whole domain of archaic Greek and Etruscan art may be said to have lain in darkness until a century ago, as that of Assyrian did until our own times.

Not more than two engraved gems, both camei, with designs in an unmistakably Gothic style, have come under my notice. Of these the first can easily be accounted for, and adds no argument to either side of the question; not so the second, which sets us as hard a problem in its class as the ruby forming the first subject of this dissertation.

To begin with the first cameo, formerly in the Uzielli Collection. The Madonna, a half-length and seen in front face, holds before her the Infant supported on a cushion resting on the balustrade of a balcony containing them. They are enshrined under a deep canopy sculptured in the latest Gothic or Flamboyant style. But since this style lingered on in France and Flanders late into the sixteenth century, in a sacred subject like this (especially as it may have been the copy of some ancient sculpture of peculiar sanctity), the introduction of Gothic ornamentation does not necessarily prove that the piece was executed before the year 1500. It may in fact have been done on this side of the Alps long after the classic style had regained its hereditary dominion in Italy. The work is very smooth and rounded in its projections, although in the flattest possible relief; and its whole manner reminds one strongly of that characterising the cameo portraits of Henry VIII. and his family, of which there are several known. In all likelihood it was the work of some French or Flemish engraver in the reign of François I. Or indeed the seal-engraver, mentioned by Agricola, in Germany and Holland towards the end of the preceding century, had they attempted cameo-cutting, would have adhered to the Gothic manner and produced something corresponding with this. The stone is a black and white onyx, the relief in the dark layer, $1\frac{1}{4} \times 1$ inch.

The second is an agate-onyx, 3 in. high by 2 wide. In the white layer is most rudely carved Christ Ascending, holding a long cross; before Him, a kneeling figure, a subject frequently seen in sculptures upon tombs. It is not possible to describe the rough chipped-out execution of the relief, the stone appearing as if cut away with a chisel. Neither work nor design bear the least resemblance to Byzantine camei, even the lowest of the class. The only plausible explanation is to suppose it the first essay of some German carver, who had acquired some slight notion of the mechanical process from the Italian inventors, and had attempted a novelty as to material, following his own national taste in everything else. The stone seems to be a true agate-onyx, perhaps of the German species, not the softer alabaster-onyx often used for camei at a later date. This curious piece is supposed to have been found in Suffolk. The outline of the stone being irregular, it is difficult to conjecture the purpose it was intended to fulfil: perhaps to be set in a cross, or some object of sacred use. Even in this case, bearing in mind that a work in the mediæval style would have been consistent with the state of art in England long after 1500 (the Gothic type was for many years retained by Henry VIII. in his coinage), this monument does not necessarily carry us back to the first period mentioned by Vasari, still less to the times anterior to the year 1417.*

After all, upon consideration of these data, the only conclusion that they justify seems to be one not very dissimilar to that generally adopted by archæologists—the purely Gothic artists, down to the early Revival (meaning thereby until after 1400), never attempted gem-engraving. Vasari, in his remark that "something continued still to be done," may refer to the feeble productions of the Byzantine cameo-cutters; but his "improvement in 1417" cannot but apply to Italy, and be the source of the singular intagli in precious stones, whose peculiar character is only to be explained upon this supposition; whilst the Gothic camei may upon internal evidence be ascribed to Teutonic apprentices in the new art, and so be in reality much posterior to the early period properly the subject of our investigation.

* Chabouillet (Glyptique au Moyen Age; Rev. Arch. 1854, p. 550) has published three camei in the French cabinet, which he considers not of Byzantine origin. The first, Christ teaching His disciples, he ascribes to the tenth century; the next, Christ in flowing robes standing under a vine, to the thirteenth; the third, the Adoration, an exquisitely finished piece, to the close of the fifteenth. He judges them Italian.

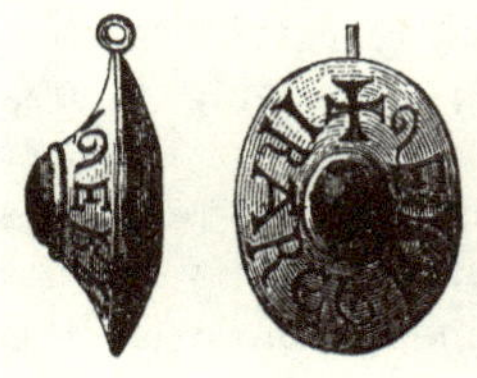

XXX.

The natural sequel to the chapter on mediæval gem-engraving, given in the preceding pages, is a brief notice of the seals and other metal work of the Middle Ages to which antique gems were so often adapted, as the inspection of any collection of old documents will show.* The subjects engraved upon such gems were interpreted by their new possessors as representing Scriptural or legendary personages and events: nor could it be otherwise in the times that saw

> . . . . "Peter's keys some christen'd Jove adorn,
> And Pan to Moses lend his pagan horn,
> Saw graceless Venus to a Virgin turned."

Thus viewed the triple Bacchic mask of the Roman stage was revered as the Trinity in person, and so declared by the added legend "Hæc est Trinitatis imago;" every veiled female head passed for a Madonna or a Magdalene, and received an appropriate motto; and Isis nursing Horus could not but serve for the Virgin and the Infant Saviour. Nor was this substitution confined to gems alone, for the long-famed "Black Virgins" of Auvergne, when at last examined by the critical eye of the antiquary, proved to be actual basalt figures of these imported Egyptian divinities, which, having merely changed names, continued to attract devotees to their shrines, and in greater flocks than before. That frequent type, Thalia holding a mask in her hand, by an ingenious interpretation becomes Herodias carrying the Baptist's head, whilst the skipping little Bacchic genius, her usual companion, is her daughter, who danced to such ill purpose, and they so appear in a seal of the fourteenth century with the allusive motto, "Jesus est amor meus." Another remarkable example of the same design and its version is supplied by an intaglio recently acquired for the British Museum on the dispersion of the Dineley Collection. It is set in a silver mounting, in the usual fashion of privy seals or *secreta* of this class, in the fourteenth century (with a loop at the top, being thus conveniently carried about the person, or by a cord around the neck); the margin bears an inscription common on amatory seals of the period—+IE SVI SEL DE AMVR LEL—"I am the seal of loyal love." This fine gem is here figured on a scale double of the original. Jupiter with his eagle at his side did duty amongst

* The documents in the muniment-room of Corpus Christi College preserve, attached to them, the wax impressions of an amazing number of such adapted intagli—the secreta of the grantors.

Charles V.'s jewels for the similarly attended Evangelist; Silenus, with his crooked *pedum*, was fittingly transformed into some crosiered abbot—

"Purple as his wines;"

whilst Cupids made very orthodox angels. But the unlucky Pan and his Satyrs were for ever banished from the finger, and their forms now appear recast as devils in pictures of the realms of torment; and all this in virtue of their caprine extremities, for *Zernibog*, "the Black God," the Evil Principle of the ancient Sclavonians, had become Zernebock in Teutonic parlance, and therefore was considered as compounded of man and goat.

Caracalla's head, with its curly locks close cropped, and its surly expression, was always taken for that of the irascible chief of the Apostles, hence such a gem is known with the name ΠΕΤΡΟϹ added, to make all sure: I have myself observed the same head (in the Bosanquet Collection) similarly *Petri-fied* by the insertion of a key in the field by some mediæval hand.*

The monks of Durham took the head of Jupiter Fulgurator for St. Oswald's, and, as such, placed it on their common seal, with the title CAPVT SANCTI OSWALDI. Serapis passed current for the authentic portrait of Christ, and in all probability was the real original of the conventional likeness adopted by Byzantine art.

The finest cameo in the world, "the great agate of France," the Apotheosis of Augustus, was long venerated in the Sainte Chapelle as a contemporary representation of the glory of Joseph in Egypt; whilst another noble work, the "Dispute between Neptune and Minerva," where a tree encircled by a vine (easily mistaken for the serpent) occupies the centre of the group, was presented to Louis XIV. (in 1685) by the authorities of a church in which, from time immemorial, it had been displayed as the picture of Adam and Eve in Paradise. But the highest glory ever attained by a work of the engraver was that of the cameo of the Abbey of S. Germain des Prés which enjoyed for an entire millennium the transcendent (though baseless) fame of adorning the espousal ring of the Virgin Mary and of preserving the portraits after the life of herself and Joseph. But, alas! antiquaries now remorselessly have restored the ownership of gem and portraits to the two *nobodies* (probably *liberti*, judging from their names) whose votive legend, "Alpheus with Aretho," is but too plainly legible in our Greek-reading times. When the Abbey was destroyed by fire in 1795, this ring, with

* Gifford, Archbishop of York, seals with a superb gem, the conjugated busts of M. Aurelius and Plato; which doubtless he took for contemporary portraits of SS. Peter and Paul.

other valuables, disappeared; it subsequently came into the hands of General Hydrow, and from him passed into the Imperial Russian Cabinet.

Seffrid, bishop of Chichester (d. 1159), chose for his actual episcopal ring the figure of the serpent-legged Abraxas deity, rudely engraved on a jasper. It had evidently been recommended to him by its numerous virtues as a sigil, whereof Camellus Leonardi gives a long list. The ring was found on the hand of the skeleton upon the accidental discovery of his stone coffin, and is preserved in the library of the Cathedral. The earliest seal of the Stuart family known, that of Walter Fitz Alan (1170), shows that he had been fortunate in obtaining a gem with the knightly subject of a warrior leaning on a cippus, his steed prancing at his side.

Antique intagli set in mediæval seals have in general a Latin motto added around the setting. For this the Lombard letter is almost invariably employed, seldom the black letter, whence it may be inferred, which indeed was likely on other grounds, that such seals for the most part came from Italy, where the Lombard alphabet was the sole one in use until superseded by the revived Roman capitals about the year 1450. Of such mottoes a few examples will serve to give an idea, premising that the stock was not very extensive, judging from the frequent repetition of the same legends on seals of widely different devices. Thus a very spirited intaglio of a lion passant found in Kent, proclaims—"SUM LEO QUOVIS EO NON NISI VERA VEHO;" another gives the admonition to secrecy—"TECTA LEGE, LECTA TEGE;" a third in the same strain—"CLAUSA SECRETA TEGO." Another lion warns us with IRA REGIA, "The wrath of a king is as the roaring of a lion:" an apt device for a courtier. Less frequently seen are legends in old French, and these are more quaint in their style; for instance, around a female bust—"PRIVÉ SUY E PEU CONNU;" whilst a gryllus of a head covered with a fantastic helmet made up of masks, gives the advice, in allusion to the enigmatical type,—"CREEZ CE KE VUUS LIRREZ," for "Croyez ce que vous lirez."

The young head of M. Aurelius, mounted in a pointed oval setting, carries the strange notice, "Credat omnis pii jaspidis" (*signo* being understood). Perhaps it was taken for the portrait of Jasper, or Caspar, the first of the Three Kings of Cologne.

Often the legend merely expresses the owner's name; thus an intaglio, Pegasus, reads—"S. JOHANNIS DE BOSCO," who, from the device he has adopted, may be supposed a Templar. An unusally large gem of the Lower Empire, a helmed head (of Mars?) between two Victories presenting him with crowns, declares itself in Early

Norman lettering + S. SIMONIS DE ROPPESLEI. The most valuable example known to me is one (Waterton) set with an intaglio of three heads, Julia's between those of her sons Caius and Lucius, exactly as the same type appears on a denarius minted by C. Marius Trogus (a moneyer of Augustus'), whose signet the gem in all likelihood was at the first. The inscription, "S. ANDREOCTI DE S'RA," proves it to have been reset for some Italian *Andreotto* di Serra (?), who doubtless thought himself happy in possessing in his seal the *veræ effigies* of the Virgin, the Infant Saviour, and His Precursor. Another (in the same collection), a finely engraved Persian vizored helmet, a type commonly entitled the "Head of Darius," is encircled with the legend S' CONRADI DE COMITE, "Corrado del Conte," also an Italian, as appears besides from the pattern of the elegant ring enchasing it.

I cannot, however, help suspecting that the earliest adaptation of antique Heads to the purpose of mediæval signets had another and a more rational motive in its origin than the one usually assigned. The Frankish successors to the name of the Cæsars also appropriated by a similar usurpation their images upon gems, by the simple expedient of adding their own superscriptions around the setting. Carloman (764) takes for his seal a female bust with the hair tied in a knot upon the head: Charlemagne, the laureated head of M. Aurelius, adding the legend, + XPE PROTEGE CAROLVM REGE FRANCR.; and later, that of Serapis; both profiles, be it observed, being almost identical in character. Louis I. (816) seals with that of Antoninus Pius, + XPE PROTEGE HLODOVICVM IMPERATORE: Pepin le Bref with the Indian Bacchus; Pepin duc d'Aquitaine with Caligula's portrait. Charles II. (843) adopts an imperial laureated head (not identified), with + KAROLVS DI GRA REX; Lothaire, that of Caracalla + XPE ADIVVA HLOTHARIV. It is usual to consider all such portraits as having been in those days mistaken for authentic likenesses of divine personages or of saints, and to have been adopted merely out of veneration for the supposed prototypes; but a circumstance has lately come under my notice almost carrying with it the conviction that these princes selected, out of the numerous antique gems at their command, such portraits as presented a resemblance either real or fancied to their own features. However remote the likeness, it could not but be more faithful to nature than aught that the decrepit art of their day could produce, even upon metal. Amongst the Anglo-Saxon charters of St Denys, two seals of our kings (published by Sir F. Madden in the Archæological Journal, vol. xiii.) have furnished me both with the first idea, and also with the strongest support of this explanation of the practice.

The first seal, that of Offa (a great patron of the art of engraving, as his coins, the best executed in the Saxon series, amply demonstrate), is a profile of himself crowned, full of an individuality perfectly marvellous in a work of that epoch, and evidently cut upon a metal seal. But the later Edgar (whose the second is) could command the services of no such skilful hand to supply him with his portrait from the life ; he, therefore, has converted into his own the diademed head of some youthful Seleucidan prince, a superb intaglio in a large *cabochon* gem, 1 inch by ¾ inch in measurement. A full description has been given above of Lothaire's attempt to resuscitate the glyptic art sufficiently to perpetuate his own image in a gem ; disappointed, however, in the results obtained, he appears finally reduced, like the others of his dynasty, to content himself with the borrowed face of a Roman predecessor. Our John follows the example and places in his privy-seal a Roman's head, with SECRETVM JOHANNIS added, The impression is found upon the reverse of his great seal. The oldest instance in this series, where a religious motive appears to have dictated the choice of the antique subject, does not occur before the date of 1176, when Louis VIII. uses for his seal, first the Abraxas-god, and, at a later period, a Diana Venatrix—legend, + LODOVICVS REX.

Ecclesiastical jewels and plate were at the same time profusely enriched with engraved stones (mostly brought back from the East by returning pilgrims), a practice, indeed, of which the example had been set long before, even under the Cæsars, for Juvenal laughs at the ostentatious patron who transferred his gems from his fingers to the exterior of his goblets.

> "Nam Virro ut multi gemmas in pocula transfert
> A digitis."

And Martial more pithily alludes to the same folly—

> "Gemmatum Scythicis ut luceat ignibus aurum,
> Aspice quot digitos exuit iste calix !"

> "How many a finger hath that cup left bare,
> That gemmed with Scythian fires its gold might glare !"

Camei of the minor class were in request as personal decorations : they were mounted as the pendent jewels for neck-chains, or, when not too large, were set as other gems in finger-rings. The estimation in which they were held when thus utilized is well exemplified by the following extracts, translated from the inventory of the jewels of the Duc de Berri (1416).

"Two fine camei, cut, the one with the figure of a man, three fingers long: the other, with the face of a woman; of the size of a full inch: both which my Lord Duke bought of Michel de Bouldue. . . . 24 livres Tournois."*

"A cameo, on which is engraved a goat, and a child riding upon it, set in a gold ring. . . . 60 sols."

"A cameo, on which are two horses harnessed, drawing a chariot, mounted in gold, and at the back, a small enamel. . . . 10 livres."

"A cameo with a *Saracen's* head (Negro's ?), set in a wreath with precious stones around it of little value; at the back is a box for holding relics. . . . 26 livres."

"A white cameo set in silver-gilt, engraved on the back with Greek letters, priced at 40 sols."

"A cameo of a head which has the mouth open (*plate*) set in silver-gilt. . . . 4 livres."

"A flat cameo, somewhat long and roundish in the shape of the bottom of a vat (sieve): whereon is a little naked image upon a pillar after the fashion of an idol, and three other images. Set in a gold *portepaix* (a pax ?). . . . 100 sols."

"A gold ring set with a cameo of a child's head with much hair. . . . 30 sols."

But the finest and most important were reserved to embellish the golden casing of the actual shrine containing the bones of the saint that gave all its spiritual virtue to the place. An early instance in this country is recorded of this usage. In a great dearth, Leofric, tenth Abbot of St. Alban's, sold all the gold and silver vessels of his church, "retentis tantummodo quibusdam gemmis preciosis ad quas non invenit emptores, et quibusdam nobilibus lapidibus insculptis quos *cameos* vulgariter appellamus—quorum magna pars ad feretrum (*the shrine*) decorandum cum fabricaretur, est reservata."† The last passage refers to the shrine made by the monk Anketil, soon after A.D. 1120. "Et cum de *antiquo* hujus ecclesiæ thesauro prolatæ fuissent gemmæ ad opus feretri decorandum, allati sunt quidam ampli lapides quos *sardiosonicleos* appellamus, et vulgariter *cadineos* [corruption of cameos] nuncupamus." ‡ Of similar works, the most ancient now existing is the *Palio* of S. Ambrogio, Milan, forming by a series of bas-reliefs in gold and silver-gilt a complete casing for the high altar, and executed before the year 850. In it appear numerous antique gems,

* The livre = 20 sols, the sol = 12 deniers. Putting the denier as equal in value to the contemporary English penny, at least representing one shilling of our money, the amounts in the text may be brought up to the present standard with tolerable correctness: in fact, will rather fall short of than exceed the true estimate.

† Matt. Paris, in Vit. Abbatum, p. 26.

‡ Ibid., p. 38.

but the most interesting is a large yellow stone, irregularly oval, engraved in coarse letters (reversed on the gem), VOTV RIADE, expressing it to be the offering *exvoto* of some pious Lombard named Riada ; by its dedicatory inscription reminding us of the Besborough nicolo offered by Ammonius to Astarte.*

In what fashion important gems were introduced into Gothic ornamentation may be learned from this example in the Trésor de S. Denys—

"Une grande image représentée de la ceinture en haut au naturel, ayant sur la teste une très précieuse mitre enrichie de grande quantité de perles et de pierreries, avec un orfray autour du col, le tout en argent doré . . . . dans le chef de l'image est aussi le chef du mesme Sainct (Hilaire), l'orfray du col est enrichi par le devant d'une très belle agathe d'une face d'homme depuis la teste jusque aux espaules ; et est l'effigie auprès du naturel de l'empereur Auguste, environnée comme est aussi tout l'orfray de grande quantité de perles et riches pierreries.

"L'orfray ou collet qui est autour du col (de S. Benoist) est enrichi de grand nombre de perles et de pierreries, et par le devant d'une excellente agathe, représentant la teste d'un homme jusques aux espaules, qui est l'effigie au naturel de l'empereur Tibére. La mitre est admirable, car elle est toute parsemée de riches agathes sur lesquelles sont représentées diverses faces d'anges, d'hommes, de femmes, et d'animaux, très bien taillées et elabourées : et outre cela de plusieurs beaux rubis et saphirs et autres pierres avec plus de 300 perles orientales. Ce reliquaire si précieux fut donné par le bon prince, Jean, Duc de Berry, l'an 1393, en reconnaissance des reliques de S. Hilaire qu'il avoit eues de l'abbé et des religieux de S. Denys."—(P. 105.)

Caylus figures several antiques, both camei and intagli, selected from nearly three hundred, at that time (1760) enchased in the sacred vessels and other ornaments belonging to the treasury of Troyes cathedral.† The majority, however, remarks Caylus, were only small intagli in cornelian, and set in the châsse, or portable shrine, containing a most precious tooth of St. Peter, and the entire head of the cheaper St. Philip. This *châsse* had been made for Bishop Garnier, almoner to the French crusaders at the taking of Constantinople in 1204, whence he piously *stole*, "conveyed, the wise it call," the apostle's skull.

* ΟΥΡΑΝΙ ΑΗΡΑ ΑΜΜωΝΙΟϹ ΑΝΕΘΗΚΕΝ ΕΠ' ΑΓΑΘω. S. Marco of Venice boasts, as I am informed on the best authority, an equally rich *palio* stuck full of precious stones and antiques.

† Caylus, 'Recueil d'Antiquités,' t. v. pl. 52.

The shrine of the Three Kings of Cologne, a work of the twelfth century, is a rich storehouse of antiques. The two gable-ends are adorned with the most important pieces at the goldsmith's disposal, large and beautiful camei, and the sides are studded with engraved stones of all kinds; for some subjects among them, Leda and the swan for instance, the devotees of that age must have been puzzled to find a Scriptural prototype.* Their original number was 226 when described by Boisserée, but the best were picked out in the *hejira* of 1794. This extraordinary specimen of mediæval metal-work was made by order of Philip von Heinsberg, *dom-probst*, or dean, in 1170, to contain the three skulls of the "Wise Men," brought from Constantinople, and presented by the Emperor Frederic I. to the Archbishop of Cologne six years before. In 1794, out of fear of the advancing iconoclast French army, all the treasures of the cathedral were hastily carried off to Arnberg, whence in 1804 they were solemnly brought back to Cologne. In this interval the shrine had been crushed, many parts of it were lost, and several gems stolen—others say, "sold for the maintenance of the ecclesiastics," in which case as it would naturally have been only the precious stones, not the antiques, that were the first to be converted into money, the original number of the latter may be supposed not materially diminished. It was therefore completely remade by the *Polacks*, artificers of Cologne, the missing pieces of the metal-work replaced by copies, and many precious stones, as well as antiques, were supplied by the devotion of the citizens to make up the deficiences. The length of the shrine was at this time reduced to 6 ft. 7 in.; the height and breadth remaining as before. The material is silver-gilt. No more than the one gable-end exhibiting the skulls, blazing with diamonds (perhaps pastes), can be seen from the choir, through a strong grating. To inspect the monument, admittance into the chapel is obtained by a fee of one thaler, and a small lantern is supplied, the vaulted strong-room being in utter darkness.

Next in importance as a mediæval storehouse of antique gems was the shrine at Marburg, constructed about 1250 to contain the bones of Elizabeth, Landgravine of Thüringen and Hesse, and

* Could they have interpreted the swan into a gigantic dove, and have discovered in the group a most materialistic representation of the descent of the Holy Ghost upon the Virgin? The frequency with which this apparently most inappropriate design is introduced into ecclesiastical ornaments, affords but too much foundation for this belief; in fact, Justinus, the boldest of the Gnostic doctors, in his application of the Greek mythology to the support of his own system of Christianity, expands this very fable, as one of those foreshowing the descent of the Saviour.

canonized in 1235. This shrine, in the usual form of a house, surrounded by a Byzantine arcade, is 6 ft. long, 2 deep, and 3½ high, above which the roof rises 1¼ ft. It is constructed of oak overlaid with copper thickly gilt. The arcade is filled with seated figures of the Apostles, in silver-gilt, of which metal are also made the elaborate bas-reliefs covering the roof. Under pediments, one in the middle of each side, corresponding in elevation with the gable ends of the edifice, are the four principal figures, two feet in height, seated on thrones, and projecting beyond the general outlines; they are, Christ seated, Christ crucified, an angel hovering above Him (stolen in 1810), the Virgin and Child, and Saint Elizabeth. The eight bas-reliefs on the roof represented scenes in the life of that saint.

The architectural portions of the metal-work were originally set with the enormous number of 824 stones, fifty-nine plates of mother-of-pearl, two large, one middle-sized, and many smaller pearls. The stones were sapphires, emeralds, amethysts, jacinths, crystals, onyxes, almandines, calcedonies, and carnelians, thus distributed; 259 in the four principal figures; 252 in the smaller; in the ornamental portions of the roof and of the frames, 313. Of these, sixty-five stones were missing, as their empty settings showed. In November, 1810, it was carried off to Cassel by the orders of the Westphalian Government, but was returned to Marburg in 1814. During its absence, however, some antiquarian thief had extracted every engraved gem but one, and these have disappeared for ever. Fortunately, Professor Ullman availed himself of its removal from under the grating which had preserved it for six centuries to take impressions in sealing-wax of thirty-four intagli and one cameo. The most famous of all the camei was placed above the Madonna, a splendid sardonyx of three layers, the heads of Castor and Pollux, regarded during the Middle Ages as a most wonderful natural production, and for which a former Elector of Mayence is said to have offered in vain the whole village of Anemöneburg. Of this, unluckily, no drawing has been preserved. Of these wax impressions Cruezer has published accurate fac-similes (in his 'Archæologie,' vol. iii.), with a long and instructive commentary upon the subject of each. These subjects may be briefly enumerated, to exhibit the strange variety of engraved gems (valuable then for their occult virtues chiefly) offered by the piety of crusaders and pilgrims. The cathedral at Marburg is the first pure Gothic building raised in Germany, begun in 1235, and finished in forty-eight years, as the church of the Knights of the Teutonic Order.

The species of the stones were not marked by Ullman; probably the settings, and the hurry of the commissioners to be off with their booty, prevented his doing more than take the impressions, which we may conclude were those of the best engraved gems.

1. Two goats under a tree; good work. 2. Cupid on a lion; very archaic. 3. Jove seated; common Roman. 4. Horse lying down, the head and neck of a cow appear above him; good. 5. Warrior seated, his helmet on a cippus in front. (I have little doubt that, in 1854, at the sale of the Webb Gems, by one of those extraordinary chances so frequent in this study, this identical gem, a nicolo, came into my possession. The exact agreement in size, and in the singular false perspective of the hero's further leg, renders this opinion almost a certainty.) 6. Warrior advancing; fine. 7. Jove seated; rude. 8. Head of Pallas; fine; a largish stone. 9. Raven, above him the Delphic E; rude. 10. Bonus Eventus, standing with cornucopia; fine. 10a. A Cufic legend. 11. Jove seated; rude. 12. Fox in a car drawn by two cocks; fine. 13. Fortuna Nemesis, winged and helmeted; fine and large. 14. A horseman, with what seems a torch over his shoulder (more probably his mantle); rude work; the only gem that has escaped, resembling a ruby. 15. Warrior seated, upon his hand a Victory, as it seems; fair. 16. A dolphin and two shells; Greek. 17. Head, laureated; rude Roman. 18. Head, perhaps Medusa's; fine. 19. Cray-fish; rude. 20. Arabic, not Cufic, legend, translated by Wahl as a Dutch name, "von Frank." 21. Roman seated between two Victories; large stone, in the rudest Roman style. 22. Arabic legend. 23. Hercules standing, his hand resting on his club; good. 24. Pegasus, or the Sassanian Winged Bull; rude. 25. Potter at work; good. 26. Persian king, slaying a monster; rude. 27. Cufic legend; very neat. 29. Fortuna, or Nemesis; good. 31. Head of Apollo, bay-crowned; in the field ΠΑΙΑΝ behind the head, and bay-sprig in front; fine Greek work; large stone. 32. Bacchante, standing, with a tray upon her head; rude. 33. Cupid mounted upon a hippocampus; fine. 34. Aquarius pouring an amphora into a crater, or perhaps a Faun; in the field four large letters, the rest on the reverse, three letters, imperfect; Cruezer proposes the reading ΤΩ ΑΜΠΕΛΩ, "to Ampelus." 35. Circular cameo, head of Pallas in the early Greek manner and flat relief. This stone, 1¼ inch wide, was placed in the centre of the canopy over the fifth apostle.

We find attached to this shrine the same story of a luminous gem, as the *osculan* in the shrine at Egmund, whereof Alardus tells so marvellous a tale; a large egg-shaped stone, placed above the grand cameo, was ever believed to give light in the hours of darkness; but Cruezer ascertained it to be no more than yellow rock-crystal, and only luminous to the eye of faith. It was famous in the Middle Ages, as the "Karfunkel" of Marburg.

The "Trésor de Conques," a secluded abbey in Auvergne, still preserves the most important monuments of Carlovingian art in existence anywhere, dedicated there by Charlemagne. Here is the statuette of Sainte Foy, Virgin and Martyr, seated on a throne, with a Byzantine crown on her head, and large square pendants in her ears, richly set with gems, the whole in gold *repoussé*, 80 c. (32 in.) high. Also the A of Charlemagne, only survivor of the complete alphabet, one letter of which was presented to each of the principal abbeys of his empire, framed of oak overlaid with silver-gilt, 45 c. high, in form a triangle, with two verticals upon the base inside. In these, in the processional cross, and in the enamelled phylacteries of the reliquaries, are set, amongst other stones, some sixty engraved gems and three camei, mostly of the Lower Empire. The most curious are, a large sard, "a head of Caracalla," very coarse work; a seated Isis, on a large "tourmaline," and most singular of all, an amethyst intaglio, a man, his head in front-face, in a pleated robe, standing, in each hand a long foliated cross, precisely the type of a Carlovingian denier, legend, CARN. The Annales Archéologiques for 1860 give many plates of the figures, and all the engraved stones.

Amongst the "*Vesselle de Chapelle*" of Louis, Duc d'Anjou, according to the inventory drawn up about 1365, we find some instructive instances of this employment of camei. No. 23, "Un tableau d'argent doré, semé par dedenz de esmeraudes granz et petites, balaiz granz et petiz, *camahieux* granz et petiz, et menues perles grant quantité. Et ou milieu dudit tableau a un très grant *camahieu vermeil*, ouquel a Nostre Dame gisant Nostre Seigneur en la cresche, et les angeles tout entour, et dessouz a Nostre Dame qui baigne son enfant, et derriere elle a Saint Josef séant. Et sieent le dit tableau sur un souage qui est semé de esmeraudes, de rubis d'Alisandre et de petites perles," &c. This cameo, with its figures in red relief, "vermeil," abounds too much in actors, although interpreted as angels, and is altogether too elaborate a composition for a Byzantine Christian work, as the minute description of the subject at first would tempt one to conclude. Doubtless it was antique, and represented that favourite theme of the Roman artist, the Education of Bacchus. The good monk who drew up the inventory for Louis saw in the nymph Leucothea the Virgin Mary; in the attendant genii, so many sportive angels; and in the seated Silenus, that ever-present actor in the history of Bacchus, the patriarchal-looking Joseph.

No. 25 is "Une crois longue et grelle d'argent doré, et y est Nostre Seigneur en la dicte croiz tout estandu; et est l'arbre d'icelle croiz semé de perles et de pierrerie. Et a ou bout du bras de la croiz par en haut un *camahieu* ouquel a ij. chevaux qui menent un chariot, et les mene un home. Et es ij. boux des travers de la croiz a ij. testes d'omme, et est l'une blanche et l'autre vermeille. Et ou bout d'icelle crois a un autre *camahieu* ouquel a une femme qui se siet en une chaire."

The following extract from the Trésor de S. Denys is extremely valuable, since it describes a most elaborate specimen of Carlovingian metal-work, as well as the manner in which remarkable engraved stones continued to retain their primary estimation, although for reasons totally diverse—for the aqua-marine here mentioned is the celebrated *Julia Titi*, the work of Evodus; the "Gem of King David" is a lump of antique *schmelze* paste, of which I have seen specimens exhibiting the same odd transition of colours on the change of light:—

"Un très riche joyau et très precieux reliquaire nommé l'escrain de Charlemagne à cause qu'il a jadis servy à la chapelle de ce sainct empereur. Cette rare pièce est en façon de tableau, composée de trois estages d'or, enrichie de grand nombre de pierres precieuses, comme d'aigues marines, saphirs, esmeraudes, cassidoines, rubis, grénats, et de très belles perles orientales toutes enchassées en or. Entre ces pierreries il y en a une admirable large comme un douzain de France, taillée en ovale et enchassée en or comme les autres, laquelle, estant posée sur la paulme de la main ou sur quelque autre lieu plat, paroist verte, et levée au jour elle semble estre de couleur de pourpre. Elle a autrefois servy au grand Roy David, comme il appert par les lettres, burinées sur l'enchaussure que disent—'Hic lapis fuit Davidis regis et prophetæ.'

"Sur la faisse de cet escrain ou buffet d'honneur on voit une aigue marine des plus belles, sur laquelle est représentée en *demy-relief* * l'effigie de Cleopatre, Royne d'Egypte, ou selon aucums de la princesse Julia, fille de l'Empereur Tite; pièce très rare et admirée de tous ceux qui la voyent. Autour de cette effigie sont gravés ces deux mots Grecs—ΕΥΟΔΟΣ ΕΠΟΙΕΙ." †

* An optical illusion due to the stone being set with the intaglio downwards, and its convex back upmost, according to the then established fashion of setting the vast engraved crystal cabochons of the period.

† 'Trésor de S. Denys,' p. 102.

"Un excellent camahieu d'agathe blanche sur laquelle est relevée la face d'une femme couronnée, qui est l'effigie de la *Royne de Saba*, laquelle se transporta de son royaume en Jerusalem pour y voir le Roy Solomen et ouyr sa sapience, comme dict l'Escriture Saincte (3 Reg. 10). Cette pièce est très antique et digne de remarque. Elle est enchassée en argent doré et enrichie de plusieurs pierres précieuses."

The Trésor also boasted of important examples of imperial "onychina et murrhina," now dedicated to the service of the altar; *e. g.*:—

"Un calice très exquis fait d'une très belle agathe, gauderonné par dehors, admirable pour la beauté et varieté des couleurs que s'y sont trouvées naturellement esparses ça et là en façon de papier marbré," a comparison aptly, though undesignedly, illustrating Pliny's description of the latter, and attesting the fitness of Martial's epithet—

" . . . *maculosæ* pocula murrhæ."

In the cathedral of Brunswick is still shown a singular adaptation of antique jewels to the decoration of a reliquary; it is the arm of St. Blaize (brought from Palestine by Henry the Lion in the eleventh century), encased in silver on the fingers of which are no less than fourteen rings.

In the Patent Roll 51 Henry III. (A.D. 1266–67) a list has been preserved of jewels collected by that king for the enrichment of the shrine of Edward the Confessor in Westminster Abbey. Some may have been obtained at Rome by the Abbot of Westminster, Richard de Ware, who was sent to Italy at that time, and brought over Peter, "civis Romanus," by whom the basement of the shrine was constructed, ornamented with glass mosaic and marbles, and upon this was placed the golden jewelled feretory wrought by two goldsmiths of London, Fitz-Otho and Edward his son. The entry on the Patent Roll, from which the following particulars regarding this shrine are derived, enumerates the costly provision made by Henry III.—"Lapides pretiosos et jocalia deputata casse sive feretro in quo corpus beatissimi Edwardi Regis disposuimus collocari." *

"Firmaculum cum camauto in medio . . . anulus cum saphiro inciso † . . . baculus continens vij. anulos cum chamahutis parvis . . . pulchrum chamahutum cum imaginibus filiorum Jacobi in capsa aurea cum rubettis et smaragdinibus in circumferentia . . .

* Extracted from Canon Rock's invaluable repertory of Ecclesiastical Antiquities, the 'Church of Our Fathers,' vol. iii. part 1, p. 393.

† Mention is made of a second ring, "cum saphiro inciso."

chamahutum cum tribus imaginibus in capsa aurea * . . . chamahutum cum imaginibus Moysis et serpentis" (Æsculapius?) ". . . chamahutum cum magno capite . . . chamahutum cum curru et equitibus . . . chamahutum cum imagine in medio . . . chamahutum cum imagine regis . . chamahutum optimum cum ij. albis imaginibus . . . chamahutum cum imagine leonis . . . chamahutum cum duabus imaginibus et arbore . . . chamahutum cum capite elevato . . . chamahutum cum ij. capitibus . . . chamahutum cum imagine beate Marie . . . chamahutum cum capite duplicato . . . magna perla ad modum chamahuti . . . chamahutum cum aquila . . ."

The list continues with a further enumeration of camei thus described—"cum ij. angelis . . . cum ymagine alba . . . cum capite albo . . . cum capite bene crinito . . . chamahutum album cum imagine mulieris cum puero et dracone" (Ceres and Triptolemus?) ". . . chamahutum cum equo . . . cum capite et leone opposito in capsa aurea ad modum crucis . . . cum capite albo barbato . . . in capsa aurea ad modum crucis cum bove . . . cum imagine alba cum magestate ex parte alba †. . . chamahutum in capsa aurea ad modum targie . . . cum ij. capitibus albis . . . cum laticibus (lyncibus?) et curru . . . cum cane . . . cum capite barbato . . . chamahutum cristallinum cum capite . . . cum capite ruffo ‡ . . . cum capite bepertito (Janus?) crinito . . . cum leone . . . j. chamahutum in anulo pontificali." The number of camei is in all not less than eighty-five.

Amongst precious stones the following are enumerated; each is described as "in capsa aurea," or "in capsa argenti."—"Onicleus —saphirus—citrinus—amatista—prasina—canis onicleus—phiola oniclea et alia cristallina—balesii—minute prasine in una chinchia —perle in una chinchia," § &c. "Saphirus *crinitus* in capsa aurea" may have been an asteria sapphire. We find also "ij. panchii calcidonii," probably for *panchri* (Pliny), multicoloured; also "decem cokille et unum album capud;" the cokille, *coquilles*, were possibly disks of mother-o'-pearl, at that time accounted very precious, and of which numerous examples are to be seen on the

* In each case, in the following items, "the camahutum" is described as "in capsa aurea," or "in capsa auri."

† Other camei are mentioned "cum magestate," *i.e.*, God the Father (a Serapis or Jupiter's bust?).

‡ This description occurs again in other instances.

§ This term here occurs repeatedly; it is somewhat obscure; the glossaries give *chinchitha* (whence *quincaillerie*), or *chinsica*, reconditorium, apotheca, &c. In old French *chinche* signifies a piece of cloth, *chiffon*, in which possibly the jewels may have been wrapped up.

Gothic crowns found at Guarrazar, and now preserved at Paris in the Musée des Thermes.* They occur also on the Marburg shrine and on the crown of the Lombard Queen Theodelinda at Monza.† Theophilus alludes to the use of mother-o'-pearl in goldsmiths' work.‡ The expression "capite elevato," repeatedly occurring in the foregoing list of camei clearly signifies work in very high relief, or more than mezzo-relievo. The "capita oniclea" I suppose to have been heads (*phaleræ*) carved *en ronde bosse.*

The feretrum was furthermore enriched by Henry III. with images representing St. Peter trampling upon Nero, St. Edmund, and other regal personages, set with precious stones, emeralds, sapphires, "balesiis, granatis, rubettis," &c. I may refer to the Patent Roll, as cited by Canon Rock, for more full details.

The following item claims notice :—" unum magnum chamahutum in capsa aurea cum cathena aurea," valued at the enormous price of 200*l.*, equal to about 4000*l.* at the present time. Also, amongst the precious stones, a sapphire of the enormous size of 54 dwts., or 324 carats.

This shrine may be supposed to have remained intact down to the time of the suppression of the monastery. All the valuable portion would then have been confiscated for the king's use, as is recorded in the case of the Canterbury shrine, of which the spoils in gold and jewels filled two chests, that required six or eight strong men, according to Stow, to carry each chest out of the church.

Numerous "Lapidaria" are extant, both in MS. and in the collection published by Camillus Leonardi in 1502 (ascribed to Solomon, Chael, Ragiel, and Rabanus Maurus), minutely describing the virtues of the different figures engraved on gems. Nonsensical as are their explanations of the designs and all their deductions thence, these doctrines were received with implicit faith during the Middle Ages. The mode of expression occasionally used makes the reader more than suspect that the compilers of these guides mistook (like the Marburghers above mentioned) the engravings upon the stones for the actual work of nature! so completely had all knowledge of this art perished. The more learned regarded them as the works of the children of Israel in the wilderness, hence their common name in those times of "Pierres d'Israel" and "Jews'

* 'Catalogue des Objets d'Art, &c., exposés au Musée des Thermes,' pp. 355, 357, edit. 1864.

† 'Arch. Journ.,' vol. xiv. p. 14.

‡ Theophilus, lib. iii. c. 95. "Secantur chonchæ marinæ per partes et inde limantur margaritæ.

stones." A few examples of the supposed virtues of these sigils will not be without interest to the reader.

Thetel Rabanus, "a most ancient doctor," says that the following figures are of the greatest potency;—

1. Man, on jasper, with shield in his left hand, and in his right an idol or some warlike weapon; with vipers instead of legs, and with the head of a cock or of a lion, and clad in a breastplate. This figure gives victory in battle and protects against poison (the Abraxas-god).

2. Man with a bundle of herbs on his neck, if found on a jasper, gives the power of distinguishing diseases, and stops the flow of blood from any part. This stone Galen is said always to have carried about with him.

3. Cross, cut on a green jasper, saves from drowning.

4. Wolf, on jasper, defends from snares, and prevents the uttering of foolish words.

5. Stag, on any stone, cures lunatics and madmen.

6. Lamb protects against palsy and ague.

7. Virgin in long robe, with laurel-branch in her hand, cut on jasper, secures against drowning and the vexation of demons, and gives success in all undertakings.

8. Man holding a palm-branch in his hand, cut on jasper, renders the wearer powerful and acceptable to princes.

A very ancient book ascribed to Solomon, by Camillo, thus begins: "In the name of the Lord. This is the precious book which the Children of Israel made in the Wilderness according to thy name, O Lord, and according to the course of the stars."

1. Old man seated on a plough (as in No. 1. of Chael) is thus proved: Take clean black wool undyed and wrap up the stone therein, place it amongst wheat straw and lie with thy head upon it: thou shalt see in thy sleep all the treasures of the kingdom in which thou art, and how to obtain them. Water, in which it has been steeped, cures all diseases of cattle.

2. Man, with helmet on his head, shield hung round his neck, and sword raised on high, and trampling on a serpent, engraved on jasper, hang round thy neck, and thou shall not fear any foe, yet be not thou slothful; in all things shalt thou be victorious, specially in war. It ought to be set in brass.

3. Horse, with a cockatrice or crocodile on his back, on a jacinth, is of power in all conferences and debates; and wearing it thou shalt be loved by all, both men and beasts. It must be set in gold.

4. Man seated and a woman standing before him with her

hair hanging down to the thighs, and casting her eyes upwards: this, engraved on carnelian, hath the virtue that every man and woman touched therewith will immediately become obedient to thy will in all things. It must be set in gold weighing as much as the stone itself: and under it the herb betony and ambergris.

5. Horse, with rider bearing a sceptre, on amethyst, renders all princes and nobles obedient to the owner. It ought to be set in twice its own weight of gold or silver.

6. Horned animal, having under him a horse which drags behind him half a goat, gives the power of taming all beasts, and must be set in lead.

7. Bird, with olive-leaf in its bill, cut on pyrites and set in a silver ring. Having this on thy right hand thou shalt be invited to every feast, and those present shall not eat, but shall gaze upon thee.

8. Scorpion and Sagittary fighting together, on any stone. Set this in an iron ring, and if thou wish to prove its efficacy impress it in wax, and whomsoever thou shalt touch therewith they shall immediately quarrel.

9. Ram, with the half-figure of an ox, on any stone, set in a silver ring, and whomsoever thou shalt touch therewith they shall immediately be reconciled to one another.

10. Woman, one half a fish, holding a mirror and a branch; cut on a marine hyacinth (pale sapphire); set in a gold ring and cover the signet with wax, and wear on thy finger. And when thou wishest to go anywhere and not be seen, hold the gem tight within thy palm, and thou shalt have thy desire.

11. Man ploughing, and over him the hand of the Lord making a sign,* and a star. If cut on any stone, and worn in all purity, thou shalt never perish by tempest, nor shall thy crops receive damage from storms.

12. Head with neck; cut on green jasper; set in a brass or iron ring engraved with the letters B. B. P. P. N. E. N. A. Wear this and thou shalt in no wise perish, but be preserved from many diseases, specially fever and dropsy; it likewise gives good luck in fowling. Thou shalt also be reasonable and amiable in all things; in battle and in law-suits thou shalt be victor. It aids women in conceiving, and in child-birth it gives peace and concord, and

* That is, a closed hand with the two first fingers stretched issuing from a cloud, as is often seen on the later Bezants. "Segnare" is the peculiar word for "to bless" in Italian.

many good things to the wearer: but he must do so in all justice and honesty.

13. Basilisk or Syren, half-woman half-serpent. With this on any gem thou shalt be able to touch any venomous creature without hurt.

14. Basilisk and Dragon entwined together, or carnelian, and also a bull's head. Put it round thy neck when thou wishest to fight with any beast of the wood or of the sea, and they shall quickly be conquered.

15. Man naked and bloated, crowned and holding a cup and a branch: if cut on jet, set in any metal, and any one having a fever and wearing this shall forthwith be cured.

16. Man, with bull's head and eagle's feet, on any stone, make an impression thereof in wax, and so long as it is upon thee no man shall speak evil of thee.

17. Man standing, and tall, holding an obolus (patera) in one hand and a serpent in the other, with the sun over his head and a lion under his feet: if cut on a diacodius (diadochus), set in a leaden ring, and put underneath wormwood and fenugreek. Carry it to the bank of a river and call up whatsoever evil spirit thou pleasest, and thou shalt have from them answers to all thy questions.

18. Aquarius, on a green turquois: the wearer shall have good luck in all his buying and selling, so that buyers shall seek after him.

19. Youth, having a crown on his head, and seated on a throne with four legs, and under each leg a man standing and supporting the throne on his neck; round the neck of the seated figure a circle, and his hands raised up to heaven; if cut on a white hyacinth (pale sapphire), ought to be set in a silver ring of the same weight as the stone, and under it put mastic and turpentine. Make the seal in wax and give it to any one, and let him carry it about on his neck or person, either the wax or the ring, and go with pure mind, and chastely, before king, noble, or wise man, and he shall obtain from them whatsoever he may desire.

20. Man, seated on a fish, cut on red jasper, being put upon the dress of any one at a feast when eating with his right hand, he shall never be satisfied.

21. Bearded man, holding a flower in his hand, cut on carnelian and set in a tin ring, the ring being made at the change of the moon, on a Friday, the 1st or 8th of the month, whomsoever thou shalt touch therewith he shall come to do thy will.

22. Serpent, with a man on his back and a raven over his tail, engraved on any stone, makes the wearer rich and crafty.

23. Man, standing on a dragon, holding a sword, must be set in a leaden or iron ring: then all the spirits that dwell in darkness shall obey the wearer, and shall reveal unto him in a low-toned song the place of hidden treasure and the mode of winning the same.

24. Man riding, and holding in one hand the bridle, in the other a bow, and girt with a sword, engraved on pyrites, set in a gold ring, it will render thee invincible in all battles. And whoever shall steep this ring in oil of musk, and anoint his face with the said oil, all that see him shall fear him, and none shall resist.

25. Man, erect in armour, holding a drawn sword and wearing a helmet, if set in an iron ring of the same weight, renders the wearer invincible in battle.

26. Man, bearing in his hand a *mutatio* (*mutande*, drawers?), cut on Euchilus, makes the wearer to be feared and respected by all people.

27. Winged horse, on any stone, is the best for soldiers, and gives speed and courage in battle; it also preserves horses from all diseases as long as they have it upon them.

28. Serpent twined round a bear, on any stone, makes the wearer cunning and steady of purpose.

29. Hercules, holding a club and slaying a lion or other monster, engraved on any stone, gives victory in battle.

30. Tree, vine, or wheat-ear, on any stone, makes one abound in food and clothing, and to have the favour of the great.

31 Mars in armour, or a Virgin in a long robe with a vestment wrapped about her, and holding a laurel-branch, cut on jasper, makes the wearer successful in all undertakings, defends him from violent death, and drowning and all accidents.

32. Mars, that is a figure holding a lance, on any stone, makes the bearer bold, warlike, and invincible.

33. Jupiter, the figure of a man with a ram's head, on any stone, makes the wearer beloved by all creatures, and to obtain whatever he may demand.

34. Capricorn, on carnelian, set in a silver ring, and carry about with thee, thou shalt never be harmed in purse or person by thine enemies, neither shall a judge pass an unjust sentence against thee; thou shalt abound in business and in honour, and gain the friendship of many, and all enchantments made against thee shall be of none effect, and no foe, however powerful, shall be able to resist thee in battle.*

* A very complete treatise on this subject has been published by G. Demay, Paris, 1877, with autotypes of ninety-seven specimens.

XXXI.

Thus the art slumbered on, seemingly destined never to be revived: all but totally extinct in the West; in the East confined to the production of the intricate convolutions of cyphers and monograms; when almost simultaneously with the first dawn of the revival of letters in Italy it not only woke up, but within the limits of a single lifetime attained to a second maturity, not merely rivalling its antique parent in skill and in taste, but in the one branch of cameo-engraving far exceeding her in the profusion, and frequently in the merit of its performances. Every experienced connoisseur has, in truth, perpetual occasion to echo the remark of the judicious Raspe, that by far the greater part of the camei one sees are works of the Cinque-cento school.

Towards the middle of the fifteenth century Italian art was fast growing more classical, having gradually freed itself from the trammels of Gothicism, "la secca maniera Tedesca," as Vasari aptly terms it, in proportion as the power of the German emperors waned away all over the peninsula. Vasari, in his 'Lives,' often alludes to the struggles going on, before this date, of men of genius to regain "Il bello," that is, the classical manner, and their blind, and mostly wild, attempts to emancipate themselves from a foreign style which they felt, not knowing wherefore, to be utterly repugnant to their nature.

The restoration of St. Peter's Chair to a native line of Popes, after its long removal and occupation by a Gallican dynasty, the creatures and the tools of the kings of France, contributed immensely to the bringing about of this complete revolution in the arts. The transition from barbarian stiffness, and the "crinkum-crankum" of the Gothic, to classical freedom and elegance, is plainly to be traced in all the works of the Quattro-cento school; in their sepulchres, bas-reliefs, ivory and wood carvings, and *nielli*. Donatello, who ended his long and industrious career in the year 1466, Vasari expressly states took *antique gems* and medals for his guide, "ritratti camei antichi e rovesci di medaglie," in the designing the eight bas-reliefs which still adorn the cortile of the Palazzo Ricardi, executed for his great patron, the elder Cosimo dei Medici. It will materially illustrate this part of our subject to specify what were these designs. They come in this order: the Rape of the Palladium—Hercules vanquished by Cupid—Hercules in the Garden of the Hesperides—an Oracle—the Triumph of Cupid—Ariadne surrounded by the Satyrs and Bacchantes—a Centaur—a

Slave kneeling before his Conqueror. All these subjects are evidently drawn from gems, most of them are very familiar to the collector—for, notwithstanding Vasari's addition (very probably made at random), none of them are to be found " on the reverses of medals."

The new-born passion for the remains of antiquity was necessarily compelled in the beginning to seek its gratification in the gems so long treasured up by their mediæval possessors for the sake of their intrinsic value or their supposed inherent and talismanic virtues, but which the newly opened eyes of a more cultivated generation had commenced to appreciate on the ground of their true merits. Pope Paul II., a Venetian by birth (whom we have already seen quoted by Vasari as inaugurating an era of *improvement* in the Glyptic art), had thus early (in 1464–71) formed a collection of gems in the spirit of a man of education and of taste, for Il Papiense records of him, " *Eruditos* oculos habens ad cernenda quæ præclari sunt operis, multa conquisivit a Græcia atque Asia atque aliis gentibus." In fact Majolo (Colloq. xvii.) makes him out a true martyr to his love for them, ascribing his death to a cold caught from the weight and chill of the rings with which the aged Pontiff was wont to overload his fingers—perhaps the most respectable occasion of death of any recorded in papal history, where the so frequent cause assigned is a dose of poison or a furious fit of passion.

To imitate these legacies of their Etruscan and Roman ancestors was the next step, and that far from a difficult one. The mechanical processes, themselves of the simplest nature, were already known to the Italians from their perpetual intercourse with the Mohammedans of the Levant, and the goldsmith who had worked from his youth at *niellatura* was, as far as drawing in miniature went, quite on a level with the Dioscorides and the Evodus of the Augustan Age. This is the reason why the art reached its second full development in so short a time, and without passing through any of the stages of infancy; for the few works that betray any influence of mediæval taste are, as the instances above collected, convincingly manifest, amongst the rarest of the rare.

By the end of the same century we find Camillo (Cesare Borgia's physician) praising four gem-engravers—Anichini of Ferrara, Gio, Maria of Mantua, Tagliacarne of Genoa, and Leonardo of Milan—as equal to any of the ancients in their profession; and furthermore stating that their works were diffused throughout all Italy—a sufficient proof of the previous length of time over which their labours had extended. And again that this art was amongst the first to revive in Italy, appears from the curious, though unsatisfactory notice, to which attention has been already directed, of the proficiency therein of the Florentine Peruzzi as early as the date 1379. The same inference is also to be legitimately drawn from the enigmatical expressions of Vasari, to interpret which an attempt has been made in the same section. But to come to historical data, they are to be found first in the continuation of the same passage of Vasari's, where, after quoting the epoch of Paul II., he goes on thus: "Thenceforward the art went on improving until Lorenzo dei Medici, a great amateur and collector of gems of all kinds, intagli, &c., and his son Piero, in order to introduce its cultivation into their dominions, invited thither a great number of masters from different countries, who, besides repairing (*rassettar*) the (antique) gems for them, brought along with them many fine things. From these masters a young man, afterwards surnamed from his occupation 'Giovanni delle Corniuole,' '*John of the Carnelians*,' learnt the art of engraving in *intaglio* through Lorenzo's encouragement." These "engravers from different countries" in all probability came from no more remote region than the north of Italy, the *ultima Thule* of a Tuscan's geography. It will be noticed that the four masters cited by Camillo as the most eminent in their profession are all from that region; and to the last Milan continued the head-quarters of the workers in crystal.

The pupil, this young Florentine, soon surpassed his instructors, for many years later, and after the Cinque-cento had burst forth in its full glory, the Grand Duke Francesco I. used to point out the head of Savonarola by him (a large intaglio in sard still preserved in the Galleria) as the finest piece in the whole collection; and this prince, despite his viciousness, was a man of exquisite taste. And besides this, his *capo d'opera*, "an infinity of his works both large and small," were to be seen when Vasari wrote.

XXXII.

The next century, the famous Cinque-cento, emblazons the familiar names of Valerio Belli il Vicentino, whose talents and industry were patronised equally by Clement VII. and Charles V.; Alessandro Cesati, surnamed *il Greco,* master of the mint to Paul III.; Matteo del Nazzaro, who served François I. in a similar capacity at Paris, where he trained up many pupils; Clement Birago and Jacopo da Trezzo, the first who engraved upon the diamond, and both enriched in the service of Philip II.; accompanied by an interminable array of others of nearly equal merit, whose works, for the most part *camei* (now in many cases passing for antique), constitute the choicest ornaments of every important cabinet.

The vast number of the practitioners of this art in the single city of Rome is clearly indicated by the quaint expression of Vasari, where, speaking of the first quarter of the century, he observes " Valerio was the cause that the profession in his time was swollen by so many recruits, that previous to the sack of Rome (1527) so vast a number had been drawn together thither from *Milan* and from other places, that it was a wonder to behold."

The recent application of the *wheel* and of the magnifying-glass to the processes of their art had enabled this newly created class to pour forth a flood of camei with a facility evidently not possessed by their brethren of antiquity; whilst the demand for them as personal ornaments for the neck-chain, for medallions to be worn in the cap, for inlaying in the elaborate pieces of plate, such favourites with the nobles of the age, far exceeded that for the works in *intaglio;* thus reversing what had been the rule in ancient times. It was the influence of this fashion that stimulated cameo-engraving to the remarkable degree which their present abundance remains to manifest—an abundance that astonishes all who are capable of recognising the stamp of the school. It is one sufficiently marked: the protuberance of the relief, often aided by *under-cutting*, and the perfect evenness of the field are technical criteria; whilst the picture-like grouping of the figures and their violent movement are artistic points strongly contrasting with the treatment of the antique works of the kind. In the latter the raised parts present the appearance of having been chiselled away with a cutting-instrument, the strokes of which are still perceptible in places; the ground is never perfectly levelled, the relief is flat, with its edges cut down perpendicularly to the lower stratum, whilst the entire design breathes the classic simplicity of the period that produced it.

To enumerate a few amongst the innumerable fine productions of Cinque-cento skill in this branch of art, that possess peculiar historical interest. First in the list stands the fatal ring, the love-gift of the Virgin Queen to Essex, the retention of which token by the treachery of the messenger Lady Nottingham, was the death-warrant of the supposed contumacious favourite. From Essex's daughter, Lady Frances Devereux, it has descended in an unbroken line of heritage from mother to daughter down to the present owner Lord John Thynne. It is set with a cameo bust of the Queen, most exquisitely cut on a miniature scale in a fine sardonyx of three layers: the ring itself is of a very simple but elegant form, and enamelled on the back with flowers in blue.

Lord Fitzhardinge again treasures a family relic of great artistic value in the celebrated "Hunsdon onyx." To quote Mr. Beck's accurate description, it is "a sardonyx of three strata, the lowest being a rich dark brown, representing the story of Perseus and Andromeda. The figure of Andromeda chained to the portico of a building on an island, the city on the coast at a distance, the animals on the trees adjoining the building, and the sea-monster in the foreground, are all most minutely and exquisitely worked. The cameo, which is on a stone of remarkable form and beauty, and the enamelled gold frame in which it is set, are works of the middle of the sixteenth century. This exquisite jewel was bequeathed by George Carey, second Lord Hunsdon, K.G. (who died in 1603), to his wife Elizabeth Spencer, and afterwards to his only daughter, Elizabeth Lady Berkeley, with strict injunctions to transmit the same to her posterity, with other jewels, to be preserved 'soo longe as the conscience of my heires shall have grace and honestie to perform my will; for that I esteeme them right jewels and monumentes worthie to be kept for their beautie, rareness, and that for monie they are not to be matched, nor the like yet knowen to be founde in this realme.' Height 3¼ inches, width the same."

A third very elaborate work of the same school was discovered by myself amongst the gems belonging to S. Bosanquet, Esq., of Dingestow House, Monmouth. It is a jewel of St. George, cut in high relief in precious sardonyx of several layers, 2 inches long by 1½ wide, in form an oval. The engraver has most skilfully availed himself of the numerous shades in his material to give effect to the different figures. The dragon is represented, the most prominent object, in the brown with a greenish reflex; the knight's body in a lighter shade of the same, but his face is rendered in an opaque white, as are likewise the forequarters of his steed—the trappings of the last are in a light brown. The Princess Saba, kneeling in the distance, is formed in the pure white of the stone; the trees have an actual shade of green assigned to their foliage. The execution of this cameo is truly wonderful—the dragon, St. George, and his horse, being in almost full relief, owing to which one fore-leg of the horse has suffered fracture. This work may, for its merit, be placed amongst the best of the Cinque-cento, and may on the same grounds be attributed either to Matteo del Nazzaro, chief-engraver to François I., or perhaps with more probability to that pupil of his (whose name is unknown) who has left us such extraordinary portraits, in cameo, of Henry VIII. and his family, two of which are in the Royal and one in the Devonshire cabinet of gems. This sardonyx is mounted in a simple gold frame, surrounded with a thin cable border, streaked with black enamel. The back presents an elegant enrichment, in green enamel, imitating a laurel-wreath. Being a piece of such extreme costliness, if we consider the estimation in which similar works were held at the period of its execution, there seems good reason to suppose it a jewel worn either by Henry himself, or by one of his three children and successors, as what is properly termed the "Jewel of the Garter,"—a distinct thing from the "George" itself, which is necessarily of *gold.* This supposition as to its first ownership is confirmed by the Tudor rose, engraved upon the lid of the massy rudely-made original silver box, which continues to serve for its receptacle.

Although its cameo-works constituted the chief glory of this school, yet one class of *intagli*, namely, those cut in square or oval plaques of rock-crystal, and upon a gigantic scale, were special favourites with its wealthy patrons. Amongst such plaques are to be found the choicest remains of Valerio il Vicentino, and of his rival Gio. del Castel Bolognese. By a return, probably undesigned, to a fashion already noticed as flourishing in the Carlovingian period, these crystals were particularly made for the decoration of church-plate, generally being framed in the precious metals for the panels of coffers, or for the other furniture of the altar, such as crucifixes and candlesticks. Hence the usually Scriptural character of the designs they present. The fewer examples with profane or amatory subjects were similarly introduced into the ornamentation of the sumptuous works of the goldsmith that loaded the beaufets of every nobleman of the times.

Camei, on the other hand, embellished the dresses, and even the armour of the noble and the wealthy, and their employment brought about a revolution in fashion, the exact converse of that we have noticed as taking place under the Lower Empire. These gem-works *now* replace the broad gold medallions of the preceding generation in the bonnet and in the pendent jewel.

XXXIII.

From the middle of this century downwards all the arts of design, this included, began to decline with lamentable rapidity. They had lost their former patrons, the grand old Popes and Cardinals, like Leo X., Clement VII., Paul III., Cornaro, Salviati, Ippolito dei Medici, Alessandro Farnese, true Romans of the Cæsarian epoch, in their lives as in their tastes, more than half Pagan by their education, magnificent even in their vices, which in truth were far less pernicious to society than the sour virtues, pushed to excess, of the bigots of the succeeding generation. In the place of Charles V., François I., and the Medicean Popes, gloomy, scrupulous bigots now rule Church and State; we have Pius IV. instead of Leo X. In the place of the old princely, *un*-moral ecclesiastics, appear, on the one side, the Jesuits, with their soul-crushing system, encountered on the other part by the equally degrading tyranny of the Calvinistic creed. In a word, the most *uncomfortable* period of European history is that lying between the death of Charles V. (1558) and the accession of Louis XIV., or nearly a complete century. War, pestilence, famine, desolated every region in its turn, and gallery after gallery of the choicest works of art accumulated in better times, fell a prey to the brutal soldiery at the successive captures of the different capitals.

Thus it was that the Seventeenth Century, the unproductive and much contemned *Seicento* of the Italians, the parent of the *Barocco* in architecture and sculpture, from all these causes combined, witnessed, not merely a decline, but even a considerable retrogression in all the arts. As a necessary consequence, there is a vast falling off perceptible in the quantity, as well as in the quality of the glyptic works of this period, that art being the first to suffer from the decay of national prosperity. Its remains, such as they are, chiefly consist in the heads of deities and philosophers coarsely and deeply cut in stones of large size; or else unskilful copies of works belonging to a better period. There is only a single artist in this line, Coldoré (Julien de Fontenay), chief engraver to Henri IV., who is now remembered from his works as having flourished in this age; and even his education, and much of his artistic career, ought rather to be referred to the closing years of the Cinque-cento. He has perpetuated the satyr-like features of his illustrious patron over and over again in the most precious materials, the sapphire, the emerald, and the ruby; the most noteworthy of his works being the portrait in the last-named stone, bearing the date 1598 (Orleans). But in point of real merit, nothing comes up to his cameo portraits of our Queen Elizabeth, on account of which his master had specially despatched him to her Court. The two most important known to me (there are everywhere to be seen a multitude of *repliche* in miniature) form, the one the chief ornament of Her Majesty's Collection, the other of the Orleans. Both are in sardonyx of considerable size, inimitable in the treatment of the face, equally so in the rendering of the elaborate costume of the splendour-loving Virgin-Queen.

XXXIV.

The next century, however, the Eighteenth, emphatically the age of the *dilettanti*, brought with its very opening a sudden and most unexpected revival in both branches of our subject. This recovery is more especially noticeable in that of intaglio-engraving, which now, from certain causes, hereafter to be explained, received as much attention from practitioners as that of cameo-cutting had met with from the most eminent of the Revival. But there is one great distinction to be remarked between the style of the school now under our consideration, and that so markedly characterising all the productions in the same department of the Cinque-cento. The latter (as Visconti has well pointed out) was no servile copyist of the antique, but borrowing thence its subjects, treated them in its own peculiar style, and this with a spirit and a vivacity which brought forth really original works. But the artists of the last century, totally disclaiming all attempts at originality, contented themselves, as a rule, with making repeated copies of the most noted antique gems, and placed the highest aim of their ambition in the successful, imposing upon credulous amateurs with their own productions as genuine and recently discovered works of antiquity.

Amongst the few to be acquitted of this charge stands the one, who is also justly regarded as the head of the school, John Pichler, who flourished during the second half of the century. He was the son of Anton Pichler, a Tyrolese engraver, likewise of some merit, established at Naples, and had a younger brother Louis, who rivalled him, especially in cameo work. Our *monetarius* Marchant, the elegant competitor of Pichler's, deserves no less praise for his honesty. The same also may be awarded to Natter and to Rega, the first at the beginning, the second at the close of the century; that is to say, after their own reputation had been established, for both of them commenced their career by executing and bringing into the market as antique many a fine piece, which still in that character embellishes royal and princely collections. Of these artists, Natter was a native of Nuremberg, but settled early at Rome, where he long worked under the auspices of Baron Stosch; and having emigrated thence to London, he was liberally patronised by our nobility, notably by the Dukes of Devonshire and Marlborough. Many of his later works may be recognised by the *snake* in the field, the rebus on the German *Natter*. Rega passed the whole of his industrial life at Naples: in my opinion he is the first of the moderns; his intagli are more than copies, they have all the spirit of the Greeks, whose coins he took for his models.

This century may justly be denominated the "Age of Forgery," fraud of every kind and degree now flourishing with wondrous luxuriance. Besides the making of the most exact facsimiles of famous antiques, a thing which at the least required and developed great technical skill, other devices infinitely more dishonourable were brought into play. The fabrication of *doublets* (where a glass-paste, moulded upon an antique work, and backed with a slice of sard carefully attached by a transparent cement, and, lastly, set so as to conceal the union, so that the combination has all the appearance of a true stone, whilst the work upon it, in point of treatment and execution, satisfies the minutest scrutiny) was now borrowed from the falsifiers of precious stones, and carried to such perfection as frequently to deceive the most practised eye; the *retouching* of antique works of the ruder class, the surest and the most hardly detected of all modes of deception; and, finally, the interpolation of imaginary artists' names upon genuine antiques, a trick engendered by the universal, though utterly baseless belief, that every ancient engraver regularly signed his best performances, and by the reluctance, springing from this belief, of wealthy but ignorant *dilettanti* to purchase even the finest monuments of his skill, unless recommended by such an indorsement. The temptation, therefore, to the interpolator was irresistible; Casanova, the painter, mentions the instance of a fine antique that, after having had its merit thus certified, readily obtained *four* times the price at which it previously had been offered in vain.

Gem-collecting had now grown into a perfect mania with the noble and the rich: the first great impetus being imparted by the arch-charlatan Baron Stosch (a Hanoverian spy over the Pretender's motions), by the formation of his enormous cabinet and its illustration by the labours of the erudite Winckelmann, with its final purchase at the enormous price of 30,000 ducats by the reputed model of the prince-philosopher, Frederic of Prussia. The Duc d'Orléans, grandson of the Regent, followed his example; our own Dukes of Devonshire and Marlborough were, concurrently with the French prince, zealously at work in forming their present magnificent cabinets, paying incredible sums for gems of any celebrity. The former acquired from Stosch, for the equivalent of 1000*l.*, the *Cow* of Apollonides, and from Sevin of Paris, at the same rate, the *Diomede with the Palladium;* the latter nobleman, says La Chaux, purchased from Zanetti, of Venice (1763), four gems for the sum of 1200*l.*: they are the *Phocion* of Alessandro il Greco, the *Horatius Cocles* (a miniature Cinque-cento cameo), the *Antinous*, and the *Matidea;* all still adorning the cabinet at Blenheim. The large cameo of *Vespasian* cost the same amateur (according to Raspe) 300 guineas. The same portrait in cameo, but restyled a *Mæcenas*, stood his emulator, Mr. Yorke, in 250. The fine intaglio, *Hercules and the Dying Amazon*, cost its acquirer, Mr. Boyd, another 300; and to conclude this list of the extravagances of the taste, the *Hercules and Lion* intaglio in sardonyx, in its antique silver mounting (found in Aleppo), was considered cheap, by Mr. Locke, at the figure of 200 guineas.

The Empress Catherine II. entered the lists with her accustomed energy, and amalgamated several well-known cabinets into a single one of unrivalled extensiveness. Such a possession (equally with that of a porcelain-fabrique of one's own establishment) was deemed an indispensable appendage for every prince making any pretensions to the character of a man of taste; and how irresistibly the tide of fashion set in this direction is exemplified, better than by anything else, by the single fact that our bucolical sovereign George III. (a man of more liking for cows than for camei) was carried away by the torrent, and sought to establish his reputation by making his own the highly-puffed collection of Consul Smith. He published his new character and his acquisition to the world of amateurs by the means of two magnificent folios, the 'Dactyliotheca Smithiana,' brought out at Venice (1767), illustrated with the finest engraving the period could supply, and with a learned text by Gori, who had then succeeded to the reputation of Winckelmann.

Last of all came the affected classicism of the Republic and the First Empire to stimulate the mania to its very highest point. Gems, antique or supposed, graced every piece of jewelry, were wrought up into *solitaires*, tiaras, and earrings, and even, after the precedent of Heliogabalus, decorated the *toes* of the sandalled feet of the Parisian *lionnes*.

The Empress Josephine was a passionate gem-collector, the choicest treasures of continental museums flowed into her cabinet, peace-offerings from their owners now trembling for their thrones. She caused a complete suite of ornaments to be made up out of the first gems of the old Royal Collection under the direction of the *savant* Denon.

It is this period, and its fruits, that have thrown so much uncertainty into the study of gems, and have rendered so difficult the deciding as to the genuineness of a fine intaglio if judged of by the work alone, irrespective of technical and mineralogical considerations. This indeed is one of the most difficult questions that can be proposed to the archæologist, however much attention he may have paid to this particular subject. From the very opening of the century, Sirletti, famed for his revival of the antique use of the diamond-point in engraving (at the suggestion, says his contemporary Giulianelli, of the experienced Stosch), Costanzi, Anton Pichler, Landi, Rossi, and innumerable others, all more or less skilful imitators of the antique manner, were indefatigably pursuing this most lucrative of trades, and have left a countless swarm of such falsifications to mislead and perplex collectors for all time to come. It may be asserted with confidence that for every antique gem of note fully a dozen of its counterfeits are now in circulation; and often so close is the imitation as to throw doubt upon the authenticity of the original itself. The larger intagli, more particularly the imperial portraits, have been the most exposed to this fraudulent reproduction.

The anxiety of these moderns in disguise to make sure of the true antique character in their designs is remarkably exemplified by a fact communicated formerly to an acquaintance of mine by a very aged amateur, Mr. Constable, who had known Rome in the palmy days of gem-engraving. These artists used to be always seeking after, and paying liberally for, antique pastes with unhackneyed subjects, which, after minutely copying in their own gems, they immediately destroyed, thus at one stroke securing the antique spirit for their own compositions, and safety against the detection of plagiarism. This multitudinousness of counterfeits, added to the discredit brought upon the critical knowledge of connoisseurs by their admission into the cabinets of persons (Payne Knight, for instance, so egregiously taken in with Pistrucci's Flora) pretending to the completest experience in this line, may be assigned as one of the main causes of that sudden and total decay of the taste for gems which prevails in our own times.

XXXV.

After Coldoré France gave birth to no engraver deserving to be remembered, except Guay, who worked for Louis XV., and who has left an admirable cameo-portrait of his patron. The goldsmith to the same King, Louis Siries, exhausted his ingenuity in attempts to achieve microscopic impossibilities, mightily esteemed at the time; even attacking the diamond, in emulation of Costanzi, but with little success. Several of his minute gems are now to be seen in English cabinets, they may be recognised by his initials, L. S., in the field.

The few *Englishmen* who have ever distinguished themselves in this walk of art, all (with the exception of T. Simon, Cromwell's inimitable medallist) flourished at different periods of the eighteenth century and through the first quarter of the present. It will here suffice to name Stuart, Seaton, the two Browns, Wray, Deane, Harris, Marchant (established at Rome, and especially patronised by the Duke of Marlborough and other English noblemen), and Burch, R.A., who closes the list in 1814. The Roman Pistrucci, on the grounds of his long residence and reputation achieved in this country, belongs rather to the category of English than Italian masters. At the beginning of his career he enjoyed the most exalted patronage, and his merit, though certainly great, was more than proportionally recompensed; receiving as much as 800*l.* for a single cameo. One of his gems, a Greek hero on horseback, had the honour to be selected by his patron, Lord Maryborough, as the type (after slight modification) of the reverse of the sovereign when issued for the first time in the great recoinage of 1816. The hero transformed thus into a St. George, besides the gold, decorates the crown-piece of the same mintage, and again on somewhat a larger scale that of George IV.; the latter, beyond all rivalry, the most elegant coin ever issued from a modern mint.

The works of this English school, *intagli* for the most part, though fine and carefully drawn, fall far short of the vigour and spirit displayed by the great names of the contemporary Italian. With the last representatives of that school, Cerbara and Girometti, who survived until within these few years, the Glyptic art may be said to have a second time expired, but to have expired with dignity. By both these its professors it had been carried to a perfection hardly ever attained before, and assuredly never surpassed.

Far from producing works embodying equal genius and commanding equal remuneration with the masterpieces of painting and sculpture, nothing of this elegant art now survives even in Rome, so long its favourite seat, except in the shape of a few miserable craftsmen—they cannot be called artists—who manufacture the small onyx cameo-studs so much in request with the visitors to that city—mere trade-articles turned out by the dozen at the least possible expenditure of time and labour—and who also, but in a small way, continue to fabricate to order *antique* intagli of the mediocre class, or to retouch such fresh discoveries as the dealers consider susceptible of improvement. In a word, the sole representatives of the once national profession who display any intelligence of beauty or tasteful workmanship in their labours (though surpassed in both by their Parisian rivals) are the cutters of camei upon shell; their material being the Indian conch, whose diversely-coloured layers cheaply counterfeit the contrasting tints of the Sardonyx. The substance is sufficiently soft to admit of being worked with the graver and scraper, by which the design in relief is brought out in the same manner as carvings in ivory and boxwood. This circumstance, therefore, removes the invention from the true province of gem-engraving to that of wood-carving.

Thus, therefore, by a most remarkable peristrophe, the art of cutting designs in the precious and hard stones may be considered as having closed its existence of thirty centuries in the same phase from which it started at the very daybreak of civilization. When the Egyptian fabricated the primal scarabæi out of the yielding steaschist, his first essay was a work in relief, a religious symbol of talismanic virtue, intended for embellishing the necklace or the bracelet; and so in our times the Roman shell-camei, formed in an equally valueless material, and manufactured for the same purpose, are the sole remains that preserve the faintest shadow of the departed glories of the Glyptic art.

FAMOUS RINGS AND SIGNETS.

THE most ancient and most wondrous in the long catalogue of famous rings recorded by the writers of antiquity, is that of Gyges, the Lydian. Plato relates in his 'Republic' how he, when a mere shepherd, espied in a chasm opened by the winter rains a monstrous horse of brass, which served for the sepulchre of some giant of old, which chamber of death he boldly entering, took off the skeleton's finger a ring. Returning to his brother shepherds, he found accidentally that by turning the face of this ring inside his hand he became invisible; whereupon, profiting by its mystic power, he murdered his master King Candaules, and took possession of his queen and kingdom, the most beautiful woman and the wealthiest region of all Asia. The crime was, after the Eastern fashion, visited upon the head of his innocent descendant Crœsus.

Next comes the love-inspiring ring of Helen, touching which Ptolemy Hephæstion relates (B. VIII.) that there is a certain fish of the whale kind, called *Pan*, and in appearance resembling that rustic deity. In its head is found the stone called *Asterites*, which, when placed in the sun, blazes forth like a flame. It is of mighty potency as a philtre, and this was the gem Helen wore for her signet, having the self-same fish, the *Pan*, engraved thereon. Suidas gives the same legend on the authority of Æsopus, "reader to King Mithridates." A proof this how universal had become the faith in the power of talismans, when even Helen's conquests were ascribed to the virtue of a philtre. These deep philosophers did not agree with the simple-minded Tibullus as to the resistless might of beauty, or hold with him that

"Forma nihil magicis utitur auxiliis."

But to descend from the regions of fable into those of authentic history, we come to the strange yet probably true story about the ring of Polycrates, the tyrant of Samos, so particularly detailed by

Herodotus. This too successful tyrant and pirate being himself alarmed by his own vast and unbroken prosperity, took counsel of the sage Amasis, the Egyptian, and following his advice, propitiated Nemesis by throwing into the sea his signet, which he regarded as the most precious of his treasures, thinking by the sacrifice of this one object he had amply, as Pliny expresses it, compounded for all the favours heaped upon him by capricious Fortune. But the ring was swallowed by a fine fish, which, being caught the same day, was brought by the captor as a present to his prince, the ring found in its belly, and restored to its astonished owner. But his end verified the predictions of the Egyptian king, atoning once for all and more than amply (as is Fortune's rule in such cases) for his past felicity; for, betrayed into the hands of the satrap Orœtes, he closed his career by impalement: his first sacrifice of atonement having been rejected and thrown back upon his hands as inadequate by the malignant ruler of events.

Kirchmann, in that wonderful repertory of curious learning, his treatise 'De Annulis' (cap. xxiii.) has collected several anecdotes in illustration of this legend of the "Fish and Ring," of which it will not be out of place to copy here the most remarkable. The first, from the character of the narrator and the publicity and recent date (at the time of its publication) of the circumstances, will doubtless be received as authentic by all who possess so much knowledge of things as to be able to judge when to believe as well as when to disbelieve—for ignorance is incredulous in the wrong place as well as credulous. Let us hear the story told by St. Augustine, bishop of the city where it happened, and who has deemed it worthy of insertion in his great work 'De Civitate Dei' (xxii. 8):—

"There lived an old man, a fellow-townsman of ours at Hippo, Florentius by name, by trade a tailor, a religious poor person. He had lost his cloak and had not wherewith to buy another. Going to the church of the Twenty Martyrs, whose memory is held in the highest veneration amongst us, he prayed with a loud voice for wherewith to clothe himself. Certain ribald youths who happened to be present overheard him, and followed him as he went down, mocking at him as though he had demanded of the martyrs the sum of fifty *folles* (6½ denarii) to clothe himself withal. But Florentius, walking on without replying to them, espied a big fish thrown up by the sea and struggling upon the beach, and it he secured through the good-natured assistance of the same youths, and sold it for 300 *folles* (37½ denarii) to a certain cook, by name Carthosus, a good Christian, for pickling, telling him at the same time all that had taken place—intending to buy wool with the money, so that his wife might make therewith, as well as she could, something to clothe him. But the cook, in cutting up the fish, found in its belly a gold ring, and forthwith being moved with compassion as well as influenced by religious scruples, restored it to Florentius, saying, 'Behold how the Twenty Martyrs have clothed thee!'"

Petrus Damianus, too, a very unlikely personage to have ever read of Polycrates, relates in his Fifth Epistle a story worth translating literally, as a specimen of the style of thought of his age:—"This Arnulphus was the father of King Pepin and grandfather of Charlemagne, and when inflamed with the fervour of the Holy Ghost, he sacrificed the love of wife and children, and exchanged the glory and pomps of this world for the glorious poverty of Christ, it chanced as he was hastening into the wilderness that in his way he had to cross a river which is called the Moselle; but when he reached the middle of the bridge thrown over it, where the river's stream ran deepest, he tossed in there his own ring, with this protestation, 'When I shall receive back,' said he, 'this ring from the foaming waves of this river, then will I trust confidently that I am loosed from the bonds of all my sins.' Thereupon he made for the wilderness, where he lived no little space dead unto himself and the world. Meanwhile the then Bishop of Metz having died, Divine Providence raised Arnulphus to the charge of that see. Continuing in his new office to abstain from eating flesh, according to the rule observed by him in the wilderness, once upon a time a fish was brought him for a present. The cook, in gutting the same, found in its entrails a ring, and ran full of joy to present it to his master; which ring the blessed Bishop no sooner cast eyes upon than he knew it again for his own, and wondered not so much at the strange mine that had brought forth the metal as that by the Divine propitiation he had obtained the forgiveness of his sins."

An exact description of this long-famed jewel of the Samean tyrant can be obtained by putting together the accounts of the event, as related by various authors. Herodotus expressly terms it "a signet of emerald, set in gold, the work of Theodorus of Samos" (iii. 41). Pausanias has (viii. 14), "a work of Theodorus was also the signet in the emerald which Polycrates, tyrant of Samos, was accustomed to wear, and on the possession of which he prided himself excessively." Clemens Alexandrinus furthermore informs us what device was engraven upon it: "the musical lyre that Polycrates had for his seal." By a singular coincidence an emerald was, a few years ago, brought to Rome, said to have been just turned up in a vineyard at Aricia, in which enthusiastic antiquaries immediately recognised this legendary signet, from the agreement both of stone and type with the ancient tradition. The emerald was large and of the finest quality befitting so wealthy an owner, the intaglio a lyre beautifully executed, above which hovered three bees, or more probably *cigale,* an insect noted by the poets for its musical powers, and which, though of much greater bulk, resembles in appearance a large drone. This type of a lyre often occurs upon gems: there can be little doubt it was adopted from the traditionary account of Polycrates' signet; it was moreover in its nature, as Apollo's attribute, a fitting device for a man of letters. Pliny, however, records a curious fact, that in his time the pretended signet of Polycrates used to be shown in the shape of a sardonyx, not engraved, "intacta illibata," set in a golden cornucopia in the Temple of Concord, and holding there but the last place amidst a multitude of other gems, all preferred to it as of higher value. It is hard to conceive how this history came to be affixed to this particular *sardonyx,* in defiance of the express testimony of Herodotus, who flourished hardly a century after the occurrence. Lessing, indeed, in order to support Pliny's tale, quibbles, like a true German critic, at a vast expenditure of learning, to prove that the term σφρηγίς does not necessarily signify an *engraved* stone, and that the expression "the work of Theodorus" only refers to the setting itself! because that artist was famous for certain ingenious works in metal, executed for King Alyattes in the preceding generation. But Herodotus and the Greeks of his day would have made little account of the goldsmith's work in the mere setting: it was the *emerald,* then a priceless stone, rendered yet more rare by the intaglio from so famous a hand (the artist, too, being in all probability then no more), that was deemed a sacrifice of such importance. But, in truth, there is no exception to the rule in classic Greek that a precious stone, regarded merely as such, is termed ἡ λίθος, or else ψῆφος, the *lapillus* of the Latins, but when *engraved* it becomes σφραγίς. As a proof, Theophrastus speaks of the λίθοι out of which σφρηγῖδες are cut. Herodotus also uses the latter word in describing the *seals* of the Babylonians, who certainly never were acquainted with the use of finger rings. But the ancient goldsmith was like his Florentine fellow-craftsman in the flourishing days of art, at once jeweller, statuary, and gem-engraver, as well as die-sinker. And Theodorus of Samos became to the Roman dilettanti what Cellini is to those of our day, the reputed author of every work of extraordinary unfathered cleverness. Thus Pliny mentions a portrait-statue of the artist himself, then preserved at Rome, holding upon his outstretched hand a four-horse car, so minute that a fly with outspread wings could cover both car, horses, and driver.

The earliest notice we have of the device upon a Greek's signet is connected with a touching anecdote. When Clearchus, Cyrus the younger's general, had been treacherously made prisoner by Tisaphernes, and was languishing in chains before his execution, he begged for a comb (for his long flowing hair, worn after the Spartan fashion), which indulgence he at last obtained through Ctesias, the royal physician. As a return for the favour, he presented the latter with his signet to serve as a means of introduction to his family, should the other ever find himself in Sparta. Its device was the maidens of Carya dancing. Ctesias himself tells the story, quoted by Plutarch in his life of Cyrus.

Alexander the Great forbade as treasonable his portrait to be engraved on gems by any less noted artist than Pyrgoteles; and from Pliny's mode of expressing himself, viz., "in hac gemma," it would appear that the *emerald* was the only stone accounted worthy of so high an honour.* After his conquest of Asia, Alexander used the "ring of Darius" for sealing his edicts addressed to the Persians, but his paternal signets for those issued to the Greeks. The device upon the latter was a lion passant, with a club in the field above in allusion to Hercules, the founder of the Macedonian line: such, at least, was the imprint on the signet wherewith Philip dreamed he had sealed up the womb of his queen Olympias, a vision interpreted both as a token of her pregnancy and also of the future greatness of the expected infant. In commemoration of this presage, Alexander subsequently founded a city, named Leontopolis.† Moreover his only coins, the hemidrachms, that

* The emerald continued set apart for the royal signet with his successors. When Ptolemy Lathyrus escorted Lucullus, returning to Rome, to his ship, he pressed upon him an emerald "of the precious sort" set in a ring: which the disinterested Roman could only be induced to accept by the monarch's showing him that it bore his own image, so that to refuse it were a personal affront.

† One of his generals and successors to his empire, Seleucus, could boast of a signet of divine origin. His mother dreamed that "she had conceived a son by Apollo, and that the god had left behind him his ring in acknowledgment of the paternity. On awaking, she actually found a signet-ring in her bed, engraved with an anchor; and the same mark was discovered impressed upon the thigh of the infant when born in due time after the vision, and continued to appear thus stamped on all his posterity for many generations."—*Justin. XV.* In commemoration of this legend, an anchor is the common reverse of the bronze coinage of the Seleucidæ.

give us his actual portrait with Ammon's horn, bear a lion for reverse. Even at this early period every man had a fixed device for his signet, as well known and as unchangeable as our armorial bearings. Quintus Curtius, in his Life of Alexander, mentions a conspiracy detected in consequence of a letter being brought to an officer of his army, bearing an *unknown* seal, which on inquiry proved to come from an agent of Darius, containing proposals for the assassination of the king.

Unfortunately no author has recorded the device upon the signet of his Persian adversary, although we may safely conclude it to have been identical with that of a Darius (perhaps the same) now preserved in the British Museum, a cylinder in a greenish calcedony (the jaspis of the Greeks), representing the king in his car, with the cuneiform legend in the field, in three different dialects, "I Darius, the king." But we labour under the "embarras de richesses" in the varying descriptions left us of the signet of his ancestor Xerxes which authenticated his communications with the Spartan king Pausanias; for the scholiast upon Thucydides (i. 129) has: "The signet of the king of the Persians bore, according to some, the monarch's own portrait; according to others that of Cyrus, the founder of the monarchy; or as others again say, the horse of Darius, in virtue of whose neighing he had been elected king." But Polyænus distinctly states that the device was a naked woman, with her hair dishevelled, a type, according to him, commemorating the tradition that their queen Rhodogune (the same story is told of the more ancient Semiramis), rushing in this state out of the bath, had quelled a revolt of her subjects—apparently a Greek fiction, coined (after their wont, rather than to confess ignorance) to explain the figure of *Anaitis*, the Babylonian Venus, so frequently represented in this guise upon the cylinders.

The frequency of the portraits of the Macedonian hero upon gems, the work of widely different ages, arose from such portraits being worn as amulets down to a very late period, Chrysostom (at the close of the fourth century) noting the custom in his own day of wearing Alexander's coins, fastened to the head or feet as charms to keep off sickness (Hom. ii.). Trebellius Pollio, speaking of the family Macriana, says that the ladies belonging to it wore the portraits of Alexander *engraved* (necessarily, therefore, on gems) in their hair-cauls in their bracelets and in their rings; adding that it was the common persuasion that persons who carried about them the likeness of Alexander in gold or silver prospered in everything they undertook.

To return once more to the poets: Sophocles, as above adduced, makes Electra recognise her brother Orestes on his producing his father's signet. The scholiast is careful to inform us, perhaps following some ancient tradition, that it was engraved "with the ivory shoulder of Pelops," meaning (the only way in which it can be understood) the bust of a youth displaying that part in a significant manner. The signet of a still older Grecian monarch, the Theban Amphitryon, is described by Plautus in the comedy of that name, in the dialogue between Mercury and Sosias:—

"*S.* Where is the bowl now?
"*M.* Locked up in my trunk,
Sealed with Amphitryon's seal.
"*S.* Say what's the impression?
"*M.* Sol rising with his car. Why seek to entrap me,
Thou gallows-bird?"

Doubtless Plautus, whose plays are all mere adaptations from the Greek, had old authority for putting such a device upon the Theban king's signet.

The Spartan magistrates in the times of the traveller Pausanias, the second century, used for their official seal the head of Polydorus, one of their ancient kings; but no reason is assigned why, above all the rest, this unknown prince should have been preferred for that distinction, in circumstances where one would naturally have looked for the image of their far-famed legislator Lycurgus, which, in fact, formed the type on the later coinage of Lacedemon.

We have an interesting notice of the signet of another Spartan monarch of the last times of the dynasty in Josephus (xxi. 5). Areius, "king of the Lacedemonians," as he there is styled, thus ends his letter addressed to Onias, the high priest of the newly re-established state of Jerusalem: "The seal is an eagle grasping a serpent in its talons." A customary conclusion to a letter was this description of the seal, in order to prevent its being opened and resealed with another signet on the way. It is singular that this group of the eagle and serpent is described by Nicetas amongst the miracles of art standing in the Hippodrome of Constantinople, and afterwards melted down for coin by the barbarian Franks on their capture of the city in 1204. The vulgar, he adds, then regarded it as a talisman delivering the city from all such venomous reptiles, set up by the most eminent of all magicians, Apollonius Tyaneus; but it was, in truth, an inheritance from the original city of Byzantium.

Callicrates, a courtier of Ptolemy III., took so great a pride in his profession of parasite, says Athenæus, in his amusing anecdotes of that class (vi. 251), that he adopted for his signet the head of Ulysses, and named his children Telegonus and Anticlea, after those of the Ithacan wanderer, who amongst the later Greeks had been put down as the prototype of the genus Parasite, upon the strength of his so long quartering himself upon the hospitality of King Alcinous. Others, besides Callicrates, were not ashamed of the same profession, for a fine intaglio in the Spilsbury Gems (No. 17) represents one carrying what Plautus (Stich. ii. 1, 55) calls the "totam supellectilem," entire stock-in-trade of the fraternity:—

"Rubiginosum strigilem, ampullam rubidam."

"A rusty scraper, a red earthen oil-cruse."

The sophist Aristion, on his return from his embassy to Mithridates, is carried in state (in the account preserved by Athenæus) into Athens, reclining upon a litter with legs of silver and coverings of purple. He takes up his quarters in the house of Dies, the richest of the inhabitants; which is furnished for his reception, at the public cost, with grand hangings, pictures, statues, and a vast display of plate. Out of this palace he used to strut, trailing behind him a gorgeous mantle, and wearing a gold ring engraved with the portrait of Mithridates. Here it may be observed that the heads of this prince are rather frequent in gems, for he was evidently very popular amongst the Greeks, who hailed him as their deliverer from the burdensome yoke of the Romans, who, like ourselves, seem to have had the fatality of making themselves universally detested to the nations subject to their supremacy. His portrait, particularly in the arrangement of the flowing locks, is evidently treated after the Apollo type in allusion to his name, which is equivalent to the Grecian Heliodorus, or "gift of the sun." He was, besides, a prince who appreciated and encouraged the arts, for his coins are amongst the most beautiful in the whole Greek regal series, a thing hardly to be expected at so late an epoch and from a semi-barbarian like the Pontic king. Being the first on record to have formed a collection of gems, his memory should be held in reverence by all lovers of the Glyptic art.

Wonderful, indeed, as a work of sportive Nature must have been the famous agate always worn by King Pyrrhus in his ring, if it actually, as Pliny quotes from some old annalist, did "represent, by its natural shades, Apollo holding his lyre and standing amidst the Muses Nine, each one bearing her proper attribute." The veins and colours of the stone must have been amazingly assisted, either by art or by the lively imagination of the beholder, to have pictured so complicated a group upon the narrow field of a ring-stone. After all, it may have been no more than a cameo, the production of a newly-invented art, and passed off by the jocose Greek upon the simple-minded Roman envoys as a natural prodigy. We have actually an analogous case already brought before us in the great sardonyx cameo decorating the shrine of St. Elizabeth at Marburg, which, during the whole course of the Middle Ages, used to be regarded with veneration by pilgrims as the unassisted workmanship of Nature. Agricola also mentions an agate naturally representing two busts with a serpent between, preserved (in the fifteenth century) in Cologne Cathedral; in all likelihood alluding to one of the camei set in the shrine of the Three Kings. Nevertheless, agates are still found adorned with designs which one feels the greatest difficulty in admitting to be the mere fortuitous result of the arrangement of their shaded strata, so exactly does that result imitate the finished production of art. Amongst the specimens of the variety called the "Egyptian Pebble," in the British Museum, there is one representing the head of Chaucer covered with the hood as in the well-known portrait of him, the resemblance of which is most astonishing, and yet this pebble is evidently in its original state, not even polished, but merely broken in two. The jewel-room of the Florentine Galleria possesses a red and yellow agate where the shades accurately depict a Cupid running; as well as some other specimens of such self-created miniatures. Among the gems of the Strawberry Hill Collection is catalogued "a rare Egyptian Pebble naturally representing Voltaire in his night-gown and cap; set in gold:" also "another representing with the utmost exactness the portrait of a woman in profile, a rock behind her and sky before, set in gold, and accounted very curious." Some others, and yet more singular, are specified in the 'Description of the Hope Precious Stones,' drawn up by B. Hertz. The known existence of these nature-paintings elucidates an epigram by Claudian, entitled "On a table of sardonyx stone;" which is somewhat obscure by reason of its too flowery style, and at first sight rather suggests the notion of a mosaic being intended, although there can be no doubt, after a careful consideration, that the poet wishes to describe the actual colouring and shades of the native stone.

Ep. XLIV. In Mensam de sardonyche lapide.

"Mensa coloratis aquilæ sinuatur in alis
Quem floris distinguit honos similisque figura
Texitur, implumem mentitur gemma volatum."

"The coloured veins that o'er my surface play
An eagle's form with dusky wings portray,
With native hues traced on the flowered stone
A life-like figure to perfection shown:
Formed in the gem, the picture seems to fly,
And, wingless, cheats the wondering gazer's eye."

Ismenias, a famous musician, and contemporary with Alexander, on hearing the description of an *emerald* engraved with the figure of the nymph Amymone, which was for sale somewhere in Cyprus at the price of six gold staters (exactly six guineas), took a fancy to it, and commissioned a friend to buy it for him. His envoy, by hard bargaining, beat down the price, and brought him back both the gem and two staters out of the six sent; but was rewarded for his pains by the complaint of the purse-proud man of music that he had done very ill, for that he had lowered by so much the dignity of the gem. This is the sole instance known to me of the then current value of an engraved gem: and even here, from the stone being intrinsically valuable, one cannot pronounce whether the *emerald* or the *intaglio* formed the chief element in the estimate. Ismenias, observes Pliny, set the example to all others of the same profession to make a mighty display of such ornaments as an essential part of their equipment in public: hence his rival Dionysiodorus attempted to outshine him in this piece of ostentation,* as did also a third artiste named Nicomachus. The collection of the last, it is recorded, though extensive, was made without either knowledge or taste, exactly what might have been expected from a fiddler dabbling in matters that demand a competent share of both.

It has been already mentioned how the great Julius is noted by Suetonius for a passionate amateur in engraved gems, as in all other branches of the antique art: *antique* being the highest recommendation even in those days. His own signet was a Venus Victrix, a fact which sufficiently explains the popularity of that subject under the reigns of his successors in the Empire. "Cæsar dedicated himself entirely to Venus, and wished to persuade the world that he had derived from her (his ancestress) a certain portion of immortal beauty. For this reason he used to wear in

* For their foppery, Aristophanes distinguishes them with an epithet of his own coining—*σφραγιδονυχαργοκομῆται*—"lazy, long-haired fellows, with fingers covered with rings down to the nails." The class were proverbial then, as now, for their empty-headedness and self-conceit, which Athenæus illustrates by a whole section of anecdotes, taking for his text the well-known epigram—"*Ἀνδρὶ μὲν αὐλητῆρι*"—which may be thus Englished:

"To men of music Heaven no brains supplies,
For with their fiddling forth their reason flies."

his signet an intaglio of the goddess armed at all points, and gave her name for the watchword in most, and in the most important of his battles" (Dio, xliii. 43).

The same amusing historian informs us (xlii. 18) that the Roman Senate refused to credit the fatal news of Pompey's death until Cæsar produced and showed to them his very signet, which bore engraved *three trophies*, like that used by the dictator Sulla before him. The motive for assuming such a device had been the same in both cases,—to commemorate the three great victories that had crowned the military career of either general: those of the first over the generals of Mithridates; of the latter, over the same king in person, the Arabians, and the Cilician pirates. But this must have been the signet used by Sulla in his later years, for Pliny writes that his favourite seal was the "Surrender of Jugurtha," the first of his successes in war. The representation of the event on the signet was doubtless identical with that still extant on one of his denarii, where the Roman general appears seated aloft on his tribunal, with two men kneeling before him; the one in a military habit with his hands bound behind his back, the captive prince; the other, his betrayer Bocchus, holding forth an olive-branch, the established emblem of a suppliant. The Mauritanian king, says Plutarch, had dedicated in the Capitol a representation of the event modelled in *gold*, containing no less than twenty figures; the principal actors, in all probability, we see in this medal—the small group being selected on account of the necessary limitation of space. These notices of Pliny's and Dio's prove that the recognised official signet of the individual was, as a matter of course, adopted for the type of the coinage issued by his authority; for another denarius of Sulla's bears for reverse these very *three trophies* between the lituus and prefericulum, accompanied by his surname of *Faustus* written in a monogram. Similarly, other types of consular coins are perpetually to be observed upon engraved stones; some such may be adduced here as examples of regular hereditary devices, or as containing a rebus on the family name:—*Crepereia*, head of the nymph Galatea (the Galene of Tryphon, celebrated in the epigram of Addæus), in the act of swimming, and consequently often mistaken for Leander's—a type allusive to the *crepitating* of the ripples on the strand, or to *crepido*, used in the same sense. *Manilia*, Ulysses recognised by his dog Argus. *Pansa*, a mask of Pan. *Scarpus*, an open hand, "carpus." *Trio*, the Moon and Seven Stars, the Septem Triones. *Acisculus*, a mandril or small pick-axe. *Lariscolus*, the sisters of Phaëthon turned into larches. Pomponius *Musa*, all the Muses one after the other, or else Hercules Musagetes. *Valeria*, the Stymphalian crane—type of strength and invulnerability. Voconius *Vitulus*, a calf,* &c., &c.

Others, again, took for their device some ancestral feat of arms in which the dread enemy of old—the Gaul—naturally plays a frequent part. Spirited pictures of such duels are to be seen on the denarii of the Minucia and Servilia families. But nothing of the kind known to me is so soul-stirring a record of some such deed of daring as the gem erst the signet of one of their contemporaries that fortune has recently brought under my notice. Upon this little sard two cavaliers are engaged in mortal combat with two Gauls: one has already despatched his man, who lies prostrate in the foreground; the other aims his spear at the survivor, a naked giant, who, one knee bent, is receiving the hit upon his broad shield, whilst swinging back his huge claymore, he is about to deal the terrific "swashing blow" of his nation at his adversary. The life and vigour put into the scene, despite its blundered perspective and inartificial execution, declare the genius of the designer if not his skilfulness.

That the portrait of a distinguished ancestor was often adopted for the signet of his representative in the next generation, exactly as it was for the type of the denarii issued by the same person (a rule, happily for the cause of inconography, generally observed during the later ages of the Republic), is a fact established by the remark made by Cicero upon the signet of Lentulus, Catiline's accomplice (In Cat. iii. 5), where the unfeeling orator thus *inproves* the occasion:—"I then showed the letter to Lentulus, and asked him if he knew the seal. He nodded assent. Yes, said I, 'tis a well-known seal, the portrait of your grandfather, that most illustrious man, who above all else loved the Republic and his fellow-citizens; 'tis a portrait which though voiceless ought to have dissuaded you from so monstrous a piece of wickedness." An objurgation, the more pointed, inasmuch as the whole P. Com. Lentulus had in his time actually been "Chief of the Senate:" a furious aristocrat, who in defending his party had received a wound in an affray with the followers of C. Gracchus, though the revolutionary measures of the latter were, it may be observed parenthetically, of an infinitely milder character than those in which his unlucky grandson had come to be implicated. Unfortunately, Cicero did not think it necessary again to "make a point" by noticing the subjects of

* Some of these types are so far fetched as to be true pictorial enigmas, for example—the curule *chair* of *Considius;* and his "squint-eyed" Venus for his cognomen, *Pœtus.*

other conspirators' seals, which authenticated their treasonable correspondence with the Allobroges; but we find each one of them in turn confronted with, and convicted beyond all possibility of denial by, the production of his own well-known family bearings.

A second precious memorial of a "tumultus Gallicus" is the signet of another member of the gens Cornelia, already alluded to, the Q. Cornelius Lupus. The type is the horse's head, the well-known national emblem (*Gaul*, in German, still means *horse*), and two Gallic shields crossed *en saltire* to express the confederation of the Insubres and Cænomani vanquished by C. Cornelius Cethegus, Consul B.C. 198. *Lupus* is a common surname in that family; the owner of the seal was probably the consul's son: the style of the intaglio would indicate that generation as its own date.

Valerius Maximus also mentions (iii. 5) that the degenerate son of Africanus the Elder "had his hand divested by his own family of the ring he wore engraved with his father's portrait:" whereupon he exclaims, "Di Boni quas tenebras ex quo *fulmine* nasci passi estis!" It must be noticed, en passant, that the "Thunderbolt" was the peculiar epithet of the Scipios, as Barcas "Lightning" was of their enemy Hamilcar—hence Virgil's "duo fulmina belli Scipiadæ;" whilst Jupiter Tonans is the type of their family-coins,—probably a rebus is intended (far-fetched indeed) between the name and σκήπτω the technical term for the lightning-stroke.

When the great Marcellus fell into the ambuscade of the Carthaginians, near Venusium, and was there slain, Hannibal having thus got possession of his signet made a treacherous use of it, to give the show of authenticity to the forged letters which he thereupon despatched in the Roman's name to the various towns in the hostile interest. Another proof this of the fixed character of the subject adopted for his own special device by every person of station, and which evidently no more admitted of capricious change than a coat of arms in our day. How provoking to the archæologist that Livy has not taken the trifling pains to add what this well-known device was. A few such particulars would now be of infinitely greater value than the long-winded, impossible orations wherewith, at a vast expenditure of labour, he has encumbered his History. However, from the hint afforded by Plautus as to the signet of the soldier Harpax bearing his own portrait, we may conjecture that Marcellus had followed the same usage, and taken his own likeness for his seal. A denarius issued by one of his family, the Claudia, a century after his death, supplies us with his authentic portrait accompanied by the *triquetra*, symbolising his conquest of Sicily; and for reverse himself dedicating the *spolia opima* of the Gallic King Viridomarus to Jupiter Feretrius. One of the most interesting gems that has ever come under my notice is a head exactly agreeing with that upon the medal in question; with a portion of the circumference of a shield introduced into the field—an allusion, it would appear, to the *spolia opima* commemorated upon the reverse of the same denarius. The execution of the intaglio is hard but vigorous, and in shallow cutting just what we should expect in the age of Marcellus, the third century before our era. There is, therefore, a possibility—and let the audacious hope be indulged—that this very sard may have sealed the missives of the two greatest generals of antiquity.

The Spaniard, whose father had been slain in single combat with Scipio Æmilianus, was so proud of the honour thus conferred on his family that he took for his signet a representation of the duel: whereupon Stilo wittily observed what would he not have done had Scipio fallen by his father's sword!

The first seal used by Augustus was a *sphinx*, for he had found amongst the valuables coming to him from his deceased mother two intagli of that subject exactly identical; and one of these he left, whenever about to be absent from Rome, in the hands of his deputy, for the authentication of such edicts or missives as a sudden emergency might require to be issued in his name. But so many satirical remarks were made upon his choice of such a device and its appropriateness to the enigmatical character of his proclamations, that he relinquished it, and for the rest of his reign sealed with a head of Alexander the Great: in all probability the original by Pyrgoteles. His successors, says Dio, used for their state seal his portrait by *Dioscorides*, until Galba substituted for it his own family device—a dog * looking forth over a ship's prow. Our office of Keeper of the Seal can boast of the highest antiquity, for the emperors had a *Custos annuli:* Trogus Pompeius states that his father served Julius Cæsar in that capacity (Justin. xxiii.).

Afterwards the custom of sealing with one's own portrait was again revived by the emperors: Spartian including amongst the omens of Hadrian's coming death the falling off from his finger of his ring, "which bore a likeness of himself," as he was taking the auspices on New Year's Day, and so obtaining a dim forecast of the events of the coming year. Commodus, however, to compliment his

* All Greek coasters and fishing-boats carry a dog on the forecastle to give warning at night of the approach of vessels—the type therefore was the emblem of vigilance.

famous mistress, Marcia, took for his seal the figure of an Amazon, as we learn from a letter of his addressed to Clodius Albinus, preserved by Capitolinus, in his life of the latter: "I have sent a letter which you will receive yourself, sealed with the figure of an *Amazon.*" And Lampridius relates of the same madman that his flatterers used to call him *Amazonius*, after the device upon his signet; but that in reality he had first got the name from his extreme devotion to his concubine Marcia, whom he had caused to be represented in the character of an Amazon—in which guise she actually figures upon some of his medallions. Gorlæus possessed in his Dactyliotheca (purchased on his death by our James I.), a ring which then passed for the true signet of Nero. The intaglio revolved on its axis; one side bearing the conjugated busts of Nero and Agrippina, a star and a lyre in the field, engraved in *gold;* the other side, a *sard* intaglio representing Apollo standing triumphant, the vanquished Marsyas bound to a tree, and his disciple Olympus kneeling at the god's feet, vainly soliciting his forgiveness. But the entire composition of both ring and signet savours too much of the Cinque-cento taste for it to be admitted as an indubitable memento of the imperial fiddler. In other respects the subject was judiciously selected as embodying an easily understood menace against all future rivals of the would-be Apollo. Its reality was felt by Lucan, whose fate is ascribed by Suetonius (in his life) to his having quoted most disrespectfully, though but too appositely, a line of the august poet descriptive of subterranean thunder, "sub terris tonuisse putes," on the occasion of an explosion of a very different nature, to the inexpressible consternation of all within hearing of his treasonable pleasantry.

One of the tokens presaging the approaching fall of this "terrible amateur" was the New Year's gift made to him by his favourite Sporus, on the same occasion as when Hadrian received from Fate a similar warning. This prophetic present was a ring engraved with the Rape of Proserpine; a most ill-omened choice, the subject being the accepted symbol of death, and set apart as a decoration for tombs alone. Nothing in the eyes of a Roman could have been more inauspicious than such a gift at such a season; as pregnant with coming woe as that legend so unaccountably put upon the marriage medal of Mary Queen of Scots and François II., "Hora nona Dominus I.H.S. expiravit, Heli clamans." Words these, so inappropriate to the occasion that they would seem to have been suggested by Atropos herself to the designer in bitter irony of the festive day: and speedily to be verified by the event.

Mæcenas's signet, Pliny tells us, was a *frog*, the sight of which, as announcing a contribution about to be levied, used to strike terror into the minds of the rich. A calcedony scarabæus in the late Praun Cabinet, thus engraved, both the beetle and the intaglio in the best style of Etruscan art, may be assigned, without overstraining probabilities, to some ancient member of the MAIKNE clan, the "regal ancestry" of Horace's patron; for it has been already shown that such devices were transmitted down through a long line of descendants. This memorable protector of literature extended his favour, and in a special degree, to this branch of the fine arts: a noble testimony to which exists in his portraits from the hand of Apollonius, of Solon, of Aulus, and above all, of Dioscorides: the last gem holding the second place amongst the eight recognised as the authentic works of that engraver.

How passionately Mæcenas loved gems—doubtless not merely for their native beauties, but, like the great Julius, for the higher value of the genius therein enshrined—appears from his lines upon the departure of Horace (preserved by Isidorus), for whose loss he declares not even the sight of his darling jewels could console him:—

"Lugens O mea vita! te smaragdos,
Beryllos mihi Flacce nec nitentes,
Nec percandida margarita quæro;
Nec quos Thynica lima perpolivit
Anellos nec iaspios lapillos."

"Whilst I thine absence, O my life! deplore,
Emeralds and lustrous beryls charm no more;
No more, my Flaccus, can the brilliant white
Of orient pearls, as erst, my soul delight;
Nor can my favourite rings my grief beguile,
Nor jaspers polished by the Thyrian file."

Augustus also evidently alludes to his passion for gems in a passage of a letter, where at the same time he mimics jocularly the affected style of his compositions (Macrob. ii. 4). "Vale mel gentium, metuelle, ebur ex Hetruria, laser Aretinum, adamas supernas, Tiberinum margaritum, Cilniorum smaragde, jaspis figulorum, berylle Porsennæ carbunculum habeas!" "Farewell, my honey of the clans, my marrow, my ivory from Etruria, my Aretine spice, my diamond of the upper regions, my pearl of the Tiber, my emerald of the Cilnian family, my beryl of King Porsenna, may you get the carbuncle!" (the last a play upon the double meaning of the word, equally good in English). Joking him at once upon his royal Etruscan descent, his weak point, and upon this his particular hobby.

It were much to be wished that Ovid had told us what tasteful device he had chosen for his own, and to which he thus prettily alludes in a letter from his place of banishment (ii. 10).

Ecquid ab impressæ cognoscis imagine gemmæ
Haec tibi Nasonem scribere verba Macer?
Auctorisque sui si non est annulus index
Cognitane est nostra litera facta manu?
An tibi notitiam mora temporis eripit horum,
Nec repetunt oculi signa vetusta tui?
Sis licet oblitus pariter gemmæque manusque
Exciderit tantum ne tibi cura mei."

Chiflet asserts, but in all likelihood upon merely monkish authority, that Augustus took for his device the 'Butterfly and Tortoise' of the old fable, to express his favourite maxim—*Festina lente*—"No more haste than good speed;" but the conceit savours too strongly of mediæval pedantry to be received as authentic.

The only Imperial signet preserved, respecting the first ownership of which no doubts can be entertained, is the celebrated sapphire of Constantius (slightly noticed above), now in the Rinuccini Cabinet, Florence. The stone of uncommon beauty and the extraordinary weight of fifty-three carats, is engraved with the representation of one of the greatest exploits of the imperial Nimrod. The Emperor is spearing a monstrous wild boar, entitled ΞΙΦΙΑϹ, in the plains of Cæsarea, that city being typified by a recumbent female, distinguished by the title (in the corrupt phonetic orthography already gaining ground) ΚΕϹΑΡΙΑ ΚΑΠ-ΠΑΔΟΚΙΑϹ. In the field the *Latin* legend, CONSTANTIVS AVG, makes it manifest that the destination of the intaglio was for the Emperor's own use: a fact furthermore confirmed by the very careful execution of the work, showing it to have come from the hand of the first engraver of the times, as well as by the enormous intrinsic value of the material. Another portrait of this prince is noticed by Visconti (Gem. Ant. 497):—"Impression of an intaglio head in crystal in the Florentine Museum; and appearing to present in its features the likeness of Constantius, son and successor of Constantine the Great. The bust is clothed in the paludamentum." But that standing next in his list is one of vastly greater historical interest: "A most singular *carnelian*,* though miserably executed, inscribed ALARICVS REX GOTHORVM. The bust is shown in front-face, and has upon the shoulder a kind of stole, called in those times *lorum*, forming part of the habit of

* Visconti is mistaken here. Biehler informs me the stone is a fine sapphire, as indeed the impression would lead one to conclude. Now in the Vienna Cabinet.

ceremony worn by the Emperors and Consuls." Probably this was the official seal of the conqueror's secretary; for had it been engraved for the royal hand, that disposed of all the accumulated treasures of the Roman world, one would have expected a gem of large intrinsic value—a sapphire or a spinel—to have been selected for so dignified a service. Unless, indeed, the expiring art of the age (a probable solution) had found itself incapable of dealing with such refractory materials. The few portraits extant belonging to this epoch are in front-face and very deeply cut, but in the softer gems—crystal and lapis-lazuli being now preferred : the mechanical side of the art having declined in the same proportion as the knowledge of design. Heads in front-face were, during the same period, fast becoming the rule upon the more important issues of the Roman and Byzantine mints, and in a short time these entirely banished profile portraits from the gold coinage.

The Mertens-Schaaffhausen Cabinet possessed the most important example of this class anywhere extant. It was the great seal of Mauricius, engraved in a large calcedony, 2 by 1½ inches in size; his bust in front-face, the orb in his hand, exactly coinciding with the type of his solidi. Above runs the legend D. N. MAVRITIVS. P. P. AVG. The engraving, though without life, is done in a remarkably neat manner. According to the sale-catalogue this gem had been dug up at Gräfin, near Bonn. M. Martigny (Paris) has in his collection the signet of the murderer of this virtuous prince, Phocas, which in all particulars of style and type coincides with the above; but the material is lapis-lazuli, and the dimensions considerably smaller.

In the De la Turbie Cabinet, No. 49 is a carnelian adorned with arabesques, encircling the legend KOMNHNOC TOY CЄBACTOY, "Comnenus, son of the Emperor," and therefore the indubitable signet of a prince of the house of Comneni, some time in the twelfth century, throughout which extent of time that family revived the faded lustre of the Byzantine purple. This is the latest example of an engraved stone, belonging to the Imperial series, the date of which can be approximately fixed; and is, as far as I have been able to discover, the unique instance of an *intaglio* produced by the palace engravers, who still continued to supply many *camei* of a religious nature. But the arabesques filling the field betray an imitation of the owner's Mohammedan rivals; for, changing into Cufic the characters in which the legend is written, the signet becomes identical in treatment with that of an Arabian Caliph.

An agreeable conclusion to this lengthy dissertation will be supplied by an extract from the flowery pages of the tasteful Bishop of Tricca, Heliodorus, who, though writing amidst the fast-gathering clouds of the fourth century, still retained a tinge of early culture, and could not extinguish a sinful admiration for artistic beauty. Like other educated men of his and still lower times, he was still able to appreciate the productions of an art even then nearly extinct; for with what enthusiasm does he enlarge upon the description of the ring worn by his heroine, Chariclea (Æthiop. v. 13)!—possibly a word, the beauty of which he had himself admired in reality, or perhaps actually possessed:—"Such is the appearance of all amethysts coming from India and Ethiopia, but that which Calasiris now presented to Nausicles was far above them in value, for it was enriched with an engraving, and worked out into an imitation of the figures of Nature. The subject was a boy tending his flocks, himself standing up on a low rock for the sake of looking about him, and guiding his sheep to their pasture by the music of his Pandean pipe. The flock seemed obedient to the signal, and submitted themselves readily to be conducted by the guidance of his notes. One would say they were themselves laden with fleeces of gold, and those not of the artist's giving, but due to the amethyst itself, which painted their backs with a blush of its own. Pictured also were the tender skippings of the lambs; while some running up against the rock in troops, others turning in frolicsome circles around the shepherd, converted the rising ground into the appearance of a pastoral theatre. Others again revelling in the blaze of the amethyst, as if in the beams of the sun, were pawing and scraping the rock with the points of their hoofs as they bounded up against it. Such amongst them as were the first born and the more audacious seemed as if they were wishing to leap over the round of the gem, but were kept in by the artist, who had drawn a border like a golden fold around them and the rock. Now this fold was in reality a stone, and not imitative, for the engraver having circumscribed a portion of the gem's edge for this purpose, had depicted what he required in the actual substance, deeming it a clever stroke to contrive a stone wall upon a *stone*." The latter part seems to express that the whole composition was enclosed within an "Etruscan border," the markings in which gave the idea of a stone-built fence.* The 'Æthiopica,' a romance, the model for the voluminous productions so fashionable in the seventeenth century, although sufficiently absurd in the nature of its most artfully complicated plot, abounds with valuable details

* A remark proving that our author is describing a real intaglio—not drawing upon his fancy merely.

respecting manners and things in Greece and Egypt in the times of the ingenious prelate-novelist: who long refused a rich bishopric rather than abjure the authorship of this very work.

We come now to the barbarian usurpers of the Roman sovereignty, the Frankish kings and the self-constituted Emperors of the West. Childeric's signet—found with other regalia in his tomb at Tournay, when accidentally opened in 1654—is not set with a gem, but has an oval beasil in the gold of the ring engraved with his bust in front-face, holding a spear, as in the type of the contemporary Byzantine aurei. He conspicuously wears the long hair of the Merovingian line. Traces remain of the legend CHILDERICI REGIS. This intaglio is very neatly cut, infinitely superior to the execution of the Merovingian coin-dies; and in fact so much in the style of Leo's aurei, that it may reasonably be supposed a present, sent with other offerings, from Constantinople. Amongst the other relics in his tomb was a cornelian Etruscan scarab, doubtless deposited therein as an amulet of wondrous virtue; also a crystal divining-ball, 2 inches in diameter. Most unfortunately this invaluable signet has disappeared with the jewels stolen from the Bibliothèque in 1831 (vide Chiflet's 'Anastasis: Thes. rep. Tornaci Noviorum effossa. 1654').

The old map-makers were accustomed to fill in the outlines of the *terra incognita* (which in their times occupied so large a proportion of the earth's surface), in default of ascertained towns and peoples, with the creations of fancy,

> "men whose heads
> Do grow beneath their shoulders,"

Sciapodes, Martichoras, unicorns, and gryphons. The same cause induces me to follow their example, and, having been unable to discover any facts of interest connected with the signets of the worthies of the Middle Ages, I shall devote this period to the 'Tale of a Ring,' extracted from William of Malmesbury, one most truly mediæval in its wildness, and in its manner of regarding the then still existing monuments of a better time:—

"But to return to Rome: a young man of that city, wealthy and of noble family, having newly married a wife, gave a grand banquet to his friends and acquaintances. After dinner, when they had made themselves merry by repeated potations, they sallied out into the fields in order to promote digestion—being gorged with food—by leaping or quoit-throwing, or other kind of exercise. The giver of the feast and leader in the sports proposed a game at ball, and, taking off his finger his *betrothal-ring*, put it upon that of a brazen statue which chanced to be standing near. But as all the rest set upon him alone, he, out of breath and overheated, was the first to give up the game; and, looking for his ring, he found the finger of the statue bent round into the palm of the hand. After long and fruitless efforts, for he was neither able to pull away his ring nor yet to break off the statue's finger, he went home without saying anything, concealing the matter from his friends from fear lest they should either laugh at him before his face, or else steal away his ring as soon as his back was turned. So returning late at night with his servants, he found to his amazement the finger straightened again and his ring gone. He dissembled the loss, and consoled himself with the caresses of his new-made bride. When bedtime was come, and he had laid down by his wife's side, he felt something like a dense cloud tumbling about between him and her; something that could be felt, but could not be seen. By this obstacle he was prevented from embracing his wife; also he heard a voice that said, 'Lie with me, for thou hast espoused me this day! I am Venus, on whose finger thou didst put thy ring: I have got it, and will not give it back!' He being astounded at this prodigy neither dared nor, indeed, had the power to reply: he spent a sleepless night, silently pondering over the matter.

"In this way a long time passed, that, whenever he wished to embrace his bride, he felt and heard the same thing; though, in all other respects, he was perfectly well and fit for all business at home and abroad. At last he was urged by his wife's complaints at his neglect of her, to communicate this strange affair to his relations. They, after some debate, seek counsel of one Palumbus, a priest in the suburbs. He was a person proficient in the science of necromancy, could construct magical figures, strike awe into the devils, and constrain them to do all his bidding. Having, therefore, agreed for a large reward that on the condition of his bringing the loving pair together, he should have his purse stuffed with coin, he strained his genius to new devices; and drew up a letter, which he gave to the young man, saying: 'Go at such an hour to the road where four ways meet, and stand silently and look out. There will pass by the shapes of people of both sexes, every age and all ranks, and of every condition; some on horseback, some on foot, some with their faces bent on the ground, some erecting their heads triumphantly; in a word, all the signs of both grief and joy shalt thou discover in their looks and gestures. Thou must answer none of them in case they speak to thee. Behind this train will come one more lofty in stature, more bulky in size than the rest, seated in a chariot. Without uttering a word, hand him the epistle to read; and forthwith, that which thou desirest shall be accomplished. Only take care thou lose not courage.'

"The youth goes as he is bid, and, standing there under the canopy of night, at the dead hour, verifies with his own eyes the truth of the priest's information. Not one particular was wanting of his description. Amongst the others that passed along before him, he remarked a woman in the attire of a harlot riding on a mule; her hair flowed dishevelled over her shoulders, and was bound with a fillet of gold. In her hand was a golden wand, wherewith she directed her palfrey; the thinness of her vesture was such, that she showed through it almost as naked, and she kept making lascivious gestures. To be brief: that One who came last, and seemed the lord of them all, fixing his terrible looks upon the youth from his proud car overlaid with emeralds and pearls, demanded the reason of his coming. Without making reply, the youth stretched up his hand and delivered unto him the epistle. The demon, daring not to slight the well-known seal, reads the letter; and then, lifting up his arms unto heaven, cries aloud, 'O God Almighty, in whose sight all sin is a foul savour, how long dost Thou put up with the wickedness of Palumbus the priest?' And forthwith he sent certain of his guards from beside him to take away the ring from Venus, and she after a long dispute at last surrendered it, but with great difficulty. Thereupon the young man, having gained his object, encountered for the future no obstacle to the consummation of his desires. But Palumbus, when he had heard of the cry of the demon unto God against himself, perceived that the end of his life was thereby announced. For which cause, having severed his limbs with his own hands, he died by this awful manner of penance, after making confession to the Pope, in the hearing of all the people of Rome, of his unheard-of enormities. This came to pass in the days of Pope Gregory VI." (A.D. 1044–7).

Of signets known in modern times, none has enjoyed so lasting and so high a reputation as the so-called "Seal of Michael Angelo," preserved for the last two centuries in the French Cabinet, into which it passed with the other antiquities of Lauthier.* Then and for many years it was received for the undoubted work of Pyrgoteles, and the design as commemorating the birth of Alexander the Great. Its value consequently was estimated at 2000*l.*; for, in addition to these high recommendations, its interest was enhanced

* A distinguished antiquary of Aix, in Provence, under Henri IV.

by the fact that it had been the favourite ring of Michael Angelo himself. More accurate criticism has, unfortunately, now stripped it of its *antique* glories and pronounced it to be merely a work of the Italian School, as its whole character unmistakably betrays. It is a sard engraved with a composition of many figures: in the exergue is a boy fishing, doubtless a rebus on the name of its author, P. M. da *Pescia*, especially celebrated in his time for his excellence in such miniature works, and, what is equally to the purpose, the intimate friend of M. Angelo. That the ring once actually belonged to the great Florentine alone seems to be a matter beyond dispute. Of this relic the following curious story is told by the witty President, Des Brosses, in his 'Lettres sur l'Italie' (ii. 27):—"Early in the century as the academician J. Hardion was exhibiting the treasures of the Bibliothèque to that celebrated amateur the Baron de Stosch, he all at once missed this very ring; whereupon, without expressing his suspicions, he privately despatched a servant for a strong emetic, which, when brought, he insisted upon the Baron's swallowing then and there, and in a few minutes he had the satisfaction of hearing the ring tinkle into the basin held before the unlucky and unscrupulous gem-collector." Such a mode of enriching his cabinet is certainly by no means inconsistent with Stosch's well-known character—Pope's

"Annius, crafty seer, with ebon wand
And well-dissembled emerald on his hand,
False as his gems, and cankered as his coins"—

by profession a Hanoverian spy on the Pretender's movements, and in practice a zealous fabricator of antiques, more especially in the class of artists' signatures wherewith to enrich the collections of noble (ill-styled) *cognoscenti.*

Of this intaglio there are a larger number of paste-copies—many admirable imitations of the sard—than of any other celebrated gem, not so much on account of the merit of the work, although that is considerable, as from its long-established reputation and the great names with which its true or legendary history is associated.

ORIGIN OF HERALDRY.

In the foregoing remarks it has been stated that the devices on the signets of the ancients were both hereditary and unalterable, like our armorial bearings. A singular confirmation of this statement is afforded by the conclusion of the Heraclean inscription, which specifies the respective seals of the magistrates therein concerned; one bearing in his signet a winnowing-fan (a noted Bacchic symbol), another a dolphin, another a bunch of grapes, &c.

Bearings, in a literal sense armorial, appear on the shields of the Grecian heroes in the most ancient pictures extant, the vase-paintings; but these seem to have been assumed at the caprice of the individual, like the knights' *cognizances* at tournaments in the days of chivalry, and not to have been hereditary. It may be supposed that Æschylus was not without some traditional authority for assigning their devices to his Seven Chiefs at the Siege of Thebes. Parthenopæus bears on his shield the sphinx devouring a prostrate Theban; Hippomedon, Typhon belching forth flames and smoke; Eteocles, a warrior scaling the city walls, &c.

So exactly did these bearings correspond to the cognizances of chivalry, that we find the traditions concerning the mythic heroes making them use engraved on their signets the same devices that decorated their shields. Thus Plutarch relates (De Solert. Anim.) that Ulysses adopted and bore on shield and signet a dolphin, to commemorate the preservation of Telemachus by its agency when in his childhood he had accidentally fallen into the sea. As his authority he quotes that early poet Stesichorus; and on the same grounds the enigma-loving Lycophron indicates Ulysses by the epithet δελφινόσημος alone. Hence in gems the portrait of the wily Ithacan is to be recognised by his shield, displaying a *dolphin* for its device.

Under the Roman Empire, when all the usages of war had become fixed and regulated by invariable and minute laws, military cognizances were also subjected to the strictest prescription. The distinguishing of the several legions by the devices painted on their shields is alluded to by Tacitus and by Ammian; and, what is more, that invaluable picture of the Lower Empire in the fifth century, the Notitia Imperii, preserves the actual designs (many of them perfectly heraldic) which distinguished not merely the legions but their component cohorts or companies from each other. Curiously enough, the figures on the shields of William the Norman's knights, as depicted in the

Bayeux tapestry, are simple and single,—birds, dragons, or circles, variously disposed,—presenting a very marked analogy in their nature to the cohort-shields: indeed it was no more than probable that such distinctions should have survived amongst the Franks and Gauls, who from Constantine's age downwards had constituted almost exclusively the material of the Roman armies, and who naturally, on founding nationalities for themselves, preserved many of the institutions of the school in which they had been trained. And what corroborates this theory is the remark of Procopius that the Armoricans, long after the establishment of the Merovingian dynasty in Gaul, continued to be distinguished from their neighbours by their Roman arms and military discipline. They, therefore, may be supposed to have maintained all the minor regulations of the old Imperial system. Now, every cohort in the service was distinguished by a special device *painted* upon the shields of its men. The invaluable MS. of the "Notitia Imperii" (Bibliothèque Nationale) preserves the whole set of these devices. In them we find everything that still exists in Heraldic usage—the Tressure, the Bend, the Pale, the Chevron—besides fantastic animals of all descriptions. Nay, what is more, where the *forms* of the device are the same for different cohorts, the necessary *difference* is obtained by giving their different *tinctures*, as strongly diversified as possible, quite after the modern rules. I give below, that of the "constantiniane," a most interesting example, for it was adopted by our Edward the Confessor for his arms, no doubt for some mystic virtue that still lingered in the acceptation of its sense.

CABINETS OF GEMS.

THE BRITISH MUSEUM.

THE Antique Gems, those hidden treasures of our interminable national collection, a portion of its contents so highly interesting and yet so little known, shall on that very account receive the first notice in the following sketch of the principal *Dactyliothecæ* of Europe. Besides, they reckon in their number some extremely interesting works; although the particular pieces that hold the first rank there, in virtue of the artists' signatures they are supposed to bear, are either copies, or else antiques with the names interpolated: fictions due to the mania prevalent at the time these collections were forming, when a work, however excellent, was thought but little of unless seemingly authenticated by such an attestation. The whole number, in rings and loose large gems, amounts to about five hundred; the former are set in gold with a few in silver, and are arranged in five cases. They come from the bequests of Townley, Payne Knight, and Cracherode. Of the last-named antiquary, the gatherings cannot indeed boast of any work of special importance, yet they are characterized throughout by his usual exquisite taste, which has admitted nothing amongst them but what is to be admired either for the elegance of the design, the fineness of the execution, or lastly, the beauty of the material itself. To take a single example from this casket—an *emerald* engraved with a Cupid teasing a goose with a bunch of grapes, is in every one of these respects the most charming intaglio that could be desired; and the same three qualities are combined in the Cupid bestriding a dolphin on a lovely aquamarine.

The Townley Gems however, number in their ranks some pieces not to be surpassed by the most princely cabinets. First amongst these is the Julius Cæsar of *Dioscorides*, a bust in front-face on sard, his brows encircled with a laurel wreath (the leaves unusually large), the face full of energy, but hard-featured, haggard, and represented with all the unflattering fidelity of a photograph: a portrait taken, it would appear, but shortly before the close of his life. The name of Dioscorides is engraved at the side in the most minute characters, which certainly have the appearance of being of the same date as the rest of the work, with however suspicious an eye so pretentious a signature is regarded by the experienced examiner. As far superior to this in beauty, as falling short of it in historical interest, is the bust, in front-face, of an empress, perhaps Livia, in the character of *Abundantia*, with veiled head, and holding the cornucopia; the stone a fine dark amethyst. It presents the letters ΕΠΙ, and has therefore been assigned to *Epitynchanus*, the engraver of the famous head of Germanicus. Another conspicuous for its excellence is the Perseus with the severed Gorgon's head in one hand, the *harpê* in the other; an exquisitely-finished engraving. Then come several excellent copies of celebrated gems, doubtless purchased for the originals by the wealthy and not too discriminating collector; a bust, in front-face, of the Indian Bacchus, a magnificent intaglio on red jasper; and Theseus, or Achilles, supporting the dying Amazon, a design full of grace, upon amethyst. Both pieces ostentatiously display the pretended signature of *Aspasius*. Next we come upon a copy, on sard, of the Tiberius, in front-face, by *Ælius*; the intaglio, indeed, may claim to be antique, though the name is certainly a modern insertion. The lovely gem for both subject and material, a ruby sard, Cupid advancing to rescue Psyche, whose foot is caught in a trap, though it is signed *Pamphilus*, betrays too much of the modern taste in its design for us to suppose it an ancient reproduction of some picture by that immortal artist.* *Heïus* also has been made to give his name in recent times to an intaglio, a Diana, of antique work: no doubt because Visconti had pronounced him the most ancient of all engravers to whom any gem can be ascribed. The Laughing Faun of *Ammonius*, a face beaming with mirth and mischief (a complete John Wilkes), is here repeated upon a dark jacinth of the finest quality that has ever come in my way.

The *uninscribed* stones are, as usual, of a more satisfactory character, and richly repay close examination. Worthy of special notice is the Sacred Hawk, in the Greco-Egyptian style, on sard;

* The composition as well as the peculiar execution bespeak the hand of a certain great master of the early Cinque-cento school, observed by me in some other reputed antiques of the highest order.

which, though of smaller size, is fully equal to the famous stone with the same subject, at Berlin, always quoted as the finest thing known in this particular period of the art. An interesting example of the style, belonging to very early date, is the intaglio of the fore part of the human-headed bull, with the legend ΓΕΛΑΣ in the field, and exactly agreeing with the type of the archaic coins of that city. A Medusa's Head, in profile, is of uncommon merit. Amongst curious subjects stands foremost that of a female sacrificing to Priapus, and placing the peculiar symbol of that deity upon a burning altar: a large sard of the finest antique work.

This part of the collection also possesses several fragments belonging to gems of extraordinary volume, and which retain portions of their engravings whose incomparable beauty makes one only the more feel the irreparable loss of the entire design. I may single out for special admiration the lower part of a female face backed by a head of Ammon, the latter having apparently formed the neckpiece to the helmet covering the head of a Minerva: an intaglio of slight depth, and belonging to the best Greek period, on brown sard. Another fragment preserves sufficient of a profile, on the largest scale, to enable us to identify the truculent physiognomy of Caracalla.

The Townley Cabinet is also very rich in Gnostic stones, many of them so well executed as to be unrivalled in their class; amongst them I recognised several of those published by Chiflet two centuries and a half ago—they having found their way through various channels into this haven of unbroken rest. Of these, and of that most rare class accompanying them, the earliest memorials of the orthodox faith, a detailed notice has been given under the proper heading in my 'Gnostics.'

The scarabæi are also numerous * and important: many of them will be found noticed in Köhler's essay. One attracted my notice particularly by the rare beauty of its material, an Indian garnet, hardly distinguishable from a spinel-ruby, and of considerable size.

As for gems still preserving their antique settings, this collection presents a rich display; and, to my great surprise, far surpassing, in this interesting particular, the cabinets of Florence and Naples. But here, as ever, the artistic value of the gem is in

* The number of scarabæi, I am informed, is about two thousand of all kinds, including many of the greatest merit. These come from the cabinets of Sir W. Hamilton, Castellani, and above all from the lately acquired Blacas, containing the most important of recent discoveries.

the inverse ratio to the costliness and singularity of the mounting. Yet one magnificent exception encountered my eye amongst their ranks, a *Hercules slaying the Hydra*, deeply cut in a rich sard, and mounted in a heavy gold ring of the fashion prevalent under the Lower Empire. Another intaglio of very fine work is to be seen forming the centre of a broad-bordered oval fibula, the surface of which is ornamented with filigree patterns in the purest Greek style. This unique example of the employment of an intaglio in the decoration of a fibula comes from Sicily: both the intaglio and the setting are evidently coeval, and date from the most flourishing period of Syracusan art. The wonderful *Canino lion-ring*, that masterpiece of the Etruscan goldsmith, has lately been added to the number of these unique remains. There is also a large and massy gold signet, having its device, *three legionary standards*, cut on the metal; an example, undoubtedly authentic, of this class of antiques, at present the favourite field for the Neapolitan forgers. Here also is preserved the most tasteful adaptation of an antique gem to mediæval fashion that has ever come before me—a pretty bust in high relief on sard, set in an elegant ring of the fourteenth century, as appears from the Lombardic legend surrounding the beasil and covering the shank. Some astrological symbols, conspicuously marked upon the shoulders, indicate an Italian origin for the jewel.

The *Camei* here, though comprising none of great importance as regards their dimensions, are several of them noteworthy for their beauty and genuineness. Conspicuous for merit amongst them are a head of Serapis, in front-face, and in high relief; profile heads of Domitian and Julia, side by side, upon a nicolo of some magnitude; and a fragment, Europa on the bull. This last, as well as the two horses, which probably once belonged to a Victory's car, certainly equal, in drawing and in careful finish, any antique camei known to me. Another, a lion passant, in low relief in the red layer of a sardonyx, exquisitely finished, has its value greatly enhanced by the LAVR. MED. cut in the field, attesting that it once belonged to the original cabinet of Lorenzo dei Medici. This stone, set in a ring, has its face protected by a glass; a proof of the estimation in which its former possessor held it. Yet more interesting, historically, is the gold snuff-box presented by Pius VII. to Napoleon upon the occasion of the Treaty of Tolentino, the lid set with an excellent antique cameo on a sardonyx of many strata; the subject, in flat relief, is a young Faun riding upon a goat, well drawn and minutely finished. This precious antique was doubtless chosen by the tasteful Pontiff to grace his offering, as really surpassing in value the diamonds that usually adorn such testimonials of regard. The fallen emperor left it as a mark of gratitude to Lady Holland, who in her turn bequeathed it to the Museum.

There remains to be noticed a class of engraved stones in which this institution, as a matter of course, stands unrivalled, the Assyrian and Persian Cylinders and Cones: their abundance here bespeaks the nation *par éminence* of Eastern travellers; and amongst them are the most precious monuments of the sort yet discovered, for example, the signets of Sennacherib and of Darius, above described. The series, also, of the Sassanian seals is very extensive. All have been lately arranged in glazed cases in one of the Assyrian galleries, and can now be conveniently studied.

Amongst the miscellanea I examined with great interest, not unmixed with amusement, the notorious *Flora*, the cameo which first brought Pistrucci into notice: it having been passed off upon Payne Knight, the "Magnus Apollo" of the cognoscenti of his day, as one of the choicest productions of Greek art. It speaks little for the practical knowledge of his set (notwithstanding the price at which they had been for many years buying experience), that they should have been thus imposed upon, for the very first aspect of the gem were sufficient, one would think, to make anyone possessing the least experience in cameo-work pronounce it, at the earliest, a piece from the Cinque-cento school, of which it betrays all the peculiarities. The head is very much under-cut, and in three-quarters relief, the hair encircled with a garland of red roses in execrable taste, and quite inconsistent with the classic period it claimed. It is broken off at the neck, the trick then in vogue for giving the colour of antiquity to a recent production; and upon this section of the neck (which the setting covers) Pistrucci is said to have cut his name, so as to be able at pleasure to vindicate the authorship of the work. In other respects the execution is fair enough, but not comparable to hundreds of other camei of the later Italian school, and falling immeasurably short of my preconceived ideas of so highly lauded a performance.

It gives me great pleasure to be able to add, that the rulers of the Museum have at last been awakened to the necessity of raising *this*, from its former feeble *status*, to a level with the high character of the other classes of antique art-treasures under their management. A spirited beginning has been made (July, 1865) by the acquisition of the small but highly-select collection, the result of the long-continued researches (aided by his exquisite taste and practical skill) of Sig. Castellani. Amongst its chief glories may be particularised a sapphirine *scarabeoid* of unusual size, with a Victory erecting a trophy in the style of the fine medals of Agathocles; a scarabæus of the rarest class, Etruscan work in relief, having its back carved into the figure of a Syren; another scarabæus with the Death of Capaneus; Hercules scaring away the Harpies from the table of Phineus; a Drunken Silenus,* archaic Greek, upon a grand agate scarabæus; the Wild Boar of Dioscorides; a Herd of Swine, a homely subject, but ennobled by Grecian treatment; a Head of Severus on an immense plasma, a masterpiece of Roman iconography; and, to conclude, three curious examples of a very uncommon but most interesting character, signets of the early Christians. With these came some unrivalled Etruscan and Greek rings; amongst the latter the most superb intaglio *in gold* ever discovered, the bust of some Berenice or Arsinoe side by side with that of Serapis; the ring itself plain and very massive; a truly royal signet.

Those here mentioned are merely such as made the deepest impression on the memory during a hurried glance over the whole, but it may be safely asserted that this choice of the choicest flowers of many a once-famous cabinet contains no one piece not recommended either by the interest of the subject or the fineness of its execution.

After this, what remains but to apostrophise the presiding Genius of the place in Virgillian phrase with

"Macte *nova* virtute senex!"

There exist in this country an infinity of inestimable gems, locked up from the public and buried in small private collections, that either by means of purchase, or through patriotic bequest (if judiciously enticed), might be made to flow into and elevate the Dactyliotheca of our National repository to the rank (as regards *intagli*) of the first in the world.

These treasures were more than doubled in the year 1866 by Disraeli's spirited purchase of the celebrated Blacas Cabinet, comprising 951 camei and intagli. Of these, the most important pieces are the grand *Augustus*, camio, converted into a Constantine, as already mentioned; the *Tityus*, crystal plaque, of Castel Bolognese, so highly eulogised by Vasari; and another, a *Sacrifice*, in the same material, with the signature of Il Vicentino. In the same style, and apparently from the same hand, are the *Hercules and Antæus*, and the *Triumphs of Neptune*, both works of extra-

* Coming, with a few others, out of the ancient Praun Cabinet—verily Numa's Sibylline Books "let him that readeth understand."

ordinary merit. The Cabinet, it is needless to say, considering the epoch of its formation, is rich in "artists' signatures," truly, in this case, the "substance of things hoped for." A full notice of the principal gems in this collection was published by me in the 'Archæological Journal,' of the year following its purchase. A finishing stroke has been given to the good work by the exhibition of our unrivalled series of Mediæval Glyptics in the room recently appropriated to that period of the Arts (1884). No other Museum can display so numerous, or so well-classified a set of seals (many literally "Great," in silver matrices) in which the Gothic artist has expended his utmost ingenuity in the devising and labour in the executing their complicated types. The *secreta* or Personal Signets in all metals are of great interest; and many of them present examples of the adaptation of antique intagli to the taste of their owner's times, and serve admirably to illustrate my remarks upon their use, to be found in the foregoing chapter upon that subject.

The Townley Pastes, also, must not pass without a word of commendation, for among them are some of the largest and finest of their kind. There is one inscribed with the engraver's name, and again the magnificent *Bonus Eventus*, which has no rival for its volume, its perfect imitation of true lapis-lazuli, and the finish of the workmanship. They have been lately brought out and arranged for public view along with the rest of the antique glass, affording an additional argument why their prototypes in real gems should be drawn from the obscurity to which they have been too long consigned. This seclusion has lasted ever since the removal of the last portion of Montague House, up to which time the cases were to be inspected under glass in the room at the top of the back stairs of that mansion. It is very much to be desired that all the more important gems should be made accessible in the same way, and placed (with their casts by each) under glass and *close to it;* according to the arrangement followed in the Bibliothèque Impériale.* This mode suffices for the exhibition of camei and *opaque* stones, but the *transparent* cannot be satisfactorily studied unless the light be allowed to pass through them. This object is ingeniously effected, by a contrivance to be described in my notice of that collection, with the gems in the Museo Borbonico. But if this be impracticable here from the want of a side light, we amateurs should be well content to see the intagli of both kinds

* This suggestion has since been carried out; but in a manner susceptible of some improvements, and the gems are now made accessible to the public, in the Jewel Room.

simply set out in horizontal cases, provided they were accompanied by their impressions.

CABINET OF THE GALLERIA, FLORENCE.*

This collection, commenced by Lorenzo, grew up under the patronage of the succeeding princes of the House of Medici (especially of Cosmo III.) until it has attained to the extent, according to Maffei, of three thousand pieces. Besides many camei of rare beauty, it possesses fourteen heads or busts in full relief in agate, turquois, sardonyx, and lapis-lazuli. The names (supposed) of their authors occur on twenty-three intagli and two camei.

To give a few particulars, full of interest, concerning the growth and vicissitudes of this the oldest cabinet in the world. Lorenzo had inherited many valuable antiques from his father Piero; to them he added the entire series accumulated by that passionate lover of gems, Pope Paul II. Of his son, Leo X., Paulus Jovius writes:—"Conspiciebatur officina nobilium artificum quoniam nullibi libentius pictores statuarii *scalptoresque gemmarum* atque antiquitatis studiosi monumenta artis deponerent quam apud Mediceos." Lelio Torelli, also, in his funeral oration upon Alessandro dei Medici (1536), notices his love for and patronage of this art. In the Uzielli Collection was a portrait of this unlucky prince, a profile cut out of plasma and *appliqué* upon a gold ground, admirably done.

Raspe thinks that the greater part of the gems inscribed LAVR. MED. are the works of *Gio delle Corniole* and his scholars, who flourished under Lorenzo's patronage. But there is no foundation for this surmise, the same inscription being found on pieces, especially the important camei, of the most varied styles and periods. It was merely used to assert the ownership in them, and prevent robbery, being the most effectual precaution that could be devised. In the same fashion the medals belonging to the old Este cabinet of Modena (now dispersed) may yet be recognised by the tiny silver imperial eagle let into their field. The ladies of the Medici family who married into the house of France appear to have carried away with them, amongst the other jewels of their *trousseaux*, many of Lorenzo's original pieces, and this will account for the wide dispersion of camei, with his name still marking them. In this way Margarita, widow of Alessandro dei Medici,

* Gori in his 'Museum Florentinum' has described 1010 intagli, and 181 camei of this collection, amongst the most valuable for either design or workmanship.

brought with her on her second marriage (to Ottavio Farnese) many fine gems out of the original cabinet into that of Parma, which, accompanying the Farnese dynasty, passed thence into the Museo Borbonico. Many more changed owners at the pillage of the Medici palace on Piero's expulsion, and were never restored.

Of the latter event a brief notice is indispensable for completing the history of this collection. Soon after the entrance of Charles VIII. into Italy, Piero (Lorenzo's son), who had put into his hands the fortresses of Sarzana and Livorno, became, in consequence of this act of cowardice, so odious to the Florentines, that, fearing for his life, he made his escape to Venice, whence he never returned home. Having followed his patron to the campaign of Naples, he was drowned by the upsetting of a ferry-boat on the Garigliano, after the great battle of that name in the year 1505. Immediately upon his flight from Florence his own allies, the French, entered the city, and being joined by the populace, with the utmost deliberation set to work to plunder the Medici palace (now the Ricardi), and dispersed or destroyed the whole of the statues, ancient MSS., and gems, long-accumulated treasures of art and literature, therein deposited. How it came to pass that so many of the latter were recovered, and the collection to so great an extent set upon its old footing, is hard to say, but is nevertheless a happy fact. Perhaps the founder's precaution of putting his name upon all the important pieces had made their retention a dangerous matter after his family were restored to power and Leo X. was labouring to rehabilitate the lost glories of his inheritance. The plunderers were (it may naturally be supposed) content with stripping the stones of their valuable mountings, more safely convertible into cash;—for at present they are mostly unmounted—a thing quite out of character with the prevailing taste in Lorenzo's times.

Giulianelli often quotes a MS. '*Istoria delle Pietre*,' written about the year 1597 by Frate Agostino del Riccio, a Dominican, and a special favourite of Francesco I. In the course of the work he names many then famous engravers, both Florentines and foreigners, and quotes many of their most noted performances Of the latter he gives drawings done by Vicenzio Doni. The MS. was then (1753) in the possession of the family Roselli. It is a pity no one has published it, for being composed under such favourable circumstances, it would form a valuable supplement to Vasari's 'Ragionamento.'

In my notices of the Modern Engravers ('Antique Gems'),

many particulars will be found as to the special patronage succeeding princes of the house of Medici extended to this particular art—the last of the race, Gian Gastone, worthily closing his career by adding to the cabinet the rare and singular gems of the Prior Vaini, which included several works by Costanzi upon the diamond and ruby (now unhappily lost through the great robbery of 1860).

In our times (1862) the collection has received an important accession by Mr. Currie's (of Como) bequest of his large and most choice series of gems, which, having an interest of their own as being for the greatest part recent discoveries and unpublished, fill Centurie V. and VI. of the *Impronte Gemmarie.* Amongst them is the celebrated Io of Dioscorides, the chief ornament of the (original) Poniatowsky Cabinet.

Of the gems bearing the attestation of Lorenzo's ownership, the finest are the Ariadne on a lion, led by Cupid; the Triumph of in Bacchus, car drawn by twin Psyches, and guided by Cupid—a both in cameo; and a Triton carrying off a Nymph, intaglio. Unique in point of *material* is the head of Tiberius, carved in full relief out of a turquois as large as a walnut. As historical monuments few camei surpass in value the Augustus and Livia, and the Julian with Helena Sacrificing, described under Historical Camei.

Of gems with artists' signatures, the Cupid with lyre on the lion, by Protarchus, stands pre-eminent. Other well-known pieces are the cameo-fragment, by Alexa Quintus; the Jupiter of Aspasius; the Apollo of Allion; the Horseman of Aulus; the Hercules and Iole of Carpus; the Vulcan forging a helmet, of Nicephorus; the Warrior Disarmed, of Nympheros; the Muse Erato, of Onesas; the Hercules of Philippus; the Diomede with the Palladium, of Polycletus; the Dancing Faun of Pygmon; the Hercules and Hebe of Teucer.

All these works will be found described and criticised in Dr. Brann's catalogue of ancient gem-engravers.

The sweeping-away of the *respectable* Grand-ducal Government, and the substitution of the blessings of "constitutional liberty" (and quadruple taxation), were appropriately followed by the mysterious disappearance of these legacies of the Medici. They were, however, soon recovered through the miraculous intervention of the very "Bird of Mercury," for a cock attracted the attention of a farmer by strutting about the barton with an antique cameo dangling from his spur, caught in his raking amongst the straw, where the thieves had concealed their booty, in waiting for the opportunity of smuggling it over to Paris.

OTHER ITALIAN COLLECTIONS.

That of the Vatican Library, though accumulated rather by means of chance acquisitions than by judicious selection, included many of excessive rarity and of extraordinary dimensions; for example, the Carpegna cameo, the largest in existence. The catalogue prepared by Visconti, but unfortunately lost, filled two folio volumes, which will give some notion of the extent of its treasures, to which access is now so difficult to be obtained that few visitors to Rome are aware that they still repose in the Library.

The STROZZI Cabinet possessed, says Visconti, a larger proportion of first-rate works than any other of its kind. Amongst them were the Hercules of Gnæus, the Medusas of Solon and of Sosthenes, the Esculapius of Aulus, the Germanicus of Epitynchanus, the Muse of Allion, the Satyr of Scylax; with many others, unsigned, but of the highest merit. By the founder's will it was attached to the Palazzo Strozzi, in Florence, from which it could not be removed under penalty of forfeiture. It has since been divided between the Russian Imperial Cabinet and the Blacas (lately acquired by the British Museum).

The LVDOVISI, belonging to the Prince di Piombino, includes many valuable gems, both antique and Cinque-cento; its chief ornaments being the Demosthenes of Dioscorides, the Augustus, a cameo by the same artist, and the Mæcenas of Solon (the replica). Casts of sixty-eight of the finest in the number are procurable in Rome.

The Cav. AZARA, minister of Spain, possessed (1790) a collection, formed by himself at a great cost and with much intelligence, and rich in both camei and intagli, valuable either for instruction or for art.

THE FRENCH COLLECTION.*

Of the finest gems in the *Cabinet des Antiques* many have been in France from time immemorial, or at least the dates at which they were brought in and the names of the persons to whom they are due are still matters of dispute.† The greatest portion of

* This historical notice is translated from Clarac's catalogue. For a description of its contents see Chabouillet's 'Cat. des Camées de la Bib. Impériale,' 1858, a work deserving the highest praise for its lucid descriptions of, and copiousness of information connected with, the most remarkable items.

† A vast amount of precious stones were brought into Aquitaine, after the sack of Rome, by the troops of Alaric, and deposited in the Gothic capital, Narbonne. These fell into the hands of the Franks, and subsequently being consecrated by the piety of the Carlovingians to embellish ecclesiastical furniture, have come down safely to our times.

them proceed from the munificence of the various kings of France, and from the travels undertaken at their command; others were presents made to themselves and given by them to the public. Many again are the fruits of conquest—S. Louis, as well as others of the Crusading princes, brought back from the East some of their number.

The covers of the royal missals and of their choice MSS. were adorned with these gems, as we see from a few examples still remaining.* Charles V. and his brother the Duc de Berri were passionately fond of jewels, and their treasures were extremely rich both in engraved gems and in precious stones, as may be seen from the curious inventory of the jewels of the former prince, preserved in the Bibliothèque. François I., to whom France owes so many masterpieces of antique sculpture (procured in Italy through his agents Primaticcio and Cellini), and who, as Vasari phrases it, had made another Rome of Fontainebleau, drew also out of Italy and other countries a vast number of engraved gems, for which he paid enormous prices. Thus the taste for them was diffused amongst his courtiers: they adorned the armour, the gold chains, the hats, the doublets of these warriors, and also served for the decoration of the dresses of the ladies of the court and of the nobility. Henri II. and Catherine de Medicis followed his example: the latter queen had also brought with her from Florence a large quantity of fine gems.

The first who brought them together into one cabinet was Charles IX., who formed in the Louvre the Cabinet des Antiquités, which, however, was plundered and dispersed shortly afterwards during the civil wars. It was not in existence on the accession to the throne of Henri IV.; but this great prince re-established it. He summoned from Provence a learned antiquary, Rascas de Bagarris, with the intention of purchasing the large collection of medals and gems formed by this amateur, in order to unite it with what was left of the old royal collection still at Fontainebleau, where the Royal library was kept at the time. This scheme was prevented by the king's death, and was not resumed until the time of Louis XIV., whose uncle, Gaston d'Orléans, had bequeathed to him a considerable collection of various antiquities, including amongst the rest a large number of gems, derived partly from that of the President De Mêmes, which had been formed out of a selection from the 2000 engraved stones got together by

* And the camei more especially served for the decoration of their fanciful and elaborate pieces of plate, of which many examples will be found in the inventory of the plate of the Duc d'Anjou (1360–8), published by Laborde.

Louis Chaduc in Italy. This cabinet was at first deposited in the Louvre; but Colbert, in 1664, replaced it in the Bibliothèque.

Louis XIV. purchased antique gems from all quarters, including the collections of Gualdi and that formed in the East by De Monceaux. Louvois in 1684 removed the medals and gems to Versailles, and appointed Carcavy keeper of them. The king often amused himself with examining these treasures, and augmented them by the addition of those of Harlai, Oursel, and Thomas le Comte. Towards the close of the seventeenth century Louis had purchased the splendid collection of Lauthier of Aix, Provence, formed with great judgment, and under the direction of the learned Peiresc, whose own gems had been purchased by Lauthier. Thus at last the king became master of the cabinet of Bagarris, which Henri IV., as already noticed, had been in treaty for, and which, on the founder's death, had come into Lauthier's hands and been incorporated with his own. To this belonged the famous "signet of M. Angelo." *

The various travels undertaken in the interests of science by Nointel, Lucas, De la Croix, and Vaillant, all carried on at this monarch's charge and at a vast cost, greatly contributed to enrich the Cabinet of Antiquities. It was still further augmented by the purchase in 1775 of the medals of Pellerin, by the bequest of Caylus, by the purchase of Foucault's collections, and by the incorporation of the Trésor de Sainte Geneviève in 1796. The total number of the gems was 1388 in 1848, when Clarac wrote. In 1858 Chabouillet gives the total as 2536 of camei and intagli, antique, and modern. The camei are 699; the Oriental, cylinders, cones, &c., 708; intagli, antique, 760; Gnostic, 187; Arabic, 29; the rest Renaissance and modern.

In this series are to be found the supposed names of the engravers, Aulus, Dioscorides, Evodus, Glycon, Gnæus, Hyllus, Midias, Pamphilus, Panæus. The intagli are distinguished as much for the beauty of the material as for the variety of their subjects. † And as regards camei, nothing can be

* Valued at the time at 50,000 fr. (2000*l.*); Lauthier himself had paid 200 pistoles (about 160*l.*) for it, an enormous sum for his times.

† This is Clarac's assertion, but must be regarded as the *fanfaronnade* of a Frenchman speaking of things French. The assemblage of intagli is, in truth, as a whole, rather poor—not comparable to that at Florence, Naples, Berlin, or even in our country to the Marlborough. The real glory of the French cabinet are the camei, the traditionary spoils of the last Roman and Byzantine Cæsars, or the magnificent works due to the patronage of the Valois dynasty.

cited as surpassing in the volume of the stone and the beauty of the work the following pieces; the Apotheosis of Augustus, better known as the Agate of the Sainte Chapelle, brought to Paris by Baldwin II. in 1244; the Apotheosis of Germanicus, also coming from Constantinople; the Augustus; the Annius Verus; the Jupiter, from Chartres Cathedral; and the sardonyx vase, designated the "Cup of the Ptolemies," or "Vase of S. Denys," the grandest specimen remaining of the ancient *onychina.*

This Collection, so "rich with the spoils of Time," has in our day received an important accession in that of the Duc de Luynes (unparalleled for its Oriental series); and which he, like a true representative of the *ancien régime*, presented to the nation in his *lifetime.*

THE NAPLES COLLECTION.

The original Cabinet formed part of the magnificent collection of antique and modern works of art accumulated by the princes of the Farnese family, in their celebrated palace, during the century and a half succeeding the papacy of Paul III., the founder of the line of the Dukes of Parma, and augmented by many rarities from the Medicean, brought into the family by Margarita, Alessandro's widow. When the family became extinct in the person of Elisabetta Farnese, wife of the first Bourbon King of Spain, early in the eighteenth century, her eldest son, Carlos IV., on his appointment to the throne of Naples, received in right of his mother the property of the ancestral palace at Rome, and lost no time in transferring all its treasures of art to decorate his newly created capital. Thus was laid the foundation of the noble Museo Borbonico, to which in despite of the oscitancy of his successors, from the constant favours of accident, notably in the discoveries of Pompeii and Herculaneum, accessions of the greatest importance were frequently made, almost without an effort on the part of the government to procure them.

The gems, to confine my description to my special subjcet, fall far short in point of number (337 intagli, 263 camei) of those at Florence, but yet rank as the second Cabinet in Italy, and perhaps equal the Paris, if not in extent, at least in value. Amongst the most important pieces may be particularised the cameo of Jupiter overthrowing the Titans, by Athenion, a work better known to the public from its perpetual reproduction than any other glyptic monument; the dispute of Neptune and Pallas about giving a name to Athens, signed with the monogram ΠΥ, and hence supposed to be the sole authentic work of Pyrgoteles now in existence; another (if genuine) by that early artist Tryphon, a replica in intaglio of the Marlborough "Marriage of Cupid and Psyche;" and a most glorious specimen of engraving in relief, the famous Farnese Vase (found in Hadrian's mausoleum), of one enormous sardonyx, for which 10,000 ducats were paid. Amongst the intagli are numbered some of the highest importance in the list of signed gems, such as the Perseus of Dioscorides; the Seahorse of Pharnaces, and the Muse of Apollonius.

Those engraved upon transparent stones are arranged according to an ingenious plan, calculated to afford a minute inspection of the work and yet defending the gems from the risk of being handled by amateurs. They are placed in perforated trays glazed on both sides, working upon a hinge and capable of being raised by turning a screw to any angle most convenient for allowing the light to pass through their body, and thus bring out all the delicate minutiæ of the figures.

VIENNA.

The Imperial Cabinet at Vienna contains 949 intagli, and 262 camei. As far as the latter are concerned, it nearly equals the French in point of numbers, and surpasses it in one thing, the possession of the finest work of the kind now in existence, the Triumph of Germanicus—better known as the "Gemma Augustea;" besides this, the Eagle, the family of Claudius, the Ptolemy and Arsinoe, the Tiberius, the Cybele rank amongst the largest and most beautiful camei in existence—already described at length. The possession of nearly the whole of Italy for two centuries by the Spanish branch of the Hapsburg line, the successive pillage of its richest capitals at various periods by the Imperial troops (Rome, Milan, Mantua, Genoa, &c.), furnished the finest opportunities for irregular acquisitions; which, backed by the good taste of a few of the first emperors of the race, as Rodolf II. and Matthias, have led to the accumulation of this large number of gems. It must, however, be admitted that but little critical discrimination has been exercised in the selection of a large proportion of the number, those of the Renaissance period greatly preponderating. Eckhel has published forty of the most important camei in a quarto volume illustrated with very correct engravings of them; and in this century Arneth has made known twelve more of considerable interest.

HOLLAND.

The Cabinet of The Hague is of considerable extent, but enjoys the unenviable reputation of being rich in forgeries. It may well be supposed that the Dutch taste in this line of antiquities is not of the most correct, and would delight more in the luxuriant and vast creations of the Cinque-cento in camei, and of Sirletti and the Pichlers in intagli, than in the minute and rigid correctness of the true antique. The collection appears to have been formed at three distinct periods, the original of small extent having been augmented by the purchase of that got together by Hemsterhuis, under the guidance of Natter, which consists as might be expected of nothing but copies more or less successful. To these was superadded the very much more numerous De Thoms Collection, abounding in pieces formerly esteemed invaluable from the artist's signature upon them, none of which, alas! have been able to bear the test of modern criticism, so that the credit of the whole stands but little higher than that of the notorious Poniatowsky.

RUSSIAN CABINET.

This Collection, kept in the palace of Zarskoje-selo, was formed by the Empress Catharine II. : "the Genius of the Arts," says Köhler, "has to thank Russia's exalted empress for this, as for so many other monuments of her taste, which manifests itself in its full magnificence in her veneration for and fine appreciation of these fairest fruits of antiquity." It was formed by the purchase of the famous Orleans Cabinet, those of Natter, Casanova, Maurice, Lord Algernon Percy (the Beverley), and many subsequent additions: making "it by far the most extensive in existence, as it numbers more than 10,000 gems," of which the camei constitute much the largest portion. Köhler specifies as the most important in their respective classes—*Egyptian*: several scarabæi in green stone, of unusual size, covered with hieroglyphics. Isis, a head in very high relief in malachite, worked out with a decision, delicacy, and finish not to be exceeded. The head is covered with the skin of a phœnicopterus, the wings of which fall on each side the face. Another Head of Isis, cameo in agate-onyx in the same attire, a sard with same bust intaglio, and another Isis suckling Horus with her finger—are in the Greco-Egyptian manner. So is a full-length figure of Osiris in cameo, distinguished for correct drawing and careful execution. A seated Harpocrates, is a cameo in a pure Greek style, showing no imitation of the Egyptian manner.

Etruscan.—Ajax carrying off the slain Achilles, inscribed with their names; the back of the scarabæus cut into the shape of a Syren tearing her robe (emblem of the departing soul). Theseus seated in Hades, with the name ΘΕΣΕ; a stone too large to have been sawn off a scarab: formerly Baron Reidesel's. The Horses of Diomedes devouring Abderus; the Horses of Achilles; Triptolemus: Pegasus; the Slave of Cadmus, carrying two amphoræ; Hippodamia in a triga driving over the corpse of a vanquished suitor; a Chimera. Many others unpublished, or wrongly explained, as the Polynices on horseback. A seated Nymph bearing on her hand the Infant Bacchus, both figures winged, in the field a caduceus. Very remarkable is a striped agate of extremely old work, a Pallas, completely armed, and advancing to the combat. A seated Old Man holding in one hand a staff, in the other a roll, an ancient rhapsodist, probably designed for Homer himself. A Wounded Tydeus remarkable for the extreme delicacy and correctness in some portions, whilst the head and muscles of the sides are only indicated by drill-holes. A scarabæus in burnt carnelian, remarked for the constrained attitude of the figure, perhaps Tydeus gnawing the skull of his enemy.

Greek gems, to a very considerable number; of which may be noticed, a cameo Head of Jupiter crowned with laurel; another on a splendid sardonyx, crowned with oak leaves. A Seated Dodonean Jove with the Dove upon his hand, the Jupiter Axur, or more probably the Augustus, signed ΝΕΙΣΟΥ in a splendid sard. Two scarabæi cut into heads of Jupiter Apomyios. A Jupiter and Leda; and Jupiter as a Satyr and Antiope. A cameo Ganymede on a large sardonyx, where the work is as perfect as the dexterity with which the strata have been employed. A small sard with bust of Pallas peculiarly treated, the ægis being represented as an actual goatskin, upon which the Gorgoneion is tied sideways by two of its snakes. A Naked Venus, cameo on a large agate-onyx, where the perfect drawing of the nude in a difficult attitude is as admirable as the delicate execution of the work. Particularly beautiful, the head of Diana, in cameo; and of Mars, in intaglio. Some Heads of Bacchus conceived with the utmost beauty. A cameo, Aurora in a biga, the horses seeming filled with divine fire; another Aurora guiding the Solar car, of no less perfect work, with the name of the artist ΡΟΥΦΟC. The cameo Hermaphroditus passes for the finest known with this subject. As especially beautiful may be pointed out, a cameo head of Victory; some figures of the Muses; a sard with head of the Youthful Hercules; an amethyst of the same head but older and seen in front; another crowned with oak-leaves, a cameo. A Bacchante where the drapery is full of spirit; a Faun sporting with a Nymph; a Sacrifice to Pan; an Eurydice; two heads of Leander; a sard with Achilles in his car; Heads of Hector and Andromache; some Children's Heads of very elegant work amongst a large number of similar design. A Cornelia, a masterpiece as to the drapery; some fine Heads of Alexander; and a little Perseus, a magnificent Greek work. One of the most famous camei in the world, quoted by Winckelmann as the ne plus ultra of the art, the cameo on agate-onyx, Perseus and Andromeda, formerly belonging to Cav. Mengs,* and of equal reputation with the Gonzaga cameo—the figures in very high relief cut in milk-white, upon a dark brown stratum. As a rare piece, may be named a Gorgon's Head in cameo, with a wing on the one side and two horns springing from the same base upon the other: Apollo perpetuating his grief on the Hyacinth into which his favourite was metamorphosed; a head signed ΥΛΛΟΥ; another, Antinous, ΕΛΛΗΝ; and the Mæcenas, ΣΟΛΩΝΟΣ. The well-known Head with the veil across the mouth, formerly called Ptolemy Auletes, but better explained by Winckelmann as Hercules in a female garb. Figure of a Youth with inverted torch on sard, the Genius of Death.

In the *Roman* department the series of imperial heads is uninterrupted from Julius to the Decline; there are here sometimes more than twenty good heads of the same prince. Perfect gems are the Heads of Augustus; Livia; the united Heads of Agrippina, Drusilla, and Livilla on the same stone; Tiberius; Poppæa; Faustina; Caracalla; two large sards, portraits of Julia Titi: and two of the Gordians, good for their period.

Of the *animals*, the most conspicuous is a Lion, an extraordinary fine Dog's Head; and many magnificent Eagles.

The Cabinet is also rich in inscriptions on gems, both in cameo and intaglio, worked out with amazing industry. "The glance of the traveller in the regions of antiquity tarries fondly amongst these memorials of affection and the finer feelings of the heart; all these stones being gifts of lovers, pledges of attachment mutually exchanged to keep up the memory of the beloved object at every moment. The vast number of such gems appears to have given occupation to a particular class of engravers, devoted solely to this branch of the art."

Of Coptic, Persian, and Turkish inscriptions on gems, this cabinet contains a large number.

It is also rich in the works of modern artists, *e.g.* Valerio

* Purchased from his heirs for 3000 scudi = 600*l.*—(Fea.)

Vicentino; Domenico di Polo; Cesati; Coldoré; Guay; Brown, and other famous masters, amongst whom Pichler deserves especial mention for his admirably executed figure of the Herculanean Dancing-girl.

Remarkable also is a set of subjects from Modern History, forming a separate collection, amongst which is a series of heads and allegorical designs relating to Russian history. "The portraits of the Imperial family in cameo are from the hand of H.I.H. the Grand-Duchess *Maria Feodorowna*, in which the accuracy of the likeness as much as the fineness and delicacy of the execution is worthy of admiration."

"In conclusion it may be remarked, that nowhere else will be found works in which rarity of material, and of its strata and colours, and the ability for their advantageous employment, are manifested so conspicuously as in the Russian Collection. As regards art, indeed, such costly productions have in themselves no real worth; but when united with masterly, ingenious treatment, why should we not coincide with the taste of the ancients in this particular, as concerns works which in the main point must ever remain to us models of perfection far beyond our reach?" From Köhler's account of the manner, the time, and the circumstances under which this Collection was formed, I strongly suspect that if examined by a critical eye it would be found to swarm with works of the last century in the department of intagli, and of the Renaissance in the camei; as indeed must be the case if it numbers above 8000 of the latter. The Orleans Cabinet, however, contained many important antiques, as may be seen from St. Aubin's exquisite engravings of the greater portion here cited, in the two sumptuous folios, the 'Pierres Gravées d'Orléans' (pub. 1780–4).

BERLIN.

The immense Collection of Berlin, by far the largest yet formed after the Russian, has for its foundation the old cabinet of the Electors of Brandenburg: the "Great Elector" having bought part of the Heidelberg Gems on the death of the Elector Charles II., in 1694; the remainder going to the Duc d'Orléans. To this were added the Collection of the Margrave of Anspach; that of Stosch, numbering 3544 stones and pastes, purchased by Frederick the Great for 30,000 ducats; that of Bertoldy, consisting entirely of antique pastes; besides later acquisitions. These form the enormous total of 4490 stones, and 848 pastes. Of these have been classed 3634, being the intagli alone, as follows:—

1. Egyptian and Oriental, 165; pastes, 31.
2. Etruscan and Early Greek, 151; pastes, 30.
3. Greek and Roman religion, 1141; pastes, 355.
4. Monuments, Heroes, 263; pastes, 172.
5. Historical subjects, 190; pastes, 70.
6. Ancient Domestic life, 138; pastes, 71.
7. Arms, Vases, Masks, 297; pastes, 66.
8. Animals, 316; pastes, 47.
9. Inscriptions and Abraxas, 125; pastes, 6.

Of these, 316 gems and 115 pastes present Heads; and 2470 gems, and 753 pastes, various subjects. Amongst them occur the names of supposed artists—Agathangelus, Agathopus, Alexa, Apollonides, Aulus, Craterus, Diocles, Diodorus, Deuton, Gnæus, Hellenius, Hermaiscus, Hyllus, Seleucus, Solon.

The finest gems to the number of 1100 are mounted in gold, the rest in silver. Of stones retaining their antique settings, there are 65, twenty-five of which are rings (in gold). Set in silver, antique rings, 9; in bronze, 15; in iron, 26; in lead, 1. By the side of each intaglio is placed a cast from it in plaster, the only mode of facilitating the study of the beauties and defects of the work, when it can only be examined through glass, not be taken in the hand. From Berlin this plan was introduced into the Collection of the Bibliothèque, Paris. Selections of 50 casts to each set, forming a chronological series of the different styles, and neatly mounted in the form of a small 4to. volume, are to be obtained at the Museum, price three thalers per volume. These casts are made in a manner superior to anything of the kind that has come under my notice during a very extensive experience in similar reproductions.

I have published already in a separate form a detailed description of Her Majesty's Camei and Engraved Gems, together with one of the Marlborough. (Reprinted from the 'Archæological Journal,' vols. xviii. and xix.)

The former of these consists principally of the 'Dactyliotheca Smithiana,' added to a few relics of the treasures of Henry VIII., Elizabeth, and Charles I.*

The latter, vying in the number and importance of its contents with almost any other cabinet in existence, has been gradually created by the incorporation into the Arundelian (formerly belong-

* 739 camei and intagli. It has since changed owners, and passed into the possession of a Mr. Broomilaw for the equivalent of £30,000.

ing to the Mæcenas of that name) of the Bessborough, collected in the early part, and finally of the numerous acquisitions made by the Ducal owner, at the close of the last century.*

Of *private gem-collections* in this country, only two of any importance are known to me as still remaining—the *Bale* and the *Rhodes.* The first of these has grown up to its present considerable extent by a very judicious selection from every cabinet brought to the hammer in London, during the last thirty years. It consists exclusively of *intagli*, and is particularly rich in specimens of the early Greek and Etruscan periods.

(*Fuit Ilium!* must be said of these collections, dispersed, the one by public, the other by private sale since the above was written; and again, in the sad category of things that *have* been, must be included the choice cabinet of nearly four hundred intagli of every antique school, formed with long-continued labour, directed by taste and judgment, by Mr. Short; and literally *sacrificed* by auction in the May of the present year, 1885.)

* The Devonshire Cabinet, and the celebrated *Parure* composed out of its choicest pieces, will be found noticed at length in my 'Antique Gems,' first edition.

ARTISTS' SIGNATURES.

Ever since the date, at the beginning of the last century, when the Regent Orleans had expressed his opinion to Baudelot de Dairval (published by the latter in 1712) that the name ΣΟΛΩΝΟϹ on the famous sard in the Vienna Cabinet was that of the *engraver*, not of the *person* thereon engraved, as had been previously believed, an unlucky mania seized all amateurs for interpreting in this sense every name occurring upon a gem, provided only it were inscribed in Greek characters. Without loss of time did Forgery also come to the assistance of this most flattering delusion in that branch of art—gem-engraving—which has ever been its especial field; and the interpolations made to the order of Andreini and of Baron Stosch swelled the list of names, and furnished Bracci with a goodly roll-call of the engravers adorning every epoch in the history of Glyptics. The first to parade before the amateur-world his treasures in this newly-discovered line was Andreini, a Florentine gem-collector, who published several then in his own cabinet, five of which Dr. Brunn allows (in accordance to his own rules) to be genuine; the rest he pronounces all works of Flavio Sirletti's (the first reviver of the antique mode of gem-engraving); but whether the latter had been passed off upon Andreini himself as genuine, or actually executed to his commission, as Köhler maintains, is a question that must ever remain undecided.

Soon afterwards Baron Stosch, besides accumulating his own vast collection, was supplying the wealthy dilettanti who visited Rome with unique pieces that would elicit sufficiently enormous offers to induce him to surrender their possession to the bidder: witness the famous Cow of Apollonides, acquired from him by the Duke of Devonshire, and the other supposititious masterpieces, already noticed, which passed through his hands. Natter, at the commencement of his career, worked at Florence under his patronage, and, beyond a doubt, supplied him with both new-made intagli and with interpolated names upon antique stones. Although this clever engraver, whilst confessing that he had put ancient artists' names upon his own works, denies that he had ever sold such for antiques, little credit can be placed in this reservation; for what possible motive, except a fraudulent one, could have induced this assumption of a borrowed name? Köhler even attributes to the crafty Baron the invention of another and yet more impudent species of fraud,—that of fabricating *signed* antique pastes from mere wax models having no actual prototype in gems.

The vast success attending the interpolation of signatures made it universal: almost every fine work of antiquity that came into the market during the remainder of the century was enriched (or rather deteriorated) by the foisting in of some supposed artist's name, borrowed either from Pliny's catalogue of noted sculptors and silver-chasers, or from the epitaphs of the freedmen of Livia Augusta (some of whom are therein described as *aurifices*), published by Gori about the same time. Sevin, of Paris, is said to have been Stosch's chief agent in this traffic, both in disposing of pieces altogether new creations, and of antique stones retouched and provided with a name to recommend them to wealthy amateurs. The interpolation of *names* upon antique works had indeed been long practised in Italy, but in an entirely different meaning, and one easily to be detected: more laughable, in fact, than injurious to the credit of the monument. Coincidently with the first dawn of the Revival in Italy, gems presenting the effigies of ancient worthies were most eagerly sought after, as we may perceive from the efforts of Fulvius Ursinus thus to augment his series, entitled, "Imagines Virorum Illustrium e marmoribus, nummis et *gemmis* expressæ." Actuated by this impulse, the clumsy fraud of those uncritical times speedily cut names upon the field of unknown portraits to convert them into likenesses of such historical characters as the features seem best adapted to represent from the coincidence of the physiognomy with the traditional reputation of the personage.* Thus I have noticed (in the Marlborough Collection) some aged Roman "nobody" transformed into a *Caius Marius* by the addition of COS VII., and some unknown Greek prince (Rhodes Collection) made invaluable in the new character of the famous Numidian by the insertion below of the name IVGVRTHA. Similarly the Mæcenas already alluded to, not being identified till long after by the fortunate discovery of a bust, was, in virtue of the profundity of its expression, considered as especially appropriate for the Athenian legislator, and on this score was equipped with the name of Solon: the true source whence have flowed all the supposed

* Portrait statues and busts of private Romans of imperial times were likewise metamorphosed by the same facile means into the sages and heroes of Greece and Consular Rome.

signatures of that imaginary artist. Fortunately, these early interpolations are cut in a lettering savouring so strongly of its own real date, and so dissimilar to the antique, that there is not the least danger of their imposing upon any experienced eye. Far different is the case with the productions of the last century, when even the finest gem was held of comparatively little value unless thus endowed with a historical certificate of its origin, and when the most eminent engravers of the day, like J. Pichler himself, condescended to further the deception by inserting names, with the utmost skill and delicacy, in the field of antique works to gratify the desire of the too unscrupulous dealer and of the too credulous amateur: the latter readily falling into the snare, having an ill-counsellor in his own avidity—

"Quis enim damnet sua vota libenter?"

But this folly having been pushed to the extreme, a reaction naturally set in, and the sagacious but too cynical Köhler undertook, in an elaborate treatise, to demolish the whole of the specious edifice that had been growing up during the previous eighty years upon the foundation of that single conjecture ventured by the tasteful Regent. Out of the whole catalogue drawn up by Bracci and republished by Clarac, *five* only have been allowed to escape his condemnation as recent insertions, and to go down to posterity as the genuine signatures of the ancient engravers. These are, the Diana of *Apollonius;* the Germanicus of *Epitynchanus;* the Julia Titi of *Evodus;* the Jupiter overthrowing the Titans of *Athenion;* and the Cupid of *Protarchus;* the two last, camei.

After a long consideration of this especial point, I myself have reluctantly been brought to agree (to even a greater extent, and on entirely different grounds) with the Russian archæologist in almost completely sweeping away the host of pretended signatures; although I differ totally from him in his constantly repeated dictum that each name passed under his judgment (justly *Draconian*) is *ipso facto* a modern insertion. For I hold on the strength of actual observation, that in many cases the inscriptions are from the same hand as the intaglio itself, and equally authentic; it is only the newly-imagined way of understanding them as referring to the artist himself that is, in my opinion, utterly untenable.

The principle from which I start is deduced from the very nature of the thing we have to deal with. It is an obvious and rational explanation that the name cut upon a signet should necessarily designate its owner,—a custom regularly established in the most ancient of the class, the Babylonian cylinders, and from them adopted in many instances by their disciples in the arts, the Ionian Greeks. For, be it remembered, these fine intagli, now treasured as mere works of art, were to the ancient household articles of the utmost importance in the affairs of life both public and private, and by no means idle objects of luxury like their silver *emblemata*, ivory carvings, and Corinthian bronzes. They were, indeed, often beautiful, displaying both taste and skill in their full perfection; but this was only in accordance to the rule that whatever came under the ancient eye assumed beauty as a matter of course (as we see manifested in the forms given to their commonest domestic utensils); and yet frequently their signet-devices, being dictated by family tradition or by religious ideas, are the commonest, nay, even grotesque, objects.

From the importance, therefore, of the articles, it cannot be supposed that the engraver (often, in the Roman period, a slave-artisan, and never, probably, holding a higher place in society than a common die-sinker of our times) should have been allowed to intrude his own ignobility upon the signet of the rich and powerful orderer of his work. For a name so inserted would inevitably have passed for that of the actual owner of the signet, in spite of the nice and arbitrary distinctions, hereafter to be detailed, whereby Dr. Brunn endeavours to discriminate the artist's from the master's signature. And this acceptation were the more natural, because the owner's name frequently accompanied and certified his family device, more especially upon the earlier Roman signets: the very time, be it observed, when the most skilful of these artists are supposed to have flourished. The hypothesis elaborated by Dr. Brunn would have been infinitely more plausible had any gems been forthcoming, presenting two different names on the same field, displaying some such marked distinction between them as should enable the casual observer to refer one to the possessor, the other to the artist.*

The same rule holds good for the ancient die-sinkers, in whose falsely assumed practice a precedent has been found to establish the credibility of the existence of artists' signatures upon gems. The names engraved in minute characters upon certain unobtrusive parts of the type occasionally to be discovered on some Greek civic medals (notably those of Velia) have always been understood as indicating the die-sinkers. This explanation, however, is in all

* Of which, indeed, a solitary instance presents itself in the supposed work of "Felix (servant) of Calpurnius Severus;" the gem being in reality his private seal.

probability erroneous, it being infinitely more consistent with the regulations of the Grecian republics that such names should indicate the mint-master or treasurer for the time being. To put upon the coinage the name of the officer responsible for its goodness (the quæstor, triumvir monetalis, monetarivs) was a very ancient law, almost universally observed under the Roman Republic, and as generally in the Frankish and mediæval periods. In certain localities, whilst Greek art yet flourished, we see the name of this officer, the Ταμίας, is printed as legibly as possible on the reverse of the coinage; for example, upon the later Athenian tetradrachms* and all the silver of Rhodes. This name, in other cases, seems to have been expressed in a rebus by the small object or figure placed behind the type, to be noticed in such endless variety upon the Corinthian didrachms, which, like the Athenian tetradrachms, were a universal currency, and therefore demanded the most complete guarantees for the maintenance of their accredited standard. It is, indeed, very possible that these accessory types represent the actual seal of the then mint-master: for in the Heraclean inscription, as already noticed, each magistrate specifies what was the device of his own signet.

It must, not, however, be concealed that some examples in which the die-sinker has placed his own name upon his work actually do exist, and that in a most conspicuous manner. Of this only two instances are known; the one a coin of Cydonia, in Crete, inscribed with ΝΕΥΑΝΤΟΣ ΕΠΟΙΕΙ; † the other the beautiful didrachm of Clazomenæ, exhibiting ΘΕΟΔΩΡΟΣ ΕΠΟΙΕΙ; but their excessive rarity proves such to have been merely trial-pieces of these artists. It may easily be imagined that as the decoration of public buildings and temples was put up for competition amongst the first sculptors of the day—a custom of which Pliny cites numerous instances,—so, similarly, the making the dies for a new and improved coinage of the same States may have been awarded to a successful candidate on the production of his trial-piece, as was actually done in our own times by the short-lived French Republic of 1848–9.

The latter consideration has now brought us back to the analogous case of our inscribed gems in those rare examples whose existence can be traced back long before this species of forgery was thought of (as the Julia of *Evodus*, once possessed by

* Some of which are extant, bearing the name of Demosthenes, who is known to have once filled that office; and also of Mithridates.

† To which M. Froehner has lately added a third, ΕΓΛΥΨΕ ΜΕΝΕΤΥΣ on a coin of Aspendus.

Charlemagne, or the Pallas of *Eutyches*, described by Cyriac of Ancona in 1445), where the names are definitely marked for the engraver's own by the addition of ΕΠΟΙΕΙ. This aquamarine, this amethyst, valuable in their time as jewels for their extraordinary dimensions, were never, as their size demonstrates, intended for signet-gems; they were probably votive offerings to the deity thereon figured or to the princess, like the crystal-portrait immortalised in the Anthology, presented by its engraver Satyreius to Queen Arsinoe. Or they may be supposed designed for ornaments for plate or for the bracelet, and intended to be employed in capacities that permitted the artist's name to exhibit itself upon them as unobjectionally as (what was then the rule) upon a bas-relief or a picture. Again, they may have been only trial-pieces, elaborate displays of skill made by the engraver to his patroness, whether divine or human. That such trial-pieces in gems were actually in use under the Empire is rendered no mere matter of conjecture by the existence of Stosch's crystal plaque, engraved with the obverse and reverse die for an aureus, and surrounded by the legend wishing a Happy New Year to the Emperor Commodus, a man of much taste in the article of coinage, as the variety and beauty of his medallions sufficiently attest. At all events, such large gems (and on such alone is the only indisputable certificate of authorship, the word ΕΠΟΙΕΙ, to be found) were not signets, and therefore they fall under the same category as the camei, on which authentic signatures of the kind are more frequent. No *genuine* example has yet been adduced of an actual signet gem of the usual size, intended for wearing on the finger, that presents a name accompanied by this distinctive declaration of its engraver. Again, in all the examples (which, in fact, form the majority of those published) where the name is written in *Greek* in the *genitive case*, it is utterly groundless to imagine that it can stand for any one but the owner's; for the same reason as (which no one has ever dreamed of disputing) when the name is expressed in *Latin* it is put in that same case, to declare that the object sealed therewith is the property or receives the attestation of the sealer. To supply, according to the now received rule of explanation, the word ἔργον, *the work of*, before this genitive, has not the slightest authority in antique practice. For in all other branches of art, sculpture, vase-paintings, mosaics, all works that are inscribed with their author's name present that name in the nominative, and followed by ΕΠΟΙΕΙ or its contraction.

One condition, much insisted upon by the former catalogue-makers such as Bracci and Clarac, that the real artist-signatures are always inscribed in the Greek character (with the conclusion built thereupon, after the very popular mode of arguing in a circle, that signatures thus written do for the most part refer to the engraver) is totally fallacious, as will appear from the following considerations. For what was more natural than that at the very time when Greek was the fashionable language amongst the polite Romans (which exactly coincided with the flourishing period of the Glyptic art), all men of taste would affect the use of that language upon their own signets, engraved, be it remembered, by artists whose native tongue was Greek. We have a somewhat analogous case in the mediæval usage of our own ancestors, where the Norman-French, as the language of polite society, is generally used upon private seals, and on *posy*-rings, Latin upon public and official ones. Together with the language the Romans adopted the Greek style of patronymic; and inasmuch as in the latter the individual possessed only a *single* name, the Roman noble, complying with this usage, had to relinquish his *nomen* (marking his *gens*) as well as his *cognomen*, and came out like a pure Greek with his *præ-nomen* alone as an ΑΥΛΟΣ, a ΓΑΙΟΣ, or a ΛΕΥΚΙΟΣ. Such names are not those of slave or freedmen artists, for such persons took the family name of their patronus upon their manumissia, as *Claudius*, *Flavius*, *Ælius*, &c., to precede their own.

On the other hand, the old-fashioned Romans who maintained the use of their own language upon their signets, kept up the ancient style, either indicating all their three names at once, more or less in full, or signing with the family name alone, as TITINI, PEDI, COPI, for the most part in the genitive case.

This is the only explanation that satisfies me for the frequent recurrence of such names as Aulus, Gaius, &c., in Greek characters upon gems; a fact so puzzling to Dr. Brunn, but which we need not settle in the summary mode adopted by the caustic Köhler, who cuts short the whole discussion by damning all such inscriptions as flagrant and palpable modern forgeries. Hence too is at last obtainable a complete solution of the difficulty why the same name —*Aulus* for example—should occur on gems evidently proceeding from different hands, in the fact of that same prænomen being necessarily borne by many hundred individuals at one and the same time. The names of persons of Greek extraction, their contemporaries, are easily to be distinguished from the former. Being generally enfranchised slaves, they present names (fancy names we may call them) appropriate to their original condition, like the La Fleur, Hyacinthe, Jasmin, the so frequent appellations borne by the French valets-de-chambre under the ancien régime. Similarly the slaves of the Roman aristocracy, their personal appearance forming their chief recommendation and value, received allusive appellations, such as Eros, Callistus, Cestus, Phlegon, Earinus, Thallus, Marathus, Narcissus, and the like.

Another criterion still much insisted upon, is the minuteness of the lettering, and its horizontal or vertical arrangement, that is to say, its occupying a *straight line* in the field, where a space appears to have been purposely reserved for its reception on the first sketching out of the design, instead of following the sweep of the circumference of the gem as do the undisputed appellatives of the owners. But this distinction seems to me altogether futile as well as arbitrary: such an arrangement having much more probably been adopted from motives of taste alone, both on account of its neater appearance, and its not in any way interfering with the effect of the design. The truth is we *do* find *Roman* names, and written in the *Latin* character, in the field similarly arranged and in a lettering equally diminutive and neat. A most convincing example is furnished by the gem No. 484 in 'Gorlæi Dactyliotheca.' The subject is Cupid sacrificing, with averted eyes, the Psyche-butterfly, and in the field on a tablet placed vertically is the owner's name T. AVCTI, engraved in the neatest and smallest characters imaginable..

But this very perfection of the lettering is in itself often the sign of a forgery, for the genuine antique signatures (like *Nicander's* on the Marlborough Julia) are cut in with bold and careless strokes such as one would expect from a great artist above troubling himself with such minutiæ. But on the other hand Pichler and his followers were adepts in a small elegant lettering where all the lines terminate in dots, a configuration which Köhler, always pushing his theory to the extreme, puts down as the surest test of falsity. These dotted terminations to the letters had however been noticed in the first days of gem-collecting: Peiresc had called attention to them in the signature of Dioscorides, and had accounted for their presence by the absurd hypothesis that they were intended for pins fastening gold letters upon the surface!

The inscription above quoted, T. AVCTI, establishes another point,—that it was not then considered absolutely necessary for the proprietor's name to stand forth in large and obtrusive characters, as if desiring to proclaim that the device itself was but of secondary consideration. It was but consistent in a man of taste who had caused his signet to be engraved by a first-rate artist, to have his own name, requisite perhaps to make his *seal* more valid, introduced in a manner that should interfere as little as possible with the effect of the masterpiece adorning it. And this consideration offers us a second reason for his adopting both the Greek brevity in that particular as well as the Greek character.

It is with regret that I acquiesce in the cruel sentence of Köhler, and abandon the pleasing delusion that we possess any true signature of the famous Dioscorides. All which present that name are ordinary signet-stones, and not of the importance of trial-pieces, or votive offerings; neither does the verifying ΕΠΟΙΕΙ appear on any: two points which authenticate the Minerva of his son Eutyches. All these examples therefore are open to the irrefutable objection applying to inscriptions giving merely a name, and that in the genitive case: occupying also the most conspicuous position. Besides, in the gems of undoubtable antiquity presenting the name of Dioscorides, both the work of the intaglio and the style of the lettering differ so much from each other (a circumstance long ago observed) as to make it impossible to ascribe them all to the same master. Again most of these inscriptions are modern additions, and what is more, the best executed amongst them, have, I suspect, the weakest claims to be accounted genuine. The *improvers* of the last century would naturally do their best in producing what was to pass for the signature of the greatest master in their art. The bolder, carelessly cut letters, on the other hand, seen upon a few of their number—for example, the Marlborough *Mercury* and Pulsky's *Muse* —are on that very account to be received as genuine and from the same hand as the engravings they accompany.

But in all such cases as the last, these inscriptions, I more than suspect, merely indicate the proprietor: for it is by no means a necessary consequence that, if not falsifications, they must signify the celebrated artist. *Dioscorides* was a very favourite name in antiquity, on account of the good augury its signification contained, "the offspring or protégé of the Dioscuri," most potent and protective genii—

"Fratres Helenæ lucida sydera."

Thus by a singular coincidence we find the illustrious father of Botanical science flourishing in the same age with the engraver; a third, a noble of Alexandria, a friend of Julius Cæsar's; with, doubtless, hundreds of others whose fame has not come down to posterity. And again another contemporary of both must have been the maker of that admirable Pompeian mosaic, the Comic Scene, who signs himself *Dioscorides the Samian.* This name, in fact, seems to have been peculiarly affected by the Greeks of Asia Minor, for the botanist belonged to Anazarbus in Cilicia, and the gem-engraver, as the trial-piece of his son Eutyches informs us, to

Ægæ in Æolia. Thus we obtain a reasonable explanation for the difference in the appearance and in the spelling of this name upon gems, as being the signets of various owners, and consequently engraved in different places and at different times, without assuming that such discrepancies betray, of themselves, a forged inscription.

With camei, however, the case stands upon an entirely different footing. Such works being intended for ornament alone, there was no more difficulty in allowing the artist to put his name upon them than upon other bas-reliefs on a larger scale wrought in marble. Accordingly we find the name occupying a corresponding position in the one to what it takes in the other, *Athenion's* in a corner of the field, *Protarchus*' in the exergue. Such inscriptions as these cannot be explained away as subsequent interpolations, for they are cut in relief in a portion of the upper layer of the sardonyx, reserved at the very time of executing the subject. But the paucity of such authentic signatures, under circumstances where there existed no moral obstacle to their insertion, furnishes in itself the strongest argument against their being admitted in that other branch where that insertion would have contravened the very purpose the engraver's work subserved.

It must be kept in mind that of the signatures upon camei, those only are to be received for genuine that are in relief; the others, common enough, merely incised in the stone, being for the most part clearly additions, and in every case to be regarded with the utmost suspicion. This is a rule laid down by Köhler as having no exception. Dr. Brunn, indeed, objects to its sweeping nature; although, in my opinion, upon no sufficient grounds.

It seems to me, however, almost certain, and it is strange the same view of the matter should not have occurred to others, that even genuine names put on camei are not necessarily those of the actual engravers, but in many cases of the famous ancient *Toreutæ* (an art already lost in the Augustan age), whose chasings in silver they were ordered to perpetuate in the more precious material which the spread of luxury had substituted, for the metal relievo, *emblema*, as an ornament for plate and armour. In this way we can satisfactorily account for the names of the masters of high renown in other branches—Protarchus, Athenion, Boethus—appearing upon camei.

There is, however, another and somewhat fanciful solution of the question. As the Greeks used in their families to repeat the same name in alternate generations, the grandson taking as a rule that of his paternal grandfather; the same appellative might be continued in a family of artists for several ages, and in such cases the Roman cameo-cutter would be called by that of his predecessor, the silver-chaser, in the century before. Here, indeed, the exact converse holds good of the rule established with regard to intagli: there is no possible room for conceiving that the name inscribed on a *cameo* is that of the proprietor; it must either designate the actual engraver or the more ancient *cælator* whose work he has reproduced. The latter supposition is the most likely to be correct, and is moreover strengthened by the great rarity of such inscriptions. None are found on the grand historic pieces: and in the minor works where they do occur, it can hardly be by a mere accident they should be exactly those of more ancient masters celebrated in the walk of *toreutice*.

The preceding are my own views upon this subject; but as gem-collectors will undoubtedly consider such a conclusion as a "hard saying," and one not to be borne, I shall proceed to give the rules generally received at present by those regarded as the highest authorities upon this head, so that the next section will serve for a commentary upon the Catalogue of Ancient Gem-Engravers, contained in Dr. Brunn's elaborate treatise, in which he thus modifies the code established by Köhler and Stephani.

RECEIVED RULES FOR ESTABLISHING THE AUTHENTICITY OF ARTISTS' SIGNATURES ON GEMS.

"From the examination of those signatures which are universally acknowledged to be authentic, and which can be traced back far beyond the time (after 1712), when this kind of forgery came into fashion, the subjoined rules have been deduced; based upon the following observations. These undoubted signatures are written in a straight line, either running vertically down the field of the stone, usually close to and parallel with some vertical portion of the design, such as a cippus: or else carried horizontally across in one of the largest unoccupied spaces; provision for its reception having evidently been made in the first sketch of the composition. The letters are reversed upon the gem (if an intaglio), so as to read the right way in the impression from it. They are always minute, so as to escape observation at first, and to appear, what they really are, subsidiary to the work itself: for the same reason they are executed with a certain freedom, totally different from the laborious minuteness so conspicuous in the modern imitations of them. They rarely exhibit the terminal dots placed in the latter with such mathematical exactitude, and connected by fine hair lines. Indeed, this style of lettering is pronounced by Stephani the most certain means of detecting the inscriptions due to the clever forgers of the last century."

"The propriety of the two positions above mentioned, and of these alone, for such memorials of the engraver, becomes self-evident, if we consider the purpose for which every antique signet was designed. As a signet it had a definite and most important use, and its subject involved usually some fixed reference to its owner, like that now claimed by armorial bearings. This being so, a name placed conspicuously would by the world necessarily be understood to designate the owner, and him alone. Of the most conspicuous positions in the field of a gem, the first is the exergue, or position immediately below the design; the second in dignity is the circumference itself of the stone. All names, therefore, occurring in these two positions, whether arranged horizontally under the line of the exergue, or sweeping round with the curvature of the circumference, show by their prominent character and magnitude that they set forth a matter of no less importance than the ownership of the signet itself. Hence it indisputably follows that names thus arranged have nothing whatever to do with the artists, and this conclusion at once reduces the list, as formerly accepted, by fully two-thirds—such names, indeed, are in many cases really antique, but are quoted, without any foundation, by Clarac as indicating the engravers. It need hardly be observed that gems of only mediocre execution cannot be expected to be endorsed with a genuine signature of their author's; the privilege of thus immortalising himself, in the rare instances in which it was conceded, was confined to the man of established reputation, and whose signature added value to his work."

"Names skilfully added, in the appropriate positions, to really antique and fine works, constitute a mode of imposture which on its first introduction met with the greatest success; the purchaser being thrown off his guard by the unquestionable authenticity and merit of the gem itself. Köhler, in fact, does not scruple to assert that such is the case (with the five exceptions already noticed) with several famous pieces, the antiquity of which even he is unable to gainsay. The only means for detecting such interpolations is to observe whether the lines forming these letters coincide in their formation with similar fine strokes entering into the composition of the design itself, for it is evident that the inscription, if genuine, must have been cut by the same instrument, and the same touch as produced such strokes, and therefore must be exactly identical with them. The modern additions, when thus examined, are at once betrayed by their disparity. Though many antique signatures are touched in with a bold and rapid hand (like that of Nicander's), yet, in spite of Stephani's dictum, some genuine inscriptions have the letters terminating in dots. But these dots are absorbed, as it were, into the lines themselves, thus forming letters exactly analogous to those used on the more carefully executed gold coinage of the same ages. The forged, on the other hand, betray themselves by the prominence given to these terminations; which also in them are united by lines almost invisible. Nevertheless forged signatures often occur scratched in with the diamond-point alone, without any attempt at finish, with the view of blinding the amateur by their apparent artistic carelessness. Such, however, can generally be detected by the absence of that wear upon their edges which has softened down similar minute cuts made by the antique graving-tool upon the same superficies." To this class belonged the numerous signatures, all devoutly believed in by their possessor, that embellished the highly-puffed and extensive Hertz Collection. As for those distinguishing the Poniatowsky Gems (of which extraordinary fabrication some details are subjoined), they display every character that the true antique does *not* possess: excessive magnitude, obtrusiveness, display of terminal dots, and faintness of the connecting hair-strokes. Marks these, that now often put the gem-collector upon his guard against intagli (especially in the class of portraits), which from their intrinsic excellence and the air of antiquity artificially imparted to the stones, would else have been accepted by him as admirable relics of ancient Roman skill. "In the case of camei other considerations are involved. These being intended merely as ornamental articles of luxury, or of personal decoration, the owner's name upon them would have been entirely out of place. As when a name is seen upon a bas-relief there can be no hesitation as to whom it designates, so in the cameo, a miniature representative of that branch of sculpture, the same conditions must hold good. In the rare instances known, the signature is found adhering closely to some portion of the design, and even following its curvature; and not necessarily, as in the intaglio, running in a perfectly vertical or horizontal direction. One invariable test of its authenticity, according to Stephani, is that it be always in relief, which is certainly a sure evidence that it was cut at the same time with the rest of the composition." This observation has obtained universal concurrence; Dr. Brunn, though admitting it generally, yet points out a few exceptions, namely, the Ludovisi Augustus of Dioscorides, and the paste from the same head by Herophilus—on the grounds that in these instances an inscription in relief would have interfered with the effect of the portrait. Still, though I hold fast to Stephani's rule, it is possible to admit that these inscriptions may indeed be antique, for they bear the strictest examination, and have been noticed during the long period the works themselves have been known to the antiquary: yet still there is much reason to believe them additions made by some ancient possessor, either to preserve the memory of their actual author, or else fraudulently, with the view of enhancing their value.*

Considering the large number of important camei preserved to us, for we probably still know all the principal pieces executed for imperial patrons, because such works were more than ever prized during the Decline, as the magnificent portraits of Constantine and his family declare; and afterwards in Gothic times, when being transferred to ecclesiastical uses, and sanctified by a Scriptural interpretation, they were reckoned amongst the richest treasures of the sacristy. Under these circumstances, the extreme rarity of any signatures upon camei is certainly a fact for which it is very difficult to account. This will be evident upon a reference to Dr. Brunn's catalogue; and my attention was the more particularly drawn to the circumstance, by my not discovering a single indisputable instance on the numerous important camei adorning the Marlborough and Devonshire Cabinets—and yet, especially under the Lower Empire, that branch of the art which occupied itself in producing inscriptions in relief (the small cameo good-wishes intended for birthday or wedding presents), was being carried to the highest perfection, whilst every other rapidly decayed.

THE PONIATOWSKY GEMS.

A notice of this, perhaps, the most audacious fabrication to be met with in the history of antique art, comes in here as the natural commentary upon the baseless creed of the amateurs of the last century; a fabrication, too, that has done more to discredit this branch of archæology, by the confusion it has introduced into it, than could possibly be imagined by the non-practical reader.

Every individual gem in this series, numbering about *three*

* A trick, Phædrus incidentally informs us, commonly practised with new-made statues in his own time—the Augustan age.

thousand (now dispersed all over Europe), presents us with the name of some supposed antique artist: Aulus, Cronius, Dioscorides, Gnæus, Pyrgoteles, Solon, and so on. The stones are generally of large dimensions and of fine quality, Oriental sards for the most part, with a few amethysts and yellow crystals, engraved in intaglio with groups or scenes taken from the Greek and Latin poets and mythologists, often executed with considerable taste and still greater technical skill; for the compositions display too much of the flighty Louis XV. manner, even in the attitudes of the persons and the treatment of the drapery. The portraits and the single figures are much the most pleasing of their number, and approach more closely to the antique spirit. The whole were executed for the Prince Poniatowsky (who died at Florence in 1833) by the best Roman artists flourishing at the beginning of the century—Cades, Ginganelli, Dies, &c. The inscriptions—that very difficult portion of the work—are from the hands of Odelli, who took upon himself that department exclusively.*

The Prince is always spoken of as the victim of an ingenious fraud practised upon him by a combination amongst these engravers: it is, however, impossible to credit such inconceivable ignorance and credulity even in a prince, whatever weight we may allow to Juvenal's dictum,—

"Rarus enim sensus communis in illa—Fortuna."

Others again defend his knowledge at the expense of his honesty, and assert that these forgeries were made to his order, that they might be palmed off upon the world as antiques: an object which, incredible as it may appear, was actually, and for some space of time, obtained.† But the true solution of the question appears to be rather the one given to me by a person above all others an adept in the mysteries of the *virtù*-dealer's craft, and who pretended to an exact acquaintance with all the circumstances (which from his large connection with Continental amateurs and dealers was probably the truth). It is, that the Prince being an enthusiastic

* Some account of this fabrication is given by Raoul-Rochette in the 'Journal des Savans' for 1831, p. 338.

† It is stated that a Mr. Tyrrell, who had somehow acquired 1200 of these gems, was so infatuated in his belief of their imaginary value as to refuse an offer of 60,000*l.* for the lot. And on the first report that the collection was on sale in London, our Government was dunned by swarms of would-be cognoscenti as to the crime of letting slip the opportunity of securing these priceless treasures for the nation. Fortunately, their usual supineness in such matters—most assuredly it was not their better knowledge—saved our authorities from committing so egregious a blunder.

lover of the Glyptic art, himself selected ideas from the classic poets, and commissioned these engravers to embody them upon gems in the antique spirit, as far as their ability allowed. And this he did from two motives—one a wish to encourage the art, the other personal vanity; believing his *protégés* to be, under his inspiration, fully competent to rival the ancients, and putting faith in Martial's promise,—

"Sint Mæcenates non deerunt Flacce Marones."

And certainly had these clever engravers set their *own* names upon their works, instead of assuming those of the ancients, or even had each adopted exclusively some antique appellative for his *nom de guerre*, under which he might still be recognised, these often masterly performances would have done them lasting honour, and have increased in value with every succeeding century. As it is, they are now looked upon as all but valueless; are sold for merely the weight of their gold settings (often extremely elaborate and beautiful), to persons understanding gems; and fill the show-cases of the lower class of London curiosity-dealers; who, by the way, often succeed in passing them off upon "country customers" as the genuine works of the artists whose names they so ostentatiously exhibit.

To show the discredit into which they have fallen, I may state that at the sale (in 1854) of Lord Monson's collection, comprising 154, and those the choicest of the series, they were knocked down at prices varying from 25*s.* to 30*s.*, though many were engraved upon the choicest of the stones above-mentioned, and mounted in open-work gold frames of the most elegant designs the taste of the Roman jeweller could devise.* Knowing all this, one cannot but be amused at the blind faith of the parties, who (1858) took the pains to publish an erudite description,† at an enormous cost, of these now discredited forgeries, illustrated with numerous elaborately executed photographs; and all this, as appears from the preface, in the full persuasion that the gems are the undoubted works of the time-honoured artists whose names figure so impudently upon them.

The motives that induced the Prince to conceive so chimerical a project, and to expend so vast a sum in carrying it out, as the remuneration then obtained by the established gem-engravers of his times necessarily entailed upon it, must ever remain a mystery,

* I have since learnt that there was a reserved price of 3*l.* on each. Some were secured afterwards for the South Kensington Museum.

† In 2 vols. 4to. Published at 20 guineas. Only 75 copies printed.

unless the explanation already hinted at be accepted: yet he *ought* to have been inspired with better taste by the possession of that incomparable cabinet of true antiques which he had inherited from his uncle Stanislaus, the last King of Poland. This collection numbered, when catalogued by Visconti, no more than 154 gems, including a few splendid camei. The intagli were all of the highest order; amongst them was the masterpiece of *Dioscorides*, the bust of Io, in three-quarter face, with small budding horns on the temples, deeply cut in a sard of singular beauty; the Eagle's Head inscribed MIΘ, and in virtue thereof assigned (with better reason than in most of such attributions) to the cabinet of the patron-saint of gem-collectors, King Mithridates; the antique paste portrait of Nicomedes IV., with the name of *Pergamus;* and last, but most curious of all, the noted Helmet, whose uniqueness demands a detailed description. The stone, a large sardonyx $1\frac{5}{8} \times \frac{7}{8}$ inch in size, is a curiosity to the mineralogist; its upper layer being a true opaque red jasper, the lower a transparent plasma or green chalcedony. The subject, deeply sunk into the latter, is a magnificent Corinthian helmet, with flowing crest of horse-hair; its crown unusually globose. This part exhibits the device of Bellerophon mounted upon Pegasus, accompanied by his dog, and spearing the Chimera engraved upon the cheek-piece below; all the figures, though on so minute a scale, being miracles of art, both for their drawing and their finish. The horse-hair crest is carefully and naturally rendered by means of the diamond-point alone. This helmet was at one time believed to be the actual signet of King Pyrrhus, for what reason it is impossible now to discover. On the dispersion of the Poniatowsky Collection (1839), it fell into Hertz's hands, who is said to have refused an offer of 150*l.* for it from the Duc de Blacas. At his own sale (Feb. 1859) it realised the very large sum, for these times, of 89*l.* It was afterwards sold to Señor Arosarena, a Mexican amateur, and is at present in his native country, but will probably (in accordance to the law that makes all rarities gravitate towards London) reappear some day in the English market. (This prophecy has been verified: the gem is now, 1885, in London seeking a *liberal* purchaser.) Winckelmann describes another in Stosch's Cabinet almost identical with this, both as to design, and, what is more singular, the species of the material. This peculiar variety (Pliny's Jasponyx) seems to have been esteemed by the artist as the most suitable vehicle for such representations of embossed metal-work; for the Hertz Collection also boasted of a second specimen engraved with a tall Corinthian Crater, the sides decorated with Bacchic compositions, almost equal in execution to the figures upon this Helmet. Curiously enough Winckelmann has noted that the gems with helmets and vases in imitation of Corinthian chasings, which occurred in the Stosch Cabinet, were all highly and carefully finished, and to be numbered amongst its choicest ornaments.

The original Poniatowsky Collection numbered, as before said, no more than 154 pieces, but all of them both masterpieces as to workmanship, and unquestioned as to antiquity. The Prince, the last possessor, added, however, so many of his own fabrications to these genuine treasures, as to swell it to the inordinate number above mentioned. By this folly the whole cabinet was discredited to that degree that, when brought to the hammer in London in the year 1839, even the established reputation of the Io was not proof against the infection of the bad company she had been keeping; and this matchless gem was actually knocked down for 17*l.*, although a few years before it would undoubtedly have realised 1000*l.*; a sum known to have been paid for other works made precious by their author's signature, yet falling infinitely short of this both in historical and artistic value. Its purchaser was Mr. Currie, domiciled at Como, who, on his decease in 1862, bequeathed it with the rest of his very important collection to the Florentine Galleria; thinking, and perhaps with justice, that his own country was as yet incompetent to appreciate the value of such a legacy:

"Ingrata patria, non habebis ossa mea!"

ENGRAVERS NOTICED BY ANCIENT AUTHORS.

It is strange that Pliny, previously so minute in describing the works and in cataloguing the names of all statuaries, sculptors, and metal-chasers, who had attained any celebrity either before or during his own times, should have been so scanty in his notice of gem-engravers; yet this last class, one would have supposed, from the passion of the greatest Romans, like Julius himself and Mæcenas, for their productions, would have then been enjoying a reputation equal to any ever gathered in the grander walks of art. But Pliny, though often enthusiastic in his description of precious stones (for instance, of the opal) seems to have regarded the whole subject treated of in Book xxxvii. of his 'Natural History' more as a mineralogist and jeweller, than as a connoisseur in the Glyptic art. In fact, he only names, and that incidentally without any notice of their works (xxxvii. 4), Pyrgoteles, for his having received the exclusive patent to engrave Alexander's portrait on the emerald; his successors, Apollonides and Cronius; and lastly, Dioscorides, for having executed a most accurate likeness of Augustus (*imaginem simillime expressit*) which was employed as the Imperial signet by his successors. Not much more information on this head is to be gleaned from other authors. Herodotus records that Theodorus the Samian had executed "the signet set in gold on the emerald stone," so highly valued by the over-prosperous Polycrates, whose romantic legend has been already told. Since the historian is thus particular as to the artist's name, we may conclude that his far-spread reputation had given additional value to the precious material his skill was exercised upon. The date of this event was about the year B.C. 529. Again, we find another native of the same island, ***Mnesarchus***, mentioned by Diogenes Laertius as a gem-engraver by trade, by Apuleius as the head of his profession, though better known as being the father of Pythagoras, and who consequently must have been practising the art before B.C. 570, the date assigned for the philosopher's birth.

Next we meet with ***Nausias***, an Athenian, described by Lysias the orator in the customary abusive style of the Grecian Bar, as carrying on three trades at once—of gem-polisher, engraver, and debauchee (*τήν τε λιθουργικὴν καὶ λιθοτριβικὴν καὶ πρὸς τούτοις τὸ τετρυφηκέναι*). It is truly unfortunate for the history of our subject, that this oration should have entirely perished, except this single paragraph. Its title, "Concerning the Seal," affords good grounds for supposing that it concerned the forgery of a seal by this same profligate Nausias; and its early date (about B.C. 400, Lysias being a contemporary of Herodotus,) would have rendered every incidental detail most instructive and interesting.

Satyreius must have been an engraver in considerable repute at the court of the Ptolemies, to judge from the extravagant eulogium bestowed upon a work of his by Diodorus in an epigram extant in the 'Anthology' (ix. 776):

"My grace and colouring Zeuxis well might claim,
Yet Satyreius is my author's name,
Who in the tiny crystal drew the form
Arsinoe's self, with life and beauty warm:
A grateful present; though minute in size,
Its fair perfection with its model vies."

From the term used, *δαίδαλον*, properly signifying a statue, it follows that this "image of the Queen," in *crystal*, was not an *intaglio* (for which, by the way, the Greeks seldom used that stone), but either a bust or a figure in full relief: like the statuette of the same queen in one single peridot, mentioned by Pliny as actually executed on the first discovery of that (in those times) much-prized gem. The "colouring of Zeuxis" is somewhat hard to apply to a work in such a material, unless by a poetical hyperbole. Perhaps, indeed, the bust was carved out of a pale amethyst, like certain antiques yet extant,—notably the grand "Cleopatra" of the Marlborough Cabinet,—in which case the allusion to the natural roseate colouring would be quite admissible. Indeed, from the connexion of time and persons, this Satyreius may be conjectured to have been the author of the celebrated peridot statuette just alluded to.

Tryphon also must have possessed distinguished merit, and at a most flourishing epoch of the art (as manifested by the excellence of the contemporary Asiatic coinage), to have obtained such high commendation from a tasteful poet like Addæus upon his intaglio of the sea-nymph Galene * (Anth. ix. 544):—

"An Indian beryl erst, famed Tryphon's skill
Hath bent my stubborn nature to his will,
And taught me calm Galene's form to wear,
And spread with tender touch my flowing hair.
Mark how my lips float o'er the watery plain,
My swelling breasts to peace the winds constrain:
But for the envious stone that yet enslaves,
Thou'dst see me sport amid my native waves."

Addæus was a favourite with King Polemo, himself an amateur in gems, as he has testified by a couple of epigrams yet extant, "On a jasper engraved with a herd of cattle." The monarch had in early life been a rhetorician, but, having ingratiated himself with M. Antony, the king-making Triumvir bestowed upon him the crown of Pontus, a donation confirmed to him by Augustus. The non-existence of the signatures of such court-engravers as Satyreius and Tryphon (for the inscription on the Marlborough cameo is a palpable modern insertion) tells strongly against the credibility of their existence in later times: for there is no doubt

* Or Leucothea, the goddess of fair weather at sea. Her bust, cleaving the waves, is very frequent upon gems, in the exact action described by the poet. On this account it is usually miscalled Leander's: but in some examples the exposure of the breasts above the waves sufficiently vindicates the claims of the nymph to this embodiment, so apt a device for the signet of a mariner. It also forms the type of a denarius of the Crepereia family; the reverse, Neptune in his car ruling the waves, tends to prove the same thing.

that in the times of independent Greece, and Greek kings, gem-engravers held the same rank as painters and statuaries. The anecdotes about Alexander and Apelles, Demetrius Poliorcetes, and Protogenes, prove that king and artist stood in the same relation to each other as François I. and Da Vinci, or Charles V. and Titian. The art of design, as Pliny has already informed us, had from the first been regarded as a liberal profession amongst the Greeks, there being a standing prohibition that no slave should ever be instructed therein.

DESCRIPTION OF THE PLATES.

"As regards my son, I desire that he will keep, as a talisman, the Seal which I used to wear attached to my watch."—*Will of Napoleon III.*

THROUGH the kind interposition of my friend General Pearse, R.A., in command at Woolwich during the years when the late Prince Imperial was a cadet there, I most happily obtained an impression of this truly historical seal.

"It is cut upon a gem [carnelian ?], octagonal, somewhat oblong, engraved in modern Arabic in a neat character, with words translated, 'The slave Abraham relying upon the Merciful' (God)." The First Consul (*l'Oncle*) picked it up with his own hands, during the campaign in Egypt, and always carried it about with him, as did his nephew afterwards. The Prince Imperial also carried the seal upon a string fastened around his neck, in obedience to the injunction of his father. At the time of his lamentable death it must, therefore, have been carried off by the Zulus amongst the other spoils when they stripped his body, and may still be preserved by them as a trophy of their success. My object in giving it the most conspicuous place amongst these illustrations is the hope that such publicity may eventually lead to the recognition and recovery of so precious a relic; which, considering the vicissitudes of Fortune with its successive owners, deserves to be deposited on her altar side by side with the signet of Polycrates. The drawing is made to double the size of the original, for the purpose of rendering the inscription more easily legible, which has also been done with all the following illustrations, unless otherwise specified.*

My own collection has in the meantime been transferred to the New York Museum of Art, and all the gems so quoted formed part of it. The Beverley Gems have also been incorporated with the other antiquities at Alnwick Castle; although not described in the lately published Catalogue of that Museum.

* It has not been thought necessary to name any but the principal cabinets, out of which the gems were selected; as those then in private hands may have changed owners repeatedly since the casts were taken.

I.

ASSYRIAN CYLINDER.

Belus seated on a throne; to whom a priest is conducting a maiden: a woman stands behind, in the attitude of adoration. The *Moon*, seen overhead, indicates the nocturnal hour, and explains the character of the ceremony. The legend is said to contain the name of *Urukh*, one of the earliest kings of Babylon; the "Orchamus" of Ovid. This cylinder, figured here of the real size in its impression, was brought from Babylon by Sir R. Ker Porter; but its present owner is not known.

The examples given in the four plates following, except the few marked otherwise, have been borrowed, through Mr. Layard's kind permission, from his great work upon the antiquities of Nineveh.

II.

1. Signet of Sennacherib. The king, standing under a canopy, receives the adoration of a subject. In the midst is placed the Tree of Life, above which soars the personification of Ormuzd. Green Amazon-stone. (Brit. Mus.)

2. Persian contending with a winged bull and a gryphon; above him, the protecting Deity. Legend in Phœnician, "Seal of Gedishmah, son of Artidadt." (Brit. Mus.)

3. Woman worshipping Ishtar, Queen of Heaven, surrounded with the moon and stars; in front sits the lion of Belus; behind is the antelope, sacred to the goddess, browsing on a tree. (Layard.)

4. Persian king contending with two lions: typical of his irresistible strength; at the side a Magus, performing his sacred rites at a fire-altar. (Layard.)

III.

ASSYRIAN STYLE.

1. Man adoring the Winged Bull, typical of Belus: overhead are seen the sun, moon, and planets.

2. Deity standing before an altar, on which stands his attribute, a cock. (Cone.)

3. The King bestowing his benediction upon a kneeling suppliant. (Cone.)

4. The King, mace in hand, attended by a guard holding a torques, offering his vows to the lunar deity.

5. Belus, elevated upon his bull, between two figures of *Nisroch*.

6. A train of captives, with the soldiers guarding them.

7. The *Hom*, Tree of Life, standing between two gryphons.

8. Belus standing upon his gryphons; Arduesher, the Giver of Waters, upon her cow, to whom a man kneels in prayer.

9. Magus about to sacrifice at an altar; before him is elevated the symbol of the Moon.

IV.

1. Sandon (Hercules) wrestling with the bull; the Minotaur with the lion; an astrological composition.

2. The *Hom*, over which soars the *Mir*, Visible Presence of the Deity; on the one side stands Oannes, attended by a winged Genius; on the other, a worshipper.

3. Warrior in a triumphal car; in front, the severed heads of his vanquished foes.

4. Cow suckling her calf; overhead, an astral symbol. (Cone.)

5. Seated figure; at her back, the planets. (Cone.)

6. The *Hom*, over which soars *Sin*, the Moon-god; the king wrestling with two winged bulls.

7. Impression in terra-cotta of the seals of Sargon, and the contemporary King of Egypt; originally attached to some covenant between them.

8. Seated figure: before him are placed a goose and a tortoise, as offerings.

V.

BABYLONIAN AND PERSIAN.

1. Man holding a knife; legend in well-cut Babylonian cuneiform, not yet read. Hæmatite. (Praun.)

2. Magus before a fire-altar; Phœnician legend, interpreted by M. Lévy, "The Herald of the Sun." On the side of the cone, a man encountering a lion-headed figure. Chalcedony. (Praun.)

3. Belus, seated, arrayed in a long Babylonish robe, to whom a worshipper presents an antelope; above is seen the *Mir;* behind, two Genii, and two women are carrying similar sacrifices. The *Crux ansata* in the god's hand betrays an Egyptian influence upon this design. Hæmatite. (New York.)

4. Gryphons and Bulls; underneath, a row of various deities, amongst whom Mylitta is conspicuous.

5. The Fish-god Oannes, or Dagon.

6. The *Hom;* above it, the great god Asshur, supported by two human-headed bulls; on each side stands a worshipper. The Phœnician legend, and the peculiar neatness of the engraving, clearly indicate its origin.

7. The Worship of Mylitta.

8. Sphinx, recumbent, in the Persepolitan style. Mottled agate. (Praun.)

9. The dwarf *Gigon* bearing up a winged deity; on each side stands a man in *Persian* dress, as distinguished from the Assyrian by the peculiar manner in which it is pleated up the front.

VI.

PARTHIAN AND SASSANIAN.

1. Two Hunters, in hooded mantles, encountering, the one a lion, the other a wild boar. Early Persian work, on a large chalcedony scarabæoid. (Leake.)

2. Another, in the same style, material, and cabinet; a Hunter spearing a stag.

3. Bust of a king wearing the tiara; about his neck is suspended the royal signet: legend, "The attestation of Sapor, fire-priest of the Hyræans." Carnelian. (Brit. Mus.)

4. Satrap, on horseback, in full attire; legend, his name "Arinanes." Amethyst. (Paris.)

VII.

INDIAN AND INDO-PERSIAN.

1. Bust of Vahrahran Kermanshah, in front face: exactly agreeing with his profile portrait on the famous Devonshire Amethyst. Deeply and exquisitely engraved in carnelian. (General Pearse.)

2. Bust of a youthful Rajah, wearing a floral crown; very well engraved, but in a totally different style from the preceding, in chalcedony. Both these gems were found buried together, and were bought at the same time by General Pearse. The political connexion of the two personages is attested by another intaglio, known to me, which bears the same two heads, but in profile, and engraved in a poor Indo-Sassanian style. Hence we may safely assume that the younger prince was the "Vitiaxa," or Satrap, of Bactria; and that these extraordinary gems were the "Great Seals" of his administration.

3. Parthian King, wearing the national *cidaris* (leathern helmet) encircled with the diadem, seated on a camp-stool; to whom a noble, also wearing the *cidaris*, is presenting a massive torques. Neatly engraved in yellowish-green chalcedony. (General Pearse.)

4. Siva, seated on the Sacred Bull, and holding in his four hands the insignia of the God of Death—the trident, the *roamal* or strangling-cord, the club, and the headsman's sword. The most ancient type of a Puranic deity that has yet been discovered on a gem. Chalcedony. (General Pearse.)

VIII.

SASSANIAN.

1. Bust of a man, wearing a necklace of great pearls, and resting upon a row of flowers—an augury of happiness; legend, "Piruz Shahpuhri" (Peroses, son, or minister, of Sapor). Yellow sard. (Praun.)

2. A similar Bust and legend, borne up on fourfold wings, emblem of deification. It is, therefore, the King's *Ferouher*, or genius: his "angel," as the Jews termed it, who had got the idea from their Persian masters. Carbuncle. (New York.)

3. Queen in full dress, holding the lotus-flower, like a goddess: at her side the young Shah, distinguished by his diadem. With her name "Almindochti," the termination, like the "Infanta" of the Spaniards, betokens royalty. Chalcedony seal. (Eastwood.)

4. Head of a King much resembling the portrait of Vahrahran Kermanshah,

and engraved in the exceptionally fine style that seems confined to the limits of his reign. Garnet. (Pulsky; now Brit. Mus.)

5. Diademed bust of a Queen, with her name, "Rozehi." Red agate. (New York.)

6. Two ladies in Sassanian costume, in conversation together. If the emblem in the field be meant for the cross, we have here a Nestorian type of the greeting of Mary and Elizabeth. Sard. (New York.)

7. Elephant's head; legend, "Masdaki Raja." Yellow sard. (New York.)

8. The Sacred Bull, emblem of Earth, recumbent. The legend seems to read, "Chosroes." Garnet. (New York.)

9. This curious symbol, of frequent occurrence in gems, and sometimes bearing the royal diadem attached to it, is usually supposed to be the Standard of the Empire. Almandine. (New York.)

IX.

SASSANIAN CHRISTIAN AND CUFIC.

1. Head of a young Indo-Sassanian Rajah; in front a star, to indicate his rank; behind, a Greek cross on a wreath to declare his religion. His name in well-cut Pehlevi letters, "Kartir," occurs also on another gem now in the New York Cabinet; but is there attached to another portrait of the regular Sassanian type and of a much older man.

This most interesting memorial of the spread of early Christianity in Bactria is engraved with superior excellence upon a garnet, which was found, set as a button, upon the jacket of an Afghan officer slain in the last war. It now forms one of the numerous exceptional rarities that enrich that unrivalled treasury of Oriental Glyptics, the collection of General Pearse.

2. A most remarkable combination of symbols. The so-called "Royal Ensign," or Buddhistic figure, to be seen on the tiara of Varanes IV. or placed singly on numerous gems; by its side a hand, holding up a long Latin cross. We have here a memorial of the Nestorians, to whom the jealous pride of Perozes afforded an asylum from the persecution of his orthodox rival, "the Byzantine emperor." The union of the two symbols was evidently intended to mark the *princely* birth of this courageous professor of Christianity; and if the legend is rightly read as "Hormasdai" (*Ahoramazdi*), we are reminded that a prince of that name was a refugee at the court of Constantius and of Julian from the tyranny of Sapor II. This garnet, found at Merv, passed from the collection of M. de Gobineau, formerly French Minister at Teheran, into that of Mr. S. S. Lewis, out of which it was "conveyed, the wise it call," during the detention of the case containing it at the custom-house of Constantinople, in December 1883. Such discrimination in the choice of plunder is so far superior to the honest dulness of a "True Believer" as to point to the refined rascality of the straitest sect of the "Oriental Church." The gem has probably ere this found its way back to Paris; and by publishing this minute description of it and its vicissitudes, I hope that some *unwished-for* light may be thrown upon the circumstances of its mysterious disappearance.

3. Head, in a pearl-bordered tiara, with bushy hair curling on the shoulders, much resembling the portrait of Khosru Parviz upon the coins. The legend (not deciphered) is in the latest Pehlevi character, fast approaching the Cufic: which latter took its name from Cufa, a town famed for calligraphers at the time of the Arab conquest, where the Koran was first transcribed out of the original Himyaritic MSS. Chalcedony. (New York.)

4. Ruby found in the ruins of Brahminabad Scinde, engraved in Cufic with "Ali ibn Hassan:" a fine example of work in so hard a material.

X.

EGYPTIAN.

The tablet, serving for a pendant jewel, is of terra-cotta, coated with blue vitreous glaze, the "artificial cyanus" of Theophrastus. The two scarabæi are cut out of dark-green jasper, or more frequently moulded in the same material as the tablet. Of the signet, the gold swivel, on account of its magnitude and value, is supposed to have belonged to royalty; the others are examples of the forms most generally in use under the Pharaohs. All are drawn to the actual size.

XI.

1. Isis, crowned with the lotus and bearing the sceptre. A pretty intaglio, of Ptolemaic date; in sardonyx. (Muirhead.)

2. Tablet in yellow jasper; bearing on one side the apis, on the other a horse. The cartouche contains the name of a very early king. (Brit. Mus.)

3. Late Egyptian talisman of Alexandrine manufacture; red jasper. The Abraxas-god, in a threatening attitude, as he is always represented, busy in his office of scaring away all evil spirits; legend in the field, EVIA, "The Serpent" (*Syriac*). Reverse: the Cnuphis Serpent, surrounded by groups of the sacred animals. This, the finest specimen of a so-called Gnostic stone that has ever come to my knowledge (here drawn of the actual size), was brought from Bombay, and is now in the cabinet of Mr. S. S. Lewis, Fellow of Corpus Christi College, Cambridge.

4. This lion-headed serpent, *Cnuphis*, a sigil prescribed by King Nechepsos for protection of the chest, is cut in a piece of veritable jade. (Same cabinet.)

XII.

ABRAXAS TALISMANS.

1. The *Abraxas*-god in the car of Phœbus; thereby identified with the solar power. Legend, "Sabao" for "Sabaoth."

1*a*. Reverse, within the coiled serpent, emblem of eternity, "Iao Abraxas." Green jasper. (Bosanquet.)

2. The *Abraxas*-god; engraved with unusual spirit and neatness. Green jasper. (New York.)

3. The same, but with the ass's head of Typhon. A unique personification. Green jasper. (Waterton.)

4. This type is the exact converse of No. 1, for here Phœbus receives the invocation, " Thou art our Father," regularly addressed to Abraxas. TVΞEVI, below, is known to be a mystic name of the Sun-god.

4*a*. Luna guiding her white cow through the heavens. Hæmatite. (New York.)

5. Abraxas, engraved in a very bold style. Legend, " Iao,"—" the Eternal Sun," as the word is usually translated; but the proper rendering is, " Sun of the Universe," *Eilam* being the Aramaic pronunciation of the Hebrew *Olam*. Black hæmatite. (New York.)

XIII.

GNOSTIC TALISMAN.

Celt of fine green jade, converted by some Gnostic of the 4th century into a talisman by the engraving upon the one side of seven lines of letters and sigils, mostly the permutation of the seven vowels that shroud from profane eyes the Ineffable Name of God; and on the other of a garland of laurel, every leaf of which bears the title of some power recognised in the theosophy of the sect. The material itself is Pliny's " Ceraunia, resembling an axe in shape, and to which the Magi ascribed wonderful virtues." The same name, translated " Donnerkeil," and the same powers, are still attributed to these articles in the popular creed of Germany. A very curious proof of the Roman estimation of the thing is the gold ring, ingeniously set with a tiny agate celt, in lieu of a precious stone, lately discovered in France and figured in the 'Archæological Journal,' vol. xl. p. 325. The one in question was brought from Egypt many years ago; and has been deposited in the Rotunda at Woolwich by its possessor, General Lefroy. A copious dissertation upon this Ceraunia and its class, with an explanation of its inscription, will be found in my 'Early Christian Numismatics,' p. 23. The immense diffusion of these talismans is again exemplified by a very important specimen of its class, an oval chalcedony, lately sent to General Pearse from India. Its face is covered with rows of Greek numerals, arranged in sets of four, which, we know from examples used in the Pistis-Sophia, are *equivalents* for the mystic names of the various persons in the Godhead. The reverse bears the following legend:

ωΝωϹΕ
ΜΕϹΙΛΑΜϹ . .
ΑΗΙΕΗΙϽ . . .
ωΝΗΓΗΙΑ . . .
ϹΑΒΑωΘ
Ʞ

a jumble of Chaldee and Greek words, cut in a square lettering for the sake of facility. The middle lines have lost their last letters through the damage of the stone, but the whole, with a few exceptions, is quite intelligible and may be thus translated: " He that *is*, Eternal Sun [then comes the usual permutation of vowels shrouding the Ineffable Name], the Living One; the Earth; Iao Sabaoth." All invoked for the protection of the wearer of the gem.

XIV.

CHRISTIAN TYPES.

1. Wheatsheaf, aptest emblem of the Church, on which is perched the Dove, placed between its enemies, the Lion and the Serpent = World and Devil. The most elegant of these devices anywhere to be found. Sard.

2. A Believer, armed with a staff tipped with the *Chrisma*, and smiting the Old Serpent, on whose body he tramples. Lapis-lazuli.

3. A Virgin-martyr, as the palm-branch gives us to understand, performing her final devotions before the fatal stroke. The name SECVNDA is that of the owner of the signet. Lapis-lazuli.

4. Fisherman's boat; Christ at the helm, its crew engaged in fishing. A type amongst those prescribed by Clemens Alexandrinus for the signets of Christians. The letters below indicate the Saviour's name. Carnelian.

5. A very curious representation of the Crucifixion, in the Byzantine style; in which the Saviour's hands are seen *bound*, not *nailed*, to the cross. The letters in monogram are IC, XP: rudely expressed. On each side stand Mary and the Centurion. Green jasper. (These last three gems are taken from the cabinet of Mr. S. S. Lewis, Fellow of Corpus Christi College, Cambridge.)

6. The Sacred Fish; a type borrowed from the Egyptians. Legend, "Iesus Christus, the One *El*,"—"El" being the name of the *comprehensible* God of the Talmudists, as distinguished from the "Ain-Soph, or Infinite." The Kabalists gave the name of *Dag*, "The Fish," to the Messiah, it being compounded in their favourite fashion out of the initial letters of his titles. They solve all the mysteries of creation by means of the twenty-two characters of the Hebrew alphabet, and the *Tash-Raq*, or retrograde reading thereof, yields (with a little amplification) this prophecy: "The Lord shall whistle for his people amongst the Gentiles. He shall make the mountains to overflow with sweetness. Who is He? The Fish cometh! (*Dag Bah*)." From these the type of the Fish passed into the symbolism of the Christians, and became still more appropriate when it was discovered that the word ΙΧΘΥΣ was composed by the initials of the Greek text "Jesus Christ, Son of God, the Saviour." Chalcedony, blanched by fire. (Captain White, Armagh.)

7. Candlestick of the Temple, the national badge of a Roman Jew. The legend LABE, "a lion," several times repeated, seems to be meant for a spell. Chalcedony; drawn here to the actual size found at Ephesus. (S. Wood.)

8. The *Chrisma* placed in a laurel wreath, and therefore proclaimed victorious. With the name of the owner, "Phœbion," EI is put for I because the accent falls upon it. (Antique paste.)

9. The Good Shepherd; a work of very early date. Sard, found at Murree, Peshawur, where many relics of the first Christians still exist. (Gen. Pearse.)

10. Medal, of Cinque-cento manufacture, *cast* not struck, of which numerous examples are current in bell-metal, and even in silver; and which are

often palmed off upon the ignorant as *contemporary* portraits of the Saviour, made by the command of Tiberius.

In connexion with this subject may be cited a singular bronze ring, formerly in the Castellani Collection. Its face, a square tablet, bears in *relief* and *reversed*, as here represented. The signet, therefore, was not meant for a signet, but as a stamp with ink for imprinting the inscription upon paper or other smooth surface. The three words may, perhaps, constitute a proper name, such compounds, in imitation of the Greek, being in fashion in those times, of which we have a notable example in "Adeodatus," the name of Augustine's son.

SPES
IN DEO

XV.

PHŒNICIAN STYLE.

Gems selected from the number discovered by General Cesnola amongst the dedicated jewels deposited in the treasure vault of the Temple at Curium, which alone yielded more specimens of Phœnician art than had previously been possessed by all our Museums put together. This art has no originality in *design*, but copies that of Assyria and of Egypt, yet with a superiority of execution that enables us at first sight to distinguish its production. These gems are either scarabæi or scarabæoids, generally sards, with a few plasmas and agates: they are all mounted as swivels in gold, or in gold collets with immense shanks of silver; not being intended for the finger, but for suspension by a cord around the neck. I have to acknowledge the kindness of Mr. John Murray in allowing me the use of these cuts, which form part of the illustrations to Cesnola's 'Cyprus.'

1. In the Assyrian style. Two men in Babylonian dress, standing on each side of the Tree of Life; over which soars the *Mir*, or winged orb, the Visible Presence of the Deity.

2. In the Egyptian taste. The Royal Vulture, supporting the flail and the sceptre; in front, the *Uræus*, serpent, badge of sovereignty.

3. Winged Deity kneeling; one of the few purely national types of Phœnicia: found also upon the coins of Malta.

4. Imitative Egyptian. The Hawk-headed *Phre* and a Man kneeling at each side of a *blank* cartouche; above it, the Mir. Behind each figure, the Symbol of Life; conjunction of Form and Matter.

5. The Tyrian Hercules wrestling with a lion; in the heavens is seen the Mir. Purely Assyrian in idea, Phœnician in fineness of workmanship.

6. The god Phre, upholding the solar orb; closely copied from the Egyptian.

7. Cypriote Warrior, with plain shield and conical helmet, spearing a Persian, recognisable by his hood and the large *umbo* of the shield. The design clearly indicates by its augury the date of the revolt of the island from Darius Hystaspes.

8. Two hawk-headed deities holding a garland between them, as a promise of victory. On the right is placed the regular Phœnician symbol of the conjunction of Baal-hammon with Ashtaroth; on the left, three Cypriote letters, probably giving the owner's name.

P

9. The Baboon of Thoth, "Scribe of the gods," busily engaged with his writing-tablet and stylus. In front, betraying a foreign hand, some blundered hieroglyphic letters, indicating an ignorant copyist.

XVI.

ETRUSCAN.

1. Sphinx confronting a winged lion; in the midst a cypress; over it the solar emblem, the usual representative of Fire. A design purely Assyrian in character, though coming from Phœnicia; incised (*graffito*) on the face of a gold ring.

2. Man in car drawn by a Sphinx and Pegasus, to whom a Harpy, emblem of Death, proffers a lotus-flower. Some doctrine of the Mysteries touching a future state must be couched in this truly mystic composition. A *graffito* on a gold ring.

3. Sard scarabæus, in the original gold setting. The Horseman engraved on its base, in virtue of the accompanying *star*, may be explained by Horace's "Castor gaudet equis." (Brogden.)

4. The Etruscan Mercury, or perhaps a *Lucomo* (his peculiar *cap* makes him the "galeritus Lucmo" of Propertius) in full dress, about to take the auspices. In the field, a Stag and a Raven, sacred to Apollo. Engraved on a gold ring.

5. Man wearing the conical Etruscan *apex*, driving a car of two winged horses. The trees in the field may convey an allusion to the proverb, "Ne extra oleas." Engraved on a gold ring.

6. Man with wings springing from his hips, in the Assyrian style, and wearing a hooded mantle and the long-toed Etruscan shoes, standing between a Sphinx and a Panther, grasping a forepaw of each in sign of mastery. Apparently allusive to some event in the history of Hercules, now lost. *Graffito* in gold.

XVII.

ETRUSCAN AND EARLY GREEK.

1. Arimaspian contending with a Gryphon, guardian of the gold mines of Scythia. Chalcedony scarabæus. (Hertz.)

2. Cadmus slaying the Serpent which haunted the fount of Dirce. Scarabæus. (Berlin.)

3. Hercules wrestling with the Nemean Lion. Intaglio, Greek scarabæus of sard. (Brit. Mus.)

4. Venus, winged in the Etruscan fashion, seated on the hymeneal altar, with an ivory distaff, and holding forth a dove as sign of amity to her worshipper. Engraved in a solid gold ring of Campanian make. (Brit. Mus.)

5. Ganymede depicted as an emasculated boy, according to the Etruscan idea of the perfection of youthful loveliness. Sard scarabæus.

6. Lion pulling down a Stag. This is the national "arms," so to speak, of Phœnicia, symbolising the power of the Sun-god, Baal. This highly-finished scarabæus, in green jasper, comes from their colony Tharros, in Sardinia.

XVIII.

EARLY GREEK AND ETRUSCAN.

1. Female Sphinx taking a necklace out of a casket: on the other side, a *crater*, emblem of conviviality. Remembering that the Theban Sphinx was the destruction of all who fell into her clutches, this graceful design was well adapted for the signet of some Laïs or Phryne of the best times of Greece. Pale green chalcedony. (Hertz.)

2. Neptune rending asunder the mountain rocks, whence issues the river Peneus, in the shape of a horse; in the field, the name of the god ΝΕΘΥΝΟΣ, converted afterwards by the Latins to *Neptunus*.

3. Icarus, with loosening pinions, tumbling backwards from the heavens. In his hands are seen the inventions of his father—the saw and the drill.

4. Telephus, wounded in the leg by the spear of Achilles, consulting Dionysus, the national god of Mysia, how to find a remedy for the incurable sore. The story is most cleverly told by the bandaged leg and agonised expression of the suppliant hero. Sard. (The late Hon. Judge Johnson, Utica, U.S.)

5. Head of Silenus, engraved on the base of a carnelian scarabæus. (Brogden.)

6. Hercules beating down the hero Ceyx: their names, in the Etruscan spelling, appear in the field. Sard. (Blacas.)

7. Hermes Psychopompos evoking a ghost from the shades, by the virtue of his mystic wand, as is indicated by his gesture. One of the finest specimens of the Etruscan style that can anywhere be found. Sard. (Berlin.)

XIX.

LATE GREEK.

1. Helmeted Head, in a very archaic manner, apparently copied from some ancient statue. The *Venus* in the field may warrant the conjecture that it represented Æneas. Many modern copies, with the face made more human, are to be met with; and ever since Agostini gave the name, they pass for the head of Massanissa, the goddess being interpreted as symbolising his amorous powers. But any portrait of the Numidian, did it exist, would be in the florid Roman manner. Sard. (Florence.)

2. Visconti identifies this noble portrait with Miltides, from its agreement with the head of the Founder placed upon a coin of Byzantium. Amethyst. (Blacas.)

3. The celebrated "Drunken Bacchus:" the finest specimen of a nude figure to be found on a gem. Winckelmann has left a copious dissertation upon its excellences in his Catalogue of the Stosch Gems. Sard. (Berlin.)

4. Ulysses leaning on his pilgrim's staff, and recognised by his old dog, Argos. A favourite type with both Greeks and Romans. That it conveyed the idea of a happy termination of one's labours, as in the case of the typical wanderer, is manifested by its being chosen to decorate an Attic tombstone, where it, no doubt, was understood in the same sense as the ship sailing into harbour on Roman monuments. Early Greek intaglio, on a chalcedony scarabæoid. (Leake.)

5. Campanian Potter, engaged in turning the rim of a great amphora, which is held up by his apprentice. The cylinder on which it rests is probably a revolving *turbo*, answering the purpose of a potter's wheel. Of extreme interest as exhibiting the actual process of manufacture in early Greek Ceramic art. At the recent sale of the Castellani Collection this fine gem reached the price of £84.

XX.

NEW YORK CABINET: RARE TYPES.

1. Minerva, preceded by her Serpent, advancing to the attack. In her right hand, instead of the usual spear, she carries what appears to be a *fire-brand*, as though leading on the Greeks to the destruction of Troy. Over her shoulders is thrown not the ægis, but a long tippet of scale-armour, of the same construction as that worn by Virgil's Etruscan warrior:

> ". . . . quem pellis ahenis
> In plumam squamis auro consuta
> Tegebat."

An intaglio valuable both for the curiosity of the subject, and the minuteness of detail in the costume; being probably copied from some celebrated statue of the Archaic school. Scarabæus of banded agate, blanched by fire.

2. Female Figure, with wings springing from her *hips*, carrying with both hands a large vase. It is uncertain whether she was meant by the Etruscan artist for Hebe, the original cup-bearer to the gods, bringing a wine-jar to the feast; or for Iris, the giver of rain to the earth, in the act pictured by Ovid: "Concipit Iris aquas, alimentaque nubibus adfert." Whatever the character intended, the lightness of motion through the air is very cleverly expressed in the engraving. The carelessness of the workmanship, and absence of finish in the details, indicate the latest period of the Etruscan school. Sard scarabæus.

3. Female Sphinx, at play: in front, an olive branch; a mystical device of unexplained signification. Her hair is drawn up into a cone, and tied in a knot at the top of the head, after the fashion of the Campanian women, the "altum Saganæ caliendrum," which (as a false one) Horace laughs at. This peculiarity, coupled with the loose freedom of its execution, proves the intaglio to belong to the Cumæan school. Dark sard, cut from a scarabæus.

4. Nero, with the *Ammon's horn* on the temples, in the character of Alexander the Great. This whimsical Cæsar often figures on gems as an Apollo, with the adjunct of his lyre—an excusable act of vanity, as every

fiddler considers himself at the summit of his art: but what possible parallelism could the most ingenious flattery have discovered between *him* and the mighty Macedonian? Bright yellow sard, of the kind popularly called "sunstone."

5. Serpent-headed Deity, on a throne, holding forth the orb, in token of universal sovereignty: before him squats the Baboon of Thoth, in the attitude of adoration. A unique figuration of Serapis; but in the same sense as that which occasionally typifies him by the Agathodæmon Serpent invested with the *modius*-crowned head of the Alexandrian god instead of its natural one; and the converse conjunction may very well be interpreted in the same sense. As Thoth or Hermes stood, in the Neo-Platonic theosophy, for the Spirit directing the movements of the universe, this picture of his attending the commands of the Supreme Deity is full of deep signification. Deeply cut in a dark-green jasper, Pliny's "molochites," in great esteem for making talismans.

6. The Good Shepherd, of the usual type, but with a very unusual adjunct, the mystic intention of which it is impossible to do more than conjecture. From beneath his tunic, behind, escapes the neck and crest of an unmistakeable *Serpent:* can this be the device of some audacious Ophite, to express the main article of their creed—the identity of Christ with Ophis? If so, this gem is the rarest of the rare—a Gnostic monument in the strictest sense of the name; the generality of the stones so denominated being no other than astrological or medicinal talismans. The V in the margin is the relic of a longer legend, destroyed by the reduction of the field to octagonal form in recent times. Fine red sard.

XXI.

APOTHEOSIS OF AUGUSTUS.

The meaning of this elaborate composition will be found fully explained at p. 44. Sardonyx of three layers; drawn to one-third of the actual size. (Paris.)

XXII.

CELEBRATED CAMEI.

1. Jupiter overthrowing the Titans, sons of Earth, as is typified by their serpent-legs. The name "Athenion" in the tablet placed below the car has always been understood of the *engraver* of the gem; but (as in many similar cases) it was also that of an eminent Greek painter. There are better reasons for believing the cameo to be a copy, made in Roman times, of some famous picture by him, thereby (so far as the design goes) assured of immortality. Sardonyx of two layers; drawn of the actual size. (Naples.)

2. "The Odescalchi Cameo." The conjugated portraits pass for those of Ptolemy II. and Arsinoë, but a comparison of the lady's profile with that of Agrippina in the "Claudian Family" will at once restore these likenesses to their proper originals—Nero and his imperious mother. Sardonyx; drawn to one-half the actual size. (St. Petersburg.)

XXIII.

HISTORICAL CAMEI.

1. The earliest work of the kind, the date of which can be fixed with certainty. Ptolemy II., distinguished by the royal asp upon his helmet, conjugated with his sister Arsinoë, in the head-dress of Isis. Sardonyx cameo; half actual size in the drawing. (Vienna.)

2. The Claudian Family. Tiberius, with his mother Livia, facing the Emperor Claudius and Agrippina, the daughter of Germanicus. The busts rest upon cornucopiæ, denoting the prosperity of their reigns; but, with ingenious flattery, the Roman eagle is made to look towards the then *reigning* powers. By comparing the portrait of Agrippina with that of the lady on the Odescalchi cameo, the latter will be restored to its true originals. Cameo; drawn to half the real size. (Vienna.)

XXIV.

WORKS IN CAMEO.

The Triumphal Procession of either Constantine, or his son, Constantius II. Although the excellence of the design of this fine cameo, so superior apparently to its professed date, may excite some suspicion as to its genuine antiquity, yet nothing can be detected in it that betrays the mannerism of the Cinque-cento school,—the usual source of such historical camei; and the accuracy of the details of costume and arrangement is far above the knowledge of the more recent forger. The gem is now in the possession of that eminent collector, Herr Tobias Biehler, of Vienna, who purchased it from the widow of a Greek, who either could not, or would not, give any information as to its *provenance.* Drawn to the actual size of the original.

I gladly embrace this opportunity of correcting my erroneous attribution, made through blindly following the traditional one, of Charles I.'s cameo, at page 51. The portrait must be restored to Claudius, and comparison with his medals will at once decide its identity. How the mistake arose it is difficult to imagine. The stone has been skilfully repaired and remounted by Mr. Spilling, and is now deposited by Her Majesty in the British Museum.

Through a similar exchange, that most exquisite of all cameo-portraits, the Augustus with the attributes of Jupiter, of the Blacas Cabinet, long passed for Constantine; and was so published by Gori in his 'Museum Florentinum.' That learned antiquary was led into error by the Byzantine jewelled *diadem,* which some centuries later had replaced the original laurel-wreath, cut away in order to admit it, not however without leaving still discoverable traces of itself. The change was probably made by Constantine himself, whose features bore a marked resemblance to those of the first Augustus, and who thereby secured a portrait of himself such as the *decadence* of contemporary art was unable to supply. Another substitution followed: in times of distress the precious stones were picked out of the diadem by the possessors of the cameo, and consequently their empty settings were filled by its purchaser, Leone Strozzi, with the little camei that now adorn it.

XXV.

ROMAN CAMEI.

1. Bacchanalian group, reclining upon a lion's hide, spread under the shade of a fig-tree. A youthful Faun is sounding the double pipes; a Nymph, holding a goblet in her left hand, pours out a libation to the god from a patera; a drowsy Cupid in the background expresses the protraction of the festivities. (Beverley; now Alnwick Castle.)

2. Polyhymnia, Muse of Heroic poetry, holding a scroll, points to the sepulchral monument of some ancient worthy, by the side of which stands a maiden with offerings to the dead. Terpsichore, seated, strikes the lyre in accompaniment; in the centre is the Bacchic *cista*, supporting a tragic and a comic mask. A good specimen of the antique style of composition in a group.

3. The same subject as the first; but here the Faun is singing, the Nymph beats time with her hands, whilst Pan supplies the music with his syrinx. (Beverley.)

XXVI.

AZTEC CAMEO.

The beneficent demi-god *Cuonlean*, seated cross-legged on a flowery cushion; on his wrists are bracelets, and hung about his neck the chalcedony cylinder, still worn in the same manner by the chiefs of certain Brazilian tribes. The figure betrays a traditional reminiscence of a Buddhist type: an idea supported by the now received theory that civilisation was brought into Peru (at least) from Japan. This extraordinary carving is executed on a slab of green Amazon stone, the highly-prized *Chalchizetel* of the Mexicans, here shown of the actual size. It was dug up by the explorer Squires, in a ruined town forty miles from Palenga.

Japanese influence upon the art of South America is both conceivable and easily accounted for, but the most inexplicable and (if genuine) the most interesting trace of the ancient connexion between the Old World and the New is the inscription still to be read upon a large stone, standing near Yarmouth, in the Bay of Fundy, Nova Scotia. This inscription, long known, has hitherto been taken for Runic, and, thus viewed, gives no sense whatever; but, when *inverted*, yields beyond all cavil, in the cursive Latin characters of the 7th and 8th centuries, the epitaph VΓCV ⊢ TALLVSANI, where the second and fourth characters are inverted, as is commonly done in Merovingian and Anglo-Saxon legends. VLCA may be intended for *Volca*, "wolf," in Sclavonic. This inscription, it will be observed by palæologists, is identical, both in sense and in lettering, with those still so numerous upon the *Maen-hirs* of North Wales, and the patriotic Cymry may be allowed to discover in it a more conclusive testimony to the famous voyage of Madoc than in the etymology of the name, "Penguin." The obvious explanation of a recent forgery is refuted by the *length of time* since it was first observed; indeed it may be questioned if any one has ever visited the locality who possessed sufficient antiquarian knowledge to perpetrate a fraud that so completely satisfies all the requirements of its professed age and destination. Although the Northmen generally made Runic their epigraphic character, yet there is no reason why they should not have been acquainted with cursive Latin, as well as the Welsh and Irish of the same time. It is also the same that is used for the Celtic inscription upon the celebrated "Newton Stone," near Aberdeen, where it is accompanied with a version in Oghams; and which that great Hebraist, Dr. Mill, by reading from right to left, converted into very satisfactory *Phœnician.* I have no doubt that the *inscription* is genuine. The question is, how it got to the Bay of Fundy? The matter-of-fact reader will reply, "As ballast in a Welsh brig bound to Yarmouth;" and so solve the problem.

XXVII.

ROMAN STYLE: MARCIA.

Posidonius records that, in the grand Dionysiac Procession celebrated by Ptolemy Philadelphus, there marched Aglaïs, "wearing a peruke with a crest fastened upon it, sounding the trumpet" (Athenæus, x. 58). Hence it may be inferred that this remarkable head-dress was an established article of costume, appropriated to certain divine personages. In this magnificent gem, the artist has certainly wished to represent an artificial head-covering, seemingly of *metal*, and not the natural hair. It has been conjectured that we have here a copy of the Pallas which adorned the *lost* pediment of the Parthenon. But, in this character, we probably have on the present gem the portrait of the Amazonian Marcia, for the face, in its stern beauty, is certainly not *ideal*, and agrees with that to be seen conjugated with Commodus upon his medallions, but in which she wears the helmet of Dea Roma. Sard; drawn here of the actual size. There is a reduced antique *replica* of this in the Blacas Cabinet, a proof of the original importance of the subject. (Florence.)

XXVIII.

RARE AND CURIOUS SUBJECTS.

1. Under a spreading Quince tree (sacred to Hymen) Vulcan is engaged in making the wedding ring; as Ovid's

"Annulus ut fiat primo colliditur aurum."

At each side stand Cupid and Psyche, who have bespoken it.

2. The youthful Bacchus offering sacrifice, under the direction of his foster-father, Silenus, who, having dropped his thyrsus, has great difficulty in keeping his legs. Sard. (Muirhead.)

3. Skeleton, emerging from a huge vase, ornamented with torches crossed, in allusion to the Eleusinian Mysteries, and plucking the branch of a palm-

tree. A speaking allegory of the reaping of posthumous fame, and expressed upon the gem with a skilfulness of workmanship not unworthy of the idea. Dark sard. (Beck.)

4. Nemesis guiding a wheel, over which is passed a rope, at which Cupid is pulling. An exemplification of Horace's

"Ingratam Veneri pone superbiam,
Ne currente retro funiseat rota."

Antique paste. (Praun.)

5. Warrior, with hammer and punch, repairing the damage done to his corslet by the foeman's spear.* This curious design may be merely the "trade-mark" of an armourer. Chalcedony. (Leake.)

6. Invaluable for the light it throws upon the ancient method of modelling life-size figures in clay. Prometheus engaged in creating Man: on each side a Ram and a Horse, whose distinctive qualities he extracts to compose the mental portion of his work. As Horace tells it:—

"Fertur Prometheus addere principi
Limo coacto particulam undique
Desectam, et insani leonis
Vim stomacho apposuisse nostro."

7. Nymph, seated upon a cork-stick (?) fixed in the ground, and balancing herself with her thyrsus, while she offers her vows to a terminal statue of Bacchus. The ceremony is explained by the history Arnobius gives of the institution of the *Phallophoria* by the same god. The most singular representation to be found in a gem. Agate, banded in a singular manner. (New York.)

XXIX.

GRECO-ROMAN STYLE.

Numbers 1, 2, 3 are various types of the goddess *Spes;* of which the third may very well be considered a copy of the famous *Spes Vetus*, one of the most ancient deities worshipped at Rome. Both the *pose* of the figure and the arrangement of the drapery bear unmistakeable evidence to the drawing's having been taken from an archaic bronze.

4. Victory reading out the announcement of some great success in war, from the scroll she holds in both hands. The *club*, so conspicuously displayed in the field, is the regular *cognisante* of the family Antonia, which claimed descent from the Heraclide Anthon: and this, coupled with the coincidence of the owner's name and the evident date of the workmanship, may justify us in assigning it to the *Eros*, the last friend, faithful to the death, of the despairing Triumvir. Sard. (S. S. Lewis.)

5. A City, under the customary personification of a tower-crowned female, soliciting the protection of the goddess Fortune; on whose arm she lays a

---

* " . . . . bis sex thoraca petitum
Perfossumque locis."—*Aen.* xi. 11.

firm grasp. The peculiar neatness of the engraving points to a Greco-Asiatic origin. Sard. (The same.) On the back of the gem, a later owner has cut

VLFIVΓ AVd (E)
NSAVACVS.

Name and lettering bespeak its Teutonic origin, and the 5th century for the addition.

6. A Citizen imploring, on bended knee, the favour of the same capricious Ruler of events by the ejaculation ΒΟΗΘΕΙ, "Help me," engraved on the reverse of the gem. A fine sard. (The same.)

7. Capaneus struck down by a thunderbolt from the walls of Thebes, which he had sworn to scale in Jove's despite. He is seen tumbling backwards, and clutching at the wall to stay himself. The gateway, with its peculiar *pinnæ*, is evidently copied from that which the Etruscan artist had before his eyes in his native town. This highly interesting intaglio once belonged to Caylus, who, viewing the subject upside down, has published it as an acrobat performing upon the *petaurum*. Sard. (The same.)

8. Woman offering a libation before a statuette of Priapus, set up on a lofty pedestal; behind her stands an aged man blowing the double flute. A bending fig-tree completes this pretty picture of a rural worship, well exemplifying Virgil's

"Inflavit cum *pinguis* ebur
Tyrrhenus ad aras."

XXX. & XXXI.

ROMAN-BRITISH.

The gems figured in this and the next plate are memorials of the Romans, who so diligently explored, during three centuries of possession, the mineral treasures of the Mendip Hills. They are chiefly in carnelian, with a few in *nicolo* (blue and black onyx) and red jasper; and a few retain their rings of iron. All proceed from a local collection made at Charterhouse-on-Mendip by a Captain of the Mines; where they were discovered by that indefatigable explorer, Mr. S. S. Lewis, Fellow of Corpus Christi College, and published by him in the Transactions of the Cambridge Antiquarian Society, and to whom I am indebted for permission to use these very interesting illustrations.

1. Virgo of the Zodiac, recognisable by her helmet, offering sacrifice upon a portable altar.

2. "Mercury of the Rocks," as the Greeks styled him, in the character of patron of sailors, seated on a rock, and proffering his money bag; evidently the signet of some "ancient mariner," who shipped the Damnonian metals for Gaul.

3. Goat browsing upon a tree. Signet of a colonist settled in the rich plains at the foot of the Mendip.

4. Bull butting. As Augustus put this exact type on a gold coin, it must have had a mystic meaning of importance, but it is not the Zodiacal Taurus.

5. Mars contemplating his own charms in the reflection from a burnished shield at his feet.

6. *Modius*, corn-measure, filled with fruits and flowers, set upon a pedestal, out of which spring two cornucopiæ. A speaking emblem of fecundity; a good augury, seen also in a similar form upon an Alexandrian coin. These last three gems retain their original *iron* settings, although much damaged.

6*a*. Hope holding forth her lily towards Abundance, who elevates a basket of fruits (*lanx satura*); in the middle, a bunch of wheat ears, to make the allegory more easily understood. This is the identical ring recorded by "that quaint old cruel coxcomb" in his 'Angler' as having been dropped into the Tyne, and refunded by a salmon. Truly, a dactyleological Jonah! Now in the possession of the Rev. Mr. Anderson.

7. Shepherd seated under a tree. Paste cast, from a fine intaglio.

8. Man and Woman joining hands; the established device for a betrothal ring (such as was found on the finger of the unfortunate wife of Pansa, in the crypt of her villa at Pompeii). Imperial coins, struck on occasion of a marriage, bear this type, with the legend "Concordia Felix."

9. Minerva Victrix. The choice of this subject points to the reign of Domitian.

10. Mars Gradibus. In a superior style of art and execution to any of the rest.

11. At once the most curious and the most tasteful of all the glyptic legacies of the Romans to the soil of Britain. Victory, wearing the winged cap of Mercury to declare her the bearer of important news, is borne along by a horse, which she urges with a whip to its utmost speed. Her attitude clearly proves that the present fashion in which a lady sits her steed was only a *re-invention* of Diane de Poitiers. As for its *meaning*, the design conveys an augury of success to some favourite racer, to be taken in the same sense as another intaglio known to me, in which the same goddess is placing the victor's crown upon the head of the winning mare "Calippa Romana." This type is, as far as I know, unpublished; but Mr. S. S. Lewis, in the winter of 1882, observed its exact counterpart upon the finger of an English railway official at Smyrna; who, however, set so extravagant a value upon the gem as to make its acquisition impossible to the most enthusiastic of amateurs. Sard; found in the ruins of the Roman *castrum* at South Shields, and now in the possession of Mr. Blair.

XXXII.

ROMAN-BRITISH (*continued*).

1. Bust of Antonia, wife of Drusus. Paste lapis-lazuli; found at Stanwix, near Carlisle. Actual size.

2. Circus; with chariot-race going on. A most accurate representation of the arrangement of the building, showing the central division (*spina*) with its dolphin fountains, and the conical *metæ*, the globes on which dropped successively at each turn of the racers around them. *Astarte* on her lion, so conspicuously placed on the *spina*, being the tutelary goddess of Carthage,

would lead to the conjecture that we see here the Circus of that important capital. Sard, much enlarged in the drawing; found at the Chesters (*Binovium*), and now in the possession of Mr. Clayton, whom I have to thank for the use of this most interesting illustration.

3. Bear: a picture from the life of the *Ursus Caledonius*, which tore Laureolus in the Roman amphitheatre in the days of Martial:

> "Nuda Caledonio sic viscera præbuit urso
> Haud falsa pendens in cruce Laureolus."

Sardonyx cameo; actual size; found at the Roman station, South Shields, and now in the collection of Mr. Blair.

4. Bust of Minerva: singularly treated, helmeted, her hair combed straight down upon the shoulder. The style of the engraving bespeaks a more early period than the Empire. (Mendip.)

5. Cupid angling: the prettiest design and neatest work of all the gems hitherto yielded by the same locality. Red jasper; now in the Lewis Cabinet.

6. Head of Omphale, clad in the lion's hide, of which she has despoiled her slave, Hercules. Sardonyx cameo, blanched by fire; lately found at Caerleon, the ancient Isca Silurum. Drawn to the actual size.

7. Bronze ring: ornamented with a Mask in low relief. This Mask is hollow and soldered on to the face of the ring: it is made with a *die;* affording a curious proof of the demand for such designs (talismanic) amongst the poorer Romans. Found at Chesterford.

This is the place to remark that in several Roman stations, but particularly at Brough on the Picts' Wall, are found large numbers of small leaden disks, stamped with various devices, often impressions of *engraved gems*. As no gem would endure, without damage, frequent application to the fused metal, we must suppose that a terra-cotta stamp made upon the officer's signet was used for the purpose. These disks, ancestors of the larger breed of Papal *Bulls*, explain the meaning of the *plumbum*, which we find from the 'Acts of St. Maximian' was given to every recruit on his first entering the service: answering exactly to the shilling now given by the enlisting sergeant. After this the *tiro*, if found fit for duty, was tattooed with the device of his own cohort (seen so frequently on tombstones), as Vegetius incidentally mentions.

XXXIII.

MEDIÆVAL USE OF ANTIQUES.

1. Jupiter, leaning on his sceptre, holding the thunderbolt downwards, in sign of peace; at his feet, the Eagle. This beautiful cameo was mounted in the present setting of gold, enamelled, and deposited in the *Sainte Chapelle*, where it was long venerated as the portrait of St. John the Evangelist, in virtue of the Eagle, his proper attribute, which accompanies the figure. Drawn to the actual size. (Paris.)

A curious example of mediæval appropriation of antique work came lately under my notice in VI⅃AΠI, cut in the most artless manner in the field before a good portrait of Nero. The blundering in the arrangement of the letters betrays the hand of a complete novice in gem-engraving, whilst the name of the great Florentine family indicates the place of the attempt.

The Inventory of the Jewels of Charles V. of France contains the following *item*:—"The King's signet: which is the head of a king without a beard, and is engraved on a fine Oriental ruby; it is with this that the King seals letters written with his own hand." I formerly identified this ring with the one of the same period now in the Marlborough Cabinet, but have since been convinced of my mistake by comparing it with a cast taken from the impression of the signet of Charles V., for which I am indebted to the kindness of Baron Pichon. The ruby of the French Royal Signet is larger; the portrait, similarly crowned and in front face, more artistically engraved, and having more the character of an actual likeness, and some vestiges of a legend completely filling the border.

2. Private Seal of William Gifford, Archbishop of York (1366–1379). The fine antique intaglio which adorns it bears the bust of M. Aurelius, *conjugated* with that of his great teacher, Plato: although, without doubt, they passed with the Archbishop's contemporaries as portraits from the life of the Apostles Peter and Paul. In fact the curly head of the emperor was then quite sufficient to identify him with the traditional likeness, as seen on the Bulls of the fiery Zelotes.

XXXIV.

CAMEO OF ST. ALBANS.

Facsimile of the drawing by Matthew Paris, done in his own MS. Chronicle, now preserved in the library of Corpus Christi College, Cambridge. A Roman Emperor, Constantine, or one of his sons, holds forth a Victory, and rests upon a spear, round which twines a serpent. The imperial Eagle stands at his side. This stone was in high repute as a talisman that assisted women in labour, the figure of Victory being interpreted in an analogous sense. It was given to the Abbey by the Saxon king Sebald; and the silver mounting is apparently of the same date. This very remarkable gem is not known to exist in any cabinet. No doubt it was carefully concealed at the time when the Abbey was dissolved, and we must hope for some lucky chance to bring it again to light: a favour of fortune not to be despaired of, when we remember the almost miraculous resuscitation of the Shrine itself a few years ago.

XXXV.

ANTIQUE GEMS IN MEDIÆVAL SETTINGS.

1. Thalia, seated, contemplating a comic mask; in front, a young Faun, balancing himself upon a pedestal. The legend "Je sui sel d'amour lel," "I am the seal of loyal love," is so disposed as to look like a religious motto. The subject was understood by the setter as Herodias gloating over the severed head of the Baptist, whilst Salome is practising her steps before her. Sard; set in a large silver seal. (Dineley; now in the British Museum.)

2. Portraits of Julia, between her sons, Caius and Lucius. The style of this most interesting intaglio coincides so exactly with the same type upon a denarius minted by Marius Trogus that it may safely be presumed to have been his personal signet. But the "Andreotto of Syracuse" who adopted this intaglio for his signet, necessarily viewing all such things with the eye of faith, converted the lively Princess and her boys into the Madonna, Bambino, and Precursor. The setting is silver. (Waterton; now S. Kensington.)

3. Vizored Persian Helmet, with monogram in the field. The signet of "Conrad del Conte;" perhaps a member of the family to which Dante disparagingly alludes (Purg. xiv. 146):

> "E mal fa Castrocan, e peggio *Conte*
> Che de figliar trai Contë più s'impiccia;"

for the make and the lettering of this elegant gold signet-ring bespeak a contemporary of the poet. Did he possibly take the trunkless head for that of the Patron Saint of Florence? Very fine work in sard. (Waterton; now S. Kensington.*)

XXXVI.

MEDIÆVAL ENGRAVINGS.

1. The so-called Seal of St. Servatius, still preserved, together with his portable altar, in Maestricht Cathedral. The obverse shows the bust of a Saint; the reverse the Gorgon's Head, regarded even to the latest time as a most potent amulet. The legend, running round both sides, is a blundered copy of the common Byzantine charm, "As a serpent thou dost writhe, but as a lamb thou shalt lie down." It was probably engraved in the 13th century, long after the times of Servatius. Green jasper; drawn of the actual size.

2. The Gnostic Gorgon; a work of the early Byzantine school. The legend is, "Holy, holy, Lord of Hosts, Osanna! Thou who art blessed in the heights." Drawn to the size of the original.

3. Ring of Siffred, Bishop of Chichester, d. 1150. The extreme rudeness of the jasper abraxas with which it is set almost proves the engraving a contemporary work. This very interesting relic is preserved in the Cathedral library.

XXXVII.

HISTORICAL RINGS.

1. Massy gold ring, set with a fine ruby, deeply engraved with the head of a youthful prince. The shank has letters in gold, upon a ground of niello,

* Of St. Bartholomew's Hospital, founded in the early years of Henry I.'s reign, the original seal was set with a large antique gem, rudely engraved with a Spread Eagle. Its style is closely allied to that of the same type on the latest *potin* coins of Alexandria; and, as the field is perfectly plane, the material was most probably the then so favourite lapis-lazuli.

containing an invocation to St. George. On these grounds, its present possessor, Baron Pichon, seems justified in attributing it to the Black Prince. This matchless specimen of mediæval jewellery was discovered in company with some human bones near the Castle of Montpensier a few years ago. Drawn to double the actual size.

2. The fatal love-token given by Queen Elizabeth to Essex, the detention of which by his treacherous messenger proved the cause of his destruction. Drawn here of the actual size. (Now preserved in the Thynne family.)

XXXVIII.

MEDIÆVAL ENGRAVING.

1. Veiled Head, probably meant for a Madonna; deeply cut in sapphire. As the motto "Tecta lege, lecta tege," was also that of Matthew Paris, the signet was formerly attributed to him. Set in a gold ring of 13th century fashion; found in an old well at Hereford. (Waterton; now S. Kensington.)

2. Ruby, engraved with a youthful head, crowned. Probably the signet of Margaret of Anjou; the setting being in the fashion of her days. (Marlborough.)

3. Royal Bust; surrounded by a *cordelière:* the *star* on the breast seems to refer it to the Douglas family. Cut in the metal of a large gold ring, supposed to have belonged to Cochrane, the favourite of James V. Found at Crawford Muir.

4. Bust of the Madonna, in the head-dress of the 13th century; her lily in the field, with the appropriate motto, "Tota pulchra." Neatly cut in a red jasper; found at Bedford.

5. Venus at Vulcan's forge; an engraving of the times of Archbishop Parker, who presented it to Elizabeth, together with an enumeration of the virtues of the gem. An agate; drawn to the actual size.

6. Triple face, deeply cut in a brown garnet (jacinth). This is the cognizance of the Trivulzi family, to whose name the "Tres Vultus" was applied. The French war-cry, "Noël," forming its legend, seems to hint that the owner was in the service of that royalty. Set in a heavy gold ring. (Waterton; now S. Kensington.)

Time, which solves all mysteries, has likewise solved the problem of the real destination of those brazen monsters of the species *Annulus*, hitherto known as "Credential rings." The various explanations as yet proposed as to their use (all of them alike unsatisfactory) I had reviewed in a former work; but now M. Castan has placed the matter out of doubt by his observations upon one now preserved in the Museum at Besançon, which by the connexion of the devices upon it plainly tells its own history. The shoulders bear respectively the shield of Pope Nicolas V. and St. George and the Dragon, with the inscription P. N. and DVX. Now it is on record that this Pope, Thomas of Sarzana, sold the sovereignty of Corsica to Fregoso, afterwards Doge of Genoa, who in his turn disposed of it to the famous Bank of St. George in that city. The ring, therefore, was the token of *investiture* of the bank with the feudal rights of both Pope and Doge. These rings were in use for the half-century between Pope Eugenius IV. and Sixtus IV. Their invention bespeaks the craftiness of the Italian and the churchman; their huge size guarded them from loss, their worthless metal from theft and the melting-pot.

Rings of the same fashion were also sent to Cardinals upon their election into the Sacred College; and this explains the fact of their having been discovered in the tombs of certain Popes who had preserved these memorials of their first step towards that supreme dignity. A copious essay upon the subject will be found in the 'Mémoires de la Société d'Antiquaires de France,' vol. xliii. p. 22.

XXXIX.

CINQUE-CENTO STYLE.

1. The Laocoon group; from a seal, formerly supposed that of W. Colyns, Prior of Tywardreth, Cornwall, but since proved to have belonged to T. Arundell, attached to a deed made between those two parties, bearing the date of 1527. As this was fifteen years after the finding of the marble, it is possible that the intaglio is only a copy of it, as restored by Michelangelo da Montorsoli.

2. The same group, represented in the fully developed manner of the Revival, with the architectural embellishments then so much in vogue.

3. An *Imperator* and a Senator, offering sacrifice before the statue of Dea Roma. The initials below refer to the engraver.

4. Head of a Turk, in a jewelled turban; clearly the signet of some Pasha, like Ali of Yannina, who had emancipated himself from the prejudices of his brethren in this respect. Green jasper. (Leake.)

5. Narcissus contemplating his naked beauties in a fountain. The attempt at pictorial effect, and the falseness of the details, strongly mark the period of this elegant composition.

6. Bellerophon watering Pegasus at the newly-risen Hippocrene; executed in the same style as the last. The legend is a bad attempt at the name of "Sostratus." Sard. (Marlborough.)

XL.

Venus and Mars taken in the toils of Vulcan; all the gods and goddesses looking on. Said to have obtained from Gregory XIII. for its artist, Calabresi, the remission of his doom to imprisonment for life; but, according to another story (much more credible), executed in 1830 by another Calabresi, who got £600 for this wonderful *tour de force.* From Prince Demidoff it has passed through various hands into Captain Peel's cabinet. The only part of the romantic history that is worthy of credit is that the work cost the artist *three* years' unremitting labour. What inconceivable pains must he have taken to completely detach the network from the figures confined therein, and then to give such exquisite finish to those figures through the small interstices of the cords! The particular Pope was evidently pitched upon for the dedicatee of this somewhat unclerical subject, on account of the notoriety he enjoys amongst Protestant amateurs as the instigator of the St. Bartholomew massacre. Cameo in blue and white agate; the net executed in the black, the figures in the white layers. Drawn to double the actual size.

XLI.

SATURN, JUPITER, &c.

1. Saturn, with head veiled, in token of seniority. The signet of some one of the family *Sentia*, who derived his hereditary cognomen from the primitive god of Latium. Sard. (New York.)

2. Faustina Mater, tower-crowned, in the character of Cybele, the Great Mother. Red jasper. (New York.)

3. Jupiter the Thunderer. The bust of Cybele in the field shows this gem to be of Tyrian work. The back of the scarab is cut into the shape of a fly. Amulets of this kind are not uncommon, and are supposed to refer to Baalzebub, "The Lord of Flies," the great god of Syria. Agate. (Praun.)

4. Serapis, as the Sun-god, uniting the characters of Ammon and Phœbus. Sapphirine chalcedony. (New York.)

5. Juno standing between Mercury and Minerva. The last holds a palm instead of her spear, as an augury of success. Sard. (New York.)

6. Ganymede borne aloft by the Eagle, as he was hunting. Sard. (New York.)

XLII.

JUPITER.

1. Head of Jupiter: the hair bound with a fillet. In the Etruscan style. (Blacas.)

2. The same head, laurel-crowned. In the best Roman manner. (Blacas.)

3. Zeus and Hera, conjugated heads, in the later Greek style. Chalcedony. (Leake.)

4. Juno, of Roman workmanship. (Berlin.)

5. Jupiter "Fulgurator" in his car. Finely engraved, but the treatment of the clouds indicates a modern date. Carnelian.

6. The shepherd Ganymede made the cup-bearer of Jove. Sard. (Blacas.)

7. Europe, holding the nuptial torch and the symbols of fertility, borne across the seas by the Bull. Sard. (St. Petersburg.)

8. Jupiter descending in thunder upon the expiring Omphale. A matchless specimen of the early Greek style. Sard. (Berlin.)

XLIII.

SERAPIS; PLUTO.

1. Serapis as the Sun-god, Lord of the Elements: the Air symbolised by the Moon, Water by the Trident, Earth by the Serpent. Sardonyx. (Wood.)

2. Genius of Death leaning on an extinguished torch: as he is often represented on sarcophagi. Not an uncommon signet-device, evidently chosen to inculcate Horace's precept:

> "Omnem crede diem tibi diluxisse supremum."

Once the property of Murat. Nicolo. (Davidson.)

3. Serapis as the Grecian Zeus, borne up by the Eagle: an idea expressed by the legend, "One Zeus, Serapis." Red jasper. (Leake.)

4. Serapis, with a stern countenance, as Lord of the Lower World; identified with the Roman Pluto. Sard. (Berlin.)

5. Magician evoking the ghost of an aged man, at the request of two women, who bend down to consult him. Etruscan sardonyx. (Hertz.)

6. *Larva,* ghost, leaning upon a tall wine-jar, and holding forth an *unguentarium:* an Epicurean hint to enjoy life whilst one can.

7. Hope throwing incense upon a portable altar, in honour of Æsculapius, for the health's sake of the owner of the signet, "Onesime," whose portrait appears above. Sard; found at Alexandria. (New York.)

XLIV.

NEPTUNE.

1. Neptune and Amphitrite borne over the waves by a sea-horse. The treatment of the water is not in accordance with the antique style in that particular. (Berlin.)

2. The Cabiri of Samothrace, inventors of navigation and commerce, conveying a wine-jar in a galley. Burnt carnelian. (Maskelyne.)

3. Scylla destroying a mariner: a design put on his coins by S. Pompey, the pirate. Sard. (Marlborough.)

4. Neptune urging his suit to the Danaid Amymone: in whose hand the *pitcher* symbolises the gift of the Fountain of Lerna. Antique paste.

5. Nymph kneeling at the side of a fountain. Either of the same signification as the preceding; or if the *cymbals* hanging on the rock have a definite meaning, she is a Bacchante fetching water for the sacred rites. Cameo. (Beverley.)

6. Giant defying the Gods; he shields himself with the lion's hide wrapped round his left hand, whilst with his right he aims a rock at his enemy.

XLV.

MINERVA.

1. Goddess with *four* wings, in the Phœnician style; but her *helmeted* head may be taken to indicate a very early type of Athene. Sard. (Blacas.)

2. Minerva, with her usual attributes. In the Etruscan style.

3. Athene Promachos encouraging the Greeks to the attack. The most spirited intaglio in the mature Greek style known to me. Sard. (Hertz.)

4. Diomede stealing the Palladium. The slain guardian lies at the foot of the altar. Onyx. (Beverley.)

5. The jealous Minerva transforming her rival Arachne into a spider. The design more in the taste of the Cinque-cento than of antiquity. Sard. (Blacas.)

6. Gorgon, or Fury: a most ancient personification of the idea of divine vengeance. Sard. (St. Petersburg.)

XLVI.

CERES.

1. Head of Ceres. Sard. (Blacas.)

2. Triptolemus, attended by the serpent of Ceres: in the field, a Punic legend in large characters.

3. Ceres presenting wheat ears to her adopted son, Triptolemus, about to start, in her own car, upon his mission of benevolence in making agriculture known to mankind. Plasina. (Paris.)

4. The Nymph Thallo, with lap full of blossoms.

5. Mother Earth reclining in the midst of her productions.

6. Ceres, seated, holding forth the figure of Justice; at her side, the corn-measure. Plasina, bleached by fire. (New York.)

XLVII.

APOLLO.

1. Apollo, clad like his rival Nero, *citharædico habitu,* singing to the *cithara* (his proper instrument) in front of the Delphic tripod.

2. The Pythia meditating on her oracles, before she ascends the tripod. Antique paste. (Berlin.)

3. Apollo seated in meditation; at his side stands the aged Herophile, the earliest priestess of Delphi.

4. Apollo standing by his tripod, about which is coiled the Python. The inscription in the field shows this gem to have belonged to Lorenzo de Medici.

5. Two Gryphons uniting with a Harpy in a mystic chorus. Etruscan scarabæus.

6. This interesting intaglio presents to us a faithful copy of the famous statue by the early artist, Canachus, placed in the Didymæum of Miletus. The stag's hind feet contained a spring, so as to allow a thread to be passed between them and the pedestal—a trick which Pliny seems to have considered the chief merit of the work. Sard. (Praun.)

7. Gryphon, emblem of the Sun, being the compound of the Eagle and Lion, holding Apollo's lyre. Amethyst. (Florence.)

XLVIII.

APOLLO, ÆSCULAPIUS, &c.

1. Apollo Pythius resting his lyre upon the head of a Delphic virgin, who holds first-fruits in her hand, represented by the branch which she extends. Sard. (New York.)

2. Bust of Apollo, which from the peculiar arrangement of the hair would seem to be a copy of the famous statue at Miletus. Amethyst. (Praun.)

3. Apollo proffering his bow in token of amity: an admirable work of the Seleucidan period. Peridot. (New York.)

4. The celebrated Æsculapius of "Aulus," the original *owner* of the signet, not the *engraver*, as was so long imagined. Sard. (Blacas; now British Museum.)

5. Cupid bearing off the trident of Neptune, and bestriding Capricorn, the "Ruler of the Western Wave," as Horace terms that sign. The type probably expresses the universal dominion of the little god. Sard. (Praun.)

6. Syren playing on the lyre. The inscription, coupled with the palm in the field, attests this to be the device of one that had gained the prize for Poetry at the *Capitoline* games instituted by Domitian. A curious historical record of the same nature has come under my notice—the intaglio of a Tragic mask, inscribed KAP CEL · COCC · COS · obtained at their celebration by the succeeding emperor, Nerva. As these contests recurred every fifth year, the frequency of similar memorials need not excite suspicion of their authenticity. Sard. (New York.)

Note upon the Apollo now in the New York Museum.

The enigmatical legend in the field, BAI CЄOV, is explained by that seen on a famous gem of the French Cabinet, in which I A BAC (Ἱερὸς Ἀπόλλων Βασιλεύς) is thanked for the restoration to health of Pescennius Niger. Similarly, on our gem, some partisan of his competitor, Severus, invokes the protection of "the Holy King Apollo" for his leader: CЄOY being the regular Greek transliteration of the Latin SEV.

XLIX.

MUSES.

1. Polyhymnia, Muse of Epic poetry, holding the *plectrum*, and contemplating the tomb of the hero whom she celebrates.

2. Clio, Muse of History, holding the scroll of records. Sard. (Marlborough.)

3. Muse, or Poetess, playing on the "many-stringed" *barbiton*. Crystal scarabæoid. (Cockerill.)

4. The same subject, on a smaller scale. Sard. (Brit. Mus.)

5. Dancing-girl making a pirouette to the sound of the double-pipe. Sard. (S. S. Lewis.)

L.

ASTROLOGICAL.

1. Aquarius, the "House" of Jupiter, as the representative of Ganymede.

2. Diana in the character of Luna; her car drawn by white stags, as that of the Hindoo *Chandra* is by antelopes. She holds forth an auspicious plant to her votary, and promises him success by the wreath placed in the field below.

3. Transportation to the Fortunate Islands of a youth, borne across the sea by the "Tyrannus Hesperiæ Capricornus undæ." Sardonyx cameo. (Beverley.)

4. Deus Lunus, the Moon-god. The chief seat of his worship was Carrhæ, where it still flourished at the date of Julian's expedition into Persia. Sard. (Blacas.)

5. Leo, the "House" of the Sun, holding in his jaws the head of the Bull, type of Earth, and trampling on Scorpio, typical of Cold.

6. The fore-quarters of Two Winged Bulls, conjoined: apparently an astrological talisman, for the idea is purely Chaldean.

LI.

DIANA.

1. The Artemis of Ephesus, here identified with Isis, as the Goddess of Earth; the scorpions in the field symbolising seed-time. Black jasper.

2. The Roman Diana, as the Lunar Power and Huntress combined.

3. The Greek *Artemis*, in the latter character only. Sard. (Leake.)

4. Niobe shielding a son from the shafts of the twin deities.

5. Nymph pouring out water from an urn. Cameo. (Beverley.)

6. Roe, the attribute of Artemis. Early Greek work.

LII.

MERCURY.

1. Mercury tuning the lyre, of which he was reputed the inventor. Sard. (Marlborough.)

2. Mercury introducing the suppliant Priam to Achilles. Sard. (Blacas.)

3. The original type of Hermes; retaining much of the Assyrian character, and adopted by Etruscan art. Sard. (Beverley.)

4. Mercury acting as cup-bearer to the Gods, carrying an *olpe*, on which rests a Soul; typifying his office in the Shades. Sard. (Paris.)

5. Mercury and Fortuna uniting their influence for the benefit of the merchant.

6. Mercury conducting a Soul to Charon, into whose hand the defunct is dropping the ferryman's fee. The design has nothing of the antique character. Peridot. (Maskelyne.)

LIII.

MARS.

1. Mars, victorious in a sea-fight, reposing after his work is done: an idea expressed by his armour lying on the ground, and by the ship's rudder displayed in his hand. (Beverley.)

2. Victory, in the character of Hygeia, feeding the Serpent of Health. Sard. (Blacas.)

3. An important historical intaglio, commemorating the restoration by the Parthians of the standards lost by Crassus. Antique paste.

4. Mars Stator, with the Roman Eagle at his side.

5. Victory pouring out a libation. (Berlin.)

6. Victory erecting a trophy: the double-headed *aclis* at the side points to the Samnite. This magnificent engraving, in a chalcedony scarabæoid, passes for Sicilian work, but the inscription on the streamer has an ugly resemblance to Pichler's signature. (Brit. Mus.)

LIV.

MARS; WAR.

1. Mars Gradibus, carrying a trophy on his shoulder. Fine early Greek work in a banded agate. (New York.)

2. Two Roman knights encountering two Gauls. A most interesting subject, as it probably commemorates Marius' famous victory over the Cimbri and Teutones. Yellow sard. (New York.)

3. Horse's Head, between two *Gallic* shields, each bearing a different national device. Another valuable monument of history, for beyond a doubt it refers to the defeat of the Insubres and Œnomanni by the Consul Lentulus Lupus, B.C. 156. Sard. (Waterton; now S. Kensington.)

4. Victory urging on her *biga:* a design copied from the reverse of the gold Philippus. A fine cameo on sardonyx; said to have been found in India early in the present century.

5. Victory holding forth the triumphal wreath, and borne along in the serpent-drawn car of Ceres: perhaps allusive to the recovery of Africa after the revolt of Clodius Macer. Sard. (New York.)

6. The "Helmet of Pyrrhus," one of the chief treasures of the *original* Poniatowsky Cabinet. It is, however, not antique, but by some unrivalled hand of the Cinque-cento, from whom I have seen another intaglio, a vase, in exactly the same style and material—a singular onyx of a red upper layer upon a translucent green base.

7. Syro-Macedonian Helmet, of the shape seen upon the coins of Tryphon. Dark sard. (Praun.)

LV.

VENUS.

1. Venus holding out a perfume-jar, and leaning upon a cippus, emblem of *stability*. Sard. (Beverley.)

2. The same, with dove perched on her hand. Early Greek sketch in sard. (Leake.)

3. Aphrodite Euplœa, patroness of mariners, borne over the waves on a sea-dragon. Sard. (Blacas.)

4. Galatea, the Sea-nymph, in the act of swimming: commonly misnamed a Leander.

5. Venus Victrix contemplating the armour of Mars. Chalcedony. (Leake.)

6. Venus in the Bath; in her hand the oil-cruse. Cameo.

7. Venus at Vulcan's forge. A design altogether in the Cinque-cento taste. (Berlin.)

LVI.

VENUS; CUPID.

1. Bust of Venus, wearing a necklace of large pearls.

2. The Goddess robing herself. Lapis-lazuli scarabæoid, found at Athens. (Maskelyne.)

3. Venus rising from the sea.

4. The Birth of Cupid: the infant deity springing out of an opening flower of the pomegranate.

5. Cupid weeping over the death of the butterfly, Psyche.

6. Cupid wrestling with Pan: the attributes of both are hung on the trees behind them. Cinque-cento taste.

7. Cupid as the Infant Harpocrates, bound with chains. A pretty conceit, hinting at secrecy and constancy in love. Cameo.

8. Cupid making his boat of an *unguentarium*, and his sail of a lady's kerchief. (Berlin.)

9. Cupid acting the schoolmaster, and brandishing the "taws" in Scottish fashion.

LVII.

CUPID; PSYCHE.

1. The Infant Cupid slumbering on the lap of Psyche, seated under a tree. The earliest representation known to me of this elegant personification of the human soul.

2. Eros and Anteros, after a contest: the victor has bound his opponent to a column.

3. Cupid, in the attitude of an archer who has just let fly his arrow: the bow is omitted from want of space. Evidently copied from a statue by Praxiteles.

4. Cupid, with averted face, quenching the torch of Love.

5. Cupid invested with the insignia of Mercury, Hercules, and Mars—in token of his resistless power.

6. Nemesis holding out the branch of ash-tree, and making the usual gesture with her hand. Of this gem innumerable modern copies are in circulation. Sard. (Blacas.)

7. Psyche, symbolised by a mere head, with butterfly wings on the temples: a type hitherto unpublished. It was a truly poetical idea thus to represent the *soul* by its proper seat, unencumbered with any portion of the body. The idea may indeed have been suggested by the form under which the Etruscans pictured their *Laverna;* who, as being the patroness of people that live by their wits, was similarly represented by a head divested of a body. The highly-finished workmanship of the present intaglio indicates a much earlier

date than that of the common type of Psyche, most of which appear to be contemporary with Apuleius' charming romance of that name. Sard; bought at the sale of the Castellani Collection by Mr. S. S. Lewis.

LVIII.

BACCHUS.

1. Bacchus, clothed in the *crocrota*, carrying the *cantharus* and the *narthex*, his proper symbols. This is the original conception of the god, and is engraved in the finest Greek style on a banded agate. (New York.)

2. The youthful Bacchus, according to the Roman idea, holding forth the *scyphus*, and backed by his vine. Banded agate. (New York.)

3. Silenus sounding the double fife. Sard. (New York.)

4. Youthful Faun, filling the bowl for the thirsty Silenus, out of a capacious *crater;* both kneeling upon the conventional representation of grass. Early Greek work, in yellow sard. (New York.)

5. Vase formed out of a triple mask of the god. At the base are laid the pastoral *syrinx* and *pedum*—emblems of Comedy. Red jasper. (New York.)

6. Goat, sacred to Bacchus, mounted by a Grasshopper. As the insect by its form suggested phallic notions, this remarkable type was probably intended as a *philtre*. Sard. (New York.)

7. Two Cupids chastising with a *pedum* the panther of Bacchus—a pretty allegory of the hostility existing between the two powers, when the latter is in the ascendant. Sard. (New York.)

8. Parrot, carrying a bunch of pistachio-nuts. The Indian bird accompanied the god on his return from the Indian campaign, and therefore figures in his triumph. Sard. (New York.)

LIX.

1. Old Faun nursing the Infant Bacchus. Fine early Greek engraving, in sard. (Blacas.)

2. Bacchus contemplating his face in the mirror of his goblet. A matchless example of the Campanian style. Sard; brought from Cumæ by Castellani.

3. Reclining Faun, represented in the archaic style, retaining more of the caprine form than in later art. Greek scarabæus, in dark agate. (Praun.)

4. Mænad, inspired by the god, casting off her robe. (Berlin.)

5. Nymph drawing water from a well, over which presides Priapus, god of fecundity.

6. Gardener at work with his hoe, before a figure of Priapus, constructed in the most primitive manner of a lopped tree. Sard. (Leake.)

7. Jupiter, in the shape of a Satyr, surprising the sleeping Antiope. Emerald. (Beverley.)

8. Silenus playing the lyre before a rustic shrine, in which is set up the *lingan* or emblem of the same god. Chalcedony. (Leake.)

LX.

1. Head of Bacchus, crowned with ivy. Magnificent Sicilian work, in brown sard. (Pulsky.)

2. Mænad, with thyrsus, full of eagerness and inspiration, as if listening to the voice of the god. (Berlin.)

3. Bust of Silenus, ivy-crowned; a drunken gravity in his features. Antique paste. (Dr. Nott.)

4. Intoxicated Bacchante, holding a wreath, and supporting herself with one hand on a tall amphora, the pattern of which clearly indicates the school and the date of this intaglio—Campanian, of the 4th century B.C. Sard. (Blacas.)

5. Nymph filling her urn at a fountain, by which stands a rock-cut figure of Priapus. Cameo.

6. The Centaur Pholos carrying a huge bowl and a tree to some Bacchic festival. Cameo. (Beverley.)

7. Ariadne, or Libera, wife of Bacchus, attired in the *nebris*, deer-skin, her distinctive costume. (Berlin.)

8. Boy carrying a goat for sacrifice, on the *thymele*, or circular Bacchic altar.

LXI.

SILENUS.

1. Silenus seated and draining his capacious bowl. Sard. (Dr. Nott.)

2. Bacchante, thyrsus on shoulder, balancing herself on one leg. Sard. (Leake.)

3. Head of Silenus, ivy-crowned: one of the finest examples of the subject known. (New York.)

4. Nymph opening the *cista mystica*, whence issues a serpent: a Faun stands by amazed. Sard. (Dr. Nott.)

5. Tall Crater, embossed with a Bacchic procession: doubtless a copy of some famous piece of plate by an ancient master. Onyx. (Pourtalès.)

6. The Panther of Baochus, equipped with wings: rapidity of intoxication. Sard. (Beverley.)

7. Young Etruscan cup-bearer, carrying a wine-jar, almost too heavy for his arms.

8. Bacchic Genius: compound of Silenus and panther. Early Greek work.

9, 10. Pan dancing against a Goat for the prize. Sard. (Leake and New York.)

LXII.

MASKS.

1. Head of Silenus, represented in the act of shouting out the Bacchanalian cry. Cameo.

2. Head of the Indian Bacchus, calm and tranquil, wreathed with ivy. Cameo.

3. Two Comic Actors: the one standing, and declaiming to the accompaniment of the other's lyre. Sard.

4. Tragic Mask, of most ferocious cast: well befitted for the character of Scythian Tyrant on the stage. Sard. (Beverley.)

5. Head of Bacchante, ivy-wreathed: her beautiful features full of wild inspiration. The most exquisite specimen of the class anywhere to be found.

6. Head of Pan: admirably expressing the jocular savagery of the God of the Shepherds.

7. Character of the Slave in Comedy—a Davus, or Dromio. The signet of some C. Clodius. The H A added, probably denotes his *cognomen*, "Habenna," or some similar word; but at the same time a joke may have been intended, as though it were the cry of astonishment which the Mask itself seems to utter.

LXIII.

HERCULES.

1. Hercules crossing the Styx, and preparing to muffle Cerberus, who awaits him on the further bank, with his cloak. The prosaic treatment of the subject is truly characteristic of Etruscan taste.

2. Hercules contending with the river-god, Achelous, for the possession of Dejanira: a very remarkable Etruscan work, in pale plasma. (Dr. Bishop.)

3. Hercules destroying the Hydra; as depicted upon the coins of Phæstum, in Crete.

4. Hercules, by the twanging of his bowstring, scaring away the Harpy Birds from the table of the blind Phineas.

5. Hercules, floating on a raft buoyed up with wine-jars, steering himself with his club, and holding up a wineskin for the sail. Rafts of this construction are still in use upon the Nile; but Juvenal poetically exaggerates them into actual *boats* in earthenware:

> "Parvula fictilibus solitum dare vela phaselis,
> Et brevibus pictæ remis incumbere testæ."

A truly Etruscan idea.

6. Death coming to the relief of the despairing Hercules. Early Greek design.

LXIV.

1. Hercules shooting the Stymphalian Cranes, invulnerable against mortal arrows. Early Greek style. Sard. (New York.)

2. The same subject, treated in the Roman manner.

3. Hercules capturing the Boar of Erymanthus: a characteristic example of the early Etruscan naturalistic treatment of such designs. Sard. (New York.)

4. Hercules about to let fly an arrow. Asiatic Greek work. Sard. (New York.)

5. Omphale, clad in the spoils of Hercules. Sard.

6. Hercules acknowledging his infant son Telephus, discovered by the shepherd whilst being suckled by a doe. Sard; found at Chiusi. (New York.)

LXV.

HEROES.

1. Bellerophon slaying the Chimera. Sard. (Dr. Nott.)

2. Atalanta pausing in her course to pick up the golden apple. Amethyst. (Berlin.)

3. Sisyphus lifting his rock up a flight of steps. Etruscan style.

4. The same subject, but treated in the modern manner. (Berlin.)

5. Prometheus chained to the rock, the vulture tearing at his side. (Berlin.)

6. Nessus, the Centaur, carrying off Dejanira. Etruscan style.

7. Theseus affixed to his iron chair at the gates of Hades. (Berlin.)

8. The sons of Hercules casting lots for the division of the Peloponnesus. A favourite subject with the ancient artists, from the earliest to the latest times. Sard. (Blacas.)

LXVI.

EPIC CYCLE.

1. The gigantic Ajax carrying off the field the slain Achilles, with the arrow still fixed in the wound. Sard. (New York.)

2. Ajax Oilei tearing away Cassandra from the altar of Pallas. Banded agate. (New York.)

3. The thirsting Tantalus grasping at the receding waters.

4. Tydeus lying in ambush. Sard. (New York.)

5. Orestes, returning home by stealth, fastens a fillet around the monument of his father. Sard. (New York.)

6. Wounded Soldier led out of the fray by two comrades: whence the old name for the subject, "Pietas Militaris." It also has, erroneously, been explained as the triple-bodied Geryon; but there is little doubt that it alludes to some Homeric incident of the above-named character.

LXVII.

TROJAN WAR.

1. Head of Priam, so called; but more probably that of some Persian king, and a portrait from the life.

2. The shepherd Paris holding out the Apple of Discord. The design betrays a modern hand. Sard. (Blacas.)

3. Æneas making his escape from the burning Troy. Sard. (Blacas.)

4. Head in a Phrygian cap, of an unknown person. Sard. (Blacas.)

5. Ulysses escaping from the cave of Polyphemus, by clinging to the belly of his Ram. (Berlin.)

6. Ulysses carried over the seas upon a turtle, which he regales with grapes.* A reference to some legend now utterly lost.

7. Penelope sorrowing for the absent Ulysses, whose bow is set before her. Etruscan work. (Blacas.)

8. The sea-monster Scylla. Early Greek style.

LXVIII.

1. Achilles in his tent, singing to the lyre "the glories of the men of old," as Homer describes him. Sard. (Blacas.)

2. Ajax meditating suicide. In the modern taste; apparently a work of Pichler's. Ruby paste. (Beverley.)

3. Achilles putting on a greave "of ductile tin," as Homer says. Early Greek engraving in chalcedony. (Leake.)

4. Achilles dragging the slain Hector at his chariot wheels.

5. Briseis raising up the suppliant Priam, at the feet of Achilles. Sard. (Palgrave.)

6. Achilles at the moment of being hit in the heel by the arrow of Paris.

7. The same, expiring from the wound.

8. The proscribed Orestes making himself known to his sister Electra. Sard. (Leake.)

LXIX.

PORTRAITS.

1. Epicurus; not antique, but evidently a modern copy from a bust.

2. Socrates and Plato. Garnet. (Paris.)

3. Plato. The Psyche-wings fastened to his temples allude to his doctrine of the immortality of the soul. A very ancient portrait. Sard.

4. Aristippus surrounded by the deities who inspired his writings. Antique paste. (Blacas.)

5. Homer chanting his verses before the monument of a hero. Cameo.

6. Generally accepted for the head of Sappho. Antique paste. (Praun.)

7. Bust of Venus, converted into a Sappho by an ignorant modern, who knew not how her name is spelt. Sard. (Marlborough.)

LXX.

1. Alexander, wearing the Macedonian bonnet. Cameo, of the time; once in the collection of Caylus.

2. Ptolemy Soter, Berenice, and their son Philadelphus. Sard; found in India. (Muirhead.)

3. Philip V. of Macedon. Sard; once in Horace Walpole's cabinet.

* This subject is exactly repeated in a bronze relief lately in the Greó Collection.

4. His son Perseus, in the character of his mythic namesake. Lapis-lazuli. (Blacas.)

5. M. Agrippa. From the De la Turbie Cabinet; as is shown by the peculiar style of the setting. Sard.

6. Bust of a youthful Prince, in the character of Alexander. The face bears a certain resemblance to the portraits of Philip V. as seen on his coins. Lapis-lazuli. (Praun; now New York.)

LXXI.

ROMAN PORTRAITS.

1. Tatius Sabinus. Early Roman work. Sard.

2. Numa. Antique copy from his statue in the Capitol, still existing in the times of Pliny, and identical with the portrait on a denarius of the Gens Pompilia, who boasted their descent from him.

3. The Second Triumvirate: in the style of the Cinque-cento.

4. Julius Cæsar; in front, the "Julium Sidus." Dark sard. (Maskelyne.)

5. Augustus in later life. The inscription seems dedicatory; not part of a name.

6. Tiberius in his younger days. Sard.

LXXII.

1. One of the finest examples of Roman art in this department anywhere to be found. It has been attributed successively to Pompey (on the strength of the tuft on the forehead), to Mæcenas, and to Tiberius in advanced life, but on no satisfactory grounds to any of them. The Apollonius whose name appears on it was the owner, not the engraver, of the gem. Brown garnet. (Hertz.)

2. Portrait of an Old Man; perhaps the physician Dioscorides, whose name is cut in front of it. Antique paste. (Nelthropp.)

3. The full face of a Child. Such were used as amulets, in a sense connected with the infant Horus. Sard. (New York.)

4. Bust of a young Cæsar, probably Geta, wielding Fortune's rudder, instead of a spear: an ingenious stroke of flattery. Sard. (New York.)

5. The most important of all Roman intagli, both for its merit and from its bearing the unimpeachable signature of the engraver, "Evodus;" for its history can be traced back to the days of Charlemagne. The subject is Julia Titi, wife of Domitian. Beryl. (Paris.)

LXXIII.

GREEK AND ROMAN PORTRAITS.

1. Socrates: good Roman work. Sardonyx. (New York.)

2. The same, in a different style; sometimes assigned conjecturally to Democritus. Sard. (New York.)

3. Scipio the Elder; his head covered with a *cudo* (leathern skull-cup), to conceal his baldness. Sard. (New York.)

4. Brutus Junior. He is represented unshaven, for towards the end of his career, as Plutarch tells us, despairing of the fortunes of the Republic, he let his beard grow as a sign of mourning. Sard. (New York.)

5. Caius Cæsar, son of M. Agrippa and Julia, daughter of Augustus: an unrivalled specimen of the art of his times. Dark sard. (New York.)

6. The Mother of the same; in the character of Isis. Sard. (New York.)

7. Lady with her hair dressed in the fashion first set by Julia Domna. The ingeniously disguised legend, "Amo te ego," indicates the use to which the signet was to be put. Sard. (New York.)

8. Julia, daughter of Titus, preposterously deified as *Juno:* distinguished by the peacock for a head-covering, and the triple ear-pendants assigned by Homer to that goddess. Yellow sard. (New York.)

LXXIV.

ROMAN PORTRAITS.

1. Augustus deified as the giver of abundance. Cameo.

2. Mæcenas; for whose portrait this head has been long accepted, though on no better authority than its resemblance to a bust, itself *conjecturally* assigned to the celebrated patron of letters.

3. Hannibal: indicated by the Ammon's horn in the helmet; but the meaning of the *lituus* below the bust cannot be explained. Sard.

4. A precious historical gem: the conjugated heads of Commodus and Marcia as Hercules and Omphale. Said to have formerly existed in the Hertz Collection.

5. Antony; a contemporary likeness. Sard. (Marlborough.)

6. Juba, "bene capillatus juvenis," as Cicero calls him. Sard. (Blacas.)

7. Caracalla and Plautilla as Ceres and Triptolemus; in the centre, the hymeneal altar, on which perches the Imperial Eagle. Sard. (New York.)

LXXV.

SYMBOLICAL TYPES.

1. Mercury, by the magic power of his *caduceus*, drawing up a soul from the Shades. The analogy of the initials C. A. D. probably led to the selection of this seal-device. Banded agate. (New York.)

2. The Nereid Galatea, the "Galene" of Addæus's epigram, breasting the waves. Sard. (New York.)

3. Cupid throwing the light of his torch into a huge vase, whence escapes a *larva*. A hint to enjoy life while life lasts. Onyx. (New York.)

4. Jupiter descending in a shower of thunderbolts upon the dying Semele. A warning against ambition.

5. Two Genii supporting a Vase, whence issues a stream. The *sun* and the *horse* painted on this vase make me see in it the Clepsydra of the Circus, as

used for timing the races. Visconti, however, interprets the design as emblematic of Spring. Banded agate. (New York.)

6. Ceres, in a *thensa*, drawn by elephants. That the type conveyed the idea of *Eternity* is manifested by a coin of Faustina's, where it is accompanied with that legend. Sard. (New York.)

7. Seated Sphinx: the type of the coins of Cos. Augustus used it for his seal; it perhaps carried a hint at secrecy to the receiver of the letter. Black jasper. (New York.)

8. Caduceus within a myrtle crown: union of the attributes of Mercury and Venus. On the reverse is the legend ΑΚΡΙꞶΦΙ, still unexplained, but clearly a charm in high repute, to judge from the frequency with which it occurs. Sard. (New York.)

LXXVI.

SYMBOLISM.

1. Type of the Province Africa, distinguished by the elephant's scalp: an idea as old as the times of the Macedonian conquest. Sard. (Blacas.)

2. The Province Sicily; the centre formed by the head of Proserpine. The *mallet* in the field indicates the owner, one "Malleolus." Sard. (New York.)

3. Morpheus pouring forth his soporiferous dews from a horn. Sard. (Praun.)

4. Head of Castor, in the *pileus;* or perhaps a boy's portrait in that character. Amethyst. (Blacas.)

5. Mercury wearing a very small *petasus*. Antique paste. (Leake.)

6. Caduceus between wheat ears: an augury of prosperous trade. Sapphire. (Maskelyne.)

7. Stork, the bird of passage, carrying *Abundantia* and Caduceus. In the same sense as the last.

8. Fortuna, as "Domina maris," mounted on Capricorn, ruler of the tides, and holding Neptune's dolphin and trident.

9. Symbolical ring; a combination of various religious symbols, noticeable amongst which are the caps of the three *Flamens*. The gryllus over the ring represents the device graven on its face. Intended to serve as an amulet for the defence of one "M. Varrius." Sard.

10. Head of Helena between her twin brothers:

> "Fratres Helena, lucida sidera."

They being the protectors of seafaring people, it is probable that this gem was supposed to possess a talismanic virtue for the benefit of that class. Chalcedony. (Leake.)

LXXVII.

RELIGIOUS RITES.

1. Sacrifice after a victory. Sard. (Blacas.)

2. Woman throwing her offerings, "libum molamque salsam," on an altar in front of a rustic shrine of Priapus, containing the emblem of the god in the

shape of a cylindrical stone; which indicates the destination of the celebrated "Pierre sacrée d'Antibes." Chalcedony. (Leake.)

3. Triumphal sacrifice to Jupiter Capitolinus.

4. Youth grasping a Serpent by the neck, and extending his right hand as though he were giving directions. Explained by Winckelmann as Telegonus, inventor of divination by the observation of serpents; but more probably Phorbas, son of Apollo, who delivered Rome from such a pest, and who therefore *must* have been honoured with a statue. The idea is allusive to the name of "Pius."

5. Insignia of a *Flamen*—the apex, aspergillum, lituus, &c.

6. Electra carrying libations to her father's tomb. A subject much in favour as a decoration for Athenian gravestones. Sard. (Blacas.)

LXXVIII.

ARTS AND SCIENCES.

1. Prometheus modelling his Man. Sard. (Blacas.)

2. Argus cutting out the stern of the first ship, to which he gave his name.

3. Water-organ (*Hydraulis*). The men below are working the forcing-pumps which drive the air into the great cylinder (*tympanum*), from which rise the pipes. The legend "Vivas" applies to the owner of the gem. Sard. The peculiar setting shows this gem to have been in the Beckford Cabinet.

4. Artist engaged in sculpturing an immense vase.

5. Diogenes ensconced in his *dolium*, oil jar, with the *dog* that gave the name to the sect: a disciple, seated before him, takes down his words of wisdom on a scroll.

6. Astrologer seated before a sun-dial, calculating a nativity.

7. Vase with doves on the handles: a restoration by a Roman hand of the famous bowl of Nestor.

8. Funeral urn, with pendant *infula.*

9. The *plectrum* for striking the lyre; and the *scabillum*, or loose shoe, for beating time to the music.

10. The Comic *soccus*, with the palm-branch: augury of success to the recipient of the gem.

LXXIX.

SPORTS AND GAMES.

1. Youth holding the *discus*, and brandishing the thong used in throwing it. The finest intaglio of the subject known. Sard. (Hertz.)

2. Youth with the metal hoop (the "Græcus trochus" of Horace), and the hooked rod used for propelling it. Etruscan style.

3. Horse's head and *Attic* helmet: the device of a Greek cavalry soldier; literally, his "armes parlantes."

4. *Quadriga* at full speed: a very characteristic example of the earliest period of Etruscan art. Sard scarabæus. (Brogden.)

5. Horse, winner of the prize; whereby is immortalised his name.

"Tiberis." On the reverse is cut a Gnostic sigil, to convert the gem, a heliotrope, into a talisman. (New York.)

6. Child scaring two others with a mask: the shape of which, as being only a *face*, betrays the modern origin of the engraving. Black jasper. (Blacas.)

7. Greek Warrior standing by his steed.

8. Boy victorious at the game of *Trochus*.

LXXX.

CAPRICES; TRADE-MARKS.

1. Female Triton charging furiously with the trident. Chalcedony. (Leake.)

2. Eagle and Tiger attacking a Rabbit: the alliance of the strong against the weak. Sard. (Leake.)

3. Sea-horse: a mariner's signet. Sard. (Leake.)

4. Corslet, interesting for the completeness of the details; exhibiting defence for the throat, like a gorget. The signet of an armourer.

5. Rabbit in a car, drawn by a pair of Ants. The more preposterous the combination could be made in these things, the greater the virtue of the amulet. Sard. (Leake.)

6. Saturn, holding the *falx* and sceptre, in his serpent car; above, Capricorn and Aquarius. The horoscope of the owner.

7. Murex-shell: a valuable type, as placing out of doubt the species that produced the Tyrian purple. The signet of a dyer, or of one like Lydia, "a seller of purple." It is evident, from their frequency, that types of this kind were used as "trade-marks."

8. Locust, as a poulterer, carrying on his pole a couple of rabbits and a fish, assailed by a scorpion and a centipede—bad-paying customers. Sard. (Leake.)

9. Caduceus, Dolphin, and Cornucopia: emblems of Trade, Navigation, Riches; the speaking device of a merchant. Chalcedony. (Leake.)

LXXXI.

GRYLLI; CAPRICES.

1. Two Gryphons pulling down a Stag: attribute of Apollo, as being typical of velocity.

2. Grasshopper perched upon ears of bearded wheat (*Triticum*). Sard. (Maskelyne.)

3. Wheat-grain between two Ants, sacred to Ceres, as the inventors of granaries.

4. Four Dormice nibbling at each corner of a vine-leaf; in the middle of which sits a *Cigala*, to furnish them with music.

5. Head of a Persian, capped with that of Aries, the guardian Sign of his country, as Manilius teaches:

> "Him Persia worships, clad in robes that flow,
> Her steps entangling as they fall below."

Sard. (New York.)

6. Locust driving a plough, drawn by a pair of Bees: Industry toiling for the benefit of Idleness and Mischief.

7. *Psittacus Torquatus*, the green paroquet of the Himalayas, and therefore playing a part in Bacchus' Indian Triumph, here combined with the face of the same god. Sard. (Leake.)

LXXXII.
ANIMALS.

1. Sow eating an apple. Greek. Animals are the favourite subjects of early art.

2. Female Panther: the *Bee* may express the owner's name, "Melissa."

3. Group of cows. Chalcedony. (Leake.)

4. Wild Sow. Etruscan work.

5. Head of great Wild Boar.

6. Wild Boar attacked by Hounds.

7. Hunter spearing Wild Boar, as he charges out from his reedy covert. Sard. (Blacas.)

8. Ass turning a cornmill, as we see in the Pompeian pictures.

9. Ass going to market, carrying panniers laden with the produce of the farm.

LXXXIII.
ARTISTS' SIGNATURES.

1. Evidently a portrait from the life, and done with infinite skill: it has been assigned to Demosthenes, for want of better, but bears no resemblance to the genuine busts of the orator. The signature of the engraver, "Dexamenos," has every appearance of being by the same hand as the rest of the work. On a particoloured agate scarabæoid; now in the possession of Admiral Soteriades, Athens.

2. Greek Lady at her toilette, unmistakably by the same hand as the last, and with his name; but the addition of another name, "Mikes," cannot be explained. The genuine antiquity of this exquisite intaglio is beyond all cavil. Sapphirine Chalcedony, obtained many years ago by Colonel Leake, but the locality not recorded.

3. Stork upon the wing. In the signature Dexamenos tells us he was a "Chian." Now this island was *Pelasgic*, which word properly signifies *stork:* the device therefore is his national emblem. No Italian forger was ever capable of so much knowledge. Agate of the same curious species as No. 1. (St. Petersburg.)

4. The celebrated Strozzi Medusa. The signature of the *imaginary* artist, "Solon," was undoubtedly added by the dealer into whose hands the gem first fell: for it was discovered soon after the unlucky conjecture of the Regent Orleans had given birth to such an artist. Chalcedony, in a Cinquecento mounting. (Blacas.)

5. Cupid engaged at the game of knuckle-bones (*astragali*); in the field, the *mitylus* shell, aptly dedicated to his mother Venus. A beautiful design, beautifully executed; but there is no reason for supposing that "Phrygillus" was other than the owner of the signet. Sard. (Berlin.)

6. Female Sphinx, scratching her head with the hind paw. The name of the ancient poet "Thamyrus" was also borne by the owner of this truly elegant signet. Sard. (Vienna.)

LXXXIV.

1. Antinous in the character of Achilles. The name has the appearance of modern insertion. Sard. (Marlborough.)

2. Augustus: used for the civic seal of the town of Valeria in Latium. A parallel to the use of the head of their ancient king Polydorus, by the magistrates of Laconia, so late as the times of Pausanias, as I have mentioned already at p. 192.

3. Cupid taming the lion by the sound of his lyre. The signature of its engraver, "Plutarchus," is amongst the very few the genuineness of which cannot be questioned, although there remains the possibility that it may only mark the copy of some noted picture by that celebrated *painter*. Cameo. (Florence.)

4. Hercules Bibax. His gladiatorial corpulence bespeaks, like that of the Hercules Farnese, a late Roman date. "Admon" is the name of the owner, or perhaps of the athlete himself, in this manner deified. Sard (Marlborough.)

5. Alexander in the character of Jupiter, after the painting by Apelles at Ephesus, as described by Pliny. The name of "Nisus" certainly designates the owner. Sard. (Orleans.)

LXXXV.

1. Cupid bearing up a huge cornucopia: an apt device for a lady of pleasure. The name of the supposed artist, "Aulus," is, as usual, a modern addition. Sard. (Marlborough.)

2. Diana standing by her Stag. That we have here a faithful copy of some very ancient and celebrated statue is proved by Faustina Junior's taking the same figure for a reverse to one of her medallions. The name "Heius" is that of the owner of the signet. Antique paste. (Blacas.)

3. The Dionysiac Bull upon a *thyrsus*, to indicate his character in this picture. "Hyllus," a name much in favour, is merely the owner's. Sard. (Paris.)

4. Mercury in cap and mantle, as patron of travellers. "Dioscorides" was one of the most popular names with the later Greeks, on account of the good augury it contained. Nevertheless, its fancied reference to the famous gem engraver made this only mediocre work obtain the price of one thousand guineas from Lord Bessborough: but, "stultitiam patiuntur opes." Sard. (Marlborough.)

5. Terpsichore tuning her lyre; at her side, a statuette of Apollo. "Allion" is an artist excogitated by the forgers out of ΔΑΛΙΟΝ, "of the Delians" (*Doric*), found accompanying a head of Apollo and misinterpreted in this manner. Nicolo. (Blacas.)

LXXXVI.

SIGNATURES, VARIOUS.

1. Head of the youthful Hercules; with the name of "Gnæus" inscribed. Beryl. (Blacas, with a facsimile by a modern hand.)

2. Sextus Pompey, with the signature of "Agathangelus," one of his officials. Sard. (Berlin.)

3. Eagle's Head, with the name "Scylax;" a gem repeatedly copied. Sard. (Beverley.)

4. This portrait so closely resembles that of Julia, daughter of Augustus, that I cannot help suspecting the Cælius who made it his signet was one of the favoured admirers of that amorous princess. Sard. (Praun.)

5. Melpomene seated: serving to authenticate the "Herophile Opobalsamum" of some oculist in the 2nd century. Sard. (Brit. Mus.)

LXXXVII.

THE EMERALD VERNICLE.

Bust of Christ, with radiated head, painted on panel, and inscribed below: "The perfect similitude of our Lord and Saviour Jesus Christ: imprinted on amerild by the predecessors of the Great Turke; and sent to the Pope Innocent the VIII. to this use, for a token that he might redeme his brother, yt was taken prisoner."

A second, almost a *replica* of this picture, exists in the Château de Pertuis, Arrondissement d'Api. Style and lettering indicate the middle of the 16th century as the date of their execution. They are copied from a large *cast* medal, a specimen of which is preserved in the British Museum, and which appears to be not much more recent than the times of the Pontiff named upon it. But the legend of the medal gives the true motive of Bajazet II.'s gift, "ut retineret fratrem," to induce the Pope to *detain*, in honourable but safe custody, a dangerous refugee, his brother Zizim. The translator, ignorant of Italian history, naturally enough rendered this by the word "redeem." The medal, therefore, is the true source of the numerous portraits of the Saviour, all claiming the *Emerald* (sometimes ascribed to Pilate) for their authority. The picture from which my drawing is made is 17 in. high by 13 wide, and has been long preserved in the School-house at Douglas, Isle of Man. The history of this curious fabrication will be found, fully traced out, in my 'Early Christian Numismatics,' p. 95.

Note upon the Gnostic Gorgon.

A very curious variety of this talisman, and which explains the primary intention of others of the sort, like the Seal of St. Servatius, has lately been communicated to me by Mr. W. T. Ready. The one face of the jasper agrees almost exactly in type and size with the former; but the other bears St. Anne, a half length, nursing the infant Madonna, with the legend, at each side, in contracted Greek, "Saint Anna," "Help, Mother of God!" Around runs the legend—VCTEPA MEΛΑΙΝΗ MEΛΑΙΝΟΜΕΝΗ OC [ὡς] ΘΑΛΑΤΑΝ (*sic*) ΓΑΛΗΝΗ CENOI (for *σαίνει*), "as the calm soothes the sea." The substitution of *ὑστερὰ* for the more common *Μοῖρα* (as in the similar gem figured by Chiflet, No. 70, "Apistopistus") proves this talisman to be intended to protect parturient women. That the worship of the "Panagia" had by this time included her mother, indicates a very low date in the Byzantine empire, probably the era of the Palæologi.

CATALOGUE OF ANCIENT ARTISTS.

CONDENSED FROM DR. BRUNN'S 'GESCHICHTE DER GRIECHISCHEN KÜNSTLER' (1859), VOL. II.

(The gems marked with a star have all been examined by myself, and several of them, unnoticed by Dr. Brunn, are now introduced into the text for the first time.)*

CLASS I.

Names handed down to us by genuine Inscriptions, and which are with confidence to be referred to the Artist.

AGATHOPUS.—Head of Sex. Pompey; behind it ΑΓΑΘΟΠΟΥϹ ЄΠΟΙЄΙ; formerly Andreini's, now Florence. Aquamarine. Köhler admits the genuineness of the intaglio, but terms the legend decidedly modern, and borrowed from that accompanying an Elephant's Head in Stosch's casts. He notes that De la Chaussée publishes this head *without* the inscription, though, as Dr. Brunn remarks, this may have been an accidental omission. [I, for my part, believe that most of these heads called Sex. Pompey's, if not all, are in reality portraits of Hadrian: certainly the lunar-shaped letters Ϲ and Є in the legend were not in use much before the reign of the latter.]

2. Head of the Laocoon, with the name spelt with an Ω, is very suspicious. (Stosch's casts.)

3. Hercules' Head in cameo, name in intaglio, is, according to Tölken, modern. (Berlin.)

4. AGATHOPI, in Latin characters, above two clasped hands, refers to the owner.

APOLLONIUS.—The Diana of the Hills, an intaglio of the greatest merit; amethyst. (Naples.) One of the few the entire genuineness of which is allowed by Köhler, who supposes it to be copied after the colossal Diana at Anticyra, the work of Praxiteles. First mentioned by De Montjosieu in 1585, who refers the name to Pliny's Apollonides. At that time in Tigrini's possession, whence purchased by Ful. Ursinus. A copy of it, but far inferior, by Lor. Masini, exists.

[*2. Head of Mæcenas, in front face; an admirable antique work: jacinth. (Hertz, now Rodes.) The signature, in minute elegant letters, undoubtedly designates the ancient owner.]

* My own observations in the *text* are enclosed in brackets, to distinguish them from the critiques of Dr. Brunn.

Aspasius.—Bust of the Minerva of Phidias; behind the neck ΑCΠΑCΙΟΥ red jasper. (Vienna.) The intaglio admitted by Köhler, but the legend condemned. First published by Canini in 1669, who takes it for the portrait of the famous Aspasia.

2. Replica of the same brought from Egypt thirty years ago by Drovetti, now Basseggio's: sard. Admitted as antique by the Roman Institute, but far inferior to the Vienna gem, though at the same time above Calandrelli's copy of the latter.

3. A well-known copy of this by Natter.

4. Serapis; lower part of the bust: red jasper. (Florence.) The legend doubtful.

5. Agrippina as Ceres: sard; erroneously described as red jasper or beryl. (Formerly Medina's, now Marlborough.) Declared by Bracci a work of Flavio Sirletti's.

Suspicious, on account of the blundered orthography, are—

6. Bust of the Bearded Bacchus; formerly Hamilton's, now Worsley: red jasper.

7. Head of Cybele: onyx. (Worsley.)

8. Juno standing, at her feet the peacock, is put down by Cades to the account of Cerbara.

9. Junius Brutus. (Stosch's casts.)

Athenion.—Jupiter in his car overthrowing the Titans; the name in relief in the ground at one side: cameo. (Naples.) Highly praised by Köhler. From the lettering Visconti attributed the work to a pre-Cæsarian age. But Tölken quotes, from Bartholdy's Collection (Berlin), an antique blue paste representing the Triumph of Drusus (whose features are clearly recognizable in the victor's), with an exactly similar signature in relief in the exergue; a proof conclusive that Athenion flourished under Augustus.*

Boëthus.—Philoctetes reclining on the earth, fanning with a wing his bandaged leg: cameo. (Beverley.) Quoted by Raspe as then in France, and supposed, by R. Rochette, to have come from Asia, because it is for the first time figured as a heading to Choiseul's map of Lemnos. Stephani, on no good grounds, calls the work modern, and the name taken from the famous *crustarius* Boëthus. [It is, however, amongst the most authentic, as far as execution goes, of any signed camei; but I have no doubt it is a copy, made in the Augustan age, of a chasing by that famous and (even then) ancient silversmith.]†

* Athenion of Maronæa, in the age of Praxiteles, was the rival of Nicias—"austerior colore et in austeritate jucundior ut in ipsa pictura eruditio eluceat"—"quod nisi in juventa obisset nemo compararetur." "Pinxit in una tabula VI Signa." An unique example of an early astrological picture this, and our Jupiter may well be a copy of some famous painting by him.—*Plin.* xxxv. 11.

† Boëthus is one of the four most famous chasers of silver quoted by Pliny (xxxiii. 55). Works of his were then extant in the Temple of Minerva at Lindus, in the Isle of Rhodes. In the same island were also preserved works by the other three; *e. gr.*, "Scyphi engraved with Centaurs and Bacchantes," whence it would appear that Rhodes was the head-quarters of the art.

Dioscorides.—*Mercury standing; the signature follows the length of the field. Quoted by Montjosieu, in 1585, as then belonging to Tigrini, afterwards by Spon, as "olim apud Fulvium Ursinum." Sard. [Apparently the gem sold by Stosch to Lord Holdernesse, whose son-in-law, the fifth Duke of Leeds, bequeathed it to the Marlborough Cabinet. The name, cut in large careless letters, has been almost effaced by the repolishing of the surface: a sufficient reply to Köhler's assertion that it is evidently an addition of the last century.]

2. Solon, or Mæcenas: amethyst. (Paris.) Shown by Bagarris, in 1605, to Peiresc; and then belonging to Fran. Perier, a nobleman of Aix. It has been repolished and retouched to all appearance, and by an unskilful hand. In 1802 it was made up with other antique gems into Josephine's parure, but returned to the Museum; unlike the fate of the rest.

3. Head of Augustus, front face, given to Colbert by the Chapter of Figéac: sard "as big as a 30-sous piece." Not known at present.

4. Augustus, with radiated head, said, by Faber, to have belonged to Ful. Ursinus. Not known.

5. Augustus, young head: large cameo. (Piombino-Ludovisi.) Name in intaglio. The relief partly ground down and effaced. This name Dr. Brunn believes genuine.

6. Head of Io: carnelian; found, in 1765, on the estate of the Duke di Bracciano; then in Poniatowsky Collection (lastly Mr. Currie's, at Como).

7. The Diomede. (Devonshire.)

8. Augustus: amethyst. (Blacas.) The inscription is below the neck; the outline of the hair seems purposely mutilated, and the work does not bear with indubitable certainty the character of antiquity.

9. A similar head, on garnet, went with the De Thoms Gems into the Hague; signature beneath the neck, a star below it. Suspected by Bracci to be a work of Sirletti's; and, with the preceding, put down by Köhler to Stosch's fabrique.

10. A modern copy, known to exist now at Paris.

*The Devonshire Diomede, purchased of Sevin, had been first mentioned by Baudelot, 1716. Its history, as given by Mariette, is that, originally in the Royal Cabinet, it was presented by Louis XIV. to his daughter the Princess de Conti; she gave it to her physician Dodart, and he to his son-in-law Homberg, on whose death it was purchased by the jeweller Hubert, and from him by Sevin. Köhler, to make it out a work of Sirletti's, says, "The Diomede is to any eye, though but slightly initiated into ancient art, a well-drawn and careful, but very timidly, meanly, and painfully highly-finished work of Flavio Sirletti's. . . . It is possible that it may have been originally a sketchy antique engraving, which Sirletti finished off with infinite industry by means of the wheel and the diamond-point. It is, however, more probable on other grounds, that Sirletti both commenced and executed this piece without any such assistance." [With this judgment of Köhler's I fully agree; the execution is slight and timid to a degree utterly inconceivable in an *ancient* artist, above all in one capable of the correct drawing that distinguishes this performance. The genuine productions of antiquity, whatever may be their other defects, are never wanting in boldness as regards their mechanical part.]

Dr. Brunn "has not the knowledge of the gem necessary for coming to a conclusion as to the justice of these remarks of Köhler's," but observes that if we compare it with the *replicas* of Solon and Gnæus, this of Dioscorides appears "not only superior in the technical execution; but also the refinement visible in the conception, the spirited intensity of the attitude, the elasticity in all the movements, awaken of themselves a favourable impression as to the antiquity of the work, which, however, requires to be verified by the careful examination of the stone itself." A copy of this gem exists at the Hague.

A similar verification is required by the *cameo* at Berlin, "Hercules chaining Cerberus," with the legend in *intaglio* in the exergue. First published by Beger, and belonging, as appears from its silver mounting, to the original treasures of that cabinet, and to the times of the Electors Joachim I. and II. (1499 and 1533); so that in this case, at least, we have not to deal with the forgers of the last century. Tölken praises its artistic merit. [It strikes me as hardly an accidental coincidence that the same should have been the subject of the *cameo* obtained by Cellini from its finders during his first sojourn in Rome (1524–7), and which M. Angelo pronounced the finest in its kind he had ever beheld. How natural, even at that early period, to enhance its value by adding so obvious a name as that of the most famous engraver on record.]

Similarly, further examination is requisite in the case of a gem of whose origin nothing is known, and which has appeared only in one single, and that a private cabinet, the **Muse* of F. Pulsky, to quote whose own words, "The most important of the Féjévari gems signed with a name, is a Muse upon a splendid dark red sard of intense fire. The signature ΔΙΟΣΚΟΥΡΙΔΟΥ is, in my opinion, genuine, for it is evident that the engraver has left somewhat more room on the left side in order to afford space for the name. The style of this gem is not that of the Blacas Augustus, nor of the Demosthenes published by Winckelmann. It is precisely that of the Poniatowsky Io, which Köhler considered too good to have been engraved by Dioscorides."

We now come to a long series of stones bearing the name of Dioscorides, all more or less suspected, many acknowledged to be forgeries. These are :—

1. Mercury Criophorus: sard. (Stosch's, now Carlisle.)

2. Perseus leaning on his shield; at his feet the rest of his armour: sard. (Naples.) Köhler thinks the gem antique, but the name added (in the exergue); but Dr. B. regards the piece as a modern copy of the Mercury of the Belvedere, or so-called Antinous.

*3. A replica of this—once Medina's, now Marlborough—Bracci calls a work of Sirletti's; Raspe, of Torricelli's or Natter's.

4. Caligula, a cameo on which, says Casanova, Amidei had the name inserted by J. Pichler, and thus obtained for it fourfold the price first asked. This is the gem seen by Winckelmann in the possession of Jenkins (the well-known Roman banker), and afterwards of General Walmoden.

5. Lower part of the head of Iole: amethyst. (Beverley.) The signature in front of the neck. [Glaringly modern.]

6. Fragment of a group, Hercules and Omphale, or more probably a Her-

maphroditic symplegma. (Cades.) The work bears the stamp of modern elegance, and at the first sight the division of the name into two lines is very suspicious.

[*Wild Boar at bay, attacked by a dog, very deeply cut, so that the body, foreshortened, comes out in the impression in nearly full relief. The inscription, partly in the exergue, follows the contour of the gem, and is inscribed in neat, almost microscopic letters of unmistakably antique work. Black agate of small size. (British Museum; purchased July, 1865, of Castellani, of Naples.)]

As no artists' signatures are known in a contracted form, so in every case where the name of Dioscorides thus appears must every other doubt acquire redoubled weight. On these grounds, as also for orthographic errors, the following gems will require a very brief notice:—

1. Giant, aquamarine (given 1720 by Crozat to Zannetti, now Worsley's). Bracci states was attributed by the two Pichlers to Sirletti.

2. Same subject, sard; Blacas: came from the De la Turbie Coll. (Turin).

3. Medusa's head, in front-face cameo, signed ΔΙΟC; regarded by Pichler as antique, and is a fine work: but the lettering differs from all the other inscriptions of this artist, and necessitates the supposition either of another Dioscorides or else of an ancient forgery. [The name is probably that of the god, taking into account the talismanic character of the subject; Jove himself being a defender:

"Saturnum que gravem nostro Jove fregimus una."]

4. Hermaphroditus reposing, attended by three Cupids—amethyst; Worsley—is given by Bracci to the same modern hand as the Giant, on the same authority.

5. Augustus: sard. Beugnot (vid. 'Impronte Gemmarie,' iv. 93). Stephani observes upon it: "The engraver exhibits, more undisguisedly than many others, that degree of empty commonplace and want of certainty in the grasping of the form, coupled with painful and clumsy diligence in the representation, which distinguishes from all others those works of the present century that are intended to pass for antique." [Certainly the work of the hair is totally different from that usually seen in the antique.]

6. Serapis, front face: garnet; in Caylus' own possession: legend ΔΙωC. [There is no necessity of referring this inscription to an artist; it being an invocation to the god.]

7. Thalia seated holding a mask: onyx of two strata; De la Turbie. The name, according to Millin, is modern. (Now in the Blacas Coll., according to Cades.)

8. Bacchus and panther: sard. (Cades.)

*9. Female head, signed ΔΙΟCΙ: topaz. (Marlborough.)

10. Silenus seated under a tree, a female Faun by his side playing the double flute: sard. (Naples.) In the exergue ΔΙοCΚοΡ. Raspe remarks of it, "A distinguished work, and worthy of Dioscorides, to whom it would be assigned if the orthography were not faulty."

11. Julius Cæsar, front face, laurel-crowned, lituus on the right: jacinth. (Blacas: signed ΔΙΟΣΚΟΡΙΔΟΣ.)

12. Augustus (unknown coll.), given by Raspe.

13. Head of Laocoon, once Dr. Mead's, broken and restored in silver by Sirletti; to whom Köhler, perhaps with justice, attributes the intaglio itself.

Epitynchanus.—Germanicus; cameo, broken below, so losing the end of the legend running downwards behind the head, ΕΠΙΤΥΓΧΑ. Belonged to Fulvius Ursinus. (Strozzi, now Blacas.) Much praised by Köhler, but doubted, as far as the legend goes, by Stephani, because the letters are in intaglio. To this objection Dr. B. replies that there is no place upon the field where an inscription in relief could appear without interfering with the cameo.

[*Same head: intaglio, sard; once Beckford's. Modern.]

All the others, with the name abbreviated, and only known by Stosch's casts, are highly suspicious.

Evodus.—The Julia Titi, on aquamarine, or, as Haüy says, green crystal. The history of the gem can be traced up to Charlemagne; it having crowned the top of a châsse belonging to his chapel, and afterwards presented by Charles the Bald to the Abbey of St. Denys.

2. Female bust, Bacchante or Muse, sard, with indistinct legend ЄΥοΔοC ЄΠΟΙ: put down by Köhler as an insignificant modern work.

3. Horse's head, ЄΥΟΔΟC: sard. Schellersheim, now Baron Roger's: if agreeing with the Blacas onyx, is but a copy of the one signed ΜΙΘ. (Berlin.)

[*4. Horse's head and neck; work bold and indubitably antique. Below ЄΥΟΔΟΥ; probably the steed's own name, "Speed away:" a fine cabochor jacinth. (Rhodes.)

*Amethyst, head of Plotina or Marciana; the work antique and good: the name a modern addition, in large coarse lettering. [Present owner unknown.]

Eutyches.—The authenticity of this inscription has been recently established in a most striking manner by unexpected testimonies, dating from a remote period, which furnish the strongest external evidence to Tölken's internal reasons in favour of the genuineness of the inscription. De Rossi has found amongst the papers of Cyriac of Ancona, in a Vatican MS., the following notice: "Eugenii Papæ, an. XV 1445) Venetum ser. ab urbe condita M.XX.III. (*i.e.* 1023 years from the founding of Venice). Ad crystallinam Alexandri capitis ymaginem. Hec antiquis Grecis litteris inscriptio consculpta videtur

ΕΥΤΥΧΗΣ
ΔΙΟΣΚΟΥΡΙΔΟΥ
ΑΙΓΕΛΙΟΣ. ΕΠΟΙ
ΕΙ.

Quæ Latine sonant: Eutychus Dioscuridis Aigelius fecit." According to the words that follow, "Bertutio Delphino Venetum Alexandreæ classis, præfecto," the gem appears to have been presented by the latter to Cyriac. The opinion of Em. Braun's, that the supposed Alexander was no other than our Pallas, has received a speedy confirmation by a further communication of De Rossi's out of another Vatican MS., which proceeds from a contemporary of Cyriac's, *i.e.* the beginning of the fifteenth century: "Ad M. Læpomagnum ex K. A. (Kyriaci Anconensis) litterarum particula de Alexandri Macedonis in cristallino sigillo comperta nuper imagine præscripta cum inscriptione. 'Præterea ut insigne admodum aliquid tibi referam, cum mihi Io. Delphin ille Ναύαρχος diligens atque Φιλοπονώτατος apud eum per noctem prætoria sua in puppi moranti pleraque nomismata pretiosasque gemmas ostentasset, alia inter ejusmodi generis supellectilia nobile mihi de cristallo sigillum ostendit, quod polliciaris digiti magnitudine, galeati Alexandri Macedonis imagine pectore tenus, miraque Eutychitis artificis ope, alta corporis concavitate, insignitum erat; et expolitæ galeæ ornamento, bina in fronte arietum capita, certa Ammonii Jovis insignia parentis, tortis cornibus impressa: ac summo a vertice thyara, cursu veloci λαργικοὺς molossos hinc inde gerere videtur; insigni artis pulchritudine: et sub galea, tenuissimis hinc inde capillamentis princeps, subtili velamine et peregrino habitu elaboratis a summitate listis amictus, dexteram et nudam cubitenus manum, vesti summo a pectore honeste pertentantem, videtur admovisse; et gestu mirifico facies, regioque aspectu acie obtuitum perferens, vivos nempe de lapide nitidissimo vultus, et heroicam quoque suam videtur magnitudinem ostentare. Cum et ad lucem solidam gemmæ partem objectares, ubi cubica corporalitate, intus sublucida et vitrea transparenti umbra mira pulchritudine membra quoque spirantia enitescere conspectantur; et tam conspicuæ rei opificem suprascriptis inibi consculptis litteris Græcis atque vetustissimis intelligimus.'"

In the last century this gem was in the possession of Salviati and Colonna, and after of Prince Avella at Naples. In recent times it belonged, if I am not mistaken, to the Schellersheim Collection, so that a second example in the Marlborough, mentioned by Clarac, must certainly be a copy. [Quite true; for the lettering of the legend is in the large peculiar style seen on the Poniatowsky Gems, and the work of the intaglio, though deep and bold, on examination is destitute of the antique finish. The dimensions of the amethyst also far exceed the "polliciari magnitudine" of Cyriac's description.]

Of very dubious credit are—

1. Sol in his quadriga; onyx. (De Thoms.)
2. Head of a Roman youth: Raspe; where the name is written Eutychianus.
3. Minerva putting her vote into the urn in favour of Orestes. (Poniatowsky.)

Herophilus.—Laureated head of Augustus: in the field in front, in two lines—

ΗΡΟΦΙΛΟΣ
ΔΙΟΣΚΟΡΙΔΟΥ

A large cameo in blue paste, now at Vienna. Figured by Winckelmann (H. A. Pl. 31 D). Said to have been found at Maintz, and to have belonged to Treves Cathedral up to the dispersion of the chapter in consequence of the French Revolution; but actually described by Pater Wilhelm (d. 1699) in his 'Luxemburgum' as then preserved in the church of Efternach, where Dr. B. thinks justly it must have lain from time immemorial, judging from its mediæval silver setting attached to a chain, as if for suspension round the neck of some holy statue. [Condemned by Köhler in perfect ignorance of the facts, but, in my opinion, one of the very few examples beyond suspicion, satisfying as it does every condition.]

FELIX.—Rape of the Palladium: sardonyx. (Marlborough.) One of the few acknowledged as indubitable by Stephani. A copy of this by Sirletti was in Andreini's Collection, whence it was stolen. Another replica in the Florentine Museum. In the original the whole of the legend

ΚΑΛΠΟΥΡΝΙΟΥ ϹΕΟΥΗΡΟΥ
ΦΗΛΙΞ ЄΠΟΙЄΙ

is in the exergue;* in Andreini's gem the ΦΗΛΙΞ ЄΠΟΙЄΙ is inscribed upon the cippus. [If Dr. B. is not mistaken here, the Marlborough gem is in all likelihood that lost by Andreini; for such is the position of the legend on the Marlborough sard—a very dark-brown sort, the French sardoine, not a sardonyx, as he calls it, misled by the Catalogue.†]

2. Cupid and Psyche, sard; Strozzi. Copy of the Capitoline group, signed ΦΗΛΙΞ by Fel. Bernabé.

3. Centaur, ΦΗΛ, probably to be assigned to the same.

4. Lucretia, altogether modern.

HERACLEIDAS.—Head of M. J. Brutus, cut in a mixed metal let into a massy gold ring, found a few years back near Capua; now in the Naples Coll.: on the side ΗΡΑΚΛΕΙΔΑΣ ΕΠΟΕΙ. Compared by Em. Braun, for the beauty of the work, to a certain coin of Catania.

HYLLUS.—Female diademed head, called Artemisia; in front, ΥΛΛΟΥ. Sard, once in the cabinet of Lor. dei Medici, Orleans; now St. Petersburg. Hence the inscription must be reckoned one of the best authenticated.

2. Head resembling Sabina, with the diadem, perhaps a row of pearls interwoven in the hair; the work very elegant and neatly finished: the lettering looks too bold. Mistaken by Stephani for the first: its present place not known.

3. Barbarian's head, common carnelian: Florence. Published by Canini 1669, and the inscription, therefore, most likely authentic.

4. Hercules, or Aventinus, standing with the club in his right hand, held downwards, his left wrapped in the lion's hide placed upon his back: sardonyx of five layers, much injured by fire, which has destroyed the surface and shows that the legend existed there previously. (In Stosch's Coll., now Berlin.) The work of little merit.

5. Dionysiac Bull: chalcedony. (Paris.) The name, carelessly and sharply cut, over the design, is pronounced by Bracci and the Pichlers a modern addition.‡ Many copies known, in the Hague, Lord Clanbrasil's, Tunstall's, Hamilton's collections.

Requiring investigation is Pulsky's Bust of Jupiter, with a sceptre, and

* Figured in Stosch's 'Pierres Gravées.'

† The extreme thinness of the stone, coupled with its large extent, and the painfully minute style conspicuous in every part, confirm the suspicion suggested by the remark of Dr. Brunn.

‡ Mr. Rhodes, after a careful examination this summer (1862), agrees in this condemnation.

upper part of an eagle; the work of a latish yet still good period, on a fiery sard. Behind the head, in almost imperceptible letters, the signature ΥΛΛΟΥ. Upon the diadem, in coarser lettering, the name ΠΕΡΙΦΑΝΤΕΣ.

The most important of all the gems with this signature is a cameo bust of a young laughing Satyr, formerly Baron Winckler's, now in the Berlin Coll. In the field, in intaglio,

ΥΛΛΟC
ΔΙΟCΚΟΥΡΙΔΟΥ
ЄΠΟΙΕΙ.

The work held by Tölken as modern, but, strangely enough, by Stephani as antique. But he rejects the inscription as being *incised.* Unfortunately its history cannot be traced beyond its first mention by Gori.

The following are in the highest degree suspicious:—

Nereid borne by a Triton, and two Cupids, stone broken below; said by Clarac to be in the Marlborough Cabinet.*

Ariadne deserted; in Baron Roger's or the Piombino Coll. The figure in the modern sentimental style, and badly accommodated to the space.

Silenus Head, amethyst; and a Hippocrates, white and grey agate. Both from De la Turbie.

Paris: sard. (Algernon Percy.) Called by Raspe a modern work.

Diana: a copy from the Diana of Heius.

Silenus Mask: sard. (Gen. Rottier.)

Seated Pallas, contemplating a Gorgoneion: ant. paste; the name the remaining portion of "Thrasyllus."

Koinos.—Adonis leaning on a column, a spear in his left hand, a hound looking up to him: small sardonyx. (Once Ficoroni's, now Lichtenstein.) The legend behind the figure reads clearly ΚΟΙΝΟΥ, though variously misread. Köhler, as usual, ascribes this work to Natter, forgetting that it had been already published by Stosch in 1724, whereas Natter did not establish himself at Florence before 1732. Besides, it had been published by Maffei long before the forgery of names had come into vogue.

2. Augustus, in a Stosch's cast, of which nothing is known.

[3. *Head of Demetrius Poliorcetes, grand antique work: sardoine: Pulsky. The name, a modern insertion, in the front.] (Now in the British Museum.)

The blundered ΚΟΙΜΟΥ, evidently arising from the false reading of the name when first published, itself testifies against every gem on which it appears. Such are—

1. Satyr running: sardonyx [dark sard?], very minute. (Once Natter's, who expresses a doubt as to the true reading of the name.) Köhler at once puts him down as its author; but in that case he would hardly have expressed himself in the above terms. The figure, however, looks like a copy after the Satyr of Pergamos, that great favourite with the forgers.

2. Pythagoras seated and handling a globe set upon a cippus before him: sard. (De Salines: a collection notorious for its forgeries.)

* The intaglio, of a grandiose character, possesses every condition requisite for certifying its antiquity; whereas the name carelessly cut into the field, where it cannot indicate the *owner*, must be an interpolation.

[*Faun, carrying a vast hydria as if ascending a rock; a delicate Greek intaglio, but the name most awkwardly foisted into the exergue: sard. (Formerly Hertz.)]

*Perseus with the Gorgon's head in his hand—feeble modern intaglio: sard. (Marlborough.)

Mykon.—1. Bust of an aged man, beardless: jasper. (Once F. Ursinus'.)

2. Cupid on a lion: small onyx. (Once Caroline Murat's.) Seemed to Clarac genuine, both work and legend.

3. Muse seated, a roll in her left hand, the right lifted, as if declaiming; before her a mask on a cippus; jacinth. Said to be at Florence. The work of no particular merit, scarcely likely to have received an artist's signature. (In Cades' casts.) [Is this the jacinth-like sard of Hertz's, now Rhodes? If so, which there is no reason for doubting, the work is far from mediocre and the sard of an extraordinary fineness: the signature, too, as antique as the intaglio, but as indubitably the owner's name, and no more.]

Neisos.—Jupiter Axur,* resting his hand on a shield, the thunderbolt in his right: large Oriental sard. (Formerly Crozat's, then Orleans, now in the Russian Coll.) Stephani decides unconditionally in favour of the inscription, and that it is of the same date as the intaglio.

2. Cock in a car drawn by two rats, legend broken off, NEI . . : black jasper. (Baron Roger.) Undecided.

Nicandros.—*Julia Titi: amethyst [*sardoine*]. (Marlborough.) Greatly abused by Köhler: "The portrait without resemblance, executed utterly without taste, and legend and all of modern origin," &c. Dr. B., though far from praising the work, says it has something harsh and unfinished, yet gives the effect of genuineness, and is quite different from the style of the forgeries of the last century. The same holds good for the signature, cut in with a certain hastiness, where angular forms of the letters and dots replace the usual curves and circles, so troublesome to execute. [These criticisms are founded upon the casts; neither writer knowing that only the lower half of the gem remains, and has been restored in gold as a Julia, though certainly of a much earlier date, the chin and neck displaying the bold treatment of the Greco-Egyptian school. The signature, fortunately, is quite perfect, and the form of its letters fixes the date beyond all dispute, the O being represented by a dot, a peculiarity of the later bronze coinage of the Ptolemies. The material is a jacinth-coloured sard.]

Onesas.—Muse, leaning against a cippus, tuning her lyre: ant. paste. (Published by Maffei, now in the Flor. Gallery.) Inscription behind the cippus, which supports a naked figure—

ONHCAC
ЄΠΟΙΕΙ.

Considering that both figure and inscription were known in the middle

* "Apelles pinxit et Alexandrum Magnum fulmen tenentem in templo Ephesiæ Danæ xx talentis auri—digiti eminere videntur et fulmen extra tabulam esse" (*Plin.* 35, 36). This famous painting was assuredly the original of the gem; indeed the youthful, heroic figure differs totally from the established type of Jupiter; and the Vejovis was unknown to Greek art.

of the seventeenth century, the last doubts as to their genuineness must vanish.

2. Bust of Hercules, olive-crowned: sard of Andreini's, now Florence. In front of the neck, ONHCAC. Köhler condemns the whole, and thinks the top part of the head was broken off purposely to hide the faulty work. Dr. B. coincides, with a reservation, in this sentence.

3. Replica, in De Thoms Coll., highly dubious; perhaps that formerly belonging to Van Hoorn, upon which C. Costanzi added the name.

4. Ulysses holding a helm: sard, broken. From the De Thoms Coll.; equally suspected.

5. Head of youthful Hercules: sapphire. (Strozzi.)

6. Apollo, head bay-crowned: sard. (Card. Albani; now Colonnuli, a Spanish marquis.) Probably the famous one belonging to the Countess Cheroffini (the Cardinal's mistress), described by Winckelmann, but having, in Dr. B.'s opinion, a very modern look. To this origin is due the uncertainty in the expression, by no means bespeaking an Apollo.

7. Drunken Woman; the inscription blundered: sardonyx. Lippert; has been attributed to Onesas.

8. Venus Victrix: sard, broken. Cades; where the signature is palpably modern.

PAMPHILOS.—Achilles, seated on a rock, playing the lyre: amethyst. (Paris.) Presented, about 1680, by Prof. Fesch of Basle to Louis XIV.

2. A copy of this, called by Lippert a caricature, the accessories slightly modified: sard. (Devonshire.) Bracci quotes Pichler as to its being a copy of the first. Two more copies known; one in Raspe, the other in Poniatowsky's. The following are more or less dubious:—

3. Youthful Hercules: Portales; modern, according to Dubois.

4. Cupid rescuing Psyche: sard. Townley (Brit. Mus.).

5. Theseus slaying the Minotaur. (Clarac.)

6. Metrodorus: Cades; certainly modern.

7. Junius Brutus: Raspe; in very suspicious company.

PROTARCHOS.—Cupid playing the lyre: cameo sardonyx. In the exergue ΠΡΩΤΑΡΧΟΣ ΕΠΟΕΙ in relief. (Formerly Andreini's, now Florence Cabinet.) One of the five allowed by Köhler to be genuine. The name at first misread Plutarchus has given rise to that signature upon the modern copies.

SOLON.—Mæcenas: COΛωNOC behind the head: first published by F. Ursinus, 1580, as the portrait of the Athenian legislator. Dairval first in 1712 published the opinion of the Regent Orleans that the *name* was the engraver's, the portrait that of Mæcenas.

2. Rape of the Palladium: COΛΩN ЄΠΟΙЄΙ. Seen in Italy by Louis Chaduc about 1600.

3. The Strozzi Medusa: chalcedony. Published by Maffei, 1709, and seen by La Chaussée at the end of the previous century. It was found on the Celio near SS. Giovanni and Paolo, came into the hands of Sabbatini, who sold it to Cardinal Albani; thence passed into the Strozzi, now Blacas Coll. Copies known: by Costanzi, for Cardinal Polignac, 1729; by Madame Preissler; and by Jeaffroy on amethyst. [The profile has none of the antique character, but much resembles a portrait from life of the sixteenth century.]

The head of Mæcenas was undoubtedly often copied during the sixteenth and seventeenth centuries; the question, therefore, is to decide which is the original. There exist—

1. A fine Oriental sard. (Farnese Coll., Naples.)

2. Sard, of the same size, in the Riccardi, afterwards Poniatowsky. The name reversed.

3. Sard, much larger than the preceding; now in the Vienna Coll., and, according to Köhler, that of F. Ursinus, and figured by La Chaussée as in his time in the Barberini.

4. Sard: the intaglio very shallow, stone shield-shaped. (Piombino.) The letters deeply cut and coarsish.

Of these four the Vienna is pronounced the best by Köhler (who, however, regards the legend as an insertion of the age of F. Ursinus). Dr. B., from the actual inspection of the Piombino gem, finds himself able to warrant its genuineness; and says that, in spite of a certain carelessness, the treatment of the head appears to him the most full of character in *this*. Taste and care cannot, indeed, be denied to the Neapolitan, but the roundness and fulness of the forms seem less appropriate to the character of the person represented.

"A large and fine bust of Mæcenas, in front face, inscribed ΣΟΛΩΝΟΣ, said to have been found, in 1794, near Palestrina," now in the Worsley Coll., deserves to be mentioned here. [Nothing further seems to be known of it.]

The Rape of the Palladium is now in the Russian Coll., according to Stephani. Dr. B. thinks it far inferior to the same subject by Dioscorides; and is inclined to agree with Köhler's suggestion, that it was done by some artist early in the last century after the description left us by Chaduc of a similar composition thus inscribed.

A second, a cameo, exactly agreeing in design with the gem by Dioscorides, but the name in relief, is highly praised by Baudelot and Caylus.* Nothing further known.

Bust of a Bacchante: large ant. paste. (Berlin.) The only other genuine work of this artist. Much praised by Winckelmann and Tölken. The surface bearing the legend greatly corroded by time.

1. Cupid standing: sard. (Schellersheim, now Bar. Roger.) Style very mannered, and probably modern.

2. Copy of the same in the Hague.

3. Hercules, bearded and crowned with laurel, in front face: sard. Tölken doubts the legend, D. B. the work also, as not bearing the antique stamp. Perhaps this is the stone once in Andreini's possession.

4. Head of an ivy-crowned laughing Faun: Oriental agate; pretended to have been found in the Columbarium of Livia's freedmen. First published by Gori, but very dubious. Dactyl. Smithiana.†

5. Livia as Ceres, veiled head: sard. The drawing betrays a modern origin.

* Figured by Caylus, Rec. I. Pl. 44. On an agate of two layers, the signature admirably cut in relief. It was then in the possession of the Comte de Maurepas.

† Not so; Gori merely says it much resembles (persimilis) a gem reported to have been found in the sepulchre, &c., in the year 1726, of which he had an impression—a hint that he suspected Smith's to be a copy of the same, as it doubtless was.

6. Head of Vulcan, in pointed cap; the hammer appears over his shoulder. (Cades.) Of very dubious stamp. [This being mentioned by Gerhard, Arch. Anz., 1851, I believe is that of the Hertz Coll.; most indubitably modern: a nicolo of neat work enough.]

7. Victory with trophies: fragment of a splendid gem.* (Westropp Coll.) Only known by a notice of Gerhard's.

8. Another fragment: Victory sacrificing a bull. (Raspe.)

9. Roman Emperor, leaning upon his shield. (Raspe.)

10. Satyr, inscribed COΛYNOC. (Raspe.)

[*Head of Neptune; behind it ΣΟΛΩ, the intaglio apparently antique: emerald, circular and very deep. (Hertz.)]

Teukros; Teucer.—Hercules seated, and drawing Iole (or Hebe) towards him: amethyst. (Formerly Andreini's, now Florence.) Authenticity unquestionable, as behind the female figure a space has evidently been reserved at the outset for the signature.

Copies of this very numerous: one in Milliotti deserves mention, on account of his assertion that it had been in the possession of the Clermont family long before the publication of Andreini's amethyst, which, if true, would be an additional warranty for the antiquity of the latter.

None of the other pretended works of Teucer can pass for antique. They are—

1. A crouching Satyr, twining a garland; left by Stosch to Guay, and by the latter to Lord Carlisle.

2. Achilles seated, holding a helmet; a lance in his right; the shield resting against a tree. Bracci affirms that both are of modern origin on his own knowledge.

3. Mask: amethyst. (De Thoms.) Style and cabinet sufficiently attest its modern origin.

4. Antinous: quoted by Raspe without further note.

5. Head of Minerva: sard. (Lippert.) Perhaps the one in the Hertz Coll., with the name blundered TEYKTOY. [No; that gem is a jacinth, with a full-length figure of Minerva of the finest work, but the name rudely scratched in.]

6. Bust of Diana: cameo. (Blacas.) The name *incised* in long deep letters; the last upon the quiver.

7. Hercules carrying a woman on his shoulders weaving a garland. An indifferent intaglio, quoted by Dubois.

* A most instructive instance this of the recent and impudent forgery of an artist's name. It is the identical stone given in the 'Impronte Gemmarie,' iv. 7, published in 1834, and in this *cast* no inscription whatever exists. It then belonged to Cav. Demidoff. Westropp bought it at Capranesi's sale: probably the name had been put in by the order of that astute *antiquario.*

Class II.

Names the genuineness or significance of which are matters of doubt.

Admon.	Demetrius.	Pharnaces.
Aelius.	Dionysius.	Philemon.
Aemilius.	Epitonus.	Phocas.
Aetion.	Evemerus.	Platon.
Agathangelos.	Gaius.	Polycletus.
Agathon.	Gnæus.	Saturninus.
Alexas.	Hellen.	Severus.
Ammonius.	Kronios, Cronius.	Scopas.
Anteros.	Lucius, Lucteius.	Scylax.
Apelles.	Midias.	Sosocles, Sosthenes.
Aulus.	Myrton.	Sostratus.
Axeochus.	Onesimus.	Thamyrus.
Classicus.	Pergamus.	

Admon.—The famous Hercules Bibax, sard; was already in the Marlborough Cabinet before 1768. Another, quoted later by Bracci and Visconti as belonging to Molinari. [A most excellent copy on sard, high *en cabochon*, was in the Hertz Coll.] Molinari's is now in the Blacas. The large size of the lettering and the nominative case of the name oblige us to assign it to the owner. Hence, highly suspicious are—

1. Hercules, aged head, signed AΔ merely; a work in the modern style. (Gori.)

2. Hercules Musagetes. (Poniatowsky.)

3. Alexander, as Hercules.

4. Hercules reposing; at his side a bull. Seen by Em. Braun at Potenza, and said to have been recently found there; but afterwards he met with a cast from the same amongst the modern class in Cades' sets. [Can this be Rega's admirable intaglio, with his signature altered ?]

Cades marks as modern also, Hercules pulling the Amazon Queen from her horse, and Theseus supporting upon his knee a slain Amazon; Dubois, the Infant Hercules strangling the serpents, in the Beck Coll.

Augustus: cameo. (De la Turbie.) Probably the one read AKMΩN by Visconti (the name in relief). Dubious from the little credit of this collection and the gem not being forthcoming.

Head of Ammon: sard. (Cades.) The lettering clumsy.

Vulcan offering arms to a youth seated by a veiled female. Raspe thinks it a work of Natter's, probably copied from the Alban sarcophagus of the Marriage of Peleus and Thetis.

Aelius.—Head of Tiberius or C. Cæsar, front face: sard. (Corsina Coll.) Dr. B. doubts the style of the work and the Greco-Latin form of the name, which too, being in the nominative, would not warrant the admission of an Ælius into the list of artists. Still more suspicious are—

1. A copy of the last, Portales: sard. EΛIOΣ.

[*Another copy (poor) in the Townley Coll., Brit. Mus. The name indubitably indicates the owner. There was in the Praun Coll. a Lion (poor work), with ΑΕΛΙΟΥ in the exergue; probably a rebus (the Solar Lion) on the name, the Æolic form of Ἥλιος.]

2. Unknown head. (Marlborough.)

3. Homer: a profile: nicolo; correctly spelt ΑΙΛΙΟΣ. But the gem comes from the Hemsterhuis Coll., and therefore is of no authority.

Aetion.—Bearded Head, covered with the Phrygian cap; in front, ΑΕΤΙΟΝΟC: sard. (Devonshire.) The gem bought by Peiresc in England, 1606; was purchased by the Duke of Devonshire from Masson in Paris (the source, says Köhler, whence all these gems with forged names got over to England). The position of the name in front of the face seems against its designating the engraver. Köhler thinks it an invention of the sixteenth century, to identify the head with that of Andromache's father, Aetion.

Two modern copies, given by Raspe and De Jonge.

A third, said to have been in the Orleans Coll., not known.

A copy, freely treated; the cap converted into a sort of helmet and an ithyphallic Herme behind the head; seems that of Gravelle's quoted by Clarac.

Bacchanalia, of nine figures in front of a temple: sard. Raspe says, exhibits Dorsch's style.

Mercury bearded, carrying a sceptre-like caduceus: sard; in the archaic style.

Same subject: sard; bought by Petrée in Egypt; is, according to Dubois, of very dubious character.

Agathangelos.—Sextus Pompey:* sard. (Berlin.) Utterly condemned by Köhler, but defended by Tölken. It was first published by Venuti and Bertoni, and was in the hands of Sabbatini, a dealer in antiques. His heirs sold it for 450 scudi to a Pole, who presented it to the Marquise Luneville at Naples. Said to have been found near Cecilia Metella's tomb, set in a massive gold ring weighing an ounce, but its authenticity doubted from the first. Winckelmann, however, believed the story, adding [a strong confirmation of its truth, in my opinion] that the sard when *drawn* was found to be backed with a gold-foil; a thing that would not have come into the head of a modern forger. [*Vid.* Pliny's remark as to the custom of foiling gems with *aurichalcum.*] Stephani notices [with justice] the modern elegance of the treatment of the hair, and points out the formation of the letters and their termination in large dots as decisive marks of their recent production. Even Tölken allows that the name, from its position under the neck, can only be referred to the owner.

2. A Sacrifice: mentioned as modern by Dubois.

Agathon. — Bacchus, with thyrsus and cup: sard. Algernon Percy (St. Petersburg); name, ΑΓΑΘWΝ; therefore its case proves it not to be the engraver's.

* Judging from the cast, I should decidedly pronounce this Hadrian's portrait, taken at an early period of his reign—certainly not the profile of Sext. Pompey.

ALEXAS.—Bull-baiting, between the feet ΑΛΕΞΑ: sard. (Berlin.) The inscription doubted by Bracci.

2. Sea-serpent, twisted about a rudder: cameo; the name in relief. Half the stone wanting: and again

3. *Lion in his cave, ΑΛΕΞΑΣ ΕΠΟΕΙ; burnt sard. Both Pulsky's, who quotes Em. Braun's judgment in favour of the latter. But *seven* unedited inscribed gems in one and the same private cabinet must excite suspicion, which is further awakened by the fragmentary state of the cameo.*

4. Serapis head; ΑΛΕΞΑ in huge letters, that can have no reference at all to the artist (Raspe).

AMMONIUS.—Head of a laughing Faun, full face; behind ΑΜΜΟΝΙΟΥ: sard. (Beverley.) [St. Petersburg.] The intaglio, from the style of expression and the treatment of the hair, very much suspected.

2. Medusa's Head: sard. Baron Roger; uncertain. The votive nicolo to the Dea Syria of the Marlborough has nothing to do with our subject.

ANTEROS.—Hercules carrying the Bull: aquamarine. (Formerly Sevin's, now Devonshire.) Pronounced by Millin and Visconti a genuine work of the age of Titus; but altogether rejected by Köhler.

*2. Head of Antinous, ANT, stone broken. (Bracci.) The name evidently of the person represented. [This is probably the grand intaglio Antinous of the Marlborough.]

APELLES.—Mask, below it ΑΠΕΛΛΟΥ; placed by Bracci in the times of Sept. Severus. Not known at present. Köhler thinks that names thus set under masks are those assumed by the actors on the stage: their favourite characters.

AULUS (ΑΥΛΟΥ).—Cupid nailing a butterfly to a tree: jacinth. Published by Faber in his edition of F. Ursinus; who interpets the name Aulus of Brutus the younger, assumed after his adoption by Au. Post. Albinus, and explains it as his signet, typifying that his soul was as firmly attached to Cæsar as the butterfly was nailed to the tree! This may be the gem now in the De Thoms Coll., unless that be a modern work done after Faber's description. Inasmuch as forgers always have followed the line of subjects suggested by some famous original, we find a series of Cupids bearing this signature:—

1. Cupid in chains, resting his head upon the handle of his mattock: cameo. (Baron von Gleichen.) In the exergue ΑΥΛΟΥ *incised.* Much lauded by Bracci, but suspected by Visconti, and the figure bears much resemblance to the children of Guido Reni and of Fiammingo.

2. Cupid, with hands bound behind his back; behind him a trophy: amethyst. (Carlisle.) Called by Köhler "a pleasing work of J. Pichler's." Dr. B. esteems it of the same fabrique as the last: the large empty space above the Cupid would not be found in an antique work.

*3. Equally modern appears the Cupid who is endeavouring to hold up a huge cornucopia; chalcedony in Raspe. [This is the Marlborough gem; a pale yellow crystal, which is certainly antique, but somewhat repolished, which

* Pulsky's lion seems antique work, and by a good master; but the legend is certainly a more recent addition.

has impaired all the outlines, but at the same time establishes the originality of the signature.]

Cavalier at full gallop : sardonyx. (Florence.)

Same subject, replica : ant. paste. (Berlin.)

Quadriga and charioteer : sardonyx. (Morpeth, or Carlisle.)

Horse, fore part of : garnet. Caylus. (Dr. Brown ; Lichfield.)

Lion pulling down a horse, like the Capitoline group : jasper. (Lord Meghan.) The name expressly said by Bracci to be a modern insertion.

Winged sow, neat work : sard. (Cades.) But the original not known.

More important is the series of heads thus signed :—

1. The famous Esculapius : sard. (Strozzi, now Blacas.) The conspicuous placing of the name upon a tablet in the field is sufficient evidence that we see here the owner's; supposed by Stephani to have been a physician, and the coincidence of the name with the supposed artist's merely accidental.

2. Bust of Bacchante : jacinth. (Ludovisi.) The work stigmatised by Köhler as "wretched, and apprenticelike, such as no man of taste should admit into his cabinet." Dr. B., having examined the original, "has no doubt as to the modern origin of the whole work."

3. Satyr's Head, front face ; prase (or sard). (Jenkins.) Pronounced by Köhler a work of the last century, and Dr. B. confirms his opinion.

4. Young Hercules, a head : sard. (Beverley.) Is probably the one called by J. Pichler a work of Costanzi's. Execution and style both have the modern stamp.

5. The Ptolemy Philopator of Stosch, or Abdolonymus of Bracci : large sard. (Paris.) Called by Köhler a good antique work, but the name added by the same hand that introduced the miserable little figures into the field. Dr. B., however, has a very low opinion of the whole, and thinks the accessories only differ from the bust in point of size, not of merit ; and though antique, the large size of the lettering proves the name to be the owner's.

6. Sextus Pompey, with a ship's beak : only known in Raspe.

7. Augustus, young head : sard. Köhler calls it "a neat but not antique work." *

8. Another : given by Raspe, from a cast of Stosch's.

9. Tiberius : sard. (Portales.) Where Dubois doubts at least the genuineness of the name.

10. Caracalla : cameo sardonyx ; the name *incised.* Modern, without a doubt, to judge from the cast. Several others, quoted by Clarac as doubtful : viz.,—Ceres : sard. (Mar. de Drée.)—Faun : nicolo. (Beck.)—Faun, copy by Jeuffroy of Nicomachus'.—Head of Laocoon.—Mæcenas.†—Helmeted Head. (Cades.)

Of many groups and whole figures the chief are :—

1. Venus seated on a rock, balancing a wand, a Cupid flying towards her :

* Apparently the gem formerly Lord Cawdor's, now Rhodes'; but I differ from Köhler as to its genuineness : it is a carefully finished Roman intaglio, and the letters (the name being divided on each side of the neck) are bold, and of the same character as the work itself.

† The Greville gem ; the face more resembles one of the Vitellian family, and the name underneath the neck, in that case, would designate the person himself.

sard. (Formerly Vettori's, now in the Townley Coll.) A composition seemingly copied from the antique pastes (Winck. Desc. ii. 573, 574), with some unsuccessful improvements attempted.

2. A copy of this by Natter, mentioned by Raspe.

3. Another copy by the same, where Venus is converted into a Danaë.

4. Mercury Criophorus, standing before a cippus, supporting an urn. (Raspe.)

5. Mercury carrying the Infant Bacchus: jacinth. De Thoms; but the name modern, according to De Jonge.

6. Pan and Olympus: sardonyx. Beck; together with

7. Leda and Swan, reclining figure: a group so often copied in modern times; are classed by Clarac among the uncertain.

8. Hercules Nicephorus: sard. Pulsky, who himself considers the name as an insertion.

9. Woman pouring out a libation, Stosch's casts, is considered by Raspe as uncertain.

10. Woman tying her sandal in front of a Priapus-Herme: sard. (Baron von Gleichen.) Seems modern in the style.

11. Victory writing on a Shield: onyx. An insignificant piece.

12. A Sacrifice: worked in the style of M. Angelo's signet.

In a few of these the inscription may be regarded as certainly, or at least as probably, authentic. But taking into account the variation in the lettering, as well as of the style of the intagli themselves, the only plausible solution of the question is to regard the name, when antique, as that of various owners. As in our days seals often bear only the first name of the possessor, the same may have been the case with the private signets of antiquity; and the frequency of this signature be explained by the commonness of the name in those times. [A probable explanation; in the familiar epistles extant, persons are generally designated by their *prænomina*, as Marcus, Quintus, &c.]

Axeochus.—Dancing Faun, wearing the lion's hide, and playing the lyre in front of a cippus supporting a statue of the Infant Bacchus. In the exergue ΑΞΕΟΧΟΣ ΕΠ: ant. paste. (Strozzi, perhaps now in the Blacas Coll.) Köhler is undecided as to the work, but condemns the inscription on account of the orthographical errors, and the abbreviation of the verb. Dr. B. also discovers something modern in the pose of the little figure, and in the movement of the Satyr.

2. Head of Omphale: sard. Countess Cheroffini; is dubious on account of the repetition of a dubious signature, and the face is strikingly deficient in expression.

3. Perseus mirroring Medusa's head upon a shield lying at his feet, on which is cut the name ΑΞΕΟΧ: sardonyx. De Thoms; is equally suspicious with

4. A Bacchante, with thyrsus and vase, rushing forwards; paste; in the same ill-famed collection.

5. Beger's agate, with ΑΞΙѠΦΙ; has nothing to do here, but belongs to the Abraxas class.

Caius. See Gaios.

Classicus.—Serapis on a throne. Crozat Cat.; assigned by Clarac to an artist, without any grounds.

Demetrius.—Hercules strangling a lion hung up to a tree: sard. (Mar. de Drée.)

2. Bull: sard. (Schellersheim.) Both uncertain, if name of artist or of owner.

Dionysius.—Bacchante's head: quoted by De Murr.

Epitonos.—Venus Victrix leaning upon a cippus: very doubtful as belonging to the De Thoms Coll.

Euemeros.—Mars in full armour, standing: sard. Quoted by Raspe as belonging to the Landgrave of Hesse-Cassel.

Gaios.—*The Sirius of the Marlborough Coll.

"A garnet on which the Head seen in front of a dog, Sirius or the Dogstar, with the inscription ΓΑΙΟΣ ЄΠΟΙЄΙ on the collar, is very deeply cut, and which formerly belonged to Lord Bessborough and afterwards passed with the rest of his gems into the Marlborough Collection, belongs to the list of very famous gems. This Head is so perfect and spirited a work that one is at a loss what most to admire in it, whether the imitation of life here carried to the highest point, or the extraordinary skill in the overcoming of all the difficulties, the licking, tender flesh in the muzzle, the inside of the jaws, the teeth, the nose, or the tongue that hangs out—'ut fessi canes linguam ore de patulo potus aviditate projiciens.' Raspe doubted as to the antiquity of this stone; Natter had practised his profession a considerable time in London, and to him has this work been ascribed." Thus speaks Köhler, p. 158. But does this report (which Murr expressly points out as resting upon an error) possess sufficient weight that, upon the strength of it, we should forthwith "number amongst those gems in which both work and legend are modern," what Köhler himself styles "a work so carefully finished that neither ancient nor modern times have produced its equal"? Nevertheless, Natter in the Bessborough Catalogue calls the stone a Bohemian garnet; a species, according to Köhler, not known to the ancient gem-engravers. On the other hand, Clarac, I know not on what authority, calls it a Syrian garnet. [It is actually an Oriental garnet of the finest quality, which might be taken for a spinel.] Natter, it is true, openly acknowledges that he did occasionally put Greek names upon his own works, yet does he as distinctly deny that he ever passed them off for antiques. But the gem in question he calls Greek, and only professes (p. 27) to have copied it with some success. Finally, as to what concerns the name which Köhler stigmatises as not happily chosen, because thereby a *Roman* engraver—Caius—appears upon the scene, on this very account would a forger have made a more "happy" choice of a designation. The name, however, in itself, is not liable to the objection that we hereafter are obliged to make good against the names "Quintus" and "Aulus:" as the example of the jurist Gaius can sufficiently prove. In addition to this, it cannot be proved in a single case that gems with the name of Gaios were known earlier than our Sirius. Upon the Berlin obsidian (to be next described) even Winckelmann had overlooked the inscription. Therefore it seems to me that as yet no sufficiently valid reasons have been adduced for its suspiciousness, although the full certainty of its genuineness can only be attained by a repeated examination of the original, which now probably is to be found in the Blacas Cabinet. [No; still in the Marlborough. But, after repeated examination, I fear this noble piece must be given to some great artist of the Cinque-cento; the work displaying none of the hieratic stiffness ever characterising this head of the *Egyptian* Solar Lion, Sirius-*Southis,* not uncommon in garnets of Hadrian's time. But—the point of most weight with me—the surface shows none of the wear of time that bites ever so deeply into the antique stone; and here this has certainly not been rectified by modern repolishing.]

2. Silenus seated on a hide, holding in each hand a flute: obsidian.* (Berlin.) Work but middling, not to be compared to the first; the name here, therefore, probably designates the owner.

3. Nemesis: only known by a cast of Stosch's.

4. Copy of this: sard. Baron Roger: and in the same collection.

5. Silenus: jacinth; after the Berlin obsidian.

GNAIOS.—Head of Youthful Hercules; below the neck ΓΝΑΙΟΣ: bluish aquamarine. (Strozzi, now Blacas.) Published by Faber as the signet of Gn. Pompey.† "The signature belongs to the best authenticated that we have, and we can prove beforehand that it cannot designate an artist, since the work of the head is of that fine quality that would justify the engraver in putting his name to it." So speaks the paradoxical Köhler.

*2. Athlete anointing himself. Published by Venuti in 1736, and then in Apostolo Zeno's Coll., afterwards in Stosch's, who sold it to Lord Bessborough. The gem was rejected by Vettori from his list of artists, whether on account of his doubting the gem itself, or merely the form of the signature. Köhler says "that Natter praises the stone so highly, that he may be suspected of being the author of it. Natter calls the stone an Oriental hyacinth (jacinth), possessing the colour of a Bohemian garnet, and notices also that the surface is flat: a convincing proof that it is modern, as all antique jacinths are cut *en cabochon*." [This criticism is based on an error: the stone is a superb *paste,* resembling indeed a dark jacinth when looked down upon, but exhibiting the true sard colour when viewed by transmitted light. A testimony this to Natter's honesty: had he been its engraver, he had certainly discovered the real nature of the piece. Dr. B. considers the work as but of insignificant merit, and points out the little skill shown in the employment of the field: certainly the large empty space left above the table has a very awkward effect; the original work, however, of the intaglio has been excellent in the Roman style, but has its outlines now destroyed by the repolishing of the surface, which must have been done before Natter described it.] ‡

3. Bust of a Queen, with the sceptre on her shoulder: sard. (Reicher Coll.) Called a Cleopatra or a Juno. Köhler only rejects the legend, and praises the intaglio as tender, tasteful, and finished; but Dr. B. suspects the style of the

* *Obsidian* probably means here a black paste, so termed pedantically by the catalogue-makers of the last century, from a misunderstanding of Pliny's description of the actual stone, which was mistaken by them for an artificial production. In the Marlborough Catalogue, *Obsidian* is always employed to designate the antique pastes of a dark colour.

† And with good foundation: the name proves it to have belonged to his *clan.*

‡ The original of this beautiful paste is a dull sardoine, also in the same cabinet; unless indeed the latter be a *copy from it.*

drawing, and the modern character of the attributes. "Though the features are pure, there is no life in the expression; the hair, too, on the brow is worked in a manner not seen in the antique."

4. Juno Lanuvina, or Theseus. (Beverley.) Bracci says the name was put in by Pichler: the whole, doubtless, modern.

5. Rape of the Palladium: ΓΝΑΙΟΥ in the exergue; present owner unknown. [This must be the Devonshire gem, a large black and white banded agate.] Pronounced by J. Pichler antique, but doubted by Köhler; and Dr. B. censures a softness in the contour of the body, and the expression of the head not suited to the character of Diomede. The design agrees with that by Dioscorides.*

6. An Apoxyomenos: sard of mediocre work, ΓΝΑΟΥ behind the figure. The name judged a modern addition by Pichler.

7. Head of Pallas, or Alexander, a Pegasus on the helmet: Mead's Museum. Raspe takes for a work of Costanzi's.

8. Head of Hercules: chalcedony; seems the gem mentioned by Natter as a copy by Costanzi of the Strozzi.

9. Muse, a bust, in front a mask on a cippus, the name behind the head. (De la Turbie.) Considered by Visconti as worthy of the artist, but suspected by Clarac, chiefly on account of the cabinet it belonged to. Dr. B. observes that the signature is clumsy and defective.

10. Alcæus, a head. (Lippert.)

11. A Theseus, perhaps identical with Raspe's Antinous.

12. Brutus. (Lippert.)

To these may be added:—

1. A Sister of Caligula's, a Head: sard; quoted by Tölken. The face exhibits traces of the modern "elegance, and is somewhat squat, and the likeness far from certain."

2. Horseman spearing a boar or bear, a reclining Faun holding a thyrsus: nicolo, Naples; very dubious.

3. Head of Mercury: Pullini, Turin; quoted by Dubois.

4. Horse's Head: fragment. (Formerly Marquis de Drée's.) Several copies of the Strozzi Hercules, of the Marlborough Athlete, and of the Apoxyomenos are known.†

HELLEN.—Bust of Antinous as Harpocrates: sard. (Orleans, now St. Petersburg.) First published by Fulvius Ursinus, as Hellen, the founder of the Hellenic race. The work praised by Köhler as of the finest antique stamp and finished with inconceivable delicacy; but the name he absurdly supposes "an addition of F. Ursinus." Though the name be genuine, yet Tölken thinks it probably indicates the owner, some Hellenios or Hellenicos.‡

* Mme. Mertens had added to the Praun Collection, as a genuine antique, another equally exact replica of this subject, but without any signature. The work is of some merit, but the stone—a common carnelian—and the intact surface make its authenticity to me extremely questionable.

† To these may be added: *Omphale, a beautiful head covered with the lion's skin, but much of a modern style. (Marlborough.)

‡ In fact, I strongly suspect ΕΛΛΗΝ in its origin to be but the signature of the famous Alessandro *Il Greco;* a most natural disguise for that artist to have assumed.

2. Mask: Blacas, from the De la Turbie Coll., and therefore extremely dubious until further examined.

3. Head of a young Satyr crowned with vine-leaves: beneath, ΕΛΛΗΝΟΥ. Tölken calls this "unmistakably modern, and copied from the chubby Bacchus-heads on tavern-signs, but the execution shows a master's hand." [The blunder in the name also is unpardonable.]*

Kronios.—Terpsichore, standing, and resting her lyre on a cippus: suspected by Bracci to be done by Sirletti. But Andreini had only the cast (published by Gori) which he had obtained fifty years before from a good engraver in the Medicean Academy, Il Borgognone. The gem not now known.

2. Jupiter caressing his Eagle: cameo. (Old Poniatowsky Coll.) Suspicious for the false reading ΚΡΩΜΟΥ.

3. Perseus with the Medusa's Head. ΚΡΩΝΙΟΥ: sard. (Devonshire.) Known to be modern. [One in the Marlborough; probably that here cited as the Devonshire, a feeble modern intaglio.]

Lucius.—Victory driving a biga at full speed: sard. (Count Wassenaer.) The work pleasing, but slight, and not of sufficient importance to presuppose the artist's signature. The name ΛΕΥΚΙΟΥ placed in the middle of the exergue with a certain nice regularity, and without any reference to the design. Finally, the hair-lines of the lettering do not correspond with those employed in the engraving itself, the whip, or wheel-spokes; and therefore Dr. B. considers the name an addition, though put in (for the owner's) in ancient times.

2. Bust of young Satyr, ivy-crowned. Köhler calls a work without the least taste, that Lippert ought to have been ashamed to admit into his series.

3. Bearded Satyr, mask, of which Raspe notices three repetitions: reading ΛΟΥΚΤΕΥ and ΛΟΥΚΤΕΙ, which probably have nothing to do with *Lucius*. [The Marl. gem reads clearly ΛΟΥΚΤΕΙΟΥ, "Lucteius;" but the position marks it the possessor's name: *this* stone, at least, is antique.]†

4. Poppæa, signed ΛΕΥ. Raspe, where no one suspects an artist.

Midias.—Gryphon trampling on a Serpent: cameo, ΜΙΔΙΟΥ incised. Paris. The stone burnt, and broken, so that the name may be part of ΑΙΜΙΔΙΟΥ, which does occur on the same subject in Cades; but the original unknown.

Myrton.—Nymph with floating veil borne upon the back of a swan with spread wings, under one of which the name ΜΥΡΤΩΝ: formerly in the

---

This theory is supported by the Omphale in the spoils of Hercules: the name, cut in the field in minute letters, seems as antique as the rest of the surface. The intaglio is in a bold, well-finished style, but clearly Cinque-cento. Sard. (My collection.)

* A magnificent head in front face, most deeply cut, of a Bacchante; ΕΛΛΗΝ in the field in extremely fine letters in Pichler's taste. The intaglio itself seems Greek of the best age; but the stone—a pale Balais of large size—and its recent surface are grounds for reasonable doubt. Left by L. Fould to Baron Roger l'aîné.

† It is figured No. 506 in Gorlæi Dactyliotheca (ed. 1695), and thence came into the Bessborough Cabinet.

Strozzi Coll. Stephani allows the name to be genuine from its evident connexion with the design, but supposes it to indicate Myrto, Pindar's mother; or else the Eulæan nymph. Dr. B. thinks the work not sufficiently important to bear an actual artist's signature: the name besides exceeds the measure allotted to such, and is more than an accessory, seeming to indicate either subject or owner: the reading, besides, is not quite certain.

Onesimus.—Jove standing holding a sceptre, parallel to which runs the name: sard. (Bar. Hoorn.) Uncertain.

2. Pallas, Helmeted Head: Raspe. Confessedly modern.

Pergamos.—Satyr dancing, in his right the thyrsus, in the left a cantharus: paste. (Florence.) The name in the field in front of the knee was read ΠΕΙΓΜΩ, or ΠΥΓΜΩΝ, or ΠΕΜΑΛΙΟ. Köhler judges from the sharpness of the letters that they are a recent addition to the antique paste. But Dr. B. observes that the inscription already existed in Agostini's time, and that, far from being recent in appearance, it has suffered corrosion equally with the rest of the surface. Hence the sole reason for not admitting Pergamos into the list of artists is the uncertainty as to the real name.

2. Other gems with this legend, where it evidently refers to the hero Pergamus, thereon represented.

3. Hercules carrying the Bull. (Stosch.) The name modern.

Pharnaces.—Hippocampus; in the exergue ΦΑΡΝΑΚΗϹ ЄΠ : sard. (Farnese Coll., Naples.) The cutting of the letters not in character with the style of the design, which is allowed by Stephani to be antique, though but mediocre. The legend therefore must be considered suspicious.

2. Capricorn and a Trident: the name awkwardly inserted between him and the waves: amethyst. (De Thoms.) The name probably taken from the Farnese gem.

3. Same subject: Poquel. (Paris.) Quoted by Dubois.*

4. Lion passant: sard. (Greville, now Beverley.) Name in the exergue. Stephani ventures upon no decision here.

5. Cupid riding on a lion: sard. (Cades.) The figure, though small, is done with cleverness and a sort of negligence, and may be antique. But in both the last, the letters are cut harshly, are furnished with dots, and proceed clearly from a modern hand; being too conspicuous for the smallness of the stones.

6. Nemesis holding a bridle; Millin: very dubious—from that attribute of the goddess, only seen in late works.

7. Wild Boar, ΦΑΡ: sard. (St. Petersburg.) Name contracted.

8. Mercury, a Head: jasper; similarly uncertain.—Fragment of a Satyr.

* Female panther passant, of the finest work; in the exergue ΦΑΡΝΑΚΟΥ. Sard. Unquestionably antique; formerly Lord Cawdor's, now Rhodes'. Where the signature is actually genuine, there is good reason to believe such gems were signets of some of the Asiatic princes bearing this name. The Bacchic panther is a rebus upon it, *Pharnaces* being, as Ausonius tells us, the Mysian name for Bacchus. By the same analogy Pharnaces II. took for reverse of his gold medals the figure of Dionysos-Helios.

. . KHC: Princess Gagarin; dubious, if it can be referred to this name. Though the signature upon one or two of the above may be genuine, yet none display any striking merit. The various forgeries prove that the supposed artist was considered eminent in the representation of animals. Stephani regards the Greville gems as the starting-point whence all the rest proceeded.

PHILEMON.—Theseus and the slain Minotaur: sardonyx. (Vienna.) A bad stone of two layers; but the work, according to Köhler, of a good modern hand. Stephani reckons it amongst the suspicious, and says the legend has much more of the modern about it than of the antique. [An exact replica of this, but without signature, a modern cameo admirably done, in the Marl. Coll.]

2. Bust of an ivy-crowned laughing Satyr: behind the head ΦΙΛΗΜΩΝ ΕΠΟΙ: paste. (Strozzi.) Köhler says, "Nothing could be more convenient at the time of forging artists' names than to get an antique paste and to ennoble it by the insertion of a few letters: in this case they bear no analogy whatever to the style of the work."

3. Hercules binding Cerberus: amethyst. (St. Petersburg.) Köhler calls modern, but of good work.

4. Bull's Head. (Bracci and Cades.)

5. Hercules strangling the Lion: onyx-cameo. (Clanbrasil.) Is known to be from the hand of Ant. Pichler.

[6. Head of Berenice; her hair, bound with a fillet, falls down in numerous curls: in the field behind, ΦΙΛΗΜΟΝΟϹ. A modern intaglio, but of the highest merit; formerly Hertz's.]

PHOCAS.—Athlete standing, holding a palm, and touching the fillet around his head: jacinth. Bracci thinks does not refer to the artist. Probably this is the true reading of ΦΩΙΛΑ on a Bacchante sard. (Schellersheim.)

PLATO.—Charioteer driving his team: not the artist's name.

POLYCLEITUS.—Rape of the Palladium. The stone broken on one side. Formerly Andreini's: condemned by Köhler; and doubted by Levezow. Subject and name are both against its being genuine.

SATURNIUS.—Antonia, wife of Drusus: cameo; the name behind the head incised: formerly Caroline Murat's, afterwards Seguin's. Stephani allows the work to be excellent, but the drapery probably retouched: only the inscription forged, as being incised. Dr. B., too, thinks the field there has the appearance of having been smoothed recently for the reception of the name.

2. The Dioscuri; between them the head of Jupiter Ammon. (Thorwaldsen Museum.) The name CATOPNЄINOC certainly has nothing to do with an artist's.

SEVERUS.—Hygeia giving the serpent to drink: plasma: Slade. Π.CЄ.-YHP.Y on a little shield in relief.

SKOPAS.—Gems bearing upon them this name are so little known, and have not been ever critically examined, that nothing certain can be advanced as to their authenticity: they are—

1. Head of Apollo Citharœdus: sard. (Formerly Sellari's.)

2. Caligula, or L. Cæsar: sard. (Leipsic Mus.) But Visconti doubts the legend, and Dr. B. objects to the weak, modern style of the work.

3. Bearded Head: sard. (Count Butterlin.) Called by Lippert a Zeno; by Raspe, an Epicurus.

4. Naked female by a vase, as if anointing herself. (Caylus.) The lines of the form very harsh, and can be hardly antique.

5. Œdipus and the Sphinx: ΣΚΟΠΑ ΕΠ. (Raspe.) Very suspicious from the abbreviation of the verb. This signature, so variously written, sometimes with round, sometimes with angular letters, in the nom. and in the gen. case, creates a very unfavourable impression as to its genuineness. And if antique in one or two cases, the exact signification must be ascertained before Scopas can be admitted into the list of engravers.

Scylax.—Mask of Pan nearly front-face: amethyst. (Strozzi, now Blacas.) Köhler says, "This mask is, both for the invention and extremely spirited execution, one of the greatest masterpieces of antique art." The name is genuine, not cut in delicate minute letters, but in a bold style to indicate the owner. This is the source whence the forgers have got the name to put upon so many of their modern gems.

2. Sirius, the entire fore-part of his body, with the paws as it were swimming through the air; in the field, CKYΛAΞ: yellow topaz, much larger than the Marl. Sirius. (Old Poniatowsky Coll.) As Natter owns to having copied the latter, this topaz may be assigned to him in Köhler's opinion.*

3. Satyr playing the flute: onyx; Cades; is a pretty work, but bears no decided stamp of antiquity.

4. Another Satyr agreeing in design with that of Pergamos; also on onyx; Cades; the manner very pointed and studied.

5. Cameo, Hercules seated playing the lyre, his weapons leant against a rock behind him; CKYΛAKOC incised in the exergue. (Formerly Tiepolo's, now Bar. Roger's.) Dr. B. doubts the work, and takes it for a copy from a small cameo in the Beverley Coll. unsigned, and figured by Enea Vico.

6. Eagle's Head; to the right, CKYΛAKOC, reading towards the neck: sard. (Formerly Algernon Percy's, now St. Petersburg.)

7. Another, to the right, and legend turned towards the border: sard. (Cades.) The letters quite bungled.

8. C. Antistius Restio, Head: sard. (Marlborough.) [A mediocre modern intaglio.]

Dubois notices in Bar. Roger's Coll., as doubtful—

1. Head of a Bald Man: garnet.

2. Man standing holding a bow: sard.

3. Satyr's mask: sard. De Murr mentions a small sardonyx (St. Petersburg), a giant drawing a gryphon out of his den, with the legend ΣΚΥΛΑΞ ΕΠ or ΣΚΥΔΑΚΙΟΣ. None of these inscriptions being entirely trustworthy, we must allow their full weight to Köhler's critique upon the Strozzi amethyst; and decide that the existence of an artist Scylax is in the highest degree problematical.

Sosocles.—Medusa's Head, CωCOCΛ in front of the neck: chalcedony. (Carlisle, now Blacas.) Köhler condemns the gem as "a stone never employed

* If antique, we should have here another rebus on the owner's name—Σκυλαξ, a puppy.

by the ancients; its origin too is betrayed by its uncommon harshness and the want of taste in the rendering of the hair; the blunders in the name could not have been made in ancient times." Visconti proposes Sosthenes as the correct reading; Dr. B., more plausibly, Sosus. The gem was published in the seventeenth century, by Stefanoni and by Licetus.

2. Copy by Natter for Hemsterhuis; in the Hague Coll.

3. Junius Brutus: sardonyx. (Aldborough.) The name CѠCOKΛ proves this to be a forgery.

Sostratus.—Cameo, Victory leading the horses of a biga. (Once L. dei Medici's; now Farnese, Naples.) In the field above, CΩCTPATOY; between the horses' feet, LAVR. MED. The work allowed antique by Köhler and Stephani; but the inscription pronounced an addition in the taste of the eighteenth century, "being scratched in with small fine lines with dots at the ends; and placed over the horses because the proper place for them was already occupied by the name of Lorenzo." It is hard to see how such an addition could have been made, inasmuch as the cameo came into the Farnese Coll. through Margaretta, widow of Alessandro de' Medici, and never subsequently passed through a dealer's hands: hence Stephani's theory cannot be admitted, without further proof.

Unfavourable, however, must be our judgment upon all other gems bearing this signature.

1. Car drawn by two lionesses bridled by a Cupid: cameo; a fragment. (Devonshire or Beverley.) The work acknowledged by all as antique and excellent, but the name an addition.

2. Meleager standing opposite the seated Atalanta: cameo. (Ottobuoni, now Devonshire.) The name incised behind Meleager. Stosch observes that the style differs essentially from that of the preceding. Dr. B. regards this piece as indubitably modern on account of the composition and the error in the costume of Atalanta, here represented as almost nude, instead of in the attire of a Diana.

3. Bellerophon watering Pegasus, reading CѠTPATOY: sard. (Raspe.) Is clearly a copy from the bas-relief of the Villa Spada.*

4. The same subject, UTIAIOY: sardonyx cut transversely. (Marlborough.) Is a further corruption of the same word.

5. Victory sacrificing a Bull: sard. (Formerly Stosch, now Devonshire.) Was judged by J. Pichler a work of the sixteenth, by Stephani of the last century.

6. Nereid riding upon a Sea-serpent: a small sard, the name above; published by Lippert; Stephani styles too insignificant a work to judge about its age: the name, however, so fine as hardly to be distinguishable, is evidently from a modern hand.

7. Nereid on a Hippocampus; cameo quoted by Winckelmann.

8. Venus Anadyomene; a cameo sold by Casanova for 300*l.* to a *Dr. Matti.* As he had received it from his brother the painter, it was most likely done from a design of his, and the buyer " what his name imports," *i.e.* a madman.

9. Seated Faun holding fast a Bacchante, OCTPAT above, quoted by Panofka, is altogether modern.

* Mediocre modern style.

The result drawn by Stephani from this review is that the Devonshire Victory was the starting-point, whence the forgers commenced with the employment of this name. This gem was in existence before 1723, though not published by Natter until 1754. Stephani thinks its style agrees with that of Natter's earliest works. Dr. B., however, believes it taken from the Farnese gem.

THAMYRUS.—Sphinx scratching her ear with her hind paw; sard. (Vienna.) The work old, according to Köhler, but the legend most suspicious. J. Pichler thought the work Greco-Etruscan, and Dr. B. notices the Etruscan border, and the style of the intaglio, rather free but marked with the sharpness of the designs upon some scarabæi; which too agrees with the character of the lettering, which, large and filling up the field, evidently designates the owner.

2. Child seated (Harpocrates), the name incised; cameo. (Beverley.) Dr. B. considers the work but sketchy; and the name, totally differing in character from the first, to be decidedly modern.

3. Warrior standing by the side of his horse; Prince Isenburg; is said by Köhler, upon the authority of Heyne, to be a work of Rega's.

CLASS III.

Names due to false readings, or which do not refer to a Gem-engraver.

ÆPOLIANUS.
AGATHEMERUS.
AKMON, for ADMON.
AKYLOS (AQUILA).
ALEXANDROS.
ALLION.
ALMELOS.
ALPHEUS AND ARETHON.
AMARANTHUS.
ANAXILAS, for HERACLIDES.
ANTIOCHUS.
ANTIPHILUS.
APOLLODOTUS.
APOLLONIDES.
ARCHION.
ARISTOTEICHOS.
ARISTON.
ATHA.
ATOU.
AXIUS.
BEISITALUS.
CÆKAS (CASCA).
CASTRICIUS.
CHÆREMON.
CHARITON.
CHELY.
CHRYSUS.
DAMNAMENEUS.
DARON.
DEUTON.
DIOCLES.
DIPHILUS.
DIVILIS.
DOMETIS.
DORY.
EUELPISTUS.
EUPLOUS.
EUTHUS.
GAMUS.
GAURANUS.
GLYCON.
HEDY.
HEIUS.
HORUS.
KÆSILAX (CÆSILAX).
KAIKISIANOS (CÆCISIANUS).
KARPOS (CARPUS).
KISSOS.
KLEON (CLEON).
KRATEROS (CRATERUS).
KRESCENS (CRESCENS).
LYSANDROS.
MAXALAS.
MENA.
MILESIUS.
MIRON.
MITH.
MUSIKOS.
NICEPHORUS.
NEPOS.
NERT.
NICOMACHUS.
NILOS.
NYMPHEROS.
PALONIANUS.
PANÆUS.
PELAGIUS.
PETRUS.
PHILIPPUS.
PHRYGILLUS.
POLYCRATES.
POLYTIMUS.

Pothus.	Rufus.	Socrates.
Priscus.	Seleucus.	Tauriskos (Tauriscus).
Pylades.	Semon.	Tryphon.
Pyrgoteles.	Sextianus.	Ythilos.
Quintil.	Silvanus.	Zenon.
Quintus.	Skymnos.	

Æpolian.—M. Aurelius, so called without sufficient reason; AEPOLIANI behind it. (Devonshire.) Stephani and Dr. B. apply the name to the owner or the person represented (probably the latter).

2. A Bacchante dancing, as Millin says, "a modern pirouette," ΑΙΠΟΛΙΦ: De la Turbie; condemns itself by style and orthography. 3. Replica of M. Aurelius, cited by Murr. 4. Roman Triumph. (Dubois.) All modern.

Agathemeros.—Socrates: sard. (Devonshire or Portland, now Blacas.) Dr. B. remarks that he has not seen the type of the Socrates head so well expressed in any of Stosch's casts as in this; and only hesitates to recognise an artist's in the name because it is divided by the neck. ΑΓΑΠΗΜΕ roughly cut in the field of a cameo head of a Greek queen of good work, in the possession of Whelar, December 1879, evidently a stupid interpolation.

Akylos.—Venus in the Bath, Cupid holding a mirror to her: sard. (Raspe.) A work of the Decline. The name in large letters, divided by the design and reversed in the impression, can only imply the owner.

2. Horse, Stosch's pastes: probably the name of the steed.

Alexandros.—Cupid, a Lion and two females, in the exergue ΑΛΕΞΑΝΔ. Ε: cameo. (Florence.) Pointed out by Raspe as the identical work of Il Greco's eulogised by Vasari. 2. Profile head of a man beardless; ΑΛΕΞΑΝΔΡΟΣ ΕΠΟΕΙ behind it: Florence; also a work of his.

3. Ptolemæus Alexander: cameo; Caylus, V., Pl. LIII., reading ΑΛΕΞΠΒ: where Caylus's reading—'Αλεξάνδρος 'Επιφανὴς Βασιλεὺς—seems very plausible.

4. Apollo, quoted by Minervini; the name running all around cannot apply to the engraver.

Allion.—Youthful Head, Hercules, laurel-crowned: small sard. (Florence, formerly Agostini's.) The legend is read by Köhler ΔΑΛΙΟΝ for ΔΗΛΙΩΝ, the god of the Delians: an explanation confirmed by the money of Delos reading ΔΑΛ. This being the case, all other gems with ΑΛΛΙΟΝ or ΑΛΛΙΩΝ become doubly suspicious, especially as all have come to light after this, which certainly cannot be an artist's name. Thus the form ΑΛΛΙΟΝ condemns as modern:—1. Same head: cameo; Raspe. 2. Head of Ulysses: sard; Worsley. ΑΛΛΙΩΝ occurs on the Dionysiac Bull: sardonyx; Hollis: but this, only known to Bracci, is a copy of the Hyllus. Inscribed ΑΛΛΙΩΝΟC is, A Muse leaning against a cippus, playing the lyre: sard; Strozzi, now Blacas. Köhler says the stone is a common dull carnelian, and therefore rejects the work. It seems a copy of the Muse by Onesas, the letters ill-cut, and the edges of the stone appear purposely broken. The Bacchanalia, aquamarine (Bessborough), is called by Natter a work of Sirletti's. To the same artist Dubois assigns three gems:—Death of Julius Cæsar, Minerva,

Venus and Cupid. The Bessborough aquamarine seems to be the one described by Bracci as engraved on such a stone by Sirletti, after an antique original, and sold to Dr. Mead.* Nessus and Deianira, quoted by Lippert; now unknown. ΑΛΛΥΩΝ on a Venus Marina: sard; Firmiano; is said by Pichler to be a modern addition. Roman head: Raspe; of no credit. Triumph of Cupid: Fejévary; modern. Hermaphroditus (legs); Demidoff: the name an insertion. Nymph upon a hippocampus: amethyst; Hemsterhuis (on which he published a dissertation); has the appearance of a modern composition. The disputed reading of the name here is, therefore, of little consequence.

Almelos.—A false reading of Pamphilos on the Orleans gem.

Alpheus and Arethon.—Male and female heads facing each other, between them incised ΑΛΦΗΟC CYN ΑΡΗΘѠΝΙ: cameo; formerly venerated as being the betrothal ring of Joseph and Mary at the Abbey S.-Germain-des-Près; now St. Petersburg. Köhler thinks the inscription votive, and added in ancient times when the stone was dedicated in some temple.†

Hence all other stones thus signed are extremely dubious:—Caligula, D'Azincourt: cameo; where the lettering is placed on each side of the head, though the stone is apparently antique. With the name Alpheus alone, we have: the Triumph of a Barbaric King: cameo, formerly Card. Albani's, now Marlborough; ΑΛΦΗΟC incised in the exergue. Köhler rejects the name, but terms the cameo a beautiful work, and the subject one of the rarest; but Dr. B. objects to the errors in the drawing, sees a want of the antique life and freshness in it, and doubts the genuineness of the cameo. Head of Juno, resembling that on the coins of Metapontum: sard; Pulsky; the name beneath the neck: doubtful, both on account of the name, and as coming from a collection professing to contain so many artists' names. Winckelmann mentions a cameo Penthesilea falling from her horse and supported by Achilles; and an Aged Warrior; both Mr. Deering's: the last by J. Pichler, says Bracci, who also added the name to the cameo. A shipwrecked Ajax seated on a rock, engraved in the scarabæus style, formerly Ant. Pichler's, is dubious for that very reason. Venus drawing a Butterfly out of a fountain: cameo; Venuti. Rape of Proserpine: Poniatowsky, quoted by R. Rochette.

Amaranthus.—Hercules and the Stymphalian Birds: sard. (Praun.) According to Amaduzzi, once belonged to Zarillo. [Not now in the Praun Coll.]

Ampho.—Bearded Head with narrow Fillet around, called Rhœmetalces. (Florence.) The name reading right upon the stone cannot be the artist's.

Antiochus.—Bust of Pallas: sard; Andreini; Bracci gives to Sirletti, who

* Diana Ephesia: sard; Libri; so highly puffed in his catalogue (May, 1864), is a regular Poniatowsky fabrication in the ruder style—large.

† The portraits are usually called Germanicus and Agrippina, but in all probability represent the pair whose names accompany them. The projecting parts of the relief, such as the hair, &c., have been worn flat by the fervent kisses of the devout during the six centuries this gem enjoyed its most sacred reputation. Stolen at the burning of the abbey in 1795, it passed into the hands of Gen. Hydrow, and thence into the Imp. Russian Cabinet.

borrowed the name from the statue of Pallas, in the Villa Ludovisi. Cupid, the name divided: sard; Raspe; Dr. B. judges modern. Female Head, of Hadrian's time, Bracci: Antiochis, the lady herself. [Blacas.]

ANTIPHILUS.—The name placed by a bent bow and arrow on a gem of the Neuville Coll., Leyden; merely the owner's.

APOLLODOTUS.—Head of Pallas, as that of Aspasius: sard. (Barberini.) In front, cut in large letters, ΑΠΟΛΛΟΔΟΤΟΥ ΛΙΘΟ, which, though antique, merely stand for the "gem of Apollodotus."

The Dying Orthryades: sard. (Raspe.) The name added.

APOLLONIDES.—Cow lying down, wanting the hind-quarters, back, and top of the head. The name in relief in the exergue.* Lippert says Stosch got 1000 guineas for this. Köhler boldly assigns the entire fabrication to Stosch himself; and remarks that the cow, though executed with the utmost delicacy and industry, betrays more than plainly by its timidity and anxiety of treatment the newness of its origin. Dr. B., too, observes that the ground on which the cow lies has more the air of a modern naturalistic than of the antique conventional treatment, and everything else shows a want of a fixed and definite style. The same design, perfect; the Hague, coming from Hemsterhuis; is a copy of the above. Œdipus and Antigone: cameo engraved by Tettelbach, of Dresden, after a design by Casanova. Mask, with the name in Roman letters; Winckelmann; necessarily designates the owner.

ARCHION.—Venus riding on a Triton, on her lap a little Cupid; paste or sard; De Thoms: the name inscribed upon a fold of the drapery. Dubious from the modern air of the design, as well as the collection to which it belongs. No genuine example occurs of a name so placed.

ARISTOTEICHOS.—Scarabæus, prase, found near Pergamus: lioness in a threatening posture. The name filling up all the field over the design is clearly the owner's.

ARISTON.—Ulysses seated before his house, the forepart of a cow visible by his feet: red jasper; Paris. In front of the figure, the name. The design within an Etruscan border shows somewhat of the hardness of the archaic style; the name is added in a later but still antique character, and reads right upon the stone.

ATHA.—Amazon, quoted by Gori.

ATOY.—Apollo and Hercules, a tripod between them. (Caylus.) The composition bears a modern air.

AXIOS.—Capricorn: opaque sard; Portales-Gorgier, the owner's name, in the field.

BEISITALOS.—Cupid standing and leaning on a sceptre: sardonyx. (Florence.) The letters large and reading right upon the stone show the name to be the owner's.

CÆKAS.—Youth standing, holding a sword: paste; the letters large and the

* Not so: by some unaccountable mistake Dr. B. (like Clarac) describes this gem as a cameo. In reality it is an *intaglio* in a red sard; the missing parts completed in gold. The work is probably antique, and so is the name; but the latter unquestionably refers to the owner, and nothing more—its agreement with that of the famous artist being a mere accidental coincidence.

name divided. [This must be a paste taken from the Devonshire Theseus, and the name wrongly read, which is clearly CASKAE.]

CHÆREMON.—Runner holding a palm: burnt sard; Brit. Mus.; stone of the Lower Empire.

CHARITON.—Cameo: formerly Casanova's, now St. Petersburg. Venus in a temple, between two female figures: the name on the base of the statue. Modern work, probably from Casanova's own design. Fragment of a head of Hercules: the name is placed behind the head. The style is affected, and of the same character as that to be seen in some other modern-made fragments.

XEΛY.—Seated Sphinx, with her forepaw raised, the inscription upon the wing: sard. (De Thoms.) The unusual position of the legend and the character of the cabinet together militate strongly against its genuineness.

XPYCOYN.—In the middle a large lunar-shaped E; above it three balls tied together by a band [or more correctly three roses or other circular flowers connected by a fillet. Euripides terms the Delphic Oracle *στέμμασι κατάσκιον*]. Uhden explains this subject as the *golden* Delphic E, a letter sacred to Apollo, and which Plutarch explains as expressing by its sound the word *εἶ*, *Thou art*, as equivalent to *ὁ ὢν*, *The living God*, or else as standing for the holy number *Five*. [A little cameo agreeing exactly with this description came into my hands at Lady Grieve's sale (1862). Caylus (Rec. vii. pl. 27) figures a third of the same type, but wanting the final N in the inscription. The ingenious Frenchman discovers in the word the name of an artist *Chrysés*, and thereupon censures him for wasting his skill upon so insignificant a memorial of himself!]

ΔAMNAMENEYC.—Mercury girt with a serpent, and surrounded by the sacred animals: touch-stone. (De la Turbie.) [A mere Gnostic talisman; *Damnameneus* occurs in the famed Ephesian Spell preserved by Hesychius, and is there interpreted as meaning the Sun.]

DARON.—Janus-head: sard. (Mariette.) Evidently nothing more than the name of the owner.

DEUTON.—A race between four chariots: paste. (De Thoms.) An insignificant work.

DIPHILI.—Vase embossed with a Sphinx, mask, and wheat-ears; upon it DIPHIL: amethyst. (Naples.) Name of the owner.

DIVILIS.—Bust of a youthful Satyr: red jasper. The largeness of the lettering manifestly declares it the owner's name.

DOMETIS.—Jupiter enthroned between Juno and Phœbus, two eagles above, &c. Winckelmann explains it as the apotheosis of Vespasian, and the legend as referring to Domitian: chalcedony. (Berlin.)

[DOMITI.—The Ephesian Diana: sard. (Bosanquet.) The name across the field.]

DORY.—Female bust, a crescent over the brow: Licetus.*

EPITRACHALOS.—False reading for Epitynchanus.

EUELPISTUS.—Chimera of an elephant's head formed out of three masks: red jasper; St. Petersburg. The owner's name cut in large letters around.

2. Nemesis seated: sard; Grivaud; the same.

* Evidently the contraction of Doryphorus, who had taken Diana for his patroness.

EUPLO.—Cupid riding on a Dolphin, legend in the exergue: sardonyx. "Prosperous voyage!" Not a name.

EUTHUS.—Silenus drunken seated on the ground, two Cupids holding flute and lyre: cameo. Köhler thinks the name Evodus blundered; Dr. B., the design modern.

GAMUS.—Spes: emerald. (Kestner.) Indifferent work.

GAURANUS.—Boar attacked by a Hound, below ΓΑΥΡΑΝΟϹ ΑΝΙΚΗΤΟΥ: bloodstone. Name of dog and his sire (or master).*

GLYCON.—Venus borne upon a sea-bull, surrounded by many Cupids: large cameo. (Paris.) "A poor work," says Köhler, "of the Renaissance, in which the accessories are better done than the goddess."

HEDY.—Medusa's Head (like Solon's): onyx. (Col. Murray.) The name probably borrowed from "Hedys aurifex" from the Columbarium.†

HEIUS.—Diana holding a stag by the horns, in the exergue ΗΕΙΟΥ: agate, according to Stosch. Letronne takes him for the Oscan Heius, the friend of Verres. The work is stiff, in an Etruscan border, but Dr. B. regards it as modern, on account of the attitude. [Paste: Blacas.]

2. Head of Apollo: sard; Greville; where the name stands for Ηως, a common title of that deity.

3. Dying Amazon: sardonyx. (Raspe.)

4. Minerva, bare Head, the helmet in the field in front: nicolo. (Raspe.) A mediocre work.

5. Dolon attacked by Diomede and Ulysses. (Blacas.)

KÆSILAX.—Roma seated, the name divided on each side of the figure: sardonyx. (Raspe.)

ΚΑΙΚΙϹΙΑΝΟΥ ΑΡΙΑ, around a Venus leaning against a column; agate-onyx; mediocre work. [Clearly the name of Arria, wife of Cæcisianus.]

KARPOS.—Fragment of the right leg of a Hercules, grandiose in style, the letters ΚΑΡΠΟΣ forming apparently the termination of a longer name. This appears to have been the origin of the modern signature, which appears on numerous gems:—1. Faun seated upon a standing panther: red jasper; Florence. Probably a modern work. 2. Muse of Onesas: cameo; Milliotti. The name on the cippus behind the figure. 3. Hercules and Omphale, heads: sard; Milliotti. Modern in design. 4. The Hercules and Iole of Teucer; formerly Medina's. 5. Group of three soldiers; also Medina's. These two works of Sirletti's.

The De Thoms Cabinet properly follows the Medina. Here we find an "antique" paste from the Satyr of Pergamus; but signed ΚΑΡΠΟΥ. Abundantia; Dr. Thomasius; Murr calls a modern copy, "as is also the Festival of Bacchus and Ariadne" [apparently meaning in the same collection]. Perseus holding up the Gorgon's head: sard. (Raspe.) Hence it results that all gems with this name are acknowledged forgeries.

* Quoted by Clarac from the St. Aignan Coll., a large stone 1½ inch in diameter, now belonging to Mrs. Stackhouse Acton. *Gauranus* means bred on Gaurus, a mountain range near Lake Avernus. Martial has an epitaph (xi. 69) on a dog, *Lydia*, killed in a similar encounter with a boar.

† Perhaps for Hedylus, which, as well as the feminine Hedylis, occur in Martial.

KASTRICIUS.—Corybant with thyrsus and vase, dragging along a kid: amethyst; found in Perugia, the residence of the Gens Castricia, therefore the signet of one of that family.

KISSOS.—Heads, called of C. and L. Cæsar, but more probably of Kissos and Sodala: Winckelmann.*

KLEON.—Apollo standing with his lyre, by a tripod set upon a lofty basis: sard; attributed to Sirletti by Bracci.

KRATEROS.—Ephesian Diana: sard; poor work. The name divided by the figure.

ΚΡΗCΚΗC.—Terpsichore, a copy of the Onesas: Poniatowsky; rejected by Dubois, for both reasons.

*ΚΥΙΝΤΙΛ.—Small comic Mask, three-quarter face, lettering very fine. (Marlborough.)

LYSANDROS.—Scarabæus of the Volterra Mus., reading ΛΥΣΑΝΔΡΟ, evidently the owner's name.

MAXALAS.—Bust of Antoninus Pius: the name beneath incised; rejected by Bracci as a modern addition.

[This name, I suspect, is merely Passaglia's usual signature ΠΑΖΑΛΙΑΣ, misread; for the latter, on the Greville gem, at first sight, would strike the eye as ΜΑΞΑΛΑΣ.]

MCIOPCIC.—Worsley. Hercules carrying the Bull. The name a false reading of M. CLOD. CIS.

ΜΗΝΑ ΤΟΥ ΔΙΟΔΩΡΟΥ, on each side of a diademed female head: De Thoms; probably modern, and the name borrowed from a sard in Gruter.

MILESIOS.—Apollo seated before a tripod: paste. (Gori.) Evidently a title of the god, if the original be genuine, which Bracci appears to doubt.

MIRON.—Head of a Muse: sard; time of the Decline. Tölken considers the name as modern. The false spelling of the name Myron with the *i* stamps as forgeries—1. Ajax killing himself upon an altar. 2. Daphne pursued by Apollo, a design in the Bernini style. 3. Lion passant, Blacas. Naked female bust, holding a mask: the legend at the side Μ ЄΠΟΙЄΙ is without any precedent: Cades.

ΜΙΘ.—Horse's Head: sard. (Berlin.) Said by Köhler to be a doublet made to Stosch's order from a wax model; but Tölken maintains that the stone is real, though the lettering, rude and large, is an addition, yet of ancient date. Eagle's Head: Poniatowsky; probably taken from the above. Sard: Wlassoff, cited by Clarac.

MUSIKOS.—Harpocrates: sardonyx; the Hague; mediocre.

NEARKOS.—Head of Sulla, name in front in neat small letters: sard; Pulsky. Head of Demetrius III.: amethyst; Pulsky. Head of Epicurus: sard; Cades: a work offering few guarantees for its authenticity.

NIKEPHOROS.—Mercury, an Eagle upon his hand: onyx; formerly Capello's, now Cassel Cabinet. The name divided by the figure. A small Victory surrounded by the name, a signet containing the rebus of the owner: Raspe. Vulcan, nude, working at a helmet: sard; Florence. The legend behind in large letters.

* Of this gem are many modern copies current.

NEPOS.—Youth playing the lyre: the name in large rude letters. (Schellersheim.)

NERT.—Bust of Cupid with his hands bound: chrysolite; a beautiful work; the Hague; suspected as modern.

NICOMACHUS.—Faun seated on a panther's skin: black agate. (Molinari.) The Latin form betokens the owner's name. [There are two pastes of this in dark-blue glass, nearly black, in the Marlborough Coll., which are, in all likelihood, Molinari's quoted as *black* agate, a stone rarely found in antique work.] Hercules, Head: Schellersheim; a perhaps modern work. Socrates, Head: Cades. [Venus in her shell, a splendid Renaissance intaglio: Uzielli.]

NEILOS.—Head, like Hadrian's, but broken: Winckelmann. The name cut in conspicuous letters, not in fine lines.

NYMPHEROS.—Warrior standing; in one hand a bay branch, in the other, resting on his shield, his helmet: name divided by the figure. The gem antique, first published by Maffei; the name probably the owner's.*

ORUS.—Silenus, mask: cameo; uncertain if antique.

P. PALONIANUS.—Merely a name upon a sard.

PANÆUS.—Satyr assailing a Nymph: ΑΦΡΟΔΙΤΗ in the exergue; ΠΑΝΑΙΟΥ in the field. Stephani thinks it a dedicatory inscription.† Replica without inscription. (Orleans Cabinet.)

ΠΑΖΑΛΙΑΣ.—Passalias is the signature of the Roman Passaglia, a Lieutenant in the Papal Guards in the last century, and a most skilful imitator of the antique style in Bacchic subjects. *Maxalas*, given in the old lists of ancient artists, seems merely his signature misread; a facile error.

PELAGI.—Diana running and drawing an arrow out of her quiver: lapis-lazuli; very mediocre work.

PETROS.—Caracalla: christened into the Apostle.‡

PHILIPPUS.—Hercules, Head garlanded: sardonyx; lettering large, the owner's name (the signet of some Macedonian prince; the head, that of the founder of the line). Horse, small Roman work. (Marlborough.)

PHILOCALOS.—Youthful Head, laureated: sard. (Florence.) The name divided in the field. A sard, in the same collection, a copy and the name blundered.

PHRYGILLUS.—Cupid playing with astragali: in the field an open mussel-shell, within an Etruscan border: sard. (Berlin.) Greatly extolled by Winckelmann, who places it at a very high antiquity, but called modern by Köhler. Stephani pronounces it a Roman work in imitation of the archaic style. The letters, large and filling up the exergue, can only stand for the owner. R. Rochette, however, identifies Phrygillus with the same name found on a coin of Syracuse. [He is right; the notion of the Etruscan style being thus revived in Roman times is a mere theory, totally unsupported by any other examples, and quite inconsistent with the ancient mode of thought.]

* In fact, Greville's Alexander taming Bucephalus bears in large lettering the name M. Ant. Nymp. . . apparently referring to the same person.

† Why should not this be an ancient reproduction, in miniature, of a picture by the famous painter Panæus?

‡ By some mediæval owner taking the curly-headed truculent portrait for that of the fiery apostle, whose traditional type it certainly strongly resembles.

Plutarchus.—Bust of Cleopatra: Murr. A forgery based upon the false reading of "Protarchus."

Poemus.—Achilles playing the lyre: Monttezun; declared by R. Rochette a genuine work, but Letronne condemns it as a blundered copy of the Pamphilus.

Polycrates.—Psyche seated, Cupid flying away; ΠΟΛΥΚΡΑΤΗΣ ΕΠΟΙΕΙ: garnet, found in the Arena at Nismes in 1743. Considered by Mariette as indubitably antique; then in the possession of the Marquis de Gouvernet. Not now known.

Polytimus.—Hercules holding the apples of the Hesperides. Insignificant work, with the legend running around.

Pothus.—Three Masks: quoted by Millingen.

Priscus.—Matidia: onyx. (Formerly Medina's, now Clanbrasil.) Bracci asserts all Medina's signed gems are forgeries [and is right as far as my experience goes].

Pylades.—Mount Argæus, on which stands an Eagle holding a wreath; name in exergue: red jasper.*

Pyrgoteles.—Neptune and Pallas: cameo. (Naples.) ΠΥ in the exergue has nothing to do with this name. [Not so certain: the letters are in monogram and seem to contain more of this great name than the first two; the chances, however, are that the monogram was an addition of some possessor after the Revival.]

Roman head, ΠΥΡΓΟΤΕΛΗϹ ЄΠΟΙЄΙ in the exergue, and ΦΩΚΙΩΝΟϹ in the field; is mentioned by Vasari as a work of Al. Cesati's. Alexander's head covered with the lion-skin; formerly Mayence Coll.; is modern The Hercules and Iolaos killing the Hydra, the antique copy mentioned by Visconti, is very dubious. Alexander, Head; Blacas; the most important of all. But Stephani thinks that, even if the stone be antique, which, to judge from the cast, is not very likely, the rudely-cut letters prove that we must not think here about the famous artist. Medusa's head: broken amethyst; Blacas. The reading of the name uncertain.

Quintil.—Neptune in a car drawn by hippocampi, the name in large letters on a frieze below: aquamarine. (Ludovisi.) Mercury with foot on a prow and regarding an "aplustre" in his right: sardonyx; name in the field behind the figure. (Spilsbury.)

Quintus.—Fragment of a cameo: the legs of a Mars Gradivus; sardonyx. (Florence.) Stephani and Dr. B. consider the inscription as a forgery. But an ant. paste—Neptune and Amymone—formerly Barberini, now Brit. Mus., is pronounced by Pulsky indubitably antique; which still does not remove Dr. B.'s doubts about this piece.

Rufus.—Head of Ptolemy VIII., an Eagle above, the name divided: sard. (Raspe.) 2. Aurora leading the horses of the sun, ΡΟΥΦΟϹ ЄΠΟΙЄΙ incised:

* The same mountain, but flanked by two Victories, below ΦΡΟΝΙΜΟΥ: red jasper. (Hertz.)

† Noble head of Jupiter, brought from India: in the field Π—Υ. Sapphire large and fine coloured. (Now Rosana, Mexico.)

Orleans ; cameo. But the stone, an Occidental onyx, and the modern character of the details, prove it a work of the sixteenth century.

SELEUCUS.—Silenus Head, ivy-crowned : sard. (Picard, now the Hague.) The work neat, but the name added, says Köhler; yet an ant. paste of Stosch's, called by Köhler a replica of this, differs, says Tölken, considerably in the expression. But the gem does not possess any great artistic merit.

The same may be said of all the others, viz. :—1. Priapus-Herme : emerald ; De Thoms. 2. Cupid playing with a Boar : paste; Raspe. 3. Hercules, Head : sard ; Blacas ; decidedly modern. In all these the abbreviation of the name, CΕΛΕΥΚ, proves it to be copied from that first quoted.

SEMON.—Water-carrier, female kneeling before a fountain issuing from a lion's mouth : scarabæus found on the plain of Troy. (Gerhard.) The name, in old Greek letters, reads right upon the stone. "Excellent work of masterly execution, in a black agate, somewhat burnt."

SEXTIANUS.—Head of Apollo radiated : sard ; the name divided, and in large letters. (Winckelmann.)

SILVANUS.—Hercules : Sellari. Bracci suspects this.

SKYMNOS.—Satyr with thyrsus running, followed by a panther : sard. (Cades.) R. Rochette identifies the name with the Cælator of Pliny ; but Dr. B. discovers in the unevenness and stiffness of the lettering, and want of freedom in the design, a modern style.

SOCRATES.—Actor standing, one hand to his head, a pedum in the other : cameo. (Bar. Roger.) The name in relief. Comedian, seen in front, leaning on his pedum : cameo, fine Oriental sardonyx. (Bar. Roger.) Fortuna Panthea helmeted : red jasper, burnt. (Borré.) The last now not known. The existence of the two camei of similar subjects in the same cabinet is very suspicious.

TAURIS(KOS).—Phœbus seated on a mountain, holding his whip ; opposite to him a chamois. Gori interprets this of the mountains of the Taurisci ; the work too mediocre for the name to denote an artist.

TRYPHON.—[Dr. Brunn's remarks upon the lovely composition, the masterpiece of this supposed artist, are so full of instruction as to admit of no abridgment ; I therefore subjoin a literal translation of his notice.] "A renowned work of the Glyptic Art is the sardonyx-cameo of Tryphon with the Marriage of Eros and Psyche. Eros pressing a dove to his breast, and with his face covered with a veil as well as Psyche's, is walking close to her, led along with the sacred ribbon, by a winged Hymen holding a torch. A Cupid lifts the covering of a sofa which is to serve as a seat for the pair, whilst another, to judge from the curled points of the wings, rather to be called Anteros, raises from behind above their heads the so-called mystic winnowing fan. This group was first made known by a drawing of Pirro Ligorio's, which Spon got from amongst the papers of Rascas de Bagarris ; that the stone itself was in Pirro's possession, as Köhler maintains, does not appear from Spon's own account. Subsequently the gem came into the Arundel, and thence into the Marlborough Coll., *out of which it has at present disappeared.* Vid. Gerhard's 'Arch. Anzeiger' for 1854, p. 443.*

* An unaccountable mistake ; it still adorns the cabinet.

An engraver Tryphon is known from an epigram of Addæus, where a beryl with the figure of Galene is extolled as a work of his. As long as people regarded the poet of the Anthology as identical with the Addæus, the acquaintance of Polemo's, and consequently as a contemporary of his and of king Antigonus, they also believed themselves warranted in placing the engraver of the Arundelian cameo in the same age: against which however the circular form of the Є would of itself be an objection, the use of which character at that period at least has not yet been satisfactorily made out. Reiske, however, has long ago pointed out that the epigram in question bears the stamp of a later epoch.* By this, at all events, should we gain the possibility of holding the artist named in the epigram and the engraver of the gem for one and the same person. But, entirely apart from this question, another possibility cannot be overlooked, viz., that in modern times the name upon the cameo has been borrowed from the epigram. Köhler, who (p. 201) first utters this suspicion, and places the stone amongst those 'the antiquity of which is dubious, as well on account of their style as of the inscription,' expresses himself indeed more cautiously than his wont, because he had only imperfect casts at his command. On the contrary, Stephani decidedly condemns the *inscription* at least—'The cutting shows indeed a character essentially different from the forgeries of the eighteenth century: the name is given in the usual style of his (Ligorio's) times, in letters equally large and sharp: the cutting of which exhibits essentially the same character as the name of Lorenzo de' Medici is wont to show upon the gems once belonging to him.' As for some other reasons of Stephani's,—the letters being in *intaglio*, the placing of the legend *above* the design, instead of in the exergue,—though I lay little weight upon them, yet am I obliged to concede that 'whatever comes from Pirro Ligorio's hands, no one in our days must take for genuine without the most weighty corroboration:' whilst in the epigram of the Anthology the possible source of the forgery clearly presents itself to us. Since by these considerations reasonable doubt has been excited, I would direct suspicion fully as much against the work itself as against the legend merely. For the design, so highly charming and so graceful, yet exhibits much of what is actually strange. The bride certainly appears in antique representations of weddings, with the veil, but where with the *face* covered? And the bridegroom also the same? The dove too, which

* He pretends it is in the taste of the late Byzantine epigrammatists, but this is a mere piece of hypercriticism. As for the somewhat forced conceit forming its point, it exactly agrees with King Polemo's "On the Herd of Cows on a jasper," and with Antipater's on Cleopatra's amethyst, engraved with Μέθη. The genuine antiquity of these two epigrams has never been disputed. But it does not by any means follow as a necessary consequence that Tryphon's "Galene" bore his signature, if Addæus was celebrating the production of a famous contemporary artist. Diodorus also has left one in praise of a certain Satyrius for his δαίδαλον (bust?) of Arsinoë in crystal, so it is clear that it was quite the fashion at the court of the Ptolemies for the poets to take these miniature works of art as the theme for their muse. The earliest example now to be found are the two of Plato the younger (B.C. 300), "On the Herd of five Cows on a jasper," and "On Bacchus engraven on an amethyst." (Anth. ix. 747, 748.)

Eros presses to his bosom, has not yet been pointed out in a similar connexion. Besides, where do we find the wedded couple chained together by the sacred ribbon and led along by this ribbon? where also the mystic fan in a wedding scene? And this fan, too, without any hint of the phallus? Even in an artistic point of view must the design awake suspicion, moving as it does in two parallel lines upon an oval ground. To all these difficulties has attention been already called by Jahn (Ant. Beiträge, p. 173); and it is therefore perhaps less bold and hazardous than it may at first sight appear, if I (with reference at the same time to the doubts raised before as to the legend) should be inclined to regard the whole as a work of the sixteenth century. Precisely at that period had the fable of Cupid and Psyche given diversified employment to the most eminent artists—as Rafaelle and Giulio Romano. And if there be nothing that controverts the opinion that the design of this cameo was composed by some such artist, but employing antique 'motives,' so will its, in other respects, great artistic merit appear sufficiently honoured under such a judgment." *

The same subject, but intaglio. (Naples.) Pronounced by Visconti a copy of the foregoing.

[Another fine copy has lately come to my knowledge. It is by a Cinque-cento hand, on a German topaz, the size of the original. (Carter.)]

Cupid on the Lion: modern. (The Hague.)

Hercules and Antæus. (The Hague.) In this the name seems a recent addition.

*Triumph of a Victor in a car drawn by elephants. (Marlborough.) [A paste taken either from a bad Cinque-cento work, or else coming, without any original, direct from a wax model of Stosch's fabrique; the latter most probable, the work being rounded and blurred as though the mould had been formed on the softer substance.]

YTHILUS.—Mars seated. (Cortona.) A blundered and suspicious inscription.

ZENO.—Serapis Head: nicolo. (Beugnot's Collection.) The name, running around the stone, must therefore indicate the owner merely.

* Careful and repeated examination of the cameo itself forces me, with regret, to endorse this judgment of Dr. Brunn's; still, however, placing the work, for beauty, grace, and execution, at the head of its class, whether antique or Cinque-cento.

INDEX.

E
E

I. ASSYRIAN.

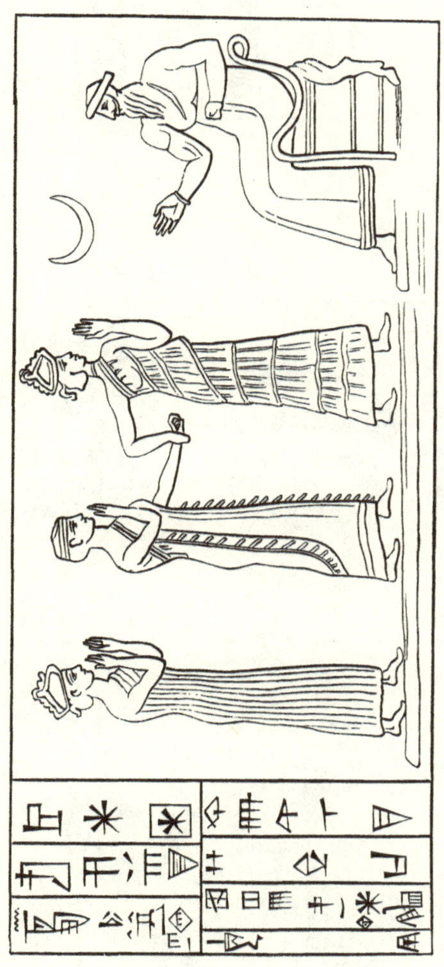

II. ASSYRIAN.

1.

2. 3.

4.

III. ASSYRIAN.

2.

1.

3.

4.

5.

6.

7.

8.

IV. ASSYRIAN.

1.

2.

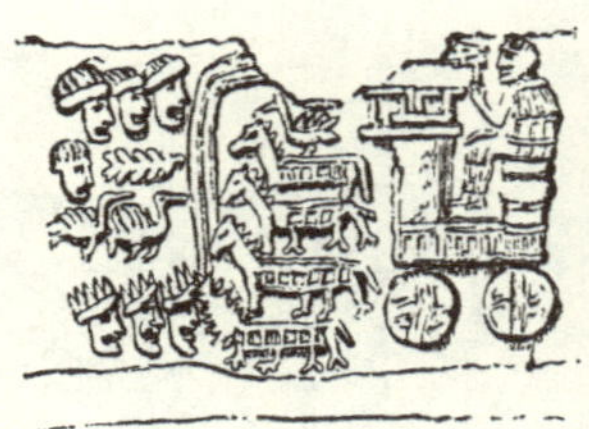

3.

4.

5.

6.

7.

V. BABYLONIAN: PERSIAN.

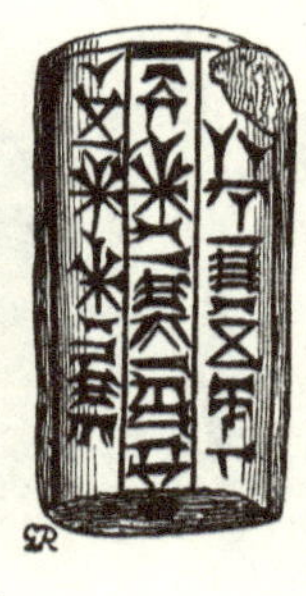

1.

2.

3.

4.

5.

6.

7.

8.

9.

VI. PARTHIAN : SASSANIAN.

3.

1.

2.

4.

VII. INDO SASSANIAN.

1.

3.

4.

2.

VIII. SASSANIAN.

1.

3.

2.

5.

6.

4.

7.

9.

8.

IX. SASSANIAN-CHRISTIAN.

1.

2

3.

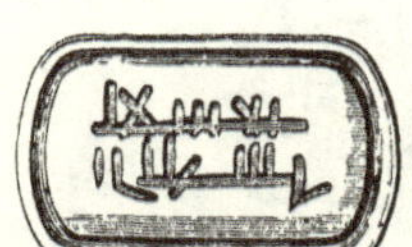

4.

X. EGYPTIAN.

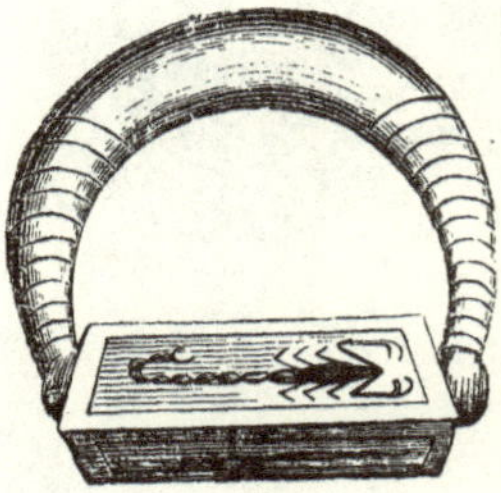

2.

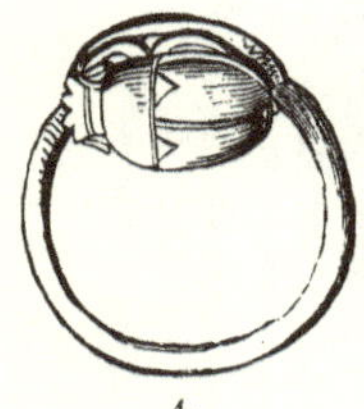

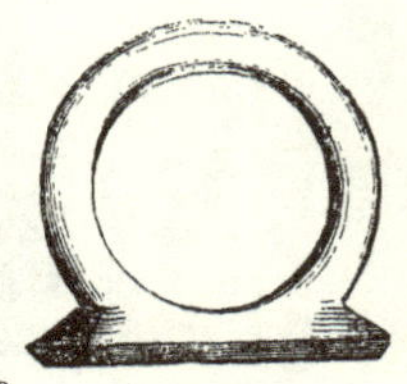

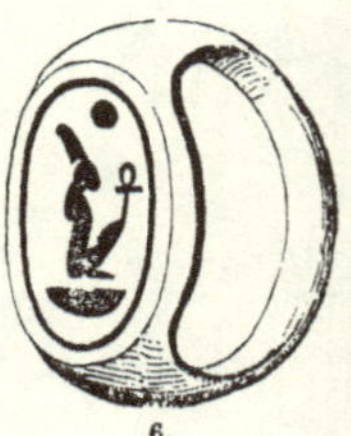

4.  3. 6.

XI. EGYPTIAN: GNOSTIC.

1.

2.

2.

3.

3.

XII. ABRAXAS TALISMANS.

1.

2.

3.

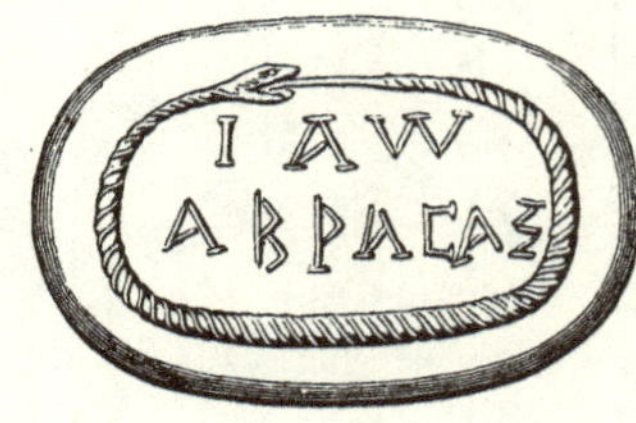

1a.

4.

4a.

XIII. GNOSTIC TALISMAN.

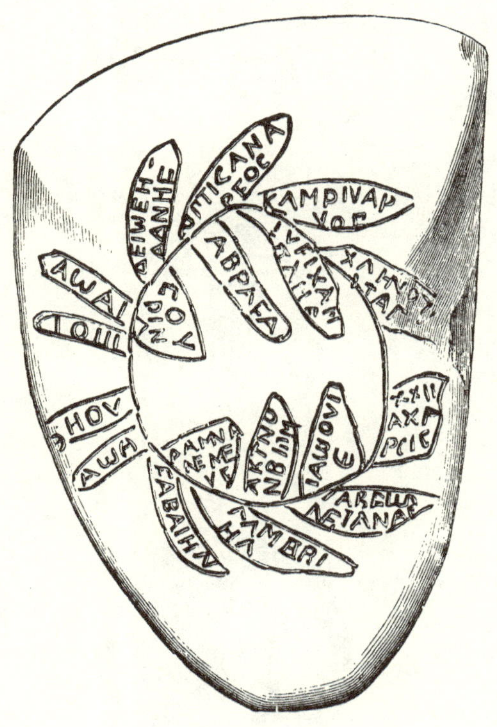

XIV. CHRISTIAN.

1.

2.

3.

4.

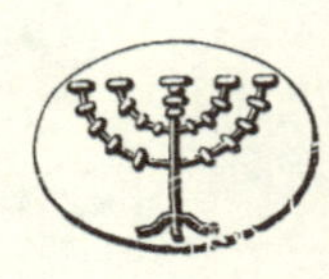

6.

7.

5.

9.

10.

8.

XV. PHŒNICIAN.

1.

2.

3.

4.

5.

6.

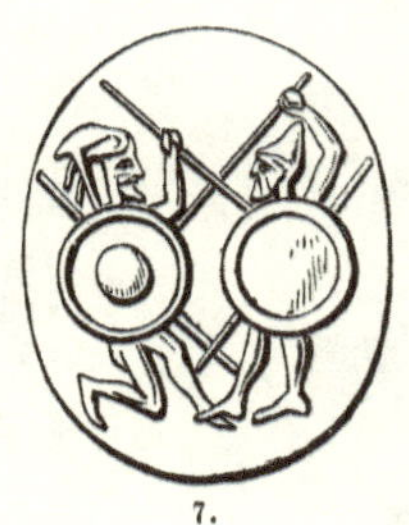

7.

8.

9.

ETRUSCAN.

2.

4.

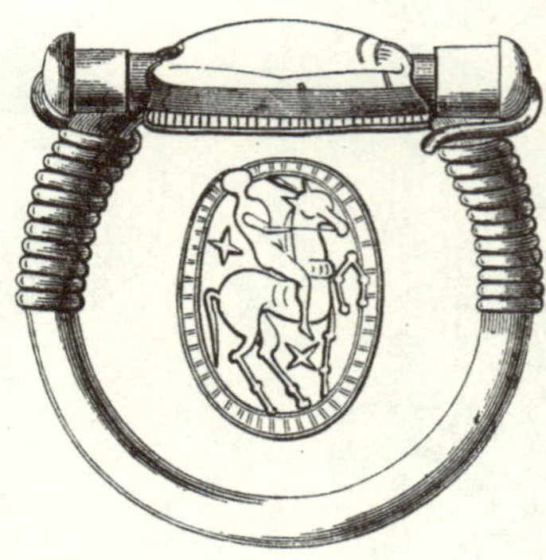

3.

1.

5.

6

XVII. ETRUSCAN.

1.

2.

3.

4.

5.

6.

ARCHAIC GREEK.

1.

2.

3.

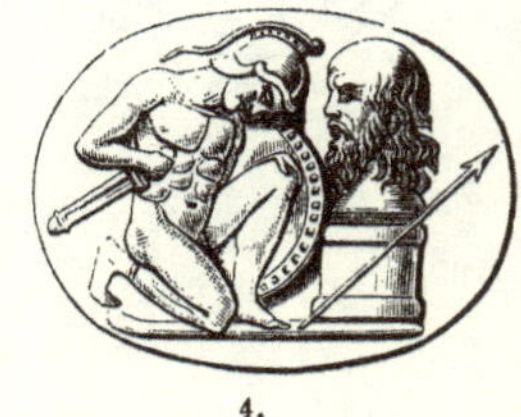

4.

5.

7.

6.

XIX. GREEK.

1.

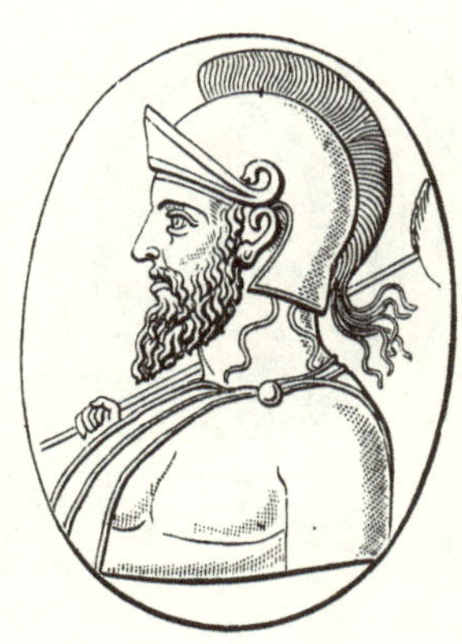
2.

3.

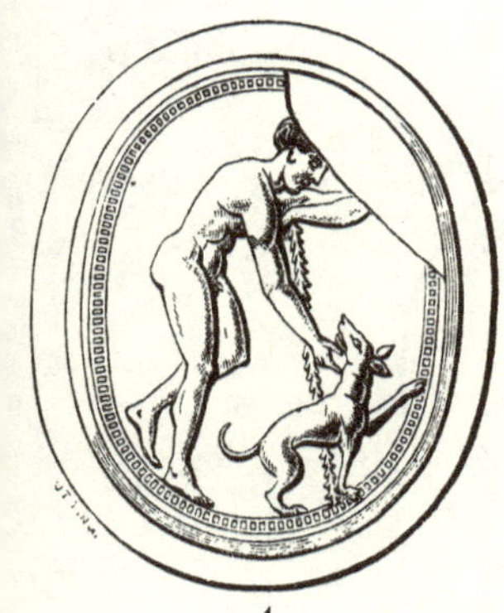
4.

5.

XX. CURIOUS TYPES, NEW YORK MUSEUM.

1.

2.

3.

4.

5.

6.

XXI. APOTHEOSIS OF AUGUSTUS.

XXII. THE NAPLES, AND ODESCALCHI CAMEI

CLAUDIAN FAMILY.

XXIV. TRIUMPH OF CONSTANTINE

XXV. ROMAN CAMEI.

1.

2.

3

XXVI. AZTEC CAMEO.

XXVII. MARCIA

XXVIII. ROMAN: RARE TYPES.

1.

2.

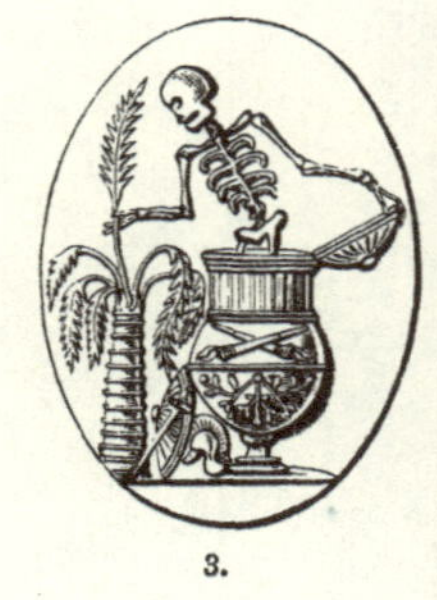

3.

4.

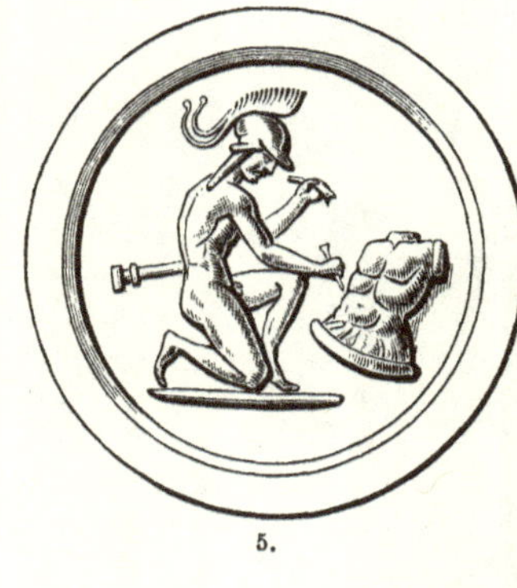

5.

6.

XXIX. GRECO-ROMAN.

1.

2.

3.

4.

7

8.

5.

6

XXX. ROMAN - BRITISH.

1.

2.

3.

6A.

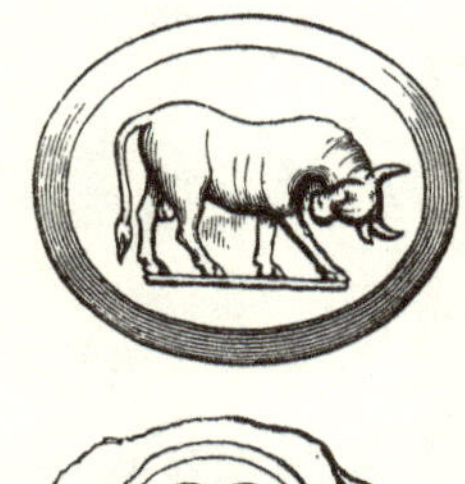

4

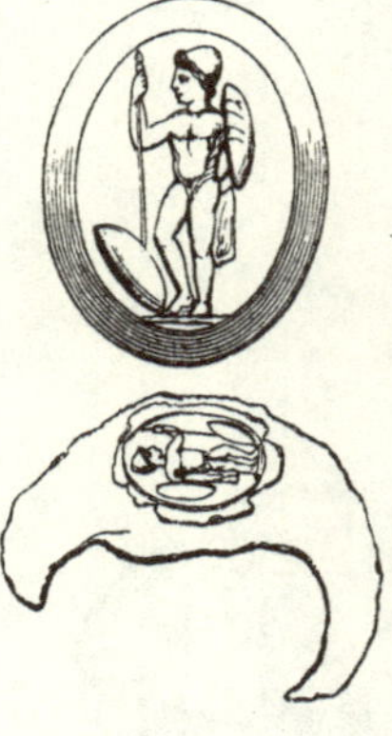

5.

XXXI. ROMAN-BRITISH.

7.

8.

11.

9.

10.

XXXII. ROMAN - BRITISH.

4. 1.

5.

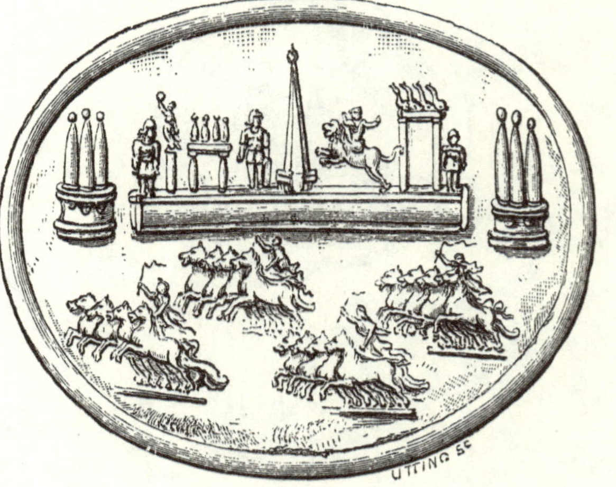

2.

6.

3.

7.

XXXIII. MEDIÆVAL USE OF ANTIQUE GEMS

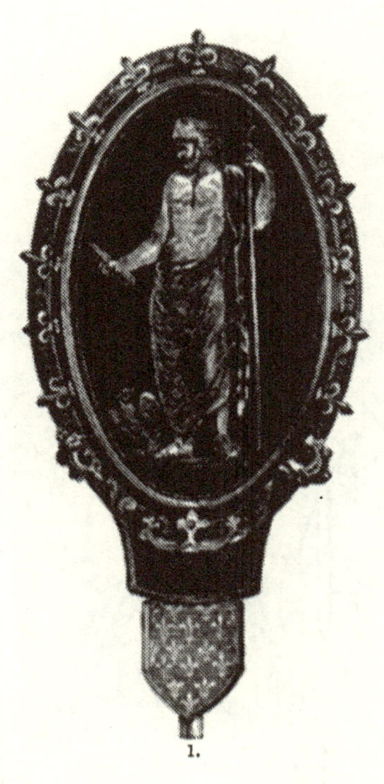

1.

2

XXXIV. CAMEO OF ST. ALBANS.

XXXV. MEDIÆVAL USE OF ANTIQUE GEMS

1.

2.

3.

XXXVI. MEDIÆVAL ENGRAVING.

1.

2.

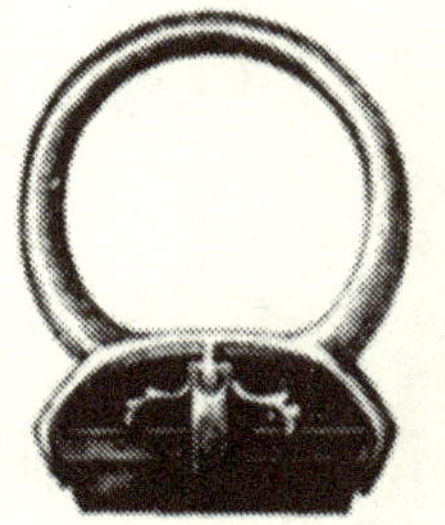

XXXVII. MEDIÆVAL ENGRAVING.

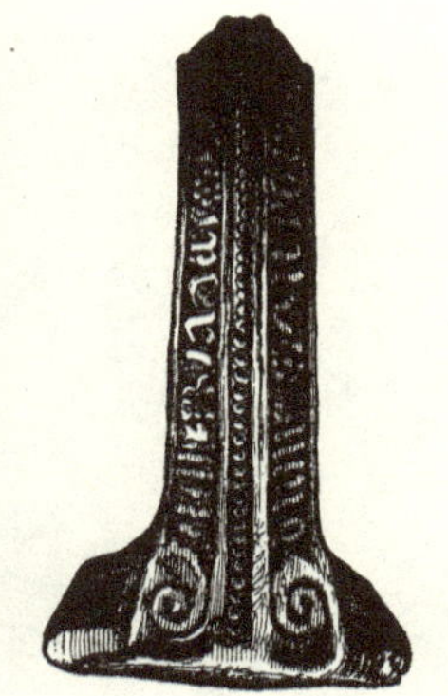

1.

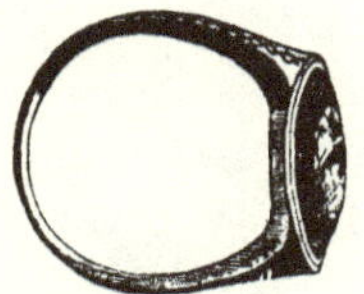

2.

XXXVIII. MEDIÆVAL ENGRAVING.

1.

3.

2.

4.

5.

6.

XXXIX. CINQUE - CENTO.

1. 2. 3. 4. 5. 6.

XL. MODERN.

SATURN: JUPITER.

1.

2.

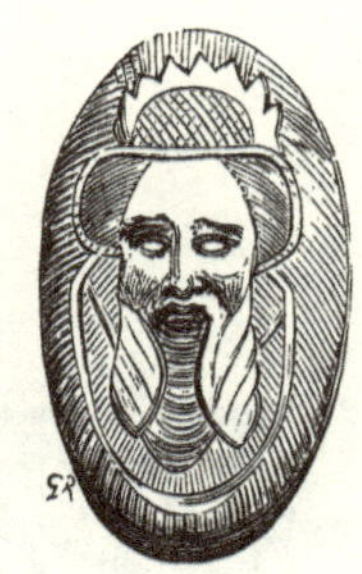

3.

4.

5.

6

XLII. JUPITER: JUNO.

2.

4.

7.

6.

5.

3

SERAPIS: PLUTO.

1.

2.

3.

4.

5.

6.

7.

XLIV. MARINE DEITIES.

1.

2.

3.

4.

XLV. MINERVA.

1.

2.

3.

5.

4.

6.

XLVI. CERES: TRIPTOLEMUS.

1.

2.

3.

4.

5.

6.

XLVII. APOLLO: PYTHIA.

1.

2.

3.

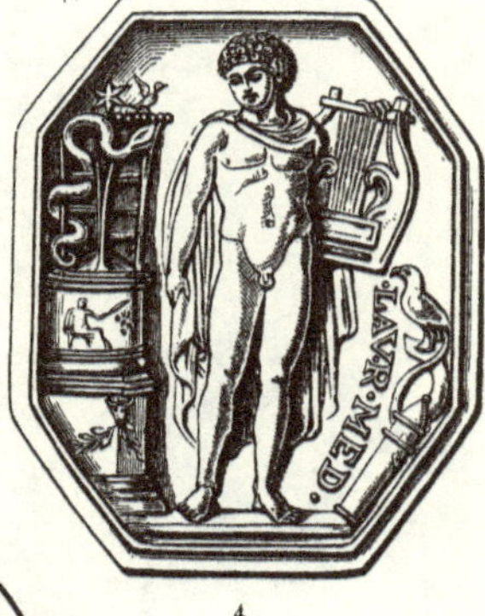

4.

5.

6.

7.

XLVIII. APOLLO : ESCULAPIUS.

1.

2.

4.

3

5.

6.

XLIX. MUSES.

1.

2.

3.

4.

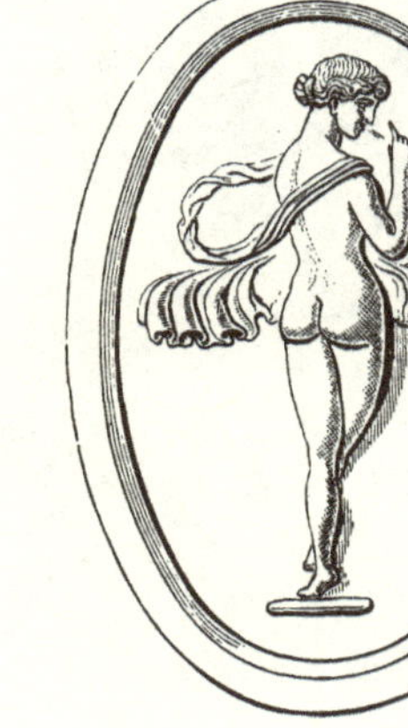
5.

L. ASTROLOGY.

1.

2.

3.

4.

5.

6.

LI. DIANA.

1.

4.

5.

6.

3.

2.

LII. MERCURY : FORTUNE.

1.

3.

2.

4.

5.

LIII.

MARS: VICTORY.

1.

2.

3.

4.

6.

5.

LIV. MARS: WAR.

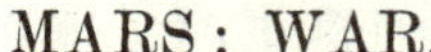

1.

2.

3.

4.

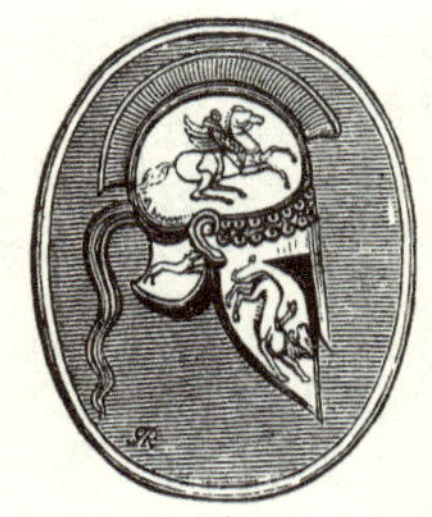

6.

5.

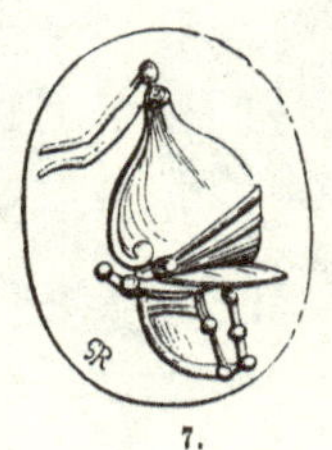

7.

LV.

VENUS.

1.

2.

4.

3.

5.

6.

7.

LVI.

VENUS : CUPID.

2. 1. 3.

6.

5. 4.

9.

8.

LVII.

NEMESIS: PSYCHE.

1.

7.

2.

3.

4.

5.

7.

LVIII. BACCHUS.

2.

1.

3.

6.

5.

4.

8.

7.

LIX. BACCHUS: FAUNS: PRIAPUS.

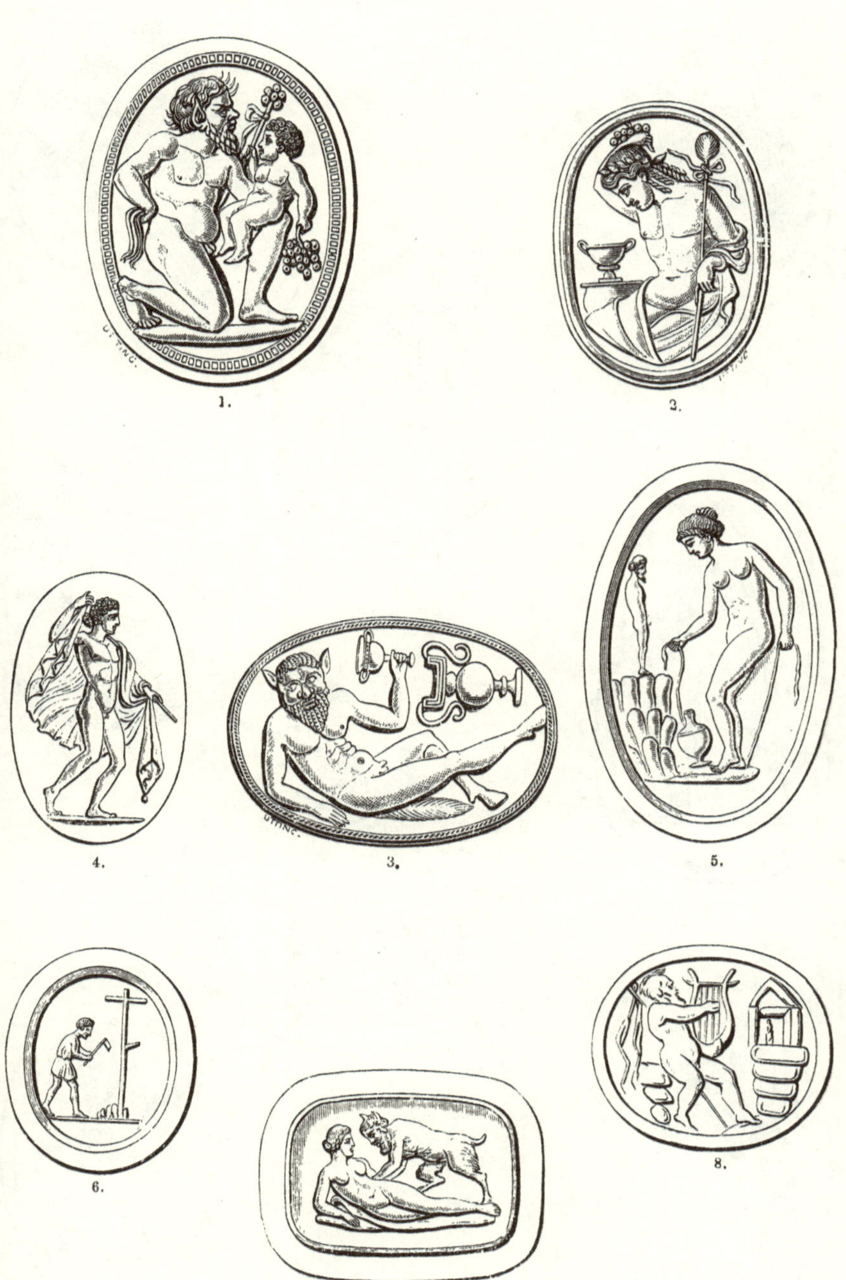

1. 2. 4. 3. 5. 6. 7. 8.

LX. BACCHANTES.

1. 2. 3. 4. 5. 6. 7. 8

SILENUS: PAN.

1.

2.

3.

4.

5.

7.

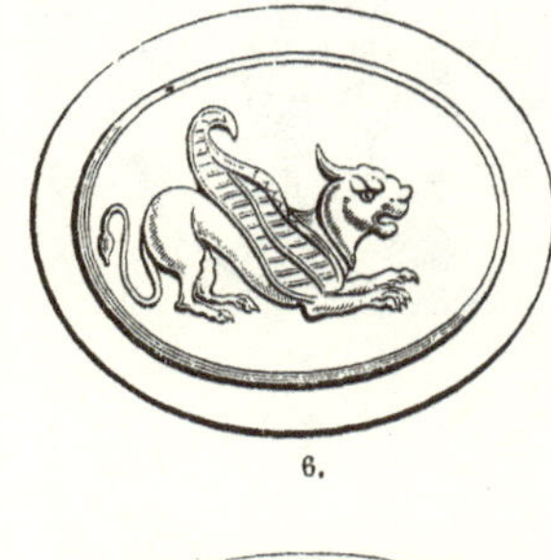
6.

9.

10.

8.

LXII. MASKS.

6.

3.

2.

4.

1.

5

9.

LXIII. **HERCULES.**

1.

2.

3.

4.

5.

6.

LXIV.

HERCULES.

1.

3.

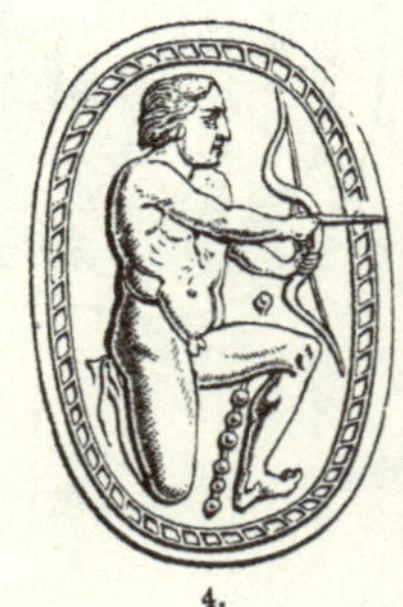

4.

2.

5.

6.

LXV. HEROES.

1.

2.

4.

3

5.

8.

LXVI. EPIC CYCLE.

1.

2.

3.

4.

5.

6.

LXVII. TROJAN WAR: ULYSSES.

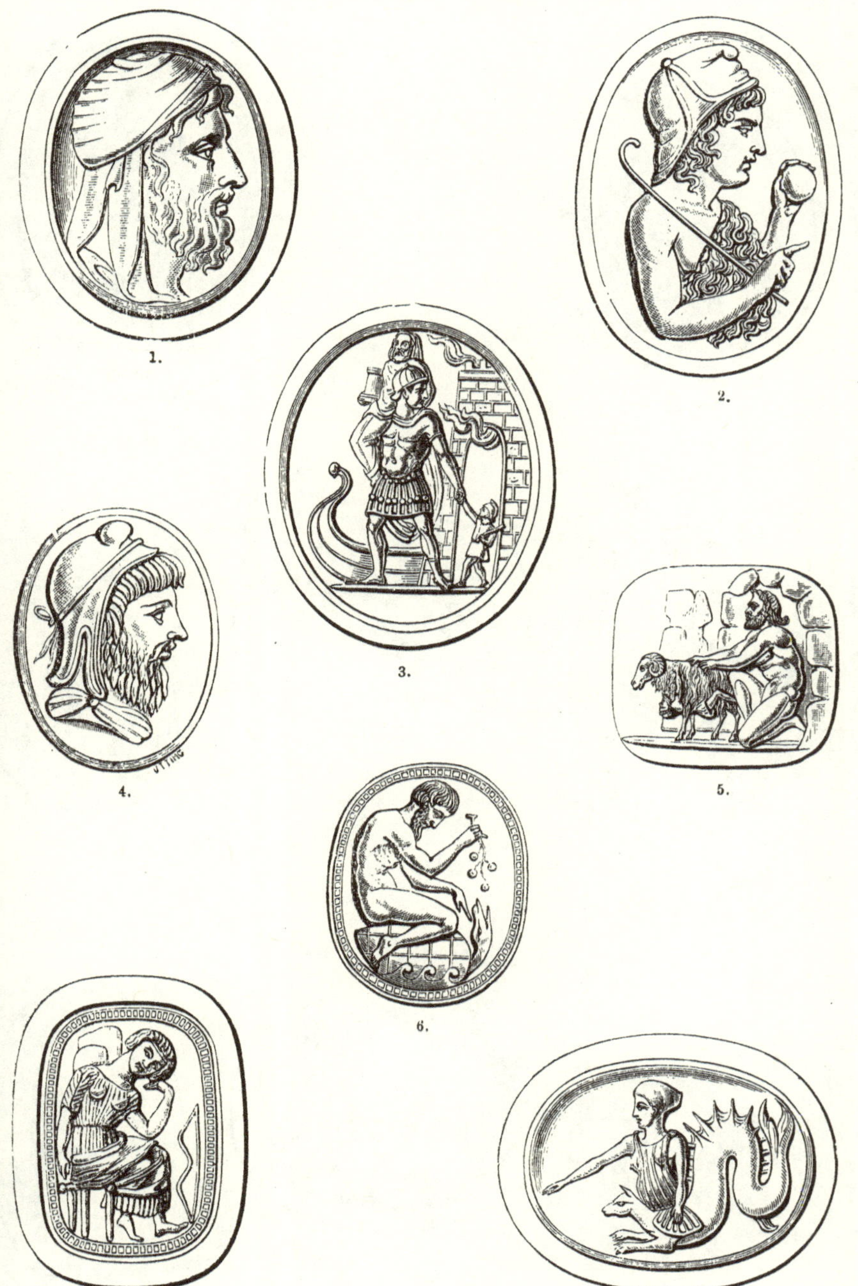

LXVIII. TROJAN WAR: ACHILLES.

1.

3.

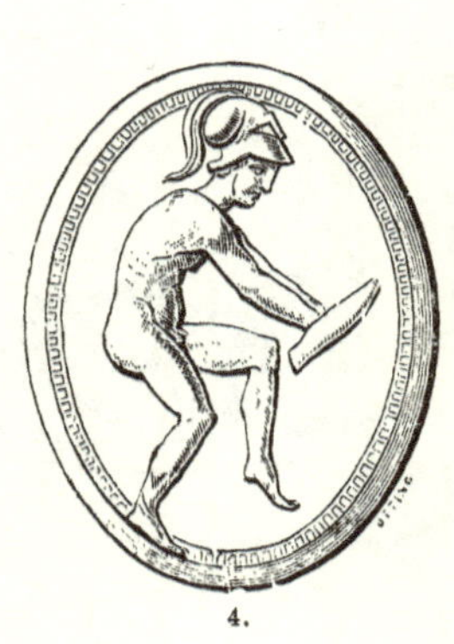

4.

5.

6.

8.

LXIX. GREEK PORTRAITS.

6.

1.

5.

2.

3.

4.

7.

LXX. GREEK PORTRAITS.

1.

4.

2.

3.

5.

6.

LXXI. ROMAN PORTRAITS.

1

2.

3.

4.

5.

6.

LXXII. ROMAN PORTRAITS.

1.

2.

3.

4.

5.

LXXIII. ROMAN PORTRAITS.

1.

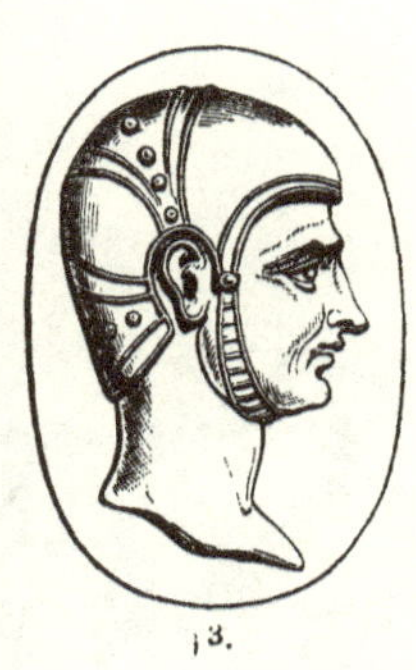

3.

4.

2.

6.

8.

7.

5.

LXXIV. ROMAN PORTRAITS.

1.

3.

2.

4.

5.

6.

7

LXXV. SYMBOLISM.

1.

2.

4.

3.

5.

6.

7.

8.

LXXVI. SYMBOLISM.

1.

2.

3.

4.

5.

6.

7.

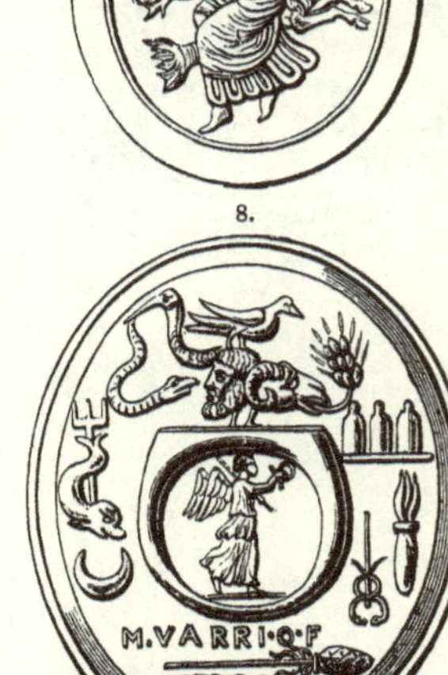

8.

9.

10.

LXXVII.

RELIGION.

2.

1.

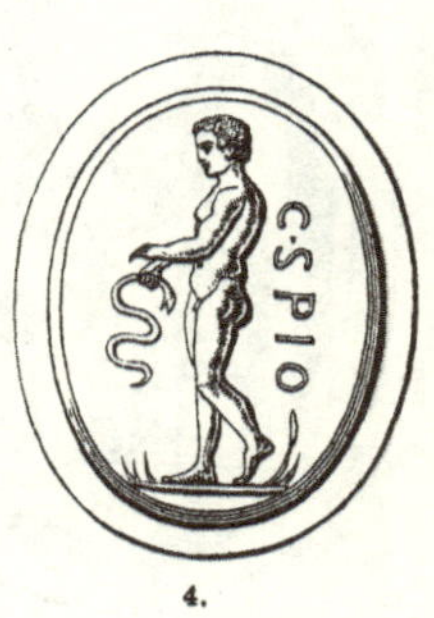

4.

3.

7.

6.

5.

LXXVIII.

ARTS: SCIENCES.

LXXIX. GAMES.

2.

1.

3.

5.

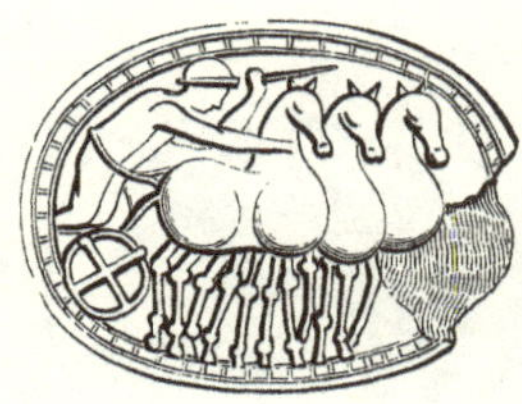
4.

6.

LXXX. CAPRICES: TRADEMARKS.

1.

2.

3.

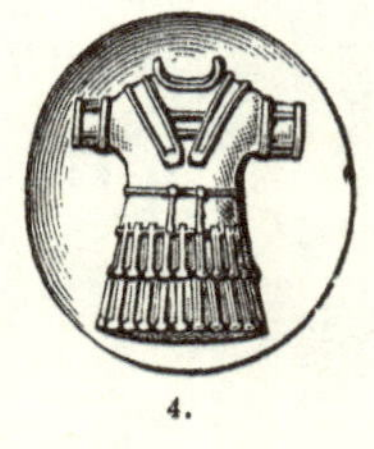

4.

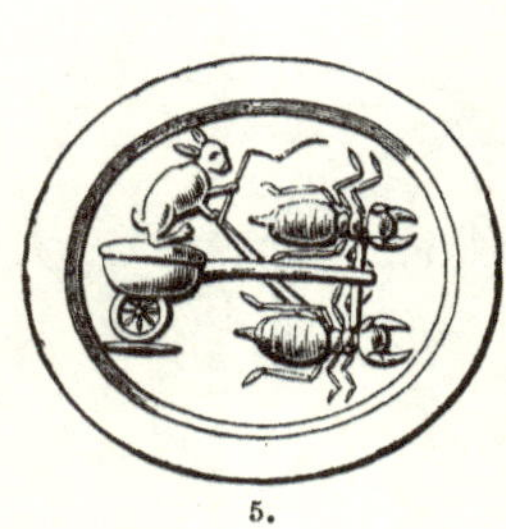

5.

6.

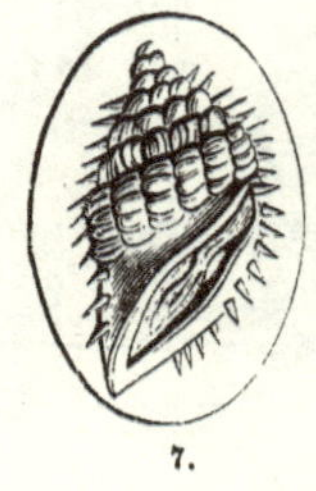

7.

8.

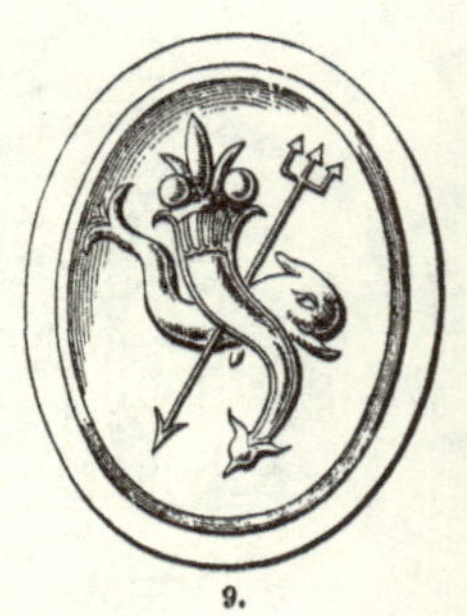

9.

LXXXI. CAPRICES: GRYLLI.

1.

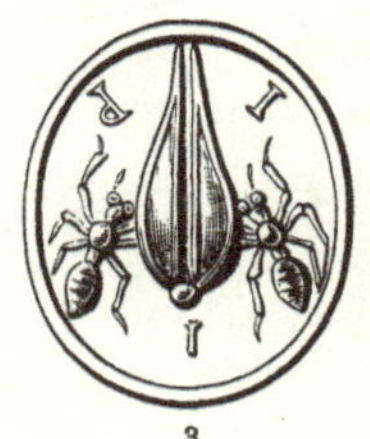

3.

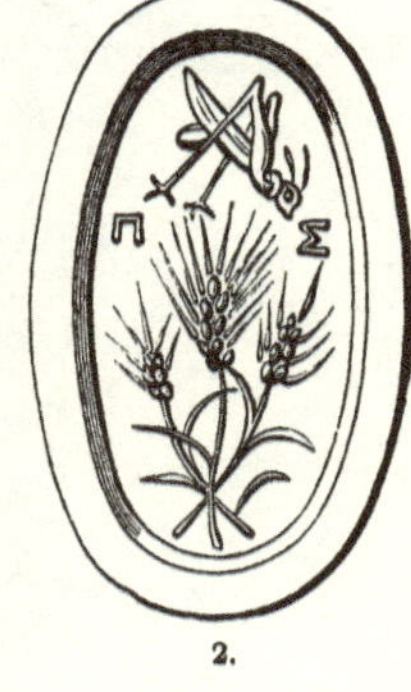

2.

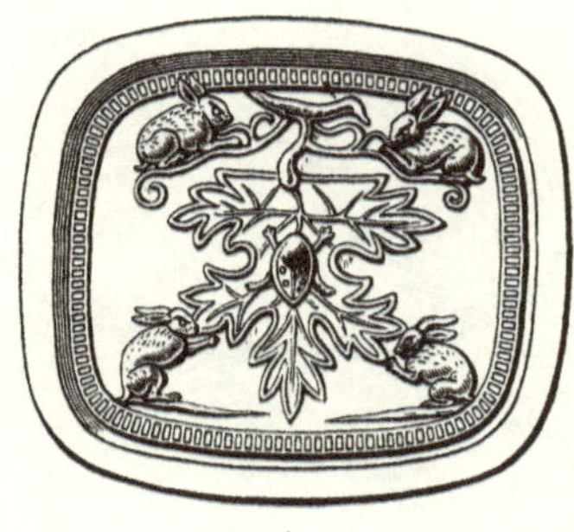

4.

5.

7.

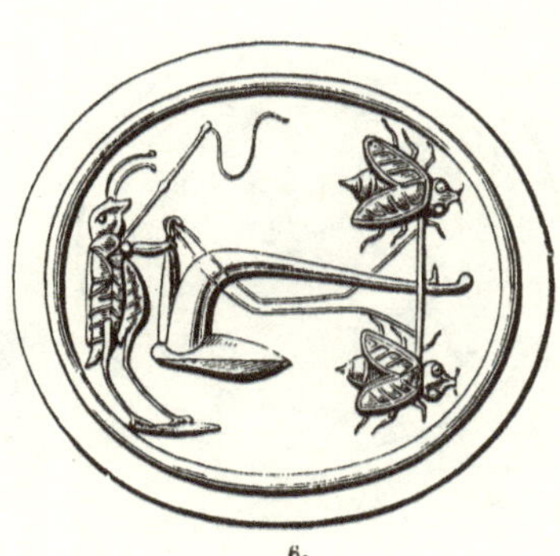

6.

LXXXII. ANIMALS.

1.

2.

3.

6

4.

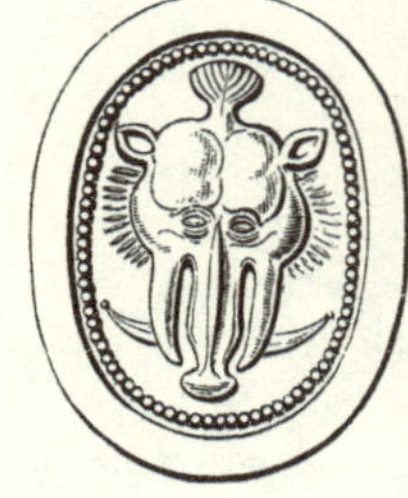

5.

7.

9.

8.

LXXXIII. ARTISTS' SIGNATURES.

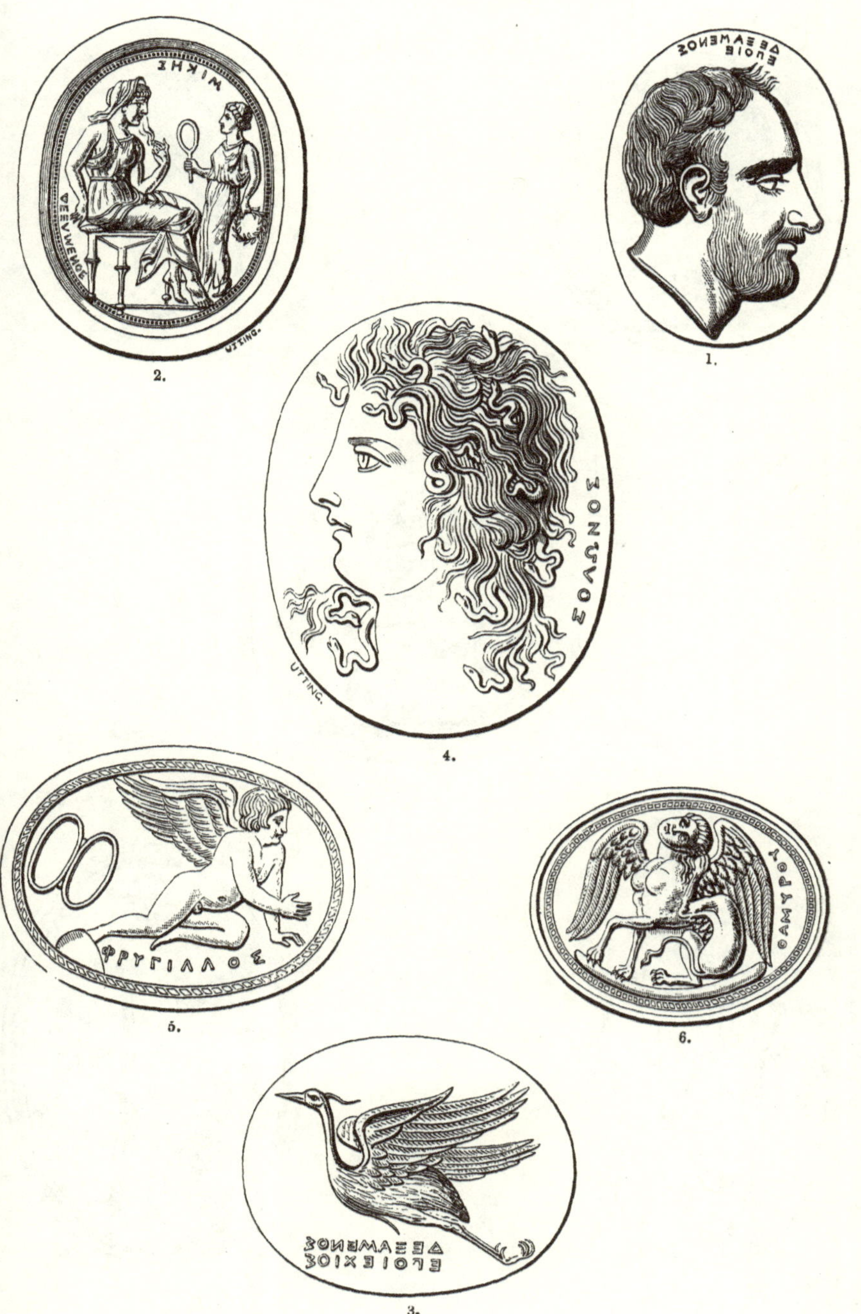

2. 1. 4. 5. 6. 3.

LXXXIV. ARTISTS' SIGNATURES.

1.

2.

3.

4.

5.

LXXXV. ARTISTS' SIGNATURES.

1.

2.

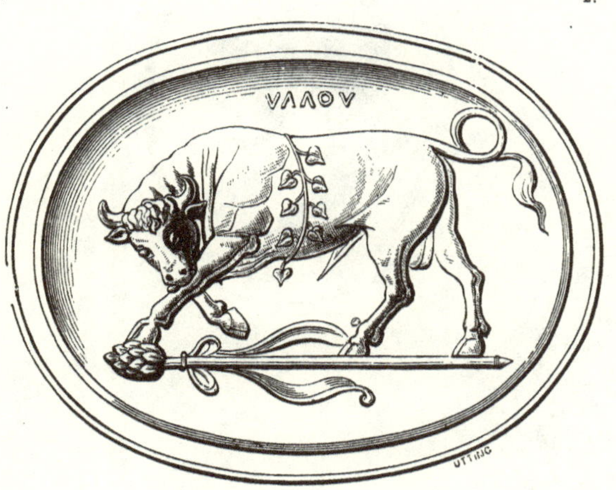

3.

4.

5.

LXXXVI. ARTISTS' SIGNATURES.

2.

3.

1.

4.

5.

7.

6.

LXXXVII. THE EMERALD VERNICLE.

www.ingramcontent.com/pod-product-compliance
Lightning Source LLC
LaVergne TN
LVHW050921080826
845145LV00001B/163

* 9 7 8 1 4 1 0 1 0 3 4 8 2 *